Students' Guide to Programming Languages

Malcolm Bull

NEWNES

Newnes
An imprint of Butterworth-Heinemann Ltd
Linacre House, Jordan Hill, Oxford OX2 8DP

 PART OF REED INTERNATIONAL BOOKS

OXFORD LONDON BOSTON
MUNICH NEW DELHI SINGAPORE SYDNEY
TOKYO TORONTO WELLINGTON

First published 1992

British Library Cataloguing in Publication Data
Bull, Malcolm, *1941*–
    Students' guide to programming languages.
    I. Title
    005.26

ISBN 0 7506 0362 3

Library of Congress Cataloguing in Publication Data
Bull, Malcolm, 1941–
    Students' guide to programming languages/Malcolm Bull.
    p.   cm.
    Includes index.
    ISBN 0 7506 0362 3
    1. Programming languages (Electronic computers) I. Title.
    QA76.7.B85   1991
    005.13–dc20   91–40722

Set by Hope Services (Abingdon) Ltd
Printed and bound in Great Britain by
Biddles Ltd, Guildford and King's Lynn

Contents

Preface

1: Why study programming languages?   1
Why should we study programming languages? –
programming languages and the end-user – programming languages and the systems analyst – programming
languages and the programmer

2: What are programming languages?   8
The development of computers – machine code –
instruction set – why have only a small instruction set?
– logical operations – comparison and branching –
instruction format – assembly code – assembler – data
names – labels – macros – stored programs – subroutines – subroutines in practice – another processor –
third generation languages – thinking of a solution –
compiler – ease of use – portability – fourth generation
languages – what is a fourth generation language? – different instruction sets – other instruction sets – binary
operations – logical operations – data format – arithmetic operations – indexing – immediate instructions –
flags and testing – input and output – interpreting –
compiling, linking and loading – linking and loading –
executing – what do we want of a programming language?

3: Data and data types   91
Types of data – converting binary numbers to decimal –
converting decimal numbers to binary – performing
binary addition – representing other data – hexadecimal
notation – binary / decimal / hexadecimal – data types –
character data type – other character sets – escape
sequences – strings of characters – strings – integer /
fixed data type – negative integer numbers – internal /
external format – fractions – very large numbers – real
numbers – floating point numbers – normalized numbers

– real numbers in storage – single-precision and double-precision – E-notation – packed decimal – Boolean data type – data types in programming languages – data types in Basic – data types in Ada – data types in APL – data types in Cobol – data types in Fortran – data types in Pascal – data types in PL/1 – data types in C – type checking – arrays – subscripts – working with arrays – homogeneous arrays – arrays with several dimensions – records – enumerated data types – implementing enumerated data types – pointers – linked lists – set types

4: Abstract data types – ADTs   185
What do we mean by data type? – an abstract data type – a simple abstract data type – ADT: queue – possible implementations – specifying an ADT – specifying an operation – formal specifications – the specification of the ADT: queue – implementing an ADT – constraints during implementation – information hiding

5: Programming structure and structures   216
Structured programming – program structures – sequence – assignment statements – arithmetic calculations – selection – logical expressions – iteration – surface structures – surface structures in structured English – surface structures in C – surface structures in Cobol – surface structures in Fortran – surface structures in Pascal – exception conditions – handling exception conditions – tree diagrams – modular programming – functions or subroutines? – internal processing modules – external processing modules – functions – arguments – scope – calling a module – COMMON data – labelled COMMON – using COMMON data

6: Specifying a programming language   263
Specifying a language – recursive rules – BNF: Backus-Naur form – deriving a sentence from a grammar – parsing – EBNF: Extended Backus-Naur form – more EBNF symbols – syntax diagrams – recursion in syntax diagrams – context-free grammars – semantics – specification by narrative description – specification by example – specification by substitution

7: Specifying functions   294
Specifying functions – sets – is a member of – operations on sets – union – difference – intersection –

writing the members of a set – primitive types in formal specifications – the input set and the domain –
mapping – the output set and the range – describing a
function – partial functions and total functions – functions with other types of data – more than one input
value – other data types – formal descriptions – recursion

8: Compilers and compiling   334
A compiler – lexical analysis – the symbol table –
constants and variables – arrays and the symbol table
– syntax analysis – syntax checking in general – syntax checking in action – syntax errors – arithmetic
expressions – reverse Polish notation – an algorithm to
convert in-fix expressions to post-fix – evaluating a
post-fix expression – an algorithm to evaluate post-fix
expressions – producing the object code – labels –
scope-checking – optimization

9: Applying languages: commercial   375
Procedural or non-procedural languages? – even
before software – report program generators – program generators – partial action of a program generator – databases – database languages – enquiry
languages – SQL – sorting – selecting specific items –
dBASE – sorting in dBASE – processing in dBASE –
QBE; query by example – processing in QBE – data
description language – fourth generation languages –
what is a fourth generation language? – the pros and
cons of using 4GLs – prototyping – 4GL / enquiry language / data manipulation language – looking at a
4GL – derived fields – using the data dictionary –
SB+ and the users

10: Applying languages: specialist   428
Concurrent processing – synchronization – condition
synchronization – mutual exclusion – deadlock –
transputers – Occam – an Occam definition – more
Occam facilities – priority and selection – simulation
problems – simulation languages – what is the problem? – queuing diagrams – a simplified simulation
language – what else is there? – linear programming

11: Other language models   464

Functional programming languages – lambda notation – orthogonality – composition of functions – LISP: list processing – processing with LISP – arithmetic in LISP – input and output – the QUOTE function – the COND function – defining your own LISP functions – heads and tails – CAR and CDR – implementing LISP – cells and binding – logic programming – Prolog: programming in logic – AND / OR – backtracking – write predicate – Prolog in business – processing data in Prolog – instantiation – expert systems – object-oriented programming – classes – messages – methods – blocks – selection and iteration – input / output

Index   523

Preface

With greater access to computers at work, at school and in the home, more and more people are now able to write programs. Only a small number of these people recognize the underlying features of the programming languages they are using, and even fewer people appreciate the features which are common to most programming languages. In this book, we shall see how most programming languages are based upon the same concepts and how a knowledge of these concepts can benefit the analyst and the programmer.

When specifying computer solutions to real problems, the systems analyst and the programmer must be able to stand back from the particular problem in hand and visualize a solution which is independent of the constraints and limitations imposed by the programming language itself. In practice, a familiarity with what programming languages can do will be helpful in selecting the right language for the right job and in designing systems which better exploit the facilities of a particular language, and a wider awareness of how programming languages behave will be of value in enabling the programmer to learn new languages and to write programs which exploit the language and to avoid inefficient coding.

The aim of the present book is to introduce you to programming languages, to show why they are needed, how they are defined and constructed, where they are used and how they are used. You will also be equipped to evaluate the various computer languages which are available with a view to selecting the one most appropriate to a particular task. We shall not teach you how to write programs in any specific language, but we shall look at some of the programming languages which are available, we shall point out the common features and concepts, and we shall see how they fit in with programming languages and other aspects of data processing which you may have already encountered. You will derive greater benefit from the book if you are already familiar with a programming language such as Basic, Pascal or Cobol, no matter whether you are very skilled in writing programs or whether you have only just begun your computer studies.

Since the successful use of a programming language demands that the programmer be fully aware of the range of data structures – sets, queues, trees – which are available, we shall also spend some considerable time looking at data types and we shall see how these can be implemented in practice.

The book is suitable for college students following BTEC and City and Guilds courses in computer studies and IT topics. It will also be of interest to those who are preparing to embark upon a university, college or polytechnic degree course in computer science.

The book will also be of general interest in the business world – particularly for those commercial users and end-users who are increasingly being confronted with a wide range of jargon and techniques in their daily work, and who feel that they would like to know what programming languages are all about and what programming languages are available for application in their particular business. By knowing what languages are available and the particular disciplines to which they are appropriate, it may be possible for end-users to help in the selection of a special programming medium – such as a simulation language or a modelling language – which will allow them to ask questions about their work and to obtain solutions which would be impossible in the more familiar languages such as Cobol and Basic.

Because of the advanced nature of the subject, we are assuming a certain preliminary knowledge of the general concepts of data processing and information technology and of the elementary features of the hardware and the software which is used. We also assume that the reader is familiar with the use and meaning of a number of fundamental terms and concepts such as **program, file, record, field, input** and **output** and – until they are discussed in detail – we shall also assume an intuitive awareness of specific programming concepts such as **loop, subroutine** and **compilation.** As other important terms are introduced, they are defined explicitly or explained implicitly by means of examples and illustrations.

There are a great many activities and assignments throughout the book. Wherever possible, you should attempt to complete the work using a computer and the appropriate software. By doing this, not only will you learn more about the compilers and the language processors, but you will also appreciate some of the areas in which there are differences between the various implementations and the descriptions given in the text.

1: Why study programming languages?

Objectives

After reading this chapter, you should be able to:

- Write down some of the ways in which the choice of a programming language affects the end-user, the analyst and the programmer.
- Describe some of the problems which can arise if an inappropriate language is chosen to implement a system.
- Write down some reasons why it is not sufficient that a program works correctly, and give some other requirements of a program.
- Write down some reasons why analysts and programmers should be aware of more than just one programming language.

Why should we study programming languages?

Before we start to look at *programming languages*, we should discuss some of the reasons why it is important to study them and to understand how they are constructed and how they behave. You may be asking yourself why is it not sufficient that we understand a programming language and use it to write programs which work as they should and which produce the required results? If you can write a program and get it working, what more could anybody want?

As we shall see, it is not enough just to be able to use a particular programming language:

- The systems analyst must be able to recommend and to choose the most suitable language for the specific problem in hand.

- The programming language must make the transition from design to final implementation as smooth as possible.
- The programming language must be capable of representing every aspects of the analyst's design.
- The programmers must be able to write programs which work, which can be seen to work and which can be proved to work.
- The structure of the language must be such that it can actually reduce the number of ways in which the programmers can introduce errors into their programs, and it must increase the likelihood of any errors being detected during the development.
- It must be easy to identify, to locate and to correct errors and to debug programs.
- It must be easy to test programs.
- It must be possible to construct a program as a series of independent units which can be linked together as required.
- It must be possible to amend one program or one program unit without having to amend several others as a consequence.
- It must be possible to amend and maintain your programs throughout their lifetime . . .

and there are many more requirements.

Programming languages and the end-user

For all intents and purposes, the end-user is (or should be) completely unaware of the language in which his/her computer system is written.

A program written in a language such as Basic, should and can be made to look like and to behave in very much the same manner as a program written in, say, Pascal. Indeed, there are sometimes occasions when a new computer system is to be introduced and the new programs must be written in different languages so as to be quite indistinguishable from the original programs.

The major differences that do exist between the various programming languages make themselves known to the end-user in a variety of ways:

- The accuracy of the results of arithmetic calculations will probably be affected by the language which is used. Some versions of Basic, for example, only allow accuracy to four decimal places. Other languages allow greater accuracy.

What does your computer display if you ask it to

PRINT 1/3

Thus, if you were writing a program to navigate a satellite around the solar system for a number of years, you would need a very high degree of accuracy in your calculations. If you only had four decimal places to play with, you might well lose the satellite somewhere around Croydon!

- The graphics capabilities, the available input and output devices, and other special facilities may not be easily accessible in some languages.

  Can your version of Basic handle the mouse or the joystick on your home computer?

- A computer system might need to handle large quantities of data, or it might need to handle that data in a particular manner. Not all languages permit these. A simple language, such as Basic, only allows data to be handled as variables, arrays and records whereas the user's requirements may be better satisfied by visualizing the data as, say, a tree structure or as a queue.

  How would you write a small routine to produce a sorted list of names which are fed to you, one at a time, in a random order?

Whilst most languages can be forced to do what the user wants, you may find that, if the programmer is not using a suitable language, he/she may have to use long, time-consuming methods to achieve the necessary effects. If the methods are long and time-consuming, the design too will be long and time-consuming, and the programming and testing will be similarly protracted. Even when the system has been delivered, a bad design or bad choice of methods may result in the system being slow and this, in turn, may lead to the users abandoning the computer system for some other alternative.

In a great many cases, new software is to run on the existing hardware, and it may only be possible for users to have their computer systems installed on a computer which is already used within the company. If a suitable language is not available on that computer system, then it may be necessary for the analyst to explain the situation to the end-users and suggest that they reduce their demands to something which can be easily and efficiently implemented on the existing computer. In an increasing number of cases, however, it is becoming possible for the organization to consider buying a special compiler for use on a small personal computer. These are fairly inexpensive and allow the correct choice of programming language to be implemented for that one application without affecting the rest of the organization.

Programming languages and the systems analyst

When an analyst is designing a computer system, it should be possible for him/her to specify the solution in a manner which is completely independent of the programming language and the computer on which the system will eventually be implemented. Indeed, if the analyst only specifies systems in terms of what he/she knows that the programming language and the computer can and cannot do, then there is a danger that this will colour the design and cripple the solution so that the resulting system is not what the users actually want.

In practice, however, the analyst must know something about the programming language and the computer which will be used to run the programs which he/she is designing. It is pointless to derive a very sophisticated solution if that solution cannot be implemented on the hardware and the operating system which is available, or, if it can be implemented, if the program is going to run slowly or inefficiently.

This makes us realize how important it is for the analyst to be completely aware of the scope of his/her design and of the hardware and software resources which are available. If the required resources are not available, is the analyst able to suggest alternative hardware and software? Is it within his/her powers to recommend that specific compilers or specific input and output devices be bought? When these questions have been answered, and the analyst knows the tools which can be used, then he/she is in a better position to design a solution which is the best one available within the constraints of the available resources.

The analyst's design for the system will be expressed in theoretical terms. For example, the design might require a set of subroutines which will simulate a *queue* of orders so that they can be processed in the correct sequence. The analyst may require one subroutine to add orders to the *end* of the queue and another subroutine to extract and process orders from the *front* of the queue. The analyst having specified these theoretical requirements, it may be left to the programmer to decide how to implement them in the physical framework of what the programming language can do. Indeed, none of the well-known languages can handle a queue, and they would probably all simulate such a queue in terms of an array. We shall spend much time looking at the ways in which it is possible to bridge this gap between what the analyst wants and what the programmer and the programming language can do.

Programming languages and the programmer

The programming language is the major (if not the only) tool which the programmer has at his/her disposal. If the correct language is not available or if an inappropriate language has been selected, the effect on the programmer and the resultant programs can be catastrophic. He/she may waste many days' work in simulating an action which could be performed very easily in another language, and the final program may be very time-consuming as it labours its way through the processing.

As we shall see, some languages are more appropriate to one type of problem than another. Cobol, for example, is ideally suited for business calculations but it is less useful in programs which perform large and complicated calculations. In contrast, Fortran, is more suited to scientific and mathematical calculations and less useful for programs which manipulate large text strings and file data.

As a further illustration, we might consider another specialized language, Simian, which is designed to solve *simulation* problems such as the flow of traffic across a busy road junction, the utilization of petrol pumps at a busy service station, or the length of the passenger queues at a railway station. These are problems in which *general statistics* are available for the volume and the flow of traffic but not the *precise* times and numbers which a language such as Cobol, Fortran or Pascal would require. Whilst it would not be impossible to write a simulation program using, say, Cobol, it would obviously be quicker, less error-prone to use a language such as Simian, and using a suitable language allows the users, the analyst and the programmer to think naturally and in terms of the problem and the requirements, rather than becoming bogged-down by the intricacies of bending the programming language to the particular problem.

No matter which programming language is used, it is, of course, essential that the programmer is able to use the language fully and efficiently. We shall see that there are a number of common features in all programming languages:

- loops and iterations,

- yes/no choices, as in IF . . . THEN . . . ELSE . . . statements,
- multiple choices, as in CASE statements,
- subroutines and procedures,
- functions,

amongst others, and by successfully applying the facilities which each language has to implement these common features, the programmer can produce a program which is quick and easy to write, debug, test and implement.

By looking at the reason which lies behind the origin and the development of programming languages, the programmer will find it easier to appreciate why:

- Computer languages demand that the programmer organizes the program and the coding in a certain manner.
  Why, for example, do Cobol and Pascal insist that all variables are declared before they are used, whereas Fortran requires some variables to be declared, and Basic does not require any variables to be declared?
- It may not always be possible to make the computer do what you want it to do.
  Why, for example, is assembly language able to handle the mouse on your computer, whereas a Basic program cannot?

Furthermore, by looking at the underlying principles which are common to all computer languages, the programmer will find it much easier to read and understand programs written in an unfamiliar language and to learn new languages.

Activity

A set of programs is required by a large organization. The users have specified their requirements to the analyst, and the analyst has designed a system which will do the required processing. The computer which is to be used has just one compiler for a language which can be used to write a suitable set of programs. The programmer has transformed the analyst's design into a set of programs but these seem to run too slowly and the users are complaining about this.
What are the reasons for this problem?

What can be done about this difficulty?
How can the situation be avoided in future?

Recap

- The choice of programming language greatly affects all those who will be involved with a computer system: the end-user, the systems analyst and the programmer. Some languages are more appropriate to one application area than to another: a commercial computer system might be more likely to use Cobol; a scientific system might be more likely to use Fortran. Some languages are suitable to a wide range of applications, commercial, scientific, industrial and so on.
- Most of the current computer languages are designed to reduce the risk of errors creeping in, and – if errors and mistakes do occur – they are designed to simplify the detection and removal of such errors.
- By equipping himself/herself to look at any programming language, the analyst and the programmer will be better able to select the correct language for any system which is being developed.

2: What are programming languages?

Objectives

After reading this chapter, you should be able to:

- List the major events in the development of the computer and of computer languages.
- Recognize and distinguish between the terms: **first, second, third** and **fourth generation computers**, and **first, second, third** and **fourth generation programming languages.**
- Describe the **von Neumann model** of a computer.
- Describe the general construction of a processor and indicate how this affects the **instruction set** for that processor.
- Make a list of the types of operations which are available on commercial processors.
- Recognize and use the terms: **register, buffer, storage,** and **program status word.**
- Describe the nature, purpose and format of the **machine code** and the machine code instructions for a processor.
- Write processing routines in machine code.
- Describe the nature, purpose and format of the **assembly code** and the assembly code instructions for a processor.
- Write processing routines in assembly code.
- Recognize and use the terms: **label, mnemonic, data names, compiling, source program, object program, linking, loading** and **executing**.
- Describe and distinguish the functions of an **assembler,** an **interpreter**, and a **compiler**.
- Describe the nature and purpose of a **macro**.
- Create macros and write processing routines using macros.
- Describe the nature of **stored programs** and the way in which they utilize the computer storage space.

The development of computers

The development of the computer has gone through many stages:

- In 1823, the mechanical difference engine of Charles Babbage was proposed.
- In the late 1890s, the electro-mechanical card-handling and tabulating machines of Hollerith (later to become the IBM Corporation) and Powers (later to become the Sperry Rand Corporation) were introduced.
- In 1944, the IBM Mark I computer was the first computer capable of performing a long sequence of arithmetic and logical operations.
- In 1946, ENIAC (Electronic Numerical Integrator And Calculator) became the forerunner of the **first generation of computers**, using vacuum tubes for storage and control.
- 1959 saw the introduction of the **second generation of computers**, building computers with transistors instead of vacuum tubes and using magnetic core storage. The use of transistors resulted in computers which were smaller, faster, cheaper and more reliable than before.
- 1965, the use of integrated solid-state circuitry in the assembly of computers and the advances made in mass storage devices and input/output equipment brought in the **third generation of computers**. The new circuitry increased the speed of operation still further, enabling millions and even billions of calculations to be performed in one second.
- Since 1970, the development of the microprocessor, a ready-made solid-state computing device, has made it possible to produce even faster, smaller and cheaper computers – the **fourth generation of computers**.

The fundamental design of all computers – known as the **von Neumann model** or **von Neumann architecture** – was developed in the 1940s by a mathematician called John von Neumann and this design has moulded the way in which the art of programming is conceived. To some extent, it has also imposed a blinkered or narrow-minded attitude to programming languages. As a result, any languages which you may have encountered so far in your studies will almost certainly be **imperative languages**. Imperative languages allow the programmer to specify his/her requirements as a sequence of instructions indicating exactly what is to be done.

9

Figure 2.1 illustrates the basic structure of a von Neumann computer.

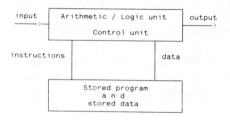

Figure 2.1 *The von Neumann model*

The von Neumann model has three main functions:
(1) it accepts input data,
(2) it processes the instructions of a stored program in a sequential manner; and finally
(3) it outputs the results.

Beyond these points, however, the history of the computer has had very little real impact upon the further development of computer languages. For example, for each new generation of computer hardware, there has been no corresponding leap forward in the programming languages used on that hardware. Indeed, the Fortran language which was developed back in the mid-1950s is still with us today.

The early electronic computers were very specialized in what they could do and in what they were expected to do, and in most cases, the people who designed the computer were the same people who used them and wrote the programs. Today, there are vast armies of analysts and programmers working behind the scenes, with the sole function of turning the users' requirements into working computer programs.

The greatest impetus given to the development of programming languages came indirectly as a consequence of computers becoming more readily available and increasingly being used by non-computer technicians. The new users wanted to use computers for themselves, but they did not have the time or the inclination to learn the arcane languages which the computers used; these users wanted a language which (with a little training) they could understand and which the computer must be taught to understand.

This motivation to provide languages which are easy and simple to use is still with us today. The very latest languages, such as SQL and

Prolog, are a natural progression arising from the need for more and more users – from managers and clerks to accountants and economists – to be able to use and live with the increasing amounts of data which are being placed at their disposal.

So let us start at the beginning and look at the basic needs behind a computer language.

Machine code

When a new computer processor – or micro-processor – is being produced, one of the first tasks of the designers is to decide the **architecture** of the processor:

- How the data is to be held.
- Whether data is to be handled as single bytes, in groups of 4, 6, 8 or 16 bytes, or whether data can be handled in strings of any size.
- Whether there are to be special fast-access areas (called **registers**) where arithmetic and other processing can be performed.
- How many registers there are to be.

The designer will then organize these and other physical aspects of the structure of the processor to produce the final design for the integrated circuit, the **chip**.

It is most unusual for anyone to sit down and design a brand-new processor. Most companies who produce a new computer use one of the standard chips at the heart of their computer and simply add their own cabinet and other extras.

There are a number of standard processors to choose from and these are used in computers produced by many different manufacturers. Foremost amongst these are the 8086 family of chips which are manufactured by the Intel Corporation. Chips from this family include the 8088 and the 8086 processors which are used in most PC computers, including those of IBM and others. The final digit of the processor number indicates the amount of data which can be passed around the processor at one time: those ending in 8 can transfer 8 bits at a time, those ending in 6 can transfer 16 bits at a time. After some time, Intel revised the design of the chips, enabling them to do more work and the results were the 80188 and the 80186 processors. In turn, these too were enhanced to make them faster and improve their capabilities to appear as the 80286 chip, the 80386 chip and more recently the 80486 chip. You may also encounter other processors such as the Mostek

11

6502 processor which is used in the Apple II series computers, the Motorola 68000 family which are used in Apple Mackintosh computers, and the Zilog Z80 processor.

Activity 1

We have said that a small number of standard processor chips are used in the manufacture of most modern computers.

Get copies of some computer magazines and make a list of the computers which are advertised there and the chip which each computer uses. The text of the advertisement will usually give a clue such as:

The AAA laptop computer gives you the 386 power wherever you need it.

telling us that the AAA laptop uses the 80386 Intel chip.

Draw up a table like that in Figure 2.2, showing which computer uses which chip.

Computer	8088	80386	80486	6502	68000	Z80
AAA laptop		X				

Figure 2.2 *Chips in use*

Instruction set

Each processor has its own set of **operations** which it is capable of performing. This range of operations, known as the **instruction set**, is determined by the engineers who designed that particular processor. The range of instructions which are available on one processor may be different from those available on another. There are several reasons for this:

● The designers may be limited by the size of the integrated circuit which is available for the processor.

● A micro-processor may be designed for a specific task. A micro-processor which is to control the workings of a washing machine, for example, will require far less operations than one which is to be used in a general-purpose desk-top computer.

The first task of the designers is to draw up the list of operations which the processor is to perform. This will depend upon the architecture of the processor, but it will normally include fundamental operations such as:

- move data into a register
- move the contents of one register into another register,
- add the contents of one register to the contents of another register,

and many more. We shall look at the other types of operations at the end of this chapter.

Assignment 1

A team of engineers has produced a design for a new processor. This is shown in Figure 2.3. The processor is to be used for arithmetic calculations and is to include a number of storage and processing areas:

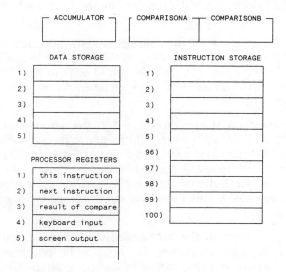

Figure 2.3 *The SG01 processor*

- The **accumulator**; this is a single storage area where all arithmetic is performed. The SG01 cannot perform arithmetic directly on data held in the data stores; the only arithmetic which can be performed is to add a number from one of the data stores to the number already held in the accumulator.

Special storage areas – such as the accumulator, the comparison stores and the processor stores – are usually known as **registers** to distinguish them from the data stores. The electronic circuitry of the registers is arranged such that operations involving the registers operate more quickly than those involving the regular data storage and instruction storage areas.

- The **comparison registers**; these are two storage areas which are used to compare one number with another. Data can only be moved from one of the data stores into either of the comparison registers, and from either of the comparison registers back into one of the data stores. The comparison operation always compares the number in COMPARISONA with the number in COMPARISONB and returns a result of:

    < if COMPARISONA is less than COMPARISONB
    = if COMPARISONA is equal to COMPARISONB
    > if COMPARISONA is greater than COMPARISONB,

- The **data stores**; the SG01 has five storage areas, each of which can hold one 10 digit decimal number.

Data can be moved from any data store to any other data store, to either of the comparison registers, to the processor registers or to the accumulator; data can also be moved back to any data store from the comparison registers, from the processor registers or from the accumulator.

- The **instruction stores**; there are 100 storage areas, each of which can hold one program instruction. When the execution begins, the processor starts at the first of the instruction stores and processes the instruction held there.
- The **processor registers**; there are several special storage areas which are used by the processor and the program for purposes such as:

- To hold a copy of the instruction which is now being processed. As each instruction is about to be processed, it is fetched from the instruction store and placed into this register where it is analysed (to see what operation is to be performed, what the data operands are, and so on). When this has been done, the instruction can be executed.

- To hold the number of the instruction store which holds the instruction which is to be executed next. The processor adds 1 to this each time an instruction is fetched and placed in the *this instruction* register. The action of a branch or jump or go-to instruction is to reset the *next instruction* register to pass control to the correct instruction.
- To hold the result of the last comparison.
- To hold an indication of whether or not the last addition in the accumulator produced a number which was too large for our processor. Thus, if we tried to add 1 to the number 9999999999, then the result would be too large for our processor (remember, we can only handle 10-digit integers) and this error indicator would be set. This condition is known as **overflow** although we shall not deal with this here.

Some processors compress much of the foregoing information into 4 bytes of storage. This is known as the **PSW**, the **program status word**.

- To hold data which has been entered at the keyboard.
- To hold the data which is displayed on the screen.
- To hold the information which will control the action of a diskette, a magnetic tape or other peripheral devices.
- To hold the data which is being sent to, or received from, such a peripheral device.

We shall only concern ourselves with a few of these registers:

- Register 1 which holds a copy of the instruction which is currently being processed.
- Register 2 which holds the number (or the **address**) of the instruction which will be executed next.
- Register 3 which holds one of = or > or < to indicate the result of the last comparison operation.
- Register 4 which holds the last number which the user typed in on the keyboard. A register such as this which is used to store to data which is to be passed between the processor and another device is known as a *buffer* or *buffer store*. We shall call this the *keyboard buffer.*
- Register 5 which holds the number which is to be displayed on the screen. We shall call this the *screen buffer.*

(1) Make a list of some of the operations for *moving data* between the various stores and registers which you think

15

should appear in the instruction set of the SG01. For example, there might be one instruction to move data from a data store to comparison register A, another to move data from comparison register B to a data store, and so on.

(2) Make a list of some of the operations which would help in performing arithmetic which you think might appear in the instruction set of the SG01.

Think about the data movement operations which you listed previously and how these might be used to add the contents of data store 1 and data store 2 together and put the result into data store 3.

Note that the only SG01 arithmetic facility is to add the contents of a data store into the accumulator; it does not allow us to subtract, divide or multiply. We can simulate multiplication by repeated addition (because 4 times 12 is equal to 12+12+12+12), and we can simulate division by repeated subtraction. We therefore need to be able to simulate subtraction. Include an instruction which would allow us to simulate subtraction by using only the addition operation.

In your solution to the first part of this last assignment, you might have suggested:

- Move the contents of either of the comparison registers to one of the data stores,

or you may have suggested this as two separate operations:

- Move the contents of the COMPARISONA register into one of the data stores.
- Move the contents of the COMPARISONB register into one of the data stores.

Exactly which of these possibilities is implemented – a single operation or two separate operations – is a matter for the design team who are developing the processor. We shall use the single operation in order to reduce the number of operations.

- Move the contents of one of the data stores into another data store.
- Move the contents of one of the data stores into either of the comparison registers.
- Move the contents of one of the data stores into the accumulator.
- Move the contents of the accumulator into one of the data stores.

You might also have suggested:

- Move the contents of a data store into the screen buffer.
- Move the contents of the keyboard buffer into one of the data stores.

You might also have recognized the need to move (or fetch) an instruction into the *this instruction* register where it can be analysed and processed. This task is handled by the processor itself and is not the concern of the instruction set or the programmer.

For the second part of the Assignment, you might have suggested the following operations:

- Add the contents of one of the data stores to the number already held in the accumulator.
- Set the contents of the accumulator to zero. This is not an essential operation.
- Change the arithmetic sign of the number in the accumulator. This will allow us to simulate subtraction.

Why have only a small instruction set?

The operations which the SG01 processor can perform are fairly simple, doing one thing at a time. This reduces the number of operations which the processor can perform and it also makes the processing faster. Since the SG01 only has facilities to add two numbers together – there are no facilities for subtraction, multiplication and division – this reduces the complexity of the electronic circuitry. Furthermore, since all addition is performed in the accumulator, this means that only one addition circuit is needed; this reduces the complexity of the electronic circuit and also makes the processing faster. For some operations which we think of as a single task (such as subtract one number from another), the problem has to be resolved into a sequence of simple steps.

Questions

Using the instructions which we discussed above, describe the steps to be taken to perform each of the tasks described below.

Check your solutions like this: draw a set of boxes on a piece of paper to represent the accumulator, data store 1, data store 2, and so on. Write a number in each box (to remind ourselves that we do not know the contents of the storage areas when we start processing) and then work through the steps changing the contents of the boxes at each stage.

1 Add the contents of data store 1 and the contents of data store 2 together and put the result into data store 3.
2 Subtract the contents of data store 1 from the contents of data store 2 and put the result into data store 5.
3 Set the contents of data store 1 to 0.
4 Set the contents of data store 1 to 9999.

Logical operations

So far, we have been concerned with data movement and the data processing aspects of the SG01. But there are also some logical capabilities.

Assignment 2

Make a list of some of the logical operations for comparing data which you think might appear in the instruction set of the SG01.

Comparison and branching

In your solution to this last assignment, you will have realized that, since all comparisons are performed in the comparison registers, there is only one such operation:

● Compare the contents of COMPARISONA register with the contents of COMPARISONB register.

You might also have recognized the need to set the result of the comparison in the processor register, but this task is handled by the processor itself and is not the concern of the instruction set or the programmer.

You probably suggested that there must also be some means of *testing* the results of the comparison. On the SG01, these instructions are:

● If the result of the last comparison was < then execute the instruction held in a specific instruction store.

This is really like a *jump* or *branch* operation and will allow us to issue instructions such as:

> If the result of the last comparison was < then execute the instruction which is held in instruction store number 30.

Basic programmers may recognize this as the operation which would be used in the execution of a Basic statement such as:

> IF A < B THEN GO TO 30

- If the result of the last comparison was = then execute the instruction held in a specific instruction store.
- If the result of the last comparison was > then execute the instruction held in a specific instruction store.

You may have realised that there is also a requirement to have an instruction which will jump to a specific instruction in the instruction store, no matter what the result of the last comparison.

- Execute the instruction held in a specific instruction store.

Basic programmers may recognize this as the operation which would be used in the execution of a Basic statement such as:

> GO TO 30

Questions

Using all the operations which we have now built up for the SGO1, write down the sequence of operations which would perform the following tasks:

5 Compare the number in data store 2 with the number in data store 7.
6 Compare the number in data store 1 with the number in data store 4, and if the result is > then jump to execute the instruction in instruction store number 76.
7 Jump to execute the instruction in instruction store number 76 if the number in data store 1 is less than the number in data store 4.
8 Compare the number in data store 1 with the number in data store 4, and if the result is > then jump to execute the instruction in instruction store number 76; if the result is = then jump

19

to the instruction in instruction store number 44; otherwise jump to the instruction in instruction store number 39.

Instruction format

We have now built up a good range of operations for the SG01 processor. The designer must now decide the format of the instructions which will carry out these operations and how these will be held in the instruction store.

Look at your list of operations. They all have one thing in common: they all *do* something. They differ in that they do different things but, and more importantly:

(1) *some always work on the same part(s) of storage.* Examples of this sort of operation are:

- Change the arithmetic sign of the number in the accumulator.
- Set the contents of the accumulator to zero.
- Compare the contents of COMPARISONA register with the contents of COMPARISONB register.

(2) *some work on one part of storage but need to know which part of storage*

- Move the contents of one of the data stores to the accumulator.
- Execute the instruction held in a specific instruction store.

(3) *some work on two parts of storage and need to know which parts of storage*

- Move the contents of either of the comparison registers to one of the data stores.
- Move the contents of one of the data stores to another data store.

From this, we see that the instructions to carry out each of our operations has a similar form:

(a) An **operation code** or **op-code** (which tells the processor what this operation does), and
(b) An **operand** (which tells the processor which part of storage this operation is working with), and possibly also
(c) A second operand (which tells the processor which other part of storage is required).

We can picture the different types of instruction as shown in Figure 2.4. Each part of the instruction occupies one byte; one byte for the op-code and one byte for each operand.

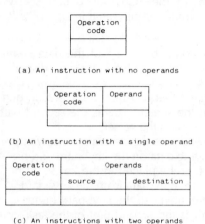

(a) An instruction with no operands

(b) An instruction with a single operand

(c) An instructions with two operands

Figure 2.4   *The format of an instruction*

If there are two operands, as in a move instruction, for example, then some processors write their instructions as:

Op-code source destination

whilst others reverse the order of the operands:

Op-code destination source

We shall use the first of these conventions on the SG01 processor.

Questions

9 Get your list of operations for the SG01 processor and for each operation:

- indicate the number of operands which that operation requires;
- suggest a suitable op-code;
- draw a diagram like those in Figure 2.4 to depict the instruction;

- write down an example of each instruction and say in your own words what that instruction does.

10 The design team has suggested that certain other operations be provided within the SG01 instruction set. Write down the instruction formats, using suitable op-codes for these operations:

- Move the contents of one of the data stores to the screen buffer. This is part of the task to display results on the screen.
- Send a signal that the data in the screen buffer is to be displayed on the screen. This is the second part of the task to display results on the screen.
- Send a signal that the program is to wait until the user has typed in some data on the keyboard and pressed return. This data will then be placed in the keyboard buffer. This is part of the task to input data from the keyboard.
- Move the contents of the keyboard buffer to one of the data stores. This is the second part of the task to input data from the keyboard.
- Abandon the program execution.
- Move a specific number such as 1234567 into the accumulator.

The suggested solutions to the previous questions are summarized in Figure 2.5. Now that we have defined our machine code instruction set,

Machine code	Meaning
A d c	move data store d to comparison register c
B d1 d2	move data store d1 to data store d2
C c d	move comparison register c to data store d
D d	move data store d to accumulator
E d	move accumulator to data store d
F d	add data store d to accumulator
G	Set contents of accumulator to 0
H	change arithmetic sign of accumulator
I	compare contents of comparison registers
J x	jump to instruction x if comparison register is <
K x	jump to instruction x if comparison register is =
L x	jump to instruction x if comparison register is >
M x	jump to instruction x
N d	move data store d to screen buffer.
O	output contents of screen buffer
P	accept data from keyboard into keyboard buffer
Q d	move keyboard buffer to data store d
R	stop execution
S n	move number n to accumulator

Figure 2.5 *Table of machine code instructions*

it should be a fairly simple matter to write entire programs for the SG01.

Questions

11 Using the machine code instruction formats and op-codes for the SG01 which we have summarized in Figure 2.5, rewrite the sequences which you produced as your solution to Questions (1) to (4).

Write machine code programs which will solve the following problems.

12 Add together the numbers 12345 and 45678 and display the result on the screen.

13 Accept two numbers from the keyboard, add them together and display the result on the screen.

14 Accept a number from the keyboard. If the number is 9999, then stop the program execution, otherwise add 1 to the number, display the result and return to ask for another number.

15 Accept a number from the keyboard. Accept a second number; if this number is 0, then stop the program execution. Otherwise compare the numbers and print out the greater of the two.

16 Accept a number from the keyboard, multiply the number by 5 and display the result on the screen.

17 How would you use this technique to produce a program which will ask the user for two numbers, multiply them together and display the result?

18 Make a list of some of the mistakes which a programmer could make when entering the machine code instructions for the SG01. Give an example of an erroneous instruction which illustrates each of the mistakes on your list saying why the instruction is incorrect.

19 How could the processor react if the programmer entered an incorrect instruction such as those in your answer to the previous question?

You should check your solutions to see that you have not fallen into any traps. In particular, there must be a stop statement at the end of the program. Otherwise, the execution will just carry on processing instruction after instruction. It may happen that the previous contents of the instruction store are still in place and you may inadvertently execute the tail end of the previous program.

So now we have developed a set of operations and the equivalent machine code language for the SG01 processor.

From our discussion, it will be clear that each set of machine code instructions is specific to a particular processor. Another processor with a different design will almost certainly have different operations and a correspondingly different machine language.

Assembly code

As you have seen, it is a fairly straightforward matter to write a program in the machine code for the SGO1 processor. A great many programs were written in such **first generation languages**. There was no alternative on the very first computers which were developed, you had to write all your programs in machine code. When the program had been written down on paper, just as you have been doing in the assignments, the programmer would go along to the computer and turn a switch which would allow him/her to type each instruction directly into the instruction store. When this had been done, the programmer would turn another switch and start the program execution.

Quite soon, however, programmers realized that, if the computer can do wonderful things like decoding war-time messages, guiding rockets and so on, then surely it should be possible for it to make their own lives a bit easier. It was proposed that instead of having to write an instruction such as:

> R

when they wanted to issue the instruction to abandon the program, they could write something meaningful, such as:

> STOP

and instead of writing

> G

to set the contents of the accumulator to zero, they could write:

> CLEAR

and instead of writing the instruction:

> D 5

to move a number from data store 5 to the accumulator, they could write:

LOAD 5

These forms of the op-codes would be easier for the programmer to remember.

Such a language is sometimes known as **assembly code** or an **assembly language** or, in the historical context, as a **second generation language**. Just as each range of machine code instructions is peculiar to each processor, so each processor has its own assembly language.

A word or abbreviation such as LOAD or CLR which is used in writing assembly code is sometimes known as a **mnemonic**; this word means *an aid to your memory*. The word sounds rather like *demonic* and the first m is not heard; some people often pronounce the whole word as if it were written *pneumonic*. Such pronunciation and such people should be avoided.

The people who design assembly languages and the mnemonics seem to like short words, preferring MV to MOVE, CLR to CLEAR, JMP to JUMP and so on. In our work we shall use longer, explicit mnemonics.

Question

20 Get your list of op-codes and instruction formats for the SG01 processor and for each operation:

- suggest a suitable assembly language mnemonic for each op-code;
- rewrite the machine code examples which you produced as your solution to Question 9 in the assembly language.

The suggested solutions to the previous questions are summarized in Figure 2.6. Now that we have defined the format of our assembly language, it should be a fairly simple matter to write entire programs for the SG01.

Questions

21 Using the assembly language instruction formats and mnemonics for the SG01 which we have summarized in Figure 2.6, rewrite the sequences which you produced as your solutions to Questions (1) to (4) and as machine code in Question (11).

Assembly	Meaning
ADD d	add data store d to accumulator
CLEAR	Set contents of accumulator to 0
COMP	compare contents of comparison registers
DISPLAY	output contents of screen buffer
IN d	move keyboard buffer to data store d
INPUT	accept data from keyboard into keyboard buffer
JUMP x	jump to instruction x
JUMPEQ x	jump to instruction x if comparison register is =
JUMPGT x	jump to instruction x if comparison register is >
JUMPLT x	jump to instruction x if comparison register is <
LOAD d	move data store d to accumulator
LOADC d c	move data store d to comparison register c
MOVE d1 d2	move data store d1 to data store d2
OUT d	move data store d to screen buffer
PLACE n	move number n to accumulator
NEG	change arithmetic sign of accumulator
STOP	stop execution
STORE d	move accumulator to data store d
STOREC c d	move comparison register c to data store d

Figure 2.6 *Table of assembly language instructions*

Write assembly language programs which will solve the following problems.

22 Add together the numbers 12345 and 45678 and display the result on the screen.

23 Ask the user for two numbers, add them together and display the result on the screen.

24 Ask the user for a number. If the number is 9999, then stop the program execution, otherwise add 1 to the number, display the result and return to ask for another number.

25 Ask the user for a number; if the number is 0, then stop the program execution. Ask the user for a second number; if this number is 0, then stop the program execution. Otherwise compare the numbers and print out the higher of the two.

26 Ask the user for a number, multiply the number by 5 and display the answer on the screen.

27 How would you use this technique to produce a program which will ask the user for two numbers, multiply them together and display the result?

28 Make a list of all the mistakes which a programmer could make when entering the assembly language instructions for the SG01. Give an example of an erroneous instruction which illustrates each of the mistakes on your list saying why the instruction is incorrect. Keep this list, we shall use it again to add further errors.
29 How could the assembler react if the programmer entered an incorrect instruction such as those in your answer to the previous question?

Assembler

In the previous assignments and questions, you have created a set of assembly codes and their equivalent machine code instructions. You have also been building up a list of the sort of errors which a programmer might make and which should be rejected as incorrect by the assembler. This information is enough for someone to specify and produce an assembler for the SGO1 processor and allow us to write programs in this language.

Now that we are able to use our assembly language, the process of developing a program becomes much easier and slightly longer. Having written the program in the assembly language, the programmer would punch the instructions into cards or type them in at the keyboard. The instructions would then be processed by a special-purpose program, called an **assembler**. The assembler would translate the assembly code instructions into machine code instructions, one by one; one assembly language instruction generating one machine code instruction.

Because the operations which the SG01 processor can perform are fixed, we cannot add new operations, such as WRITE TO DISK. This is a limitation of the SG01 processor and there is no solution to this and similar problems, no matter whether we use machine code or assembly language (or any other programming language).

We have seen that it is also difficult – or at best, long-winded – to write the coding for some fairly simple tasks which the SG01 *can* perform, such as MULTIPLY DATA STORE 1 BY DATA STORE 2 AND PUT THE RESULT INTO DATA STORE 3. But the assembler is a different matter; the assembler is just a program, and like any other program it can be changed and made to let us do what we like. Provided that the program produced by the assembler is a valid sequence of SG01 machine code instructions, our assembly code

27

instructions can be more flexible. So let's see how we make the programmer's life easier.

Data names

One useful job which the assembler could perform would be to let us use **names** to identify the data stores instead of the numbers which the machine code uses. Thus, instead of issuing instructions such as:

LOAD 1

to move the contents of data store 1 into the accumulator, or:

ADD 2

to add the contents of data store 2 to the number in the accumulator, it would be useful if we could use meaningful names to identify the data stores. The assembler can let us do this, but first we must define the **data names** which we will use. This could be done by means of statements such as:

DEFINE STORAGE NUMBER 1
DEFINE STORAGE ANSWER 2

which will tell the assembler that we shall use the names NUMBER and ANSWER to identify data store 1 and data store 2 respectively. It is not usual to be able to assign names to the registers, although there is no reason why an assembler could not permit this.

Having declared the names for our data stores, we can issue assembly code instructions such as:

LOAD NUMBER
ADD ANSWER

The assembler will, of course, reject an instruction such as:

LOAD VALUE

if we have not previously defined the name VALUE. Usually, all such names must be declared at the start of the program and before they are used in the assembly language instructions.

The person who writes the assembler will decide what is to be an acceptable data name. He/she may impose some restrictions such as:

- they must consist of letters only
- they must be from 1 to 6 characters in length;

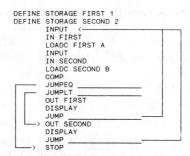

```
DEFINE STORAGE FIRST 1
DEFINE STORAGE SECOND 2
         INPUT   <
         IN FIRST
         LOADC FIRST A
         INPUT
         IN SECOND
         LOADC SECOND B
         COMP
         JUMPEQ
         JUMPLT
         OUT FIRST
         DISPLAY
         JUMP
      -> OUT SECOND
         DISPLAY
         JUMP
      -> STOP
```

Figure 2.7 *Jumps in a program*

- they must not be the same as an assembly code mnemonic.

The more rules there are, the easier it is to enable the assembler to accept a valid data name and to reject an invalid data name.

We use the term **directive** or **declarative** to describe a statement such as DEFINE STORAGE because it provides information to the assembler and is not converted into a machine code instruction. A directive does not occupy any space in the machine code program. A piece of information such as:

STORE 4

is an assembly code **instruction** because it can be translated directly into a machine code instruction. We shall use the general term **statement** to refer to either a compiler directive or an instruction.

Questions

30 Write down some of the differences between the three statements:

DEFINE STORAGE AGES 1
ADD 5
ADD AGES

and describe what action the assembler takes when it meets each of these statements

31 The action of the assembly code program shown in Figure 2.7 is to input two numbers and display the larger. If the two

numbers are equal, then the program will stop. There are several jump statements in the program – I've drawn arrows to show where they jump to – and I want you to fill in the missing instruction numbers of the destinations for these jump statements.

Labels

We could also arrange for the assembler to make our life even easier and help us work out the destinations of any of the JUMP statements in our program. At the moment, if we want to jump ahead in our program we must write a statement such as:

JUMPGT_____

leaving the destination blank, and then, when we have written the entire programme, we can count up the statements and go back and insert the number of the instruction store that we wish to jump to. This is a great source of errors, especially if you amend your program and insert more statements and forget to change the destination of the JUMP statement.

The assembler will let us do this by means of a **label** or a **statement label**. A label is an identifier which is written at the front of the statement like this:

FINISH STOP

or

RESTART MOVE 1 2

When we wish to jump to the labelled statement, we could use a statement such as

JUMPGT FINISH

or

JUMP RESTART

As with data names, the person who writes the assembler will decide what is to be an acceptable label. He/she may impose some restrictions such as:

- they must consist of letters only;
- there must be no spaces before the label;
- they must be followed by a space before the op-code;

- they must be from 1 to 6 characters in length;
- they must not be the same as an assembly code mnemonic or a data name.

We may even specify a requirement to declare all labels before they are used, as we did with the DEFINE STORAGE directive. This might take the form:

DECLARE LABEL FINISH
DECLARE LABEL RESTART

and would allow the assembler to know what labels to expect, although (unlike the DEFINE STORAGE directive) it would not specify the actual instruction stores with which the labels are associated.

The more rules there are, the easier it is to enable the assembler to accept a valid label and to reject an invalid label. The assembler may have other rules concerning the layout of the instructions which it is able to convert:

- the label – if any is used – must be the first part of the instruction;
- there must be at least one space before the op- code;
- there must be at least one space between the op-code and the operands;
- there must be at least one space between the operands.

Questions

32 When it encounters an instruction such as:

JUMP JOBEND

what work must the assembler do to translate this into a machine code instruction such as:

M 22

What actions do you think the assembler must carry out in order to be able to handle labels?

33 Carry out the operations which you gave as your answer to the previous question to check that they would work on the program shown in Figure 2.8.

34 Look at the suggested solution for Question 25, and rewrite this program using suitable data names and labels.

35 You having been building a list of errors which a programmer

```
DEFINE STORAGE FIRST 1
DEFINE STORAGE SECOND 2
START INPUT
      IN FIRST
      LOADC FIRST A
      INPUT
      IN 2
      LOADC 2 B
      COMP
      JUMPGT AISBIG
BISBIG OUT FIRST
      DISPLAY
      JUMP START
AISBIG OUT 2
      DISPLAY
      JUMP START
```

Figure 2.8 *An assembler program with labels: 1*

might make when writing an assembly code program. Add to this list any new errors which a programmer might make when using data names.

36 To the list of errors which a programmer might make when writing an assembly code program, add any further errors which a programmer might make when using labels.

37 How could the assembler react if the programmer entered an incorrect statement such as those in your answer to the previous questions?

Macros

Even in the few small programs which you wrote in the preceding assignments, you probably recognized that certain tasks keep coming up again and again. A sequence of the form:

PLACE 12345
STORE 1

PLACE 9999
STORE 4

appeared several times to move a specific value into one of the data stores. You may have even felt that it would be convenient if there were an operation to the SG01 repertoire to do just that; possibly a new PUT statement, something like:

PUT 12345 1

or

PUT 9999 4

The assembly code programmers also felt that it would be useful to be able to add more operations, but, since it is not possible to add more operations to the processor once it has been manufactured, they came up with the idea of **macros**. A macro is an assembly code statement – looking very much like any other assembly code instruction. The difference is that, whereas an assembly code instruction generates one machine code instruction, a macro instruction generates a sequence of one or more assembly code instructions into play. This means that, with the help of macros, we **can** include our PUT instruction and make it do precisely what we want.

First, we must define our new macro statement. This is done by a sequence like this:

```
DEFINE MACRO PUT $1 $2
PLACE $1
STORE $2
MACRO END
```

which tells the assembler than that the PUT macro will have two operands, identified by the **dummy operands** – or **parameters** – $1 and $2 in this definition.

So when the programmer writes an instruction such as:

```
PUT 9999 4
```

in his/her program, the assembler will recognize that this is not standard SG01 assembly code, but before rejecting the instruction, the assembler will look for a macro definition for PUT and, finding our DEFINE MACRO sequence, it will use that. The assembler will first match the statement:

```
DEFINE MACRO PUT $1 $2
```

with the statement

```
PUT 9999 4
```

and associate the parameter $1 with the number 9999, and the parameter $2 with the number 4. Then it will use these new values, *slotting* them into the appropriate positions in the statements:

```
PLACE $1
STORE $2
```

to produce the two assembly code instructions:

33

PLACE 9999
STORE 4

A macro definition can use assembly code instructions or machine code instructions. It may even use another macro. All macros must be defined *before* they can be used in a program.

Sometimes, it may be required to use a label within a macro. This will allow you to repeat a sequence of processing or even to jump to the end and abandon the macro under certain conditions. In this case, the labels in the macro definition will have the form:

L$1

and

L$2

and so on. For example, we might need a macro which will compare two data stores and, if they are equal, put the value 9999999999 into data store 1. A suitable definition is shown in Figure 2.9.

```
        DEFINE MACRO COMPSET $1 $2
        LOADC $1 A
        LOADC $2 B
        COMP
        JUMPEQ L$1
        JUMP L$2
L$1     PUT 9999999999 1
L$2     MACRO END
```

Figure 2.9   *A macro definition with labels*

You will notice that we can jump to the MACRO END statement, if necessary.

We shall construct some useful macros in the questions which follow. Most assemblers are provided with a standard set of macros, and there may be facilities to set up your own library of macros, so that you don't have to declare every macro whenever you need it.

Questions

Using the above format for the DEFINE MACRO, define the following macros:

38 A macro with the op-code FETCH which will have the combined effect of the instructions:

> INPUT   get data from keyboard
> IN XXX   move keyboard buffer to data store xxx

and let me input a value into any of the data stores.

39 A macro with the op-code WRITE which will have the combined effect of the instructions:

> OUT yyy   move data store yyy to screen buffer
> DISPLAY   display the contents of the screen buffer

40 A macro with the op-code STOREN which will allow me to write an instruction such as:

> STOREN 12345 3

in order to put the value 12345 into data store 3.

41 A macro with the op-code SUM which will allow me to write in instruction such as:

> SUM 1 2 3

in order to add the contents of data store 1 and the contents of data store 2 and put the results in data store 3.

42 A macro with the op-code DECR which will allow me to write an instruction such as:

> DECR 3

an order to subtract 1 from the number in data store 3.

43 A macro with the op-code COMPARE which will allow me to write an instruction such as:

> COMPARE 3 5

in order to compare the contents of data store 3 with the contents of data store 5. It will set the comparison result register to < if the contents of data store 3 are less than the contents of data store 5, and > if the contents of data store 5 are less than the contents of data store 3.

44 A macro with the op-code COMPNUM which will allow me to write an instruction such as:

> COMPNUM 3 5

in order to compare the contents of data store 3 with the number 5. It will set the comparison result register to < if the contents of data store 3 are less than 5, and > if the contents of data store 3 are greater than 5.

45 Use your macros to write a program which will do the following:

- Get two numbers from the user.
- If either or both of the numbers is 0, then stop the program execution.
- Multiply the two numbers together.
- Display the result.

46 Apply the same techniques which you used in the previous program to write a macro with the op-code MULTIPLY which will allow me to write an instruction such as:

    MULTIPLY 1 2 3

in order to multiply the contents of data store 1 by the contents of data store 2 and put the result in data store 3.

47 A macro which will allow me to write an instruction like:

    RDADIS 1 2

in order to read two numbers into data store 1 and data store 2 respectively, add them together and print out the result. Our assembler will let you use one macro within another so you can use the macros which you defined in the previous questions.

48 If you consider the format of the DEFINE MACRO declaration, you will probably have realized that part of the declaration is superfluous. Which part(s) and why?

Activity 2

This activity offers further practice in the use of macros and extends the facilities of the assembly language.

Define macros for other frequently-required processes such as:

(a) JUMPNE

Such that a statement such as:

    JUMPNE LABEL1

will jump to the instruction at label LABEL1 if the comparison register is set found to show a condition of either < or >

(b) LOOPFOR

Such that a sequence such as:

LOOPFOR 10

assembly language statement(s)

ENDLOOPFOR

will execute the statement(s) between the LOOPFOR statement and the ENDLOOPFOR statement 10 times.

(c) LOOPUNTIL

Such that a sequence such as:

LOOPUNTIL =

assembly language statement(s)

ENDLOOPUNTIL

will execute the statement(s) between the LOOPUNTIL statement and the ENDLOOPUNTIL statement until the comparison register is found to show a condition of equality.

(d) LOOPWHILE

Such that a sequence such as:

LOOPWHILE =

assembly language statement(s)

ENDLOOPWHILE

will execute the statement(s) between the LOOPWHILE statement and the ENDLOOPWHILE statement whilst the comparison register is found to show a condition of equality.

Stored programs

There are several useful facilities that we could propose in order to make the writing and development of programs much simpler. These would be programs or **utilities** – written in machine code or assembly code – which would help with the development of our programs. Typically, these programs will include:

- An INPUT utility to read in the instructions of a program as they are typed in at the keyboard.

- A SAVE utility to save the program on disk, and a DELETE utility to remove unwanted programs from the disk.
- A PRINT utility to display or print a listing of the instructions in a program.
- An EDIT utility to allow us to add, change and/or delete the instructions of a program.
- A LOAD utility to recall a program which has previously been saved on disk.

These utilities, together with the assembler itself, would become a standard set of programs – the **software** – which would be available to anyone writing programs for the SG01 processor.

Then, when we have typed in the statements of a program – our **source program** – and we are satisfied that the program is correct, there will be other pieces of software which will allow us to:

- submit a program to the assembler, and the assembler will then
- produce an error report if we have made any mistakes in writing the program, or it will
- convert the program into the equivalent machine code program. This form of our program is known as the **object program**.

We could even ask that the software should be able to save the object program on disk so that, next time we want to execute that program, we can ask for the *object program* without having to reassemble the source program every time.

In the case of the SG01, it might not be possible to implement all of these facilities because we have not discussed any means of reading and writing data to disk. This would be achieved by means of registers and buffers, in much the same manner as we have described for input from the keyboard and output to the screen.

Activity 3

If you have written and used any programs on a computer, make a list of the software which was available to help you to develop the program.

Were there any pieces of additional software which you would have liked to have had? How would these have helped you in your work?

Subroutines

You may remember that we insisted there be a STOP statement at the end of our program. Otherwise, the processing would continue into the instructions which just happened to be left in the instruction store by the last program which was executed before our program was loaded. This is illustrated in Figure 2.10. Diagram (a) shows a picture of the instruction store at 10 a.m. when program A was loaded and executed; the statements of program A are shaded dark. Diagram (b) shows the instruction store at 11 a.m. when the shorter program B was loaded; the statements of program B are shaded lighter. If there were no STOP statement at the end of program B, then we should plough straight into the remnants of program A and continue to execute the darker-shaded statements there.

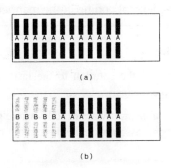

Figure 2.10   *Loading one program after another: 1*

The fact that our program does not clear the instruction store can be used to our advantage. We could arrange to load some program instructions at the bottom end of the instruction store and this would remain there indefinitely, provided that we did not overwrite it. This is illustrated in Figure 2.11. Diagram (a) shows a useful routine called S which has been loaded into the bottom end of the instruction store and remains there for use by both program A and program B. When a program – say, program A – needs to use that routine, the processing can jump to the instruction store where routine S starts; routine S will then be executed and when it has finished, the processing can jump back to where it came from in program A.

39

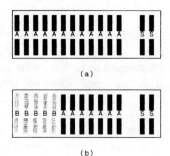

Figure 2.11 *Loading one program after another: 2*

Question

49 Write down some of facilities that we should need in order to be able to use a piece of coding in the manner described.

Subroutines in practice

The facilities suggested in the solution to the last question could be achieved by fairly simple means.

(a) We could tell the loading software exactly where routine S is to be loaded by including an assembly code directive such as:

   START 78

   if we wanted the first statement of routine S to be placed in instruction store 78.

(b) In order to reach routine S from our main program (program A or program B), we would simply use a statement such as:

   JUMP 78

Remembering *where to go back to* when we leave routine S is slightly more complicated. Have you any ideas? We need two new facilities, as illustrated in Figure 2.12. In this diagram, the first section of the instruction store is used by program A, the section from 78 to 91 is used by routine S.

The first facility which we need is to be executed *just before we jump to routine S*. Do you remember that one of the processor registers holds the number of the instruction which will be executed next? The new

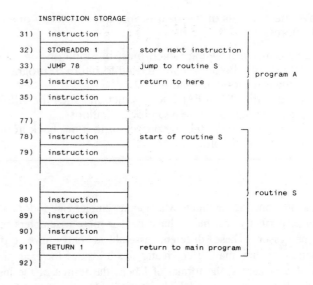

INSTRUCTION STORAGE

31)	instruction		
32)	STOREADDR 1	store next instruction	
33)	JUMP 78	jump to routine S	} program A
34)	instruction	return to here	
35)	instruction		
77)			
78)	instruction	start of routine S	
79)	instruction		
88)	instruction		} routine S
89)	instruction		
90)	instruction		
91)	RETURN 1	return to main program	
92)			

Figure 2.12 *STOREADDR and RETURN*

facility will store the contents of the next-instruction register in one of the data stores. I have shown the new instruction:

STOREADDR 1

which will move the current contents of the next-instruction register into data store 1.

The second facility, which I have represented by the instruction:

RETURN 1

will take the contents of data store 1 and use the address held here to return to the main program A.

Questions

We now discover that the SG01 processor has these two new operations:

- Move the contents of one of the data stores to the *next instruction* register.

- Move the contents of the *next instruction* register to one of the data stores.

50 Indicate any processing which must be done on the contents of data store 1 before it can be used to return to program A in the situation shown in Figure 2.12.

51 How do the STOREADDR instruction and the RETURN instruction relate to these two new operations?

52 How do we actually tell the processor to jump back from routine S to the main program A?

So these are some of the things which an assembler can do for us. It is, of course, perfectly feasible to have two or more assemblers for the same processor. These different assemblers may have different mnemonics or they may offer greater flexibility in, for example, the length of data names, the format of labels, the format of the instructions, the library of macros which are available, and so on. But they will all produce a machine code program for, in our case, the SG01 processor. Could we use the same assembler for the SG01 processor as for, say, the Intel 80386SX processor? Justify your answer.

The names given to the different assemblers usually indicate the processor or the computer on which they can be used. You might encounter Intel 8085 assembler, the IBM System/370 assembly language, the ICL 1900 assembler, and so on.

Another processor

The SG01 processor has been in use for some time, and the manufacturers have made the decision to produce a newer version to meet the changing requirements of the computer industry. The features of this new model – the SG02 – are to include:

- All the registers and the accumulator are to be one **word**, that is, four bytes in length. The registers are to be used as they were in the SG01.
- There are to be variable-length instruction formats. An instruction will no longer occupy a word (as it did in the SG01), but only 1 byte (for an instruction with no operands), 2 bytes (for an instruction with one operand), or 3 bytes (for an instruction with two operands).

- There is to be no distinction between data stores and instruction stores. Both data and instructions are to be held in a single storage area called **memory**.
- A piece of data may occupy one or more bytes of memory.

The memory consists of a sequence of single bytes of storage. There are 1,000,000 bytes of memory in the basic model, although this may be increased, if required. Each byte is identified by its position within memory (this is known as the **address** of the byte): the first byte is byte number 0 so its address is 0; the next byte is byte 1, so its address is 1; then come byte 2, byte 3 and so on. Data will be identified by the address of the first byte of the word which holds the data, and instructions will be identified (in jump operations) by the address of the first byte of the instruction.

A diagram of the new processor is shown in Figure 2.13.

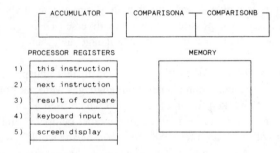

Figure 2.13 *The SG02 processor*

Activity 4

Consider the changes which will be necessary to the design of the assembler.

(1) What changes will there be to the operations which the SG02 processor can perform?
(2) How will the op-codes change in the new machine language?
(3) How will the operands change in the machine language?
(4) How will the format of the instructions change in the machine language?
(5) How will the variable-length nature of the data affect the instructions?

(6) Since data and instructions are mixed, how can you avoid using data when you should be using an instruction, and vice versa?

(7) How will the assembler deal with labels?

Third generation languages

We have followed the progression of the computer language for the SG01 processor. We saw that the first generation language – the machine code – is peculiar to each particular processor. The SG01 has its own machine language, the Intel 8085 has its own machine language, the Intel 80386 has its own machine language, and so on, and they are all different; a different language for each processor. These differences will be fewer for processors which are related to each other.

Even when we move on to the second generation of computer languages, the assemblers, we find that they are just as diverse as the machine languages; possibly even more diverse. There is usually at least one assembler for each machine language and, therefore, for each processor.

During the 1950s, computer users began to feel unhappy about the fact that the first and second generation languages were not **portable.** If a programmer worked for an organization which used a computer with an SG01 processor and then left to join another company which used a computer with, say, an Intel 8088 processor, he/she would have to learn a completely new assembler. If a company used a computer based upon a Zilog Z80 processor and then bought a more powerful computer based upon an Intel 80836 computer, all the programmers would have to be retrained to write programs in the new language and all the existing programs would have to be rewritten. It was not possible just to load the existing programs on to the new computer. Neither the languages nor the programs were **portable**, they could not be moved across to another computer without a great amount of work in modifying them for use on the new processor.

The solution came in the form of the **third generation** of computer languages. The requirements of these languages were:

- They should allow the programmer to express a problem in a more natural language and in terms with which he/she was familiar, not in the stilted manner of machine code and assemblers.

- They should be easier to use than the previous languages.
- They should make it easier to write, debug, test, implement and maintain a program.
  Machine code and assembly language programs are fairly easy to write, but it is often difficult to maintain a program written in these languages. Being asked to amend someone else's assembly language program can be a nerve-racking experience.
- They should offer more programming facilities. We shall look at the techniques of structured programming and modular programming later.
- They should be portable, permitting a program written for one processor to be used – with few, if any, changes – on another, completely different processor.

Thinking of a solution

In the period from 1954 to 1956, an American called John Backus was working for IBM when he proposed a new language translation program which would accept instructions as a series of algebraic formulae and translate these into the appropriate machine code. It was really just an extension of the ideas which we have already met in assemblers and in macros. The name given to the finished product was Fortran, the *FOR*mula *TRAN*slator.

We have already designed an SG01 assembly language macro to add two numbers together and put the result in a third data store:

    ADD 1 4 5

or, if we have declared names for our data stores, we might write

    ADD A B C

and the assembler would convert this into the appropriate machine code. In exactly the same manner, Fortran would allow a programmer to write the statement as a mathematical formula such as:

    C = A + B

and then this would be converted into the appropriate machine code.

At much the same time, there was much interest in the same problems in Europe. In 1958, a meeting at the Swiss Federal Institute of Technology in Zurich laid the foundations of IAL (an International

Algebraic Language) which was subsequently published as Algol 58 – the *ALGO*rithmic *L*anguage.

There were slight differences between the grammar of Fortran and that of Algol. In Algol, we should represent the same problem by the expression:

A := B + C

With the advent of third generation languages, the programmer was allowed to think in his/her own terms. No longer was the programmer to be constrained to think in terms of registers and buffers, as the computer did. This is a most important feature and it marks a significant advance for programming languages. To remind us that these language are removed from the detail of machine code and assembly code, the term **high-level languages** is often used to describe them.

Activity 5

(1) Make a list of the sort of people who would be able to use computers in their work if only the computer spoke the appropriate language.
(2) Add the following potential users to your list and write down some of the special requirements of the computer system which each of these groups of people might use in their work.

   (a) An accountant.
   (b) An electrical engineer.
   (c) A designer who plans kitchen layouts and calculates the cost.
   (d) A statistician who is concerned with the flow of traffic at a road junction.
   (e) An author who is writing books and articles.
   (f) A teacher producing programs to teach the English language to foreign students.
   (g) An artist who is designing wallpaper patterns.
   (h) A radio talk-show presenter who uses a screen to display details of the people who are waiting to speak to her.
   (i) A lexicographer who uses the computer to maintain and print the pages of an English dictionary.

Compiler

Just as the name *assembler* is given to the software which converts an assembly language source program into machine code, so a **compiler** takes a source program comprising a set of third generation language statements and produces an equivalent object program. This is illustrated in the diagram in Figure 2.14.

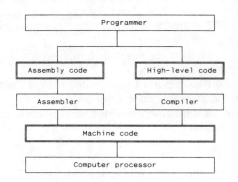

Figure 2.14 *Programming languages*

Activity 6

(1) Look at the diagram in Figure 2.14. Imagine that you have written a program in a first generation language. Highlight the box where your program would appear on the diagram.

(2) Indicate where each of the following would appear in Figure 2.14:

    (a) A second generation language program.

    (b) A third generation language.

    (c) A Fortran program.

    (d) An Algol program.

    (e) A Basic program.

    (f) A sequence of SG01 instructions such as:

        D 1
        F 2
        E 3

    (g) A sequence of SG01 instructions such as:

        PLACE 12345

```
STORE 1
ADD I
STORE 2
```

(3) Write a sequence of machine code instructions for the SG01 processor which will subtract the contents of data store 1 from the contents of data store 2 and put the result into data store 3.

Now write the same processing using the SG01 assembly code. You have been asked to explain your program to someone who knows very little about computers and programming, so you should use any or all of the facilities which you know to make the program *readable*.

Now write the same problem as a mathematical formula, or as an arithmetic expression.

Indicate how each part of your mathematical formula is represented in the assembly code solution.

(4) Write down the equivalent SG01 assembly code to represent the Fortran statement:

A = B * C

given that the * represents multiplication.

Ease of use

A program written in a high-level language is considerably shorter than the equivalent assembly code or machine code. In turn, this means that there are fewer opportunities for the programmer to make mistakes when writing in the high-level language. Because the high-level language statements are more intelligible and more meaningful than the low-level languages, any mistakes will be easier to spot. If I write a piece of assembler code to take a certain course of action if VALUE1 is greater than VALUE2:

```
DEFINE STORAGE VALUE1 1
DEFINE STORAGE VALUE2 2
LOADC A VALUE2
LOADC B VALUE1
COMP
JUMPGT 22
```

it is less easy to see that I have made three mistakes than it would be to spot the single mistake in the equivalent Fortran coding:

IF (VALUE1.GT.VALUE2) OG TO 22

It is also much easier to see what is happening in the Fortran coding.

Obviously, it is going to be much easier to write programs in a high-level language. But the people who developed these languages were concerned with other aspects besides their being easy to use.

Backus was concerned that the object program produced by the Fortran should be *fast and efficient*. The Algol team were concerned that the language should have *structured programming* capabilities and that it should force the programmer into good programming habits; for this reason, Algol and Pascal (a descendant of Algol) are ideal languages for teaching programming skills.

Portability

Because a high-level computer language is less closely tied to a particular processor, the source programs are to a large extent machine independent – they are *portable*. A Fortran program written for one computer can be used very easily on another completely different processor; all that is needed is a suitable compiler. In order to use a Fortran program on the SG01 processor, I need a Fortran compiler for the SG01; to use the same Fortran program on an IBM System/370 computer, I need a Fortran compiler for the IBM System/370 computer. For various practical reasons, there may be slight differences between the various Fortran compilers, but the amount of work required when transporting a high-level language program between computers is minimal compared to the task of moving a machine code program or an assembly language program.

Of course, someone has to write a Fortran compiler for each processor, but that is a *once-only* task. The same Fortran compiler for the SG01 processor can compile any Fortran program into a form suitable for use on the SG01 processor.

Fourth generation languages

Third generation languages have been used for over 30 years and almost all commercial programs are nowadays written in a third generation language such as Cobol or Basic, or for more detailed processing, in a second generation assembler.

Since the late 1970s, there has been great concern over certain other aspects of the programming activity over and above those of Backus and the Algol team. Users now demand more of the language than that it is merely a means to express a problem in computer terms. Nowhere has this concern been more noticeable than in commercial data processing. The troublesome aspects when producing systems in third generation languages are:

- The specification, design, development and testing cycle is too long when a new computer system is required. The time-scales must be reduced.
- There is often a loss of information or a dilution of ideas as the problem makes the transition from the end-user, via the analysts and programmers, through to the final solution.
- Once it has been expressed as a written specification, the system becomes inflexible and cannot respond to last-minute additions or other changes required by the user.
- The task of maintaining an existing program is difficult and requires the program to be tested thoroughly once again in order to identify any errors introduced by the amendments.
- The programs and the database are quite separate entities. It would be desirable to use parts of the database, such as the data dictionary, as an active part of the programming task.

The solutions to these problems lay in the area of **fourth generation languages**, or 4GL.

What is a fourth generation language?

At the moment, there is no real definition of a fourth generation language. But, if we look at some of the pieces of software which are described as a 4GL, we can identify a number of common features:

- 4GLs are predominantly used in commercial programming environments.
  Commercial systems are concerned more with manipulating and organizing large quantities of data, rather than just performing calculations.
- 4GLs use a data dictionary to specify the format of the data records and values which are being processed.
- 4GL programming tools are easy to learn and to apply.
- 4GL tools are suitable for all users, from non-technical end-users (such as clerks, managers) through to highly skilled technical staff

(such as analysts and programmers). Each user is able to learn and apply the language to the extent that he/she requires.

- 4GL programs are easy to read, write and maintain.
- 4GL programming tools reduce the time and effort needed to develop a system.

Tasks such as opening files, reading and writing records, and closing files, which are required in almost every program, are performed automatically by the 4GL processor.

The production of screen displays and printed reports is done automatically by the 4GL, based upon pictures or images painted by the programmer.

These programming tools improve the productivity of the analyst and programmer.

- 4GL processing descriptions are **non-procedural**.

This means that you do not write a sequence of statements which are to be executed one after the other. Instead, the programmer fills in a series of forms and paints a set of screens and report images describing the task which is to be carried out.

- 4GL programming tools focus on the **functionality** (what the program must do) rather than on the mechanics of programming (how the programmer and the program must do it).

In Chapter 9, we shall look at 4GLs in more detail when we consider the fourth generation language known as SB+.

Different instruction sets

The diagram in Figure 2.15 illustrates some important points about the instruction set of the processor and the instructions in a particular programming language.

The instructions which a high-level programming language – such as Cobol or Pascal – is able to carry out are shown at the top of the diagram. The individual programming language instructions are represented by the boxes marked HL1, HL2 and so on.

The instructions which the processor is capable of performing – the machine code operations – are shown along the centre of the diagram. The individual machine language instructions are represented by the boxes marked OP1, OP2 and so on.

The instructions which the assembly language for the processor is capable of performing are shown at the bottom of the diagram. The

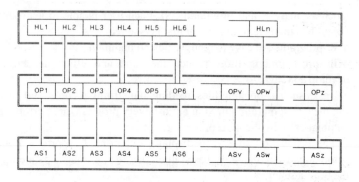

Figure 2.15   *Machine language/programming language*

individual assembly language instructions are represented by the boxes
marked AS1, AS2 and so on.

The diagram illustrates several points:

(1) The processor is invariably capable of performing many more operations than a high-level programming language.

For example, the processor may be able to play music on a
speaker attached to the terminal, but the programming language
may not have statements to use that facility. In the diagram, the
high-level language has no means of using the machine language
instructions OP5, OPv and OPz.

In general, the higher the level of the language, the greater the
separation between the HL boxes and the OP boxes, and the more
OP boxes are used by each HL box.

(2) A programmer writing in a low-level programming language, such
as the assembler for the processor, is capable of using all the facilities of the machine language.

The diagram shows this by having a link from AS1 to OP1, AS2
to OP2 and so on.

(3) A single high-level language statement may invoke a single
machine language instruction or a single high-level statement may
call upon several operations in the machine language.

These situations are shown in the diagram where HL1 invokes
OP1 and HL3 uses OP2, OP3 and OP4.

(4) A single machine language instruction may be used by several
high-level language statements.

In the diagram, OP6 is used by both HL5 and HL6.

Assignment 3

A certain processor – the SG07 – uses 5 storage areas identified by the number 1, 2, 3 and so on.

There are instructions which will:

- Clear the contents of storage area number 1.

    In the assembly language for the processor, this instruction is CLR.

- Move a number from storage area number 1 into any one of the other storage areas, overwriting the previous contents of that storage area.

    These assembly language instructions are MV2 (move into storage area 2), MV3, MV4 and MV5.

- Print the contents of storage area number 1.

    This assembly language instruction is PR.

- Add the contents of one storage area to the number in storage area number 1.

    These assembly language instructions are AD2 (add into storage area 2), AD3, AD4 and AD5.

- Accept a number from the keyboard and place this into storage area number 5.

    This assembly language instruction is IN.

(1) Draw a diagram like that in Figure 2.15 which shows one set of boxes to represent the SG07 processor instructions and another set of boxes to represent the assembly language instructions.

(2) Write a program in the assembly language which will:
   - (a) ask the user for two numbers;
   - (b) add these together;
   - (c) print out the sum of the two numbers.

(3) On your diagram, draw a new set of boxes which includes one which will add two numbers together. Link this box to those representing the SGO7 processor instructions to show which machine language instructions your addition operation uses.

(4) I want you to consider any computer which you may have used to write and execute programs. This may be a small microcomputer, a PC-compatible computer at college or a large mini or main-frame computer, and you may have written programs in Basic or Pascal or any other language.

    Make a list of all the features which are available on that computer:

- The screen and terminal effects: music, sound, colour, graphics, and so on.
- The hardware devices, such as mouse, diskette, magnetic tape, printer and plotters.

(5) I want you to think about each programming language which you have used on this computer and check through your list of features and alongside each feature:

    (a) Indicate whether or not you are able to use this feature from the programming language which you have used.

    (b) If the feature can be used, write down a statement (or sequence of statements) which will use the feature.

Use your lists to answer the following questions:

- Are there any features of the computer which you cannot use? What are the features?
- Are there any features which you can use in one language but not in another? What are the features and what are the languages?

(6) Why is it not possible to use all the features of the processor from some languages? Is this desirable or undesirable? Justify your answer.

Other instruction sets

The SG01 processor is a simple device and does not offer the full range of operations which are found on commercial microprocessors. In this section, I want to summarize some of the other types of instruction which you will encounter as you look at other computers and microprocessors.

One of the major differences between our SG01 instruction set and that of other processors is that most offer facilities for operating upon data held:

- in memory only,
- in registers only, or
- in both memory and registers.

These instructions simplify the handling of data in that it can be processed wherever it is held without having to move it to a special location.

Binary operations

Several machine code instructions are dedicated to the processing *binary* data. These include facilities to shift a binary number to the left (filling with zeros at the right), shift a binary number to the right (filling with zeros at the left). The use of such operations speeds up the multiplication and division of binary values by 2. There are also operations to rotate a binary number to the left, and to rotate a binary number to the right.

Logical operations

A subset of many instruction sets performs *logical* operations on the data.

The AND instruction takes two binary strings and performs a logical AND operation on the corresponding bits: if both bits are set to 1, then the result is 1, otherwise the result is 0.

The NOT instruction takes a single binary string and performs a logical NOT operation, flipping the bits, that is, changing a 1 to a 0, and a 0 to a 1.

The OR instruction takes two binary strings and performs a logical OR operation on the corresponding bits: if either or both bits are set to 1, then the result is 1, otherwise the result is 0.

The exclusive OR instruction takes two binary strings and performs a logical exclusive OR operation on the corresponding bits: if one (but not both) of the bits is set to 1, then the result is 1, otherwise the result is 0.

Data format

The SG01 processor could only handle positive and negative integer numbers of 10 or fewer digits in length. We cannot handle fractions, very large numbers (such as the distance from the earth to the sun in metres), very small numbers (such as the diameter of a virus in millimetres), strings of data (such as words and sentences), or binary numbers.

Arithmetic operations

A wider range of arithmetic operations are usually available for numeric data, allowing us to perform addition, subtraction, multiplication and division of integers and *floating point* numbers. These avoid the use of the complex processing and repetition which we had to use when we wanted to subtract or to multiply on the SG01 processor.

Indexing

There will be facilities for *indexing* memory addresses, adding the contents of a special register – known as an **index register** – to the specified address before the data is retrieved. For example, our SG01 machine code has the operation:

D 1

to move the contents of data store 1 into the accumulator. If we had an indexing facility, then there would be an instruction such as

Z 1

meaning add the contents of the data store whose number is 1 plus whatever is held in the *index register*. So, if the index register contained the number 0, then the instruction

Z 1

would move the contents of data store 1+0 (that is, data store 1) into the accumulator; but if the index register contained the number 3, then the instruction

Z 1

would move the contents of data store 1+3 (that is, data store 4) into the accumulator.

This facility makes it very easy to handle *arrays* if the **base address**, that is the start address of the array, is held in storage (in data store 1, in our example) and then the index register is incremented by the size of each element in order to access the successive elements of the array. This is illustrated in Figure 2.16.

Immediate instructions

Some instruction sets have facilities for storing one byte of data – one of the operands – within the instruction itself. This is particularly valuable because it reduces the time taken to access the second operand.

Examples of such instructions might be:

CI xxxx +

(the compare immediate instruction) will compare the data at address xxxx with the character +

MVI ! xxxx

(the move immediate instruction) will move the single character ! into the byte at address xxxx

ADDI 1 xxxx

(the add immediate instruction) will add 1 to the data at address xxxx.

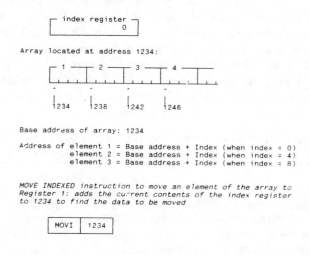

Figure 2.16 *Indexing to access elements of an array*

Flags and testing

The SG01 processor used a register to store the result of the last comparison operation. Most processors and their instruction sets use single binary **flags** to indicate this and many other conditions within the processor. Typically, these flags will include:

- Carry flag which is set when the last addition operation resulted in a digit being carried over to the left.

- Overflow flag to indicate whether the last arithmetic operation resulted in an overflow because the result was too large for the storage location.
- Parity flag which is set to indicate whether the current value contains an odd or an even number of 1-bits.
- Sign flag which is set to indicate the sign of the current value.
- Zero flag which is set when the current value is zero.

Input and output

The basic principle of input and output on our SG01 processor is very similar to that of other microprocessors. There are a series of buffers which are used to store the data prior to transmission to a device (for output), and to receive the data being read in from a device (for input). The major difference is that we had only one input device and one output device. In practice, there may be a great many pieces of equipment. Each of these devices will be connected to a **port**, and each port is identified by a unique port number. The required port number is included within the IN and OUT instructions and the processor uses this to transfer data between the port and memory.

Activity 7

Get a copy of the assembly language manual for one of the computers or microprocessors which you will be using, and write down some brief notes on the instruction set which is available.

Pay particular attention to the:

- binary operations;
- logical operations;
- data format;
- arithmetic operations;
- indexing;
- immediate instructions;
- flags and testing;
- input and output,

and any other special facilities which are offered by the instruction set.

Interpreting

On some operating systems, the statements of a program are processed immediately they are typed in. For example, some versions of Basic will allow you to type in a statement such as:

    12*34*56

and the result:

    22848

will be displayed on the screen and another statement awaited. You can even type in a sequence of statements such as:

    A=4
    B=7
    PRINT A+B

and the Basic processor will display the result:

    11

If you make a mistake and type an incorrect statement such as:

    12(34*56

then this will be rejected with some suitable error-message and no action will be taken. A language processor which works in this manner is known as an **interpreter** because it takes each statement and interprets (or translates) it into a suitable form for processing.

Some languages – Basic is one such language – will allow you to type in a whole sequence of statements, possibly also allowing you to store these for later use. Then, when you want to use that program, the interpreter is called into play to look at, translate and perform the action of the statements, one by one. If there is an error in any statement, then the interpreter may take any of several possible courses of action: it may:

- tell you about the error and skip the offending statement; or
- tell you about the error and let you correct the statement; or
- tell you about the error and abandon the entire program.

Exactly what happens depends upon the people who wrote the interpreter.

Activity 8

(1) Look at the Basic program shown in Figure 2.17 (a) and work through it using each of the four sets of data shown in Figure 2.17 (b).

If you have access to a Basic interpreter, then you may prefer to use it for this exercise; otherwise, work through the program on paper. As you do this, locate any errors in the program and say when the interpreter would detect the errors, how the error would be notified to the user, and what action you might reasonably expect the interpreter to take. Correct each error *only as it is revealed by the interpreter*; do not correct any other errors which you may spot by reading through the program.

```
100 DIM A(10)
110 PRINT HOW MANY READINGS DO YOU WANT?
120 INPUT N
130 IF N=99 THEN GO 270
140 TOTAL=0
150 FOR X=1 TO N
160 PRINT "ENTER READING NUMBER ";X:": ";
170 INPUT A(X)
180 TOTAL=TOTAL+A(X)
190 NEXT X
200 DISPLAY ANSWER = ";TOTAL/N
210 END
```

(a) the program

	N	Readings
a)	3	5, 6, 9
b)	5	4, 2, 3, 2, 1
c)	11	7, 5, 5, 5, 1, 4, 1, 7, 9, 8, 1
d)	99	

(b) the data

Figure 2.17 *Using a basic interpreter*

(2) Make a list of some of the advantages of using an interpreter to execute your programs.
(3) Make a list of some of the disadvantages of using an interpreter to execute your programs.

Compiling, linking and loading – some jargon

We have encountered the concept of interpreting and compiling. In order to simplify the explanation of the various programming languages which we shall consider later in the book, we need to have a working understanding of some other concepts which are involved in the use of these languages. This section introduces the major terms. Many of these will be discussed in detail later.

Earlier, we saw that a *compiler* is a piece of software provided to perform several functions:

- It reads in all the statements for the program. This version of the program which you write in Basic or some other language is known as the **source program**.
- It checks the grammar of each statement in your source program and reports any errors there and then. This sort of error is sometimes called a **syntax error** or a grammatical error.
- It translates each statement into the equivalent machine code.
- It produces a list – known as the **symbol table** – of the variables which are used in the program (we used A, N, TOTAL and X in our program) and makes a note of how much storage space they require. For example, we would probably find that all the simple variables require 4 bytes of storage and the array A requires 10 times 4 bytes of storage. The compiler would then be able to draw a map of the storage requirements and use this to work out the address of the memory location where variable N is to be found, the address of TOTAL and so on. These addresses might be recorded as the number of bytes from the start of the program.
- If there are no errors in the source program, it allows the translated form of the program to be saved on disk. This machine-code version of your program is known as the **object program**.

When we want to use this program, we can call up the object version and use this. When we test our program, we may find that there are still **logical errors** in the program – for example, we may have multiplied by 10 when we meant to multiply by 1000 – so we shall have to correct the source program and recompile the program again. This will produce a new version of the object program. When we have removed all the errors, we are left with a clean, object program which we can use over and over again, whenever we want to perform our calculations.

Linking and loading

So now we have our object program and we can ask to execute this. But before we can execute the program, the operating system must load the object version into memory. This is not just a matter of fetching the object program from disk and putting it into memory. The software must perform the following tasks:

- The software must link in any other routines which we have used. For example, we may have used a statement such as:

  A=SQRT(49)

  so the software must go to a library of standard routines for the SQRT process and link it into our object program. If we have written in a language such as Pascal which lets us build our program out of many smaller routines and procedures, these too will be linked in at this stage. This task of **linking** is usually performed by a piece of software known as a **link editor**.
- The software must also determine in which part of memory the program and the additional standard routines can be placed ready for execution, and then load the object code into that position. This is performed by the **loader**.
- The software must look at the table of addresses of the variables (which the compiler worked out relative to the start of the program) and convert these into the true physical address of the storage in the computer's memory.

On many operating systems, both these last two tasks are performed by a single piece of software: the **linker-loader**.

Executing

Finally, when the object program has been loaded, the execution of the program will begin under the control of the **run-time processor**. It is this processor which is responsible for passing each statement for execution and reporting any run-time errors such as attempts to take the square roots of negative numbers, attempts to read non-existent elements of an array, attempts to produce numbers much larger than can be handled by the processor.

What do we want of a programming language?

We have now seen what a computer language will let us do. Later, we shall see that there are a great many languages available and we shall look at some of the ways in which these various languages let us use the facilities offered by the processor.

So, if there are so many languages to choose from, how are we to know whether one language is better than another? How are we to know which language is best for the job we have in mind?

Almost any computer language can be used to write a program to perform any given task. I can use the Cobol language to write a program to calculate and print out the wages for an entire company, to write a program to control a satellite around Mars and Jupiter and back, to write a program to monitor the operation of an atomic power station. I could use the Basic language to write programs to solve the same problems, or the Fortran language, or . . . .

However, it is not sufficient that the program should *work*. There are other important criteria.

- The language must be suitable. We have said that almost any problem can be solved in almost any language. Nevertheless, some languages are more suitable for certain types of application. A program which is heavy in computation would be easier to write in Pascal, Fortran or APL than to attempt to struggle with the inappropriate facilities of, say, Cobol. On the other hand, it might be more appropriate to use Cobol to write a program to read a set of clock-cards, use these to calculate the employees' wages and then print the necessary documents and update the payroll file.
- The program must be readable. It must be possible for someone, unfamiliar with the problem, to look at a listing of the program and follow what is happening.

  If the program is readable, it will also be possible for the users to check that the programmer has done what is required.

  The syntax of the language itself has a great impact on its readability. Just ask your grandmother to take a look at the sections of machine code or assembly language code and compare these with equivalent sections of a Fortran, Cobol or Pascal program, and then ask her to comment on what is happening.

  Even the way in which the programmer applies the conventions for the names of variables can have significant impact on the

63

program's readability. Thus, a name such as TAX_TO_DATE (of Cobol) or Tax_to_date (of Pascal and others) are more meaningful than the TAXDAT which Fortran would demand, or VALUE2 which an inexperienced programmer might use.

The readability of the program has a further impact on the other criteria.

- The program must be easy to write.
  The extent to which a programming language uses a relatively small number of primitive constructs to build a large number of more complex constructs in known as **orthogonality**. The more orthogonal the language and the fewer the constructs, the easier it is to learn and to use, and the more likely it is that the programmer will exploit the full potential of the language.

  If the language has a great vocabulary of instructions and there are several ways of performing the same task, the typical programmer will come to use just a subset of the entire range. This subset will probably be just the instructions which he/she can remember and which they like to use, without any regard for the efficiency or suitability of the various options.

  Furthermore, the programmer will make fewer mistakes if he has little choice about the ways in which he/she can perform a certain operation.

- The program must be easy to debug. The more facilities the language provides for detecting errors, the greater will be the risk of undiscovered errors creeping into the finished product.

  The compiler can assist in this regard by reporting any dangerous areas, such as mixing real numbers and integers.

- The programs must be easy to use. The run-time processor can help by taking suitable corrective action in the event of an error, such as dividing by zero, running out of storage space, or the program attempting to use a non-existent element of an array.

- Correct use of the facilities of the language – its control structures, its modularity – will result in programs which are easy to write, to read and to debug.

- The program must be maintainable. During their life, most programs undergo a process of evolution and development. What starts out as a simple program may, over a period of time, be amended many times to meet the changing requirements: as they gain confidence in the system, the users will want the program to do more and more for them; the ways of performing calculations will change; the ways in

which the organization operates will change; there will be new legis-
lation. The program must adapt to respond to all of these.

- The language must be economical. There are various costs implicit
in the use of a programming language and many of these costs are
incurred by the wages of the people who are involved in (or waiting
for) each stage of the program development: the purchase cost of the
compiler, the cost of training programmers to use the language, the
cost of transforming the design specification into the program
specification, the cost of writing the program code, the cost of compiling each program, the cost of debugging and testing the program,
the cost of executing the program, and the cost of maintaining the
program.

Throughout this book, we shall emphasize the fact that a programming
language must be *easy to use*. This does not imply that programmers
are – or should be – lazy people. It is simply that programmers are like
ordinary people; the easier it is to use a programming language, the
fewer mistakes and errors there will be in the final program. In turn,
this will mean that the programs are produced more quickly and with
fewer problems, thereby benefiting the organization by reducing the
time-scales and the costs of the programming effort.

Activity 9

At various points in this chapter, we have discussed the various
demands which users, programmers, analysts and others make
upon a programming language.

(1) Make a composite list of the requirements of a programming
     language.
(2) Give reasons why each requirement is important.
(3) How do the SG01 machine code and the SG01 assembly lan-
     guage match up to these requirements?
(4) Consider any programming language which you have used
     and comment upon each of the requirements in your list.
(5) Make a list of the people who are involved and the reasons
     why time and money are spent during each stage of a pro-
     gram's life:

     (a) Training programmers to use the language.
     (b) Transforming the design specification into the program-
          specification.

(c) Writing the program code.
(d) Compiling the program.
(e) Debugging and testing the program.
(f) Executing the program.
(g) Maintaining the program.

For each language with which you are familiar, write down a few comments at each stage.

Recap

- The evolution of computers and computing equipment led to concept of the von Neumann model of a computer which has dominated most of our programming thinking for 30 years.
- We considered the fictitious SG01 micro-processor and used this to follow the development of computer languages through the first, second, third and fourth generation of programming languages.
- The SG01 exhibits many features of a real processor, both in terms of the types of operations which are available and the architecture.
- The action of a processor is ordained by the machine code instruction set (the first generation language). An assembly language (the second generation language) with its facilities for using data names, labels and macros, makes it easier to write low-level programs for the processor.
- Third generation languages, such as Cobol, Fortran and Pascal, make it even easier for non-technical programmers to design and produce programs for a computer. Fourth generation languages will eventually allow non-technical users, such as clerks, managers, secretaries, and accountants, to use the computer to develop their own processing and reporting routines.
- A great deal of supporting software is required to support the programmer (and others) in using the processor: an assembler (to translate assembly language programs), a compiler (to translate third generation language programs), a linker-loader (to prepare programs for execution), and a run-time processor (to control and monitor the performance of the executing program).

Answers to questions

1 The following steps could be taken:

(a) Move the contents of data store 1 into the accumulator.
(b) Add the contents of data store 2 into the accumulator.
(c) Move the contents of the accumulator into data store 3.

You might also have suggested:

(a) Set the contents of the accumulator to zero.
(b) Add the contents of data store 1 into the accumulator.
(c) Add the contents of data store 2 into the accumulator.
(d) Move the contents of the accumulator into data store 3.

2 The following steps could be taken:

(a) Move the contents of data store 1 into the accumulator.
(b) Switch the sign of the number in the accumulator.
(c) Add the contents of data store 2 into the accumulator.
(d) Move the contents of the accumulator into data store 5.

3 The following steps could be taken:

(a) Set the contents of the accumulator to 0.
(b) Move the contents of the accumulator into data store 1.

4 The following steps could be taken:

(a) Set the contents of the accumulator to 9999.
(b) Move the contents of the accumulator into data store 1.

5 Your sequence of operations might be:

(a) Move the contents of data store 2 into the COMPARISONA register.
(b) Move the contents of data store 7 into the COMPARISONB register.
(c) Compare the contents of COMPARISONA register with the contents of COMPARISONB register.

6 Your sequence of operations might be:

(a) Move the contents of data store 1 into the COMPARISONA register.
(b) Move the contents of data store 4 into the COMPARISONB register.
(c) Compare the contents of COMPARISONA register with the contents of COMPARISONB register.

(d) If the result of the last comparison was > then execute the instruction in instruction store number 76.

7 Your sequence of operations would be the same as in the previous question.

8 Your sequence of operations might be:

(a) Move the contents of data store 1 into the COMPARISONA register.
(b) Move the contents of data store 4 into the COMPARISONB register.
(c) Compare the contents of COMPARISONA register with the contents of COMPARISONB register.
(d) If the result of the last comparison was > then execute the instruction in instruction store number 76.
(e) If the result of the last comparison was = then execute the instruction in instruction store number 44. Note that we do not have to make the comparison again because the result is still held in the processor register.
(f) Execute the instruction held in instruction store number 39.

9 You may have suggested other op-codes than those which I have shown here. For example, you may have preferred to use the op-code

C

where I used

I

for the operation which compares the two comparison registers. This does not matter. The points to remember are:

• the design team should all agree on the op-codes which are to be used
• each op-code should be just one character; and
• each op-code should be unique.

Here are my suggestions:

(a) Move the contents of either of the comparison registers to one of the data stores. See Figure 2.18 (a).
This particular instruction would move the contents of COMPARISONA register to data store 1.
You may have decided to use 1 and 2 instead of A and B

Operation code	Operands	
	source	destination
A	A	1

(a) First suggestion

Operation code	Operands	
	source	destination
A	1	1

(b) Alternative form

Figure 2.18   *Operation code A*

to identify the comparison registers, as in Figure 2.18 (b). Although it would seem natural to use A and B, since the registers are called COMPARISONA and COMPARISONB, this is perfectly acceptable, provided that the design team agrees with you.

Operation code	Operands	
	source	destination
B	2	5

Figure 2.19   *Operation code B*

(b) Move the contents of one of the data stores to another data store. See Figure 2.19.

This particular instruction would move the contents of data store 2 to data store 5.
(c) Move the contents of one of the data stores to either of the comparison registers. See Figure 2.20.

Operation code	Operands	
	source	destination
C	3	B

Figure 2.20   *Operation code C*

This particular instruction would move the contents of data store 3 to COMPARISONB register.

69

(d) Move the contents of one of the data stores to the accumulator. See Figure 2.21.

Operation code	Operand
D	5

Figure 2.21 *Operation code D*

This particular instruction would move the contents of data store 5 to the accumulator.

(e) Move the contents of the accumulator to one of the data stores. See Figure 2.22.

Operation code	Operand
E	3

Figure 2.22 *Operation code E*

This particular instruction would move the contents of the accumulator to data store 3.

(f) Add the contents of one of the data stores to the number already held in the accumulator. See Figure 2.23.

Operation code	Operand
F	4

Figure 2.23 *Operation code F*

This particular instruction would add a number which is held in data store 4 to the number already held in the accumulator.

(g) Set the contents of the accumulator to 0. See Figure 2.24.

Operation code
G

Figure 2. 24 *Operation code G*

(h) Change the arithmetic sign of the number in the accumulator. See Figure 2.25.

Figure 2. 25 *Operation code H*

(i) Compare the contents of COMPARISONA register with the contents of COMPARISONB register. See Figure 2.26.

Figure 2. 26 *Operation code I*

(j) If the result of the last comparison was < then execute the instruction held in a specific instruction store. See Figure 2.27.

Operation code	Operand
J	99

Figure 2. 27 *Operation code J*

If the result of the last comparison was < then execute the instruction held in instruction store number 99.

(k) If the result of the last comparison was = then execute the instruction held in a specific instruction store. See Figure 2.28.

Operation code	Operand
K	76

Figure 2.28 *Operation code K*

If the result of the last comparison was = then execute the instruction held in instruction store number 76.

(l) If the result of the last comparison was > then execute the instruction held in a specific instruction store. See Figure 2.29.

Operation code	Operand
L	44

Figure 2.29 *Operation code L*

If the result of the last comparison was > then execute the instruction held in instruction store number 44.

(m) Execute the instruction held in a specific instruction store. See Figure 2.30.

Operation code	Operand
M	32

Figure 2.30 *Operation code M*

Execute the instruction held in instruction store number 32.

10 You may have suggested other op-codes than those which I have shown here. The rules that we listed in the previous answer still apply.

(n) Move the contents of one of the data stores to the screen buffer. See Figure 2.31.

Operation code	Operand
N	5

Figure 2.31 *Operation code N*

This particular instruction would move the contents of data store 5 to the screen buffer.

(o) Send a signal that the data in the screen buffer is to be displayed on the screen. See Figure 2.32.

Figure 2.32   *Operation code O*

(p) Send a signal that the program is to wait until the user has typed in some data on the keyboard and pressed return. This data will then be placed in the keyboard buffer. See Figure 2.33.

Figure 2.33   *Operation code P*

(q) Move the contents of the keyboard buffer to one of the data stores. See Figure 2.34.

Operation code	Operand
Q	2

Figure 2.34   *Operation code Q*

This particular instruction would move the contents of the keyboard buffer to data store 2.

(r) Abandon the program execution. See Figure 2.35.

Operation code
R

Figure 2.35   *Operation code R*

(s) Move a specific number into the accumulator. See Figure 2.36.

Operation code	Operand
S	1234567

Figure 2.36   *Operation code S*

This particular instruction would move the number 1234567 into the accumulator.

11 (a) A possible machine code solution to Question 1 is given in Figure 2.37.

```
D 1        move the contents of data store 1 into the
           accumulator.
F 2        add the contents of data store 2 to the
           number in the accumulator.
E 3        move the contents of the accumulator into
           data store 3.
R          stop the execution.

           (a)

G          set the contents of the accumulator to 0.
F 1        add the contents of data store 1 into the
           accumulator.
F 2        add the contents of data store 2 to the
           number in the accumulator.
E 3        move the contents of the accumulator into
           data store 3.
R          stop the execution.

           (b)
```

Figure 2.37   *Suggested solution: Question 11(a)*

(b) A possible machine code solution to Question 2 is given in Figure 2.38.

```
D 1        move the contents of data store 1 into the
           accumulator.
H          change the arithmetic sign of the number in
           the accumulator.
F 5        add the contents of data store 5 to the
           number in the accumulator.
E 5        move the contents of the accumulator into
           data store 5.
R          stop the execution.
```

Figure 2.38   *Suggested solution: Question 11(b)*

(c) A possible machine code solution to Question 3 is given in Figure 2.39.

74

```
G               set the contents of the accumulator to 0.
E 1             move the contents of the accumulator into
                data store 1.
R               stop the execution.
```

Figure 2.39   *Suggested solution: Question 11(c)*

(d)   A possible machine code solution to Question 4 is given
in Figure 2.40.

```
S 9999          set the contents of the accumulator to 9999.
E 1             move the contents of the accumulator into
                data store 1.
R               stop the execution.
```

Figure 2.40   *Suggested solution: Question 11(d)*

In the first of these suggested solutions, I have shown the
instructions as they would appear in the instruction store,
in the rest, I have simply numbered the instructions. This
will also help you to identify the destinations of any jump
operations.

12 See Figure 2.41.

```
1   | S 12345 |    move 12345 to accumulator

2   | E 1     |    move accumulator to data store 1

3   | S 45678 |    move 45678 to accumulator

4   | F 1     |    add data store 1 to accumulator

5   | E 1     |    move accumulator to data store 1

6   | N 1     |    move data store 1 to screen buffer

7   | O       |    display on screen

8   | R       |    stop the execution
```

Figure 2.41   *Suggested solution: Question 12*

13 See Figure 2.42.

```
P               get data from keyboard                     (1)
Q 1             move keyboard buffer to data store 1        (2)
D 1             move data store 1 to accumulator            (3)
P               get data from keyboard                     (4)
Q 2             move keyboard buffer to data store 2        (5)
F 2             add data store 2 to accumulator             (6)
E 3             move accumulator to data store 3            (7)
N 3             move data store 3 to screen buffer          (8)
O               display on screen                           (9)
R               stop the execution                         (10)
```

Figure 2.42   *Suggested solution: Question 13*

14 See Figure 2.43.

```
P                    get data from keyboard                      (1)
Q 1                  move keyboard buffer to data store 1        (2)
A 1 A                move data store 1 to COMPARISONA            (3)
S 9999               move 9999 to accumulator                    (4)
E 2                  move accumulator to data store 2            (5)
A 2 B                move data store 2 to COMPARISONB            (6)
I                    compare                                     (7)
K 15                 jump if equal                               (8)
S 1                  put 1 in accumulator                        (9)
F 1                  add data store 1 to accumulator            (10)
E 1                  move total to data store 1                 (11)
N 1                  move data store 1 to screen buffer         (12)
O                    display on screen                          (13)
M 1                  jump back to instruction 1                 (14)
R                    stop the execution                         (15)
```

Figure 2.43   *Suggested solution: Question 14*

15 See Figure 2.44.

```
P                    get data from keyboard                      (1)
Q 1                  move keyboard buffer to data store 1        (2)
A 1 A                move data store 1 to COMPARISONA            (3)
S 0                  move 0 to accumulator                       (4)
E 3                  move accumulator to data store 3            (5)
A 3 B                move data store 3 to COMPARISONB            (6)
I                    compare                                     (7)
K 22                 jump if equal                               (8)
P                    get data from keyboard                      (9)
Q 2                  move keyboard buffer to data store 2       (10)
A 2 A                move data store 2 to COMPARISONA           (11)
I                    compare                                     (12)
K 22                 jump if equal                              (13)
A 1 B                move data store 1 to COMPARISONB           (14)
I                    compare                                     (15)
J 20                 jump if A < B                              (16)
N 2                  move data store 2 to screen buffer         (17)
O                    display on screen                          (18)
R                    stop the execution                         (19)
N 1                  move data store 1 to screen buffer         (20)
O                    display on screen                          (21)
R                    stop the execution                         (22)
```

Figure 2.44   *Suggested solution: Question 15*

16 See Figure 2.45.

```
P                    get data from keyboard                      (1)
Q 1                  move keyboard buffer to data store 1        (2)
G                    set the accumulator to 0                    (3)
F 1                  add data store 1 to accumulator            (4)
F 1                  add data store 1 to accumulator            (5)
F 1                  add data store 1 to accumulator            (6)
F 1                  add data store 1 to accumulator            (7)
F 1                  add data store 1 to accumulator            (8)
E 2                  move accumulator to data store 2            (9)
N 2                  move data store 2 to screen buffer         (10)
O                    display on screen                          (11)
R                    stop the execution                         (12)
```

Figure 2.45   *Suggested solution: Question 16*

17 I shall leave you to work out your own solution to this question. The program must accept the two numbers (call these A and B), then it must repeatedly add A into the accumulator and subtract 1 from B. This is repeated until B reaches the value 0.

18 Your list should include all of the following:

(a)   A blank instruction is unacceptable.

(b)   An incorrect op-code. For example:

   Z 1 2
   ! A 1
   m 77

   Only the letters A to S are available in our instruction set.

(c)   Too many operands:

   A 1 2 3 4

   Each instruction has none, one or two operands.

(d)   Operands when none required:

   G 1 2

   Some instructions have no operands.

(e)   Too few operands:

   A A

   Each instruction must have the correct number of operands.

(f)   An incorrect comparison register:

   A X 1

   The comparison register may only be A or B.

(g)   An incorrect data store number:

   A A 9
   A 1 – 99

   The data store number must be a positive integer in the range 1 to 5, inclusive.

(h)   Too large a number in the S (place a value in the accumulator) instruction:

   S 99999999999999

   The number must be a positive integer of ten digits or less in length.

(i) A non-numeric value in the S (place a value in the accumulator) instruction:

S abcde

The number must be a positive integer of ten digits or less in length.

(j) Jump to an incorrect instruction:

K –4
K 99999

The instruction store number must be a positive integer in the range 1 to 99, inclusive.

19 The processor can do little – if anything – constructive about an incorrect instruction. Most processors will signal the error to the programmer and abandon the program execution. Some may invoke a piece of debugging software and allow the programmer to amend the incorrect instruction and restart the program either from the beginning or from the corrected instruction.

20 You will almost certainly have suggested other mnemonics than those which I have shown here. As before, the points to remember are:

- the design team should all agree on the mnemonics which are to be used;
- each mnemonic should be just one (short) word;
- each mnemonic should be unique;
- each mnemonic should be meaningful to a human programmer.

There is an unwritten convention that we use the mnemonic STORE when we want to move data *from a register into the ordinary data store,* and the mnemonic LOAD when we want to move data *from the ordinary data store into one of the registers..* My solution goes along with that convention.

(a) Move a number from either of the comparison registers to one of the data stores:

STOREC A 1

This particular instruction would move a number from COMPARISONA register to data store 1.

(b) Move a number from one of the data stores to another data store:

MOVE 2 5

This particular instruction would move a number from data store 2 to data store 5.

(c) Move a number from one of the data stores to either of the comparison registers

LOADC 3 B

This particular instruction would move a number from data store 3 to COMPARISONB register.

(d) Move a number from one of the data stores to the accumulator:

LOAD 5

This particular instruction would move a number from data store 5 to the accumulator.

(e) Move a number from the accumulator to one of the data stores:

STORE 5

This particular instruction would move a number from the accumulator to data store 1.

(f) Add a number from one of the data stores to the number already held in the accumulator:

ADD 2

This particular instruction would add the number which is held in data store 2 to the number already held in the accumulator.

(g) Set the contents of the accumulator to 0:

CLEAR

(h) Change the arithmetic sign of the number in the accumulator:

NEG

(i) Compare the contents of COMPARISONA register with the contents of COMPARISONB register:

COMP

(j) If the result of the last comparison was < then jump to the instruction held in a specific instruction store:

JUMPLT 99

If the result of the last comparison was < then jump to the instruction held in instruction store number 99, and then continue from there.

(k) If the result of the last comparison was = then jump to the instruction held in a specific instruction store:

JUMPEQ 76

If the result of the last comparison was = then jump to the instruction held in instruction store number 76, and then continue from there.

(l) If the result of the last comparison was > then jump to the instruction held in a specific instruction store:

JUMPGT 44

If the result of the last comparison was > then jump to the instruction held in instruction store number 44, and then continue from there.

(m) Jump to the instruction held in a specific instruction store:

JUMP 32

This particular instruction would jump to the instruction held in instruction store number 32, and then continue from there.

(n) Move the contents of one of the data stores to the screen buffer:

OUT 5

This particular instruction would move the contents of data store 5 to the screen buffer.

(o) Send a signal that the data in the screen buffer is to be displayed on the screen:

DISPLAY

(p) Send a signal that the program is to wait until the user has typed in some data on the keyboard and pressed return. This data will then be placed in the keyboard buffer:

INPUT

(q) Move the contents of the keyboard buffer to one of the data stores:

IN 2

This particular instruction would move the contents of the keyboard buffer to data store 2.

(r) Abandon the program execution:

STOP

(s) Move a specific number into the accumulator:

PLACE 1234567

This particular instruction would move the number 1234567 into the accumulator.

21 (a) Possible assembly language solutions to Question 1 are given in Figure 2.46.

```
LOAD 1        move the contents of data store 1 into the
              accumulator.
ADD 2         add the contents of data store 2 to the
              number in the accumulator.
STORE 3       move the contents of the accumulator into
              data store 3.
STOP          stop the execution

              (a)

CLEAR         set the contents of the accumulator to 0.
ADD 1         add the contents of data store 1 into the
              accumulator.
ADD 2         add the contents of data store 2 to the
              number in the accumulator.
STORE 3       move the contents of the accumulator into
              data store 3.
STOP          stop the execution

              (b)
```

Figure 2.46 *Suggested solution: Question 21(a)*

(b) A possible assembly language solution to Question 2 is given in Figure 2.47

```
LOAD 1        move the contents of data store 1 into the
              accumulator.
NEG           change the arithmetic sign of the number in
              the accumulator.
ADD 5         add the contents of data store 5 to the
              number in the accumulator.
STORE 5       move the contents of the accumulator into
              data store 5.
STOP          stop the execution
```

Figure 2.47 *Suggested solution: Question 21(b)*

(c) A possible assembly language solution to Question 3 is given in Figure 2.48.

(d) A possible assembly language solution to Question 4 is given in Figure 2.49.

```
CLEAR          set the contents of the accumulator to 0.
STORE 1        move the contents of the accumulator into
               data store 1.
STOP           stop the execution
```

Figure 2.48   *Suggested solution: Question 21(c)*

```
PLACE 9999     set the contents of the accumulator to 9999.
STORE 1        move the contents of the accumulator into
               data store 1.
STOP           stop the execution
```

Figure 2.49   *Suggested solution: Question 21(d)*

22 See Figure 2.50.

```
PLACE 12345    move 12345 to accumulator            (1)
STORE 1        move accumulator to data store 1     (2)
PLACE 45678    move 45678 to accumulator            (3)
ADD 1          add data store 1 to accumulator      (4)
STORE 1        move accumulator to data store 1     (5)
OUT 1          move data store 1 to screen buffer   (6)
DISPLAY        display on screen                    (7)
STOP           stop the execution                   (8)
```

Figure 2.50   *Suggested solution: Question 22*

23 See Figure 2.51.

```
INPUT          get data from keyboard               (1)
IN 1           move keyboard buffer to data store 1 (2)
LOAD 1         move data store 1 to accumulator     (3)
INPUT          get data from keyboard               (4)
IN 2           move keyboard buffer to data store 2 (5)
ADD 2          add data store 2 to accumulator      (6)
STORE 3        move accumulator to data store 3     (7)
OUT 3          move data store 3 to screen buffer   (8)
DISPLAY        display on screen                    (9)
STOP           stop the execution                   (10)
```

Figure 2.51   *Suggested solution: Question 23*

24 See Figure 2.52.

```
INPUT          get data from keyboard               (1)
IN 1           move keyboard buffer to data store 1 (2)
LOADC 1 A      move data store 1 to COMPARISONA     (3)
PLACE 9999     move 9999 to accumulator             (4)
STORE 2        move accumulator to data store 2     (5)
LOADC 2 B      move data store 2 to COMPARISONB     (6)
COMP           compare                              (7)
JUMPEQ 15      jump if equal                        (8)
PLACE 1        put 1 in accumulator                 (9)
ADD 1          add data store 1 to accumulator      (10)
STORE 1        move total to data store 1           (11)
OUT 1          move data store 1 to screen buffer   (12)
DISPLAY        display on screen                    (13)
JUMP 1         jump back to instruction 1           (14)
STOP           stop the execution                   (15)
```

Figure 2.52   *Suggested solution: Question 24*

25 See Figure 2.53.

```
INPUT          get data from keyboard                           (1)
IN 1           move keyboard buffer to data store 1             (2)
LOADC 1 A      move data store 1 to COMPARISONA                 (3)
PLACE 0        move 0 to accumulator                            (4)
STORE 3        move accumulator to data store 3                 (5)
LOADC 3 B      move data store 3 to COMPARISONB                 (6)
COMP           compare                                          (7)
JUMPEQ 22      jump if equal                                    (8)
INPUT          get data from keyboard                           (9)
IN 2           move keyboard buffer to data store 2            (10)
LOADC 2 A      move data store 2 to COMPARISONA                (11)
COMP           compare                                         (12)
JUMPEQ 22      jump if equal                                   (13)
LOADC 1 B      move data store 1 to COMPARISONB                (14)
COMP           compare                                         (15)
JUMPLT 20      jump if A < B                                   (16)
OUT 2          move data store 2 to screen buffer             (17)
DISPLAY        display on screen                               (18)
STOP           stop                                            (19)
OUT 1          move data store 1 to screen buffer             (20)
DISPLAY        display on screen                               (21)
STOP           stop                                            (22)
```

Figure 2.53 *Suggested solution: Question 25*

26 See Figure 2.54.

```
INPUT          get data from keyboard                           (1)
IN 1           move keyboard buffer to data store 1             (2)
CLEAR          set the accumulator to 0                         (3)
ADD 1          add data store 1 to accumulator                 (4)
ADD 1          add data store 1 to accumulator                 (5)
ADD 1          add data store 1 to accumulator                 (6)
ADD 1          add data store 1 to accumulator                 (7)
ADD 1          add data store 1 to accumulator                 (8)
STORE 2        move accumulator to data store 2                 (9)
OUT 2          move data store 2 to screen buffer             (10)
DISPLAY        display on screen                               (11)
STOP           stop                                            (12)
```

Figure 2.54 *Suggested solution: Question 26*

27 I shall leave you to work out your own solution to this question. The program must accept the two numbers (call these A and B), then it must repeatedly add A into the acumulator and subtract 1 from B. This is repeated until B reaches the value 0.

28 Your list should include all of the following:

(a) A blank instruction is not acceptable.

(b) An incorrect op-code. For example:

S PRINT 1 2
! A 1
add 5

Only the specific mnemonics are available.

(c) Too many operands:

ADD 1 2 3 4

Each instruction has none, one or two operands.

(d)   Operands when none required:

STOP 1 2

Some instructions have no operands.

(e)   Too few operands:

LOADC I

Each instruction must have the correct number of operands.

(f)   An incorrect comparison register:

LOADC 1 X

The comparison register may only be A or B.

(g)   An incorrect data store number:

STOREC A 9
STOREC B –99

The data store number must be a positive integer in the range 1 to 5, inclusive.

(h)   Too large a number in the PLACE (place a value in the accumulator) instruction:

PLACE 99999999999999

The number must be a positive integer of ten digits or less in length.

(i)   A non-numeric value in the PLACE (place a value in the accumulator) instruction:

PLACE abcde

The number must be a positive integer of ten digits or less in length.

(j)   Jump to an incorrect instruction:

JUMP –4
JUMPGT 99999

The instruction store number must be a positive integer in the range 1 to 99, inclusive.

29 The assembler could signal the error to the programmer and indicate the nature of the error. In some circumstances, it may even be possible for the assembler to suggest a possible correct version of the statement. Having done this, the assembler should continue with the rest of the program. If there are any incorrect assembly code instructions, then it will not be possible for the assembler to produce an object program. The programmer must amend the incorrect assembly code instruction(s) and reassemble the program.

30 The DEFINE STORAGE directive passes information to the assembler but it does not produce an equivalent machine code instruction; the ADD instruction can be converted directly into a machine code instruction; the ADD AGES instruction can be converted into a machine code instruction (provided, of course, that a DEFINE STORAGE directive has been found for the name AGES).

31 The solution is shown in Figure 2.55. You should remember that the DEFINE STORAGE directives do not occupy any space in the final program. I've numbered the statements to show how the correct instruction addresses can be found.

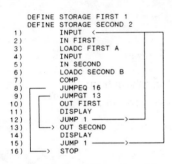

```
        DEFINE STORAGE FIRST 1
        DEFINE STORAGE SECOND 2
  1)        INPUT    <───
  2)        IN FIRST
  3)        LOADC FIRST A
  4)        INPUT
  5)        IN SECOND
  6)        LOADC SECOND B
  7)        COMP
  8)   ┌──  JUMPEQ 16
  9)   │ ┌─ JUMPGT 13
 10)   │ │  OUT FIRST
 11)   │ │  DISPLAY
 12)   │ │  JUMP 1 ──────>──┐
 13)   │ └─> OUT SECOND
 14)   │    DISPLAY
 15)   │    JUMP 1 ──────>──┤
 16)   └──> STOP
```

Figure 2.55   *Suggested solution: Question 31*

32 The assembler must read through the program twice: once to find out which instructions (if any) the labels are attached to, and then again to translate the assembly code into machine code and insert the correct addresses for the labels as it does so. This is exactly the same operation that you would perform yourself, as we described at the start of this section.

33 The assembler would read through the program instructions to find the addresses identified by the labels. These numbers are shown in Figure 2.56 (a).

By doing this, it would find the addresses at which each label was defined:

START is attached to instruction (1)
BISBIG is attached to instruction (9)
AISBIG is attached to instruction (12)

Then it would read through the program, translating the instructions into machine code and replacing the label references by the appropriate addresses. This is illustrated in Figure 2.56 (b).

```
 1) START INPUT
 2)       IN 1
 3)       LOADC 1 A
 4)       INPUT
 5)       IN 2
 6)       LOADC 2 B
 7)       COMP
 8)       JUMPGT AISBIG
 9) BISBIG OUT 1
10)       DISPLAY
11)       JUMP START
12) AISBIG OUT 2
13)       DISPLAY
14)       JUMP START

                         (a)

 1)       INPUT
 2)       IN 1
 3)       LOADC 1 A
 4)       INPUT
 5)       IN 2
 6)       LOADC 2 B
 7)       COMP
 8)       JUMPGT 12      <== replace AISBIG by 12
 9)       OUT 1
10)       DISPLAY
11)       JUMP 1         <== replace START by 1
12)       OUT 2
13)       DISPLAY
14)       JUMP 1         <== replace START by 1

                         (b)
```

Figure 2.56   *An assembler program with labels: 2*

Notice that the label BISBIG is not used by any of the jump statements in the program. This is not usually regarded as an error; indeed, this can be quite useful in identifying the various parts of the program. However, an attempt to jump to a label which had not been defined *would* be an error from which the assembler could not recover.

34 Your solution should look something like that shown in Figure 2.57. The indentation is not important, although some assemblers require that a label is not preceded by a space.

35 Your list should include all of the following errors which might occur when using data names:

(a)   An incorrect DEFINE STORAGE statement.

```
DEFINE 1
define storage FIRST1 1
DEFINE STORE FIRST 1
DEFINESTORAGE FIRST 1
```

The statement must begin with the words DEFINE STOR-AGE. The words must be spelt correctly, in capital letters, separated by a space and in the right order.

(b) An invalid data name in a DEFINE STORAGE statement.

```
DEFINE STORAGE 1FIRST 1
```

We have not specified the actual rules which our assembler will use. Typically, however, the name must begin with a letter and may contain only letters and digits and may be no more than 6 characters in length.

(c) An incorrect data store number in a DEFINE STORAGE statement.

```
DEFINE STORAGE THIS1 99
```

The data store number must be a positive integer in the range 1 to 5, inclusive.

(d) Using a data name which has not been defined on a DEFINE STORAGE statement.

```
        DEFINE STORAGE FIRST 1
        DEFINE STORAGE SECOND 2
        INPUT
        IN FIRST
        LOADC FIRST A
        PLACE 0
        STORE 3
        LOADC 3 B
        COMP
        JUMPEQ FINISH
        INPUT
        IN SECOND
        LOADC SECOND A
        COMP
        JUMPEQ FINISH
        LOADC FIRST B
        COMP
        JUMPLT PRINT1
        OUT SECOND
        DISPLAY
        STOP
PRINT1  OUT FIRST
        DISPLAY
FINISH  STOP
```

Figure 2.57 *Suggested solution: Question 34*

36 Your list should include all of the following errors which might occur when using labels:

(a) An invalid label.

We have not specified the actual rules which our assembler will use. Typically, however, the label must begin with a letter and may contain only letters and digits and may be no more than 6 characters in length.

(b) Using a label which is the same as an op-code. Such an error would probably be identified when the instruction is analysed as a valid op-code.

(c) Using a label on a JUMP instruction which does not appear in the program.

37 The assembler could signal the error to the programmer and indicate the nature of the error. Having done this, it should continue with the rest of the program. If there are any incorrect assembly code instructions, then it will not be possible for the assembler to produce an object program. The programmer must then amend the incorrect assembly code instruction(s) and reassemble the program.

38 See Figure 2.58 (a)

39 See Figure 2.58 (b)

```
a)    DEFINE MACRO FETCH $1
      INPUT
      IN $1
      MACRO END

b)    DEFINE MACRO WRITE $1
      OUT $1
      DISPLAY
      MACRO END

c)    DEFINE MACRO STOREN $1 $2
      PLACE $1
      STORE $2
      MACRO END

d)    DEFINE MACRO SUM $1 $2 $3
      LOAD $1
      ADD $2
      STORE $3
      MACRO END

e)    DEFINE MACRO DECR $1
      PLACE 1
      NEG
      ADD $1
      STORE $1
      MACRO END

f)    DEFINE MACRO COMPARE $1 $2
      LOADC $1 A
      LOADC $2 B
      COMP
      MACRO END
```

```
g)           DEFINE MACRO COMPNUM $1 $2
             LOADC $1 A
             PLACE $2
             STORE $1
             LOADC $1 B
             COMP
             STOREC $1
             MACRO END

h)           FETCH 1
             COMPNUM 1 0
             JUMPEQ FINISH
             FETCH 2
             COMPNUM 2 0
             JUMPEQ FINISH
             STOREN 0 3
AGAIN        SUM 2 3 3
             DECR 1
             COMPNUM 1 0
             JUMPGT AGAIN
             WRITE 3
FINISH       STOP

i)           DEFINE MACRO MULTIPLY $1 $2 $3
             STOREN 0 3
AGAIN        SUM 2 3 3
             DECR 1
             COMPNUM 1 0
             JUMPGT AGAIN
             MACRO END

j)           DEFINE MACRO RDADIS $1 $2
             FETCH $1
             FETCH $2
             SUM $1 $2 3
             WRITE 3
             MACRO END
```

Figure 2.58 *Macro definitions*

40 See Figure 2.58 (c)

41 See Figure 2.58 (d)

42 See Figure 2.58(e)

43 See Figure 2.58(f)

44 See Figure 2.58 (g)

45 See Figure 2.58(h)

46 See Figure 2.58(i)

47 See Figure 2.58(j)

48 The specification of the parameters $1, $2 and so on on the DEFINE MACRO line could be omitted if we accept the convention that the first parameter is $1, the second is $2 and so on.

49 We should need all of the following
   (a) Some means of telling the software which loads our programs that routine S is to be placed at the end of memory.
   (b) Some means of jumping from program A to routine S. One of the JUMP instructions will do this for us.
   (c) Some means of remembering where in program A we must go back to when we leave routine S.
   (d) Going back to program A.

50 The STOREADDR instruction stores the current contents of the next-instruction register. When we execute STOREADDR 1 at instruction number 32, it will put the number 33 into data store 1. We really want the contents of data store 1 to point to instruction number 33, so before we can use the contents of data store 1 to return from routine S to the main program A, we must add 1 to the contents of data store 1. Figure 2.59 shows how the instructions at the end of routine S might look.

51 The instruction STOREADDR 1 will move the contents of the next-instruction register to data store 1, and the instruction RETURN 1 will move the contents of data store 1 to the next-instruction register.

52 Because the RETURN instruction places the appropriate instruction number into the next-instruction register, and the processor uses this to determine what to do next, we need take no further action once we have loaded the correct address into the register.

89

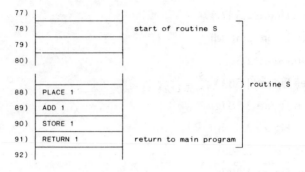

Figure 2.59 *Preparing to go back*

3: Data and data types

Objectives

After reading this chapter, you should be able to:

- Describe the nature of **binary** data.
- Perform binary arithmetic.
- Convert binary values to their decimal equivalents, and vice versa.
- Describe how a binary pattern may have more than one significance.
- Describe and use the **hexadecimal** notation.
- Convert hexadecimal values to their binary and decimal equivalents, and vice versa.
- Describe the nature and physical appearance of the elementary data types: **integer, real, character, string, Boolean, packed decimal, arrays, records, enumerated, pointers, linked lists,** and **sets.**
- Describe and use **floating point** numbers.
- Convert floating point values to their decimal equivalents, and vice versa.
- Describe and apply the naming conventions by which data types are handled in various programming languages.
- Describe the concept of **type checking**.

Types of data

The computer holds all its data as a sequence of **bits** – binary digits. These are small, physical elements which are capable of carrying one of two possible electrical signals. These two states are conventionally used to represent the values 0 and 1 respectively, although we could equally well have chosen **on** and **off**, **up** and **down**, **yes** and **no.**

Because each bit may be set to either of two states, 0 or 1, data represented in this form is known as **binary** data.

These bits are organized into groups of eight bits, and each group is called a **byte**. If we were to look at the state of the bytes on a computer we might find that one contained bits which were set to:

01110001

whilst another was set to:

01011100

Since there are 8 bits in a byte, and each bit is capable of being in either of two states, the bits in any particular byte may be set to any one of 256 possible patterns (that is, 2 to the power 8).

By convention, we record the first of these as:

00000000

and the next as:

00000001

and the next as:

00000010

and the next as:

00000011

Questions

1 Write down the next 12 patterns in the sequence shown in the text.
2 Write down the last 12 patterns in the sequence ending with the final pattern:

11111111

Converting binary numbers to decimal

If you are already able to convert binary numbers to their decimal equivalents, you may wish to skip this section.

We can regard these patterns as representing **binary numbers** (that is numbers counting in twos), then we can convert them to the equivalent decimal numbers (that is, numbers counting in tens), as shown in Figure 3.1.

```
             0 (binary) = 0 (decimal)
             1 (binary) = 1 (decimal)
           1 0 (binary) = 2 (decimal)
           1 1 (binary) = 3 (decimal)
         1 0 0 (binary) = 4 (decimal)
           (a) without leading zeroes
0 0 0 0 0 0 0 0 (binary) = 0 (decimal)
0 0 0 0 0 0 0 1 (binary) = 1 (decimal)
0 0 0 0 0 0 1 0 (binary) = 2 (decimal)
0 0 0 0 0 0 1 1 (binary) = 3 (decimal)
0 0 0 0 0 1 0 0 (binary) = 4 (decimal)
           (b) with leading zeroes
```

Figure 3.1   *Binary numbers/decimal numbers*

Note that it is usual (although not essential) to write down the leading zeros of a binary number – as in Figure 3.1 (b) – just to remind ourselves that we are working with eight binary digits.

As we move across from right to left, we go up in *powers* of two:

(1) a 1 in the right-most position represents 1 (in decimal), that is 2 raised to power 0;
(2) a 1 in the second from right-most position represents 2 (in decimal), that is 2 raised to power 1;
(3) a 1 in the third from right-most position represents 4 (in decimal), that is 2 raised to power 2;
(4) a 1 in the fourth from right-most position represents 8 (in decimal), that is 2 raised to power 3, and so on.

We can picture the eight bits and their decimal equivalents as in Figure 3.2 (a). We can then use this correspondence to convert any binary number to its decimal equivalent by adding up the decimal values for those bits which are set to 1 in the binary number, as illustrated in Figure 3.2 (b).

This tells us that the binary number 10110110 is equivalent to the decimal number 182.

```
                    left <——————————— right

binary          1    1    1    1    1    1    1    1

decimal        128   64   32   16    8    4    2    1

two to          7    6    5    4    3    2    1    0
the power
                                        (a)

binary          1    0    1    1    0    1    1    0

decimal        128   0   32   16    0    4    2    0

adding       128+  0+  32+  16+  0+   4+   2+   0   = 182 (decimal)

                                        (b)
```

Figure 3.2   *Binary notation*

Another way of converting from binary to decimal is by using the **multiply by 2 and add** rule. Using this rule, we:

(1) start with the left-most binary digit;
(2) multiply this by two;
(3) add the next binary digit;
(4) if there are any more binary digits to the right, then go back to step (2), otherwise the result is the decimal equivalent of the binary number.

Applying this to the binary number 10110110 we take the following steps:

(a) take the left-most digit, 1
(b) multiply this by 2 (result = 2)
(c) add the next binary digit, 0 (result = 2)
(d) multiply this by 2 (result = 4)
(e) add the next binary digit, 1 (result = 5)
(f) multiply this by 2 (result = 10)
(g) Add the next binary digit, 1 (result = 11)
(h) multiply this by 2 (result = 22)
(i) add the next binary digit, 0 (result = 22)
(j) multiply this by 2 (result = 44)
(k) add the next binary digit, 1 (result = 45)
(l) multiply this by 2 (result = 90)
(m) add the next binary digit, 1 (result = 91)
(n) multiply this by 2 (result = 182)

(o) add the next binary digit, 0 (result=182)

(p) there are no more binary digits, so the result is the decimal number 182.

This confirms our previous result.

Question

3 Look at the binary numbers in the answers to Questions (1) and (2) above and write the decimal equivalent alongside each binary pattern.

Converting decimal numbers to binary

If you are already able to convert decimal numbers to their binary equivalents, you may wish to skip this section.

The simplest way to convert a decimal number to its binary equivalent is by repeated division by two, and recording the *remainder* at each stage. We illustrate this by means of an example. Let us convert the decimal number 182 to its binary equivalent.

```
182 / 2 = 91 remainder 0
91 / 2 = 45 remainder 1
45 / 2 = 22 remainder 1
22 / 2 = 11 remainder 0
11 / 2 = 5 remainder 1
5 / 2 = 2 remainder 1
2 / 2 = 1 remainder 0
1 / 2 = 0 remainder 1
```

Then we write down the *remainders*, starting with the *last* one:

10110110

So the binary equivalent of the decimal number 182 is 10110110, confirming our previous result.

Question

4 Convert the following decimal numbers to their binary equivalents:

(a) 203
(b) 244
(c) 11
(d) 0115
(e) 1010
(f) 15
(g) 127
(h) 217

Performing binary addition

If you are already able to add together two binary numbers, you may wish to skip this section.

One advantage in holding numbers in this form is that, for the computer, binary arithmetic can be performed much more easily than decimal arithmetic. To add two binary numbers together, the computer only needs to remember *four* rules:

$$0 + 0 = 0$$
$$1 + 0 = 1$$
$$0 + 1 = 1$$
$$1 + 1 = 0 \text{ carry } 1$$

So we need four electronic circuits if we are going to perform binary arithmetic. This makes calculations much faster than they would be using decimal arithmetic.

Question

5 How many rules would there be if we were to equip our computer to add two *decimal* digits together?

Using these four rules to add the two binary numbers:

01001101 and 00111010

we write the two numbers down, one beneath the other, as with decimal arithmetic:

01001101

00100110

and apply the four rules of binary addition, starting from the right. First, we add the two right-most digits:

01001101
00100110
1

then, the two second from the right-most digits:

01001101
00100110
11

then, the two third from the right-most digits:

01001101
00100110
1   carry
011

carrying 1 over to the left.

Then, we include this *carry* value and complete the addition obtaining the sum:

01001101
00100110
01110011

giving us the answer:

01001101 + 00100110 = 01110011

Of course, pure binary numbers (like pure decimal numbers) may be of any length. But remember that we are only concerned here with the *eight* bits which make up a byte of computer storage.

Questions

6 Look again at the numbers which we used to illustrate the principle of binary addition. Convert the two binary numbers and their binary sum to the equivalent decimal numbers. Is the answer correct?

7 Add the following binary numbers together. Convert the binary numbers to the equivalent decimal numbers to check your answers.
   (a) 00000110 + 10100011
   (b) 01000001 + 10001001
   (c) 00010110 + 11011010
   (d) 00000011 + 11101010
   (e) 01101000 + 10010011
   (f) 00100110 + 10000100
   (g) 00000101 + 11010010
   (h) 01010000 + 10000000

8 What is the smallest decimal number which we can represent by a pattern of eight bits?

9 What is the largest decimal number which we can represent by a pattern of eight bits?

10 How many different binary patterns can we represent by the eight bits? How many different values can be represented by one byte?

Representing other data

All possible forms of data have to be represented by these 256 possible patterns. As we have seen, a byte can only represent a decimal value in the range 0 to 255. So we cannot even represent the decimal number 256, nor −50, nor the letter A, nor the £ sign. So what are we to do? How can we use the 256 patterns to represent all the data which we shall require our computer to hold? One possibility is to have some form of coding whereby one pattern represents the letter A, another represents the letter B, another the £ sign, another the number 1, another the number 9, another the number 0 and so on. There are many such codes. One of the most commonly encountered is the American Standard Code for Information Interchange (ASCII for short). In your studies, you may also encounter the EBCDIC (Extended Binary Coded Decimal Interchange Code) representation.

Some of the 256 ASCII character representations are shown in the table in Figure 3.3. This table shows the binary patterns, their decimal equivalents (obtained in the way we described earlier), and the equivalent ASCII *graphic* character. We have omitted the patterns before decimal 32 and those after decimal 122 as these are usually reserved for special signals to control the hardware and transmission devices and have no graphical value.

Binary	Dec	Char	Binary	Dec	Char
00100000	32	space	01001011	75	K
00100001	33	!	01001100	76	L
00100010	34	"	01001101	77	M
00100011	35	£	01001110	78	N
00100100	36	$	01001111	79	O
00100101	37	%	01010000	80	P
00100110	38	&	01010001	81	Q
00100111	39	'	01010010	82	R
00101000	40	(	01010011	83	S
00101001	41	)	01010100	84	T
00101010	42	*	01010101	85	U
00101011	43	+	01010110	86	V
00101100	44	,	01010111	87	W
00101101	45	–	01011000	88	X
00101110	46	.	01011001	89	Y
00101111	47	/	01011010	90	Z
00110000	48	0	01100000	96	'
00110001	49	1	01100001	97	a
00110010	50	2	01100010	98	b
00110011	51	3	01100011	99	c
00110100	52	4	01100100	100	d
00110101	53	5	01100101	101	e
00110110	54	6	01100110	102	f
00110111	55	7	01100111	103	g
00111000	56	8	01101000	104	h
00111001	57	9	01101001	105	i
00111010	58	:	01101010	106	j
00111011	59	;	01101011	107	k
00111100	60	<	01101100	108	l
00111101	61	=	01101101	109	m
00111110	62	>	01101110	110	n
00111111	63	?	01101111	111	o
01000000	64	@	01110000	112	p
01000001	65	A	01110001	113	q
01000010	66	B	01110010	114	r
01000011	67	C	01110011	115	s
01000100	68	D	01110100	116	t
01000101	69	E	01110101	117	u
01000110	70	F	01110110	118	v
01000111	71	G	01110111	119	w
01001000	72	H	01111000	120	x
01001001	73	I	01111001	121	y
01001010	74	J	01111010	122	z

Figure 3.3   *Some ASCII codes*

From the table, we can see that if a byte contains the pattern:

01001010

then it will be displayed on the screen as the letter:

J

Those programming languages which have the CHAR or the CHR or CHR$ function might display the letter J by means of either of the statements:

PRINT 'J'

or

PRINT CHR$(74)

99

or

> PRINT CHAR(74)

Some programmers use the decimal equivalents to identify any non-graphic characters (that is, those characters which cannot be written down). For example, I could say that:

> 'In order to sound the bell on the terminal, I must print character 7.'

or

> 'The statement:
>
> > PRINT CHR$(7)
>
> will sound the bell on the terminal.'

Questions

11 What ASCII graphic character is represented by the binary pattern 00111101?

12 What ASCII graphic character is represented by the binary number 00101111?

13 What ASCII graphic character is represented by the decimal value 122?

14 What is ASCII character 65?

15 What is the decimal equivalent of ASCII character j?

16 What is the binary pattern for ASCII $ character?

17 What is the decimal equivalent of the binary pattern 01101100?

Hexadecimal notation

If you are already familiar with hexadecimal notation, you may wish to skip this section.

It is obviously difficult to memorize or to dictate a binary pattern such as:

> 01011010

we could tell someone that this is the binary pattern for the capital letter Z, or that it is the binary equivalent of the decimal number 90. The pattern:

01011011

would be more difficult, since there is no graphic character corresponding to this pattern.

It is more convenient to use **hexadecimal notation** to write down these patterns. To use hexadecimal notation to represent a value such as:

01011011

the binary string is split into two **quartets** of four binary digits:

0101

and

1011

and these two quartets are written as hexadecimal digits according to the table shown in Figure 3.4.

Decimal	Binary	Hexadecimal
0	0000	0
1	0001	1
2	0010	2
3	0011	3
4	0100	4
5	0101	5
6	0110	6
7	0111	7
8	1000	8
9	1001	9
10	1010	A
11	1011	B
12	1100	C
13	1101	D
14	1110	E
15	1111	F

Figure 3.4 *Table of hexadecimal digits*

From the table, we see that:

0101 in binary is equivalent to 5 in hexadecimal

1011 in binary is equivalent to B in hexadecimal

so, the binary number:

0101 1011

would be written as:

5 B

in hexadecimal notation, and the binary number 01011011 is equivalent to the hexadecimal number 5B.

Questions

18 It is important for you to realize that decimal numbers, binary numbers and hexadecimal numbers (and others, such as octal numbers) are only a means of recording a numeric value. Look at the boxes in Figure 3.5.

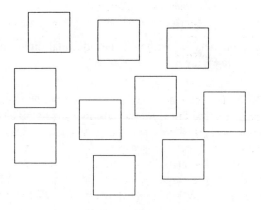

Figure 3.5 *How many boxes?*

Write down the number of boxes as:

(a) a decimal number,
(b) a binary number
(c) a hexadecimal number.

These are three different ways of recording the same information.

19 Write down the hexadecimal equivalents of the following binary numbers:

(a) 00001011
(b) 00000100
(c) 01110011
(d) 01111111

(e) 11001011
(f) 11011001
(g) 11110000
(h) 11110010
(i) 11110100
(j) 11111111

Binary / decimal / hexadecimal

Binary, decimal and hexadecimal are simply ways of writing down numeric values, such as the number of boxes in Figure 3.5. They are all equally valid ways of representing information. It's just that one may be more convenient than others at certain times.

Decimal notation is really just one way of recording numbers that increases in powers of 10 as you move from right to left across the number. That is, if we write the decimal number:

333

the first 3 (which is worth 300) is ten times the value of the next 3 (which is worth 30), and this is worth ten times the value of the last 3 (which is worth just 3). Similarly, binary notation is just a way of recording numbers that increases in powers of 2 as you move from right to left across the number. We used this when we were converting binary values into their decimal equivalents.

And finally, hexadecimal notation is really just a way of recording numbers that increases in powers of 16 as you move from right to left across the number. We could use this fact if we needed to convert a hexadecimal number to its decimal equivalent by adapting our rule for converting from binary to decimal using the **multiply by 16 and add rule**. In this case, the rule tell us to:

(1) start with the left-most hexadecimal digit;
(2) multiply the decimal value of this (taken from the above table) by sixteen;
(3) add the decimal equivalent of the next hexadecimal digit;
(4) it there are any more hexadecimal digits to the right, then go back to step (2), otherwise the result is the decimal equivalent of the hexadecimal number.

Applying this to the hexadecimal number 5B we take the following steps:

(a) take the left-most digit, 5
(b) multiply the decimal equivalent of this (5) by 16 (result = 80)
(c) add the decimal equivalent of the next hexadecimal digit, B (= 11) (result = 91)

There are no more hexadecimal digits, so the result is the decimal number 91.

Data types

The fact that the binary pattern in a byte may be interpreted in many ways raises another question: if the pattern:

01001010

is to represent the letter J, how can we represent the decimal number 74? If we represent 74 by the same pattern, how do we know it means the number 74 and not the character J?

You might suggest that we represent the number 74 by *ASCII characters* 7 and 4. If we wish to do this, then we should need **two bytes**: one to hold the ASCII character 7 and one to hold the ASCII character 4. The two bytes would look like this:

00110100 00110111

Now, if we wish to perform arithmetic with this version of the number 74, we have a much greater problem because we have agreed that our computer only performs binary arithmetic. So we shall have a great deal of work to convert this binary pattern to the correct binary number.

What we really want it is to be able to hold the number 74 in one byte as a binary pattern, and then some way to tell the computer:

- that the byte contains a pattern which represents binary data for use in arithmetic calculations,

and when we want to represent the letter J,

- that the byte contains a pattern which is to represent an ASCII character for use in messages and text output.

Most programming languages allow you to specify these requirements. You indicate that a certain variable is to hold numeric data or that it is to hold character data. This leads us to the concept of **data types**. Let us look at some of the important data types.

Character data type

We have already seen the need to be able to hold non-numeric values, such as letters of the alphabet. If we can hold letters on the computer, then we can print messages, text and so on.

Question

20 What other information might we need to hold inside the computer besides letters of the alphabet and numbers?

Other character sets

Since we have only 256 possible bit patterns at our disposal, how can we handle all the possible letters and other characters of all the world's languages in our computer? This can only be done with considerable effort. That is why most computers use just a small subset of the possible characters. An English user might need the ordinary character set with just the numbers, upper-case (capital) letters, lower-case (small) letters, and a few special characters. A French user might need the ordinary character set plus the accented letters, the cedilla and the « and » quotation marks. A Spanish user might need the ordinary character set plus the letters ñ and Ñ, the currency symbol Pt and the special punctuation marks ¿ and ¡. But, if a user does have additional characters then he/she may have to lose some of the special characters, because there are only 256 patterns. The internal representation is of little concern to the computer; it is the hardware which determines whether a particular pattern is going to print as the symbol ¿ or the symbol ¥.

In some situations, 256 might not be sufficient to hold all the characters which a user needs. In that case, a sequence of stored characters would be used to represent a single graphic character. This is what happens when you attempt to use a language such as Chinese on the computer. The Chinese language has over 60,000 different symbols – a single symbol representing an entire word or a phrase – and each Chinese character is represented inside the computer by a sequence of data: the first part of the sequence indicates that this is a Chinese character and the remainder of the sequence indicates which particular symbol is to be displayed or printed.

105

Escape sequences

The same method is used when we need to send special information to take advantage of the facilities offered by a graphics screen or a laser printer. For example, in order to tell my laser printer that I want to print at 12 characters per inch, I must send the sequence of five characters:

<ESC> & k 4 S

and to instruct the printer to output italic characters, I must transmit the sequence:

<ESC>) s 1 S

The **escape character**, shown here as <ESC>, is the binary pattern corresponding to the decimal number 27, and is frequently used for invoking special actions on output devices. When I am using the printer, the computer sends a stream of information to the printer. Most of this will be letters, numbers and spaces which are to be printed, but when the printer receives the <ESC> character from the computer it knows that a special *control sequence* follows and not a string of information which is to be printed. For obvious reasons, such strings of data are called **escape sequences**.

Strings of characters

According to the software which you are using, a sequence of characters may be held:

● Exactly as it is created. Thus the string:

NO

would occupy 2 bytes, and the string:

THE CAT SAT ON THE MAT

would occupy 22 bytes.
● Up to a certain length. Thus a very long string may be truncated to, say, 1000 bytes.
● In a whole number of words (that is, groups of 4 bytes), using as many words as necessary to accommodate the string. If the number of characters does not exactly fill the words, any additional bytes might be filled with special null characters. Thus the string:

NO

would occupy one word, that is, four bytes (possibly with two bytes of null characters to round it up to four bytes), and the string:

THE DESK IS OLD

would occupy four words, that is, 16 bytes.

In this situation, we might visualize the actual storage as in Figure 3.6 where a shaded box represents the *null* character.

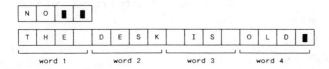

Figure 3.6   *Strings in storage*

Strings

If we imagine that a program variable called NAME is able to hold the value:

JONES

at one point in the program, and the value:

FEATHERSTONEHAUGH

at another point, this clearly presents a problem for the compiler and the run-time processor: how much space is it to allocate for the variable NAME?

Many languages overcome the problem by requiring the programmer to declare the maximum space which will be allowed for the variable. This may be done by statements of the form:

Pascal: type NAME = packed array [30] of char
Fortran: CHARACTER NAME*30
C: char NAME[30]

The various languages may handle names of other than 30 characters in different ways. If the name is shorter than 30 characters, as with JONES, then it may be padded out with spaces or with nulls, as we saw earlier, or there may be a special *end-of-string* marker character after the final letter of the name. If the name is longer than 30 characters, as

107

with FEATHERSTONEHAUGH-FITZWILLIAM-SMYTHE, then it will be truncated to just the first 30 characters.

When the programmer has already specified the maximum size of the string, it is fairly straightforward to allocate storage for the string.

Basic places no such limitation on strings, and a variable such as NAME$ may be built up to virtually any length. In practice there will be some finite (if very large) limit imposed, and typically this will be 32000 characters. The way in which this is handled in practice is by assuming that NAME$ will be an ordinary variable of one word – that is, four bytes – in length. This is satisfactory whilst NAME$ takes values such as:

MARY
JOHN
BILL

If the name is shorter than four characters – as with YES – then an end-of-string marker will be placed at the end of the string.

But when the name exceeds four characters – as with FEATHER-STONEHAUGH – the run-time processor resolves the problem – as illustrated in Figure 3.7 – by looking around memory for a piece of unused storage space and placing the name FEATHERSTONEHAUGH there. When this has been done, a pointer to this location is placed in the original four bytes, together with a marker (represented by the asterisk) to show that this storage space contains an address pointer and not a value.

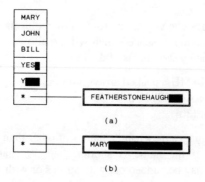

Figure 3.7 *Strings in practice*

The amount of space allocated to a long name depends upon the compiler and the run-time processor which are used. It may be just long enough to hold the string and an end-of-string marker, or it may be a sufficient number of four-byte chunks (as in the case illustrated here), or it may one of a number of fixed length areas (possibly 50 bytes or 100 bytes or 250 bytes and so on up to 32000 bytes). Again, different operating systems may behave differently if the name shrinks back to MARY; some may discard the overflow space and revert to the simple variable, others may continue to hold the short name in the overflow space, as illustrated in Figure 3.7 (b).

Integer / fixed data type

When a byte represents a binary number, the value can easily be used in arithmetic. We have already seen this. We have also seen that one byte can only represent numbers in the range 0 to 255. This is not much use for large numbers, for fractions or for negative numbers. So what can we do? The solution to the first problem can be found by using several adjacent bytes together to hold a larger number. Thus, if we decided to use two bytes to hold our number, a typical pattern might look like this:

0 1 0 1 0 1 1 1 0 1 0 1 0 1 0 1

Questions

21 Extend the process we described earlier to convert the binary number:

0101011101010101

to its decimal equivalent.

22 What is the largest binary number which can be held in two bytes? What is the equivalent decimal number?

23 What is the largest decimal number which can be represented by three bytes?

24 What is the largest decimal number which can be represented by four bytes?

Some computer systems will allow you to use a sequence of 2 bytes, others 4 bytes, and so on, to store your numeric data. A group of four bytes is frequently encountered and is sometimes known as a **word**, two bytes as a **half-word**, and eight bytes as a **double-word**.

This is one way of solving the problem of holding large numbers. The more bytes which may be used to hold a number, the larger the number can be.

The next question is 'How can we hold decimal fractions?' Unfortunately, it is not possible to hold fractions and numbers such as:

1.5

or

3.14159265358979323846

using binary numbers in this way. For this reason, these binary values are called **integer numbers**, **binary integers**, or just **integers**. We shall leave this question of fractional numbers until later.

Negative integer numbers

If you are already familiar with the way in which negative numbers are handled in binary arithmetic, then you may skip this section.

The final question concerning integer values is 'How can we hold negative numbers?' This problem is handled by the convention of using the left-most bit of the pattern to indicate the **sign** of the number. Thus, if we use two bytes to store an integer value, then a pattern such as:

0101010101010101

would represent a positive number (because the left-most bit is set to 0) and a pattern such as:

1010101010010101

would represent a negative number (because the left-most bit is set to 1).

In order to see how negative numbers are represented, we shall employ a trick to produce the required results. Before we look at negative binary numbers, let us consider how we might handle negative numbers in **decimal** arithmetic calculation using numbers which are four digits long:

0004 − 0003 = ?

We impose this restriction because, as we have seen, binary numbers have a fixed length. Since our computer can only perform addition, the calculation must be rearranged to:

0004 + (–0003) = ?

We know that the answer must be:

0001

but the *trick* is to produce the answer:

10001

which, since we are only using four digits, is truncated to:

0001

losing the left-most digit and giving us the answer which we want. This tells us that the way of representing the number:

–0003

is to look at the new calculation:

0004 + ? = (1)0001

and rearrange this to get:

? = (1)0001 – 0004

so we know that the missing number is:

9997

because:

0004 + 9997 = (1)0001

The 1 in brackets is lost (or it *overflows*) because we have only four digits available to represent the number. This tells us that 9997 is a way of representing –3 in our four-digit numbers. We apply the following rules or *algorithm* to convert the number –3 into the correct form:

(1) For each digit of the number (of which we want the negative form), subtract that digit from 9 (the highest value in a decimal system). So:

0003

becomes:

9996

(2)   Add 1 to the result, giving us:

   9997

So 9997 is the representation of −0003 in our decimal, four-digit numbers.

   We can check this by adding the positive and the negative values together:

   0003   the positive number
   9997   the negative number

(1) 0000

which gives us 0 since:

   $0003 + (−0003) = 0$

Question

25   Using the above algorithm, write down the representation of the following negative decimal numbers using four-digit arithmetic as we have done above.

   (a)   −87
   (b)   −144
   (c)   −255
   (d)   −390
   (e)   −493
   (f)   −530
   (g)   −626
   (h)   −766
   (i)   −883
   (j)   −942

Check your answers by adding the positive number and the negative number together; the result should be (1)0000 in each case.

A similar algorithm is used to represent negative binary numbers, whatever the length of the binary field. We illustrate this by converting the 16-bit binary number:

   0010101010101110

to its negative counterpart:

1. For each digit of the number (of which we want the negative form), subtract that digit from 1 (the highest value in a binary system. So:

   0010101010101110

   becomes:

   1101010101010001

   Since there are only two possible values (0 or 1), this step is frequently written as:

   'flip the bits'

   that is, change a 0 to a 1 and change a 1 to a 0.
2. Add 1 to the result, giving us:

   1101010101010010

   which is the representation of:

   −0010101010101110

   as a binary number.

We can check this by adding the positive and the negative values together:

   0010101010101110 the positive number
   1101010101010010 the negative number

(1) 0000000000000000

We can summarize both steps of the algorithm in the simple rule

flip the bits and add one

This way of holding negative binary numbers is often known as the **twos complement** form.

Question

26 Write down the negative equivalent of the following positive 16-bit binary numbers. Check your results by adding the positive and negative numbers together.

(a)   0001010100111111
(b)   0000010011110000

(c)	0001000010011001
(d)	0000010111101000
(e)	0001010011111110
(f)	0000000000101001
(g)	0000011011101110
(h)	0000110101101110
(i)	0001011100010110
(j)	0000101100101101

Internal / external format

It is important for you to remember that, although the numbers are held internally inside the computer as a binary pattern, they are converted to and from the required external form automatically by the software. Thus, you might write a Pascal statement such as:

    counter := 36;

but the Pascal processing software will convert this to the binary pattern:

    00100100

and store this pattern in the area allocated to the variable called **counter**. If you execute a sequence such as:

    increment := 1;
    counter := 36;
    counter := counter + increment;

then the binary pattern in the variable counter will be:

    00100101

but when we come to execute an output statement such as:

    write (counter);

the value represented by the binary pattern will be converted to its decimal equivalent (37) and the number:

    37

will be displayed on the screen.

The binary patterns are purely for internal storage. The external equivalents of these patterns are always decimal values or characters.

The external format depends upon the type of data which the variable – *counter* in this case – can hold.

Question

27 Complete the following summary, giving some examples of values which *can* be held in integer numbers, and some examples of values which *cannot* be held in integer numbers. In this section, we have seen that the computer can use integer numbers to represent values such as:

(a) _____
But integer numbers cannot be used to represent values such as:

(b) _____

Fractions

We still need to have some means of holding fractions such as

123.456

There are very few languages that allow us to handle fractions (or quotients) such as

1/2

and

22/7

and we shall ignore any requirement to handle these.

Some programming languages ignore the decimal point and use the integers to hold such numbers. They adopt a convention of assuming that a number has a fixed number of decimal places. For example, if the number is assumed to have 2 decimal places, then a value such as:

4294967295

would be interpreted, used in arithmetic calculations and displayed, as

42949672.95

For this reason, such values are called **fixed point numbers**.

When the language supports such a feature, there may be a means of specifying the **precision** (that is, the number of decimal places) for the numbers. In any one program, the precision is usually the same for all the fixed point numbers in the program. As before, the larger the number, the more space you need to hold that number.

Very large numbers

It would be useful if we could have some means of holding very large numbers such as:

$$1 \times 10^{25}$$

that is, 1 followed by 25 zeros:

10000000000000000000000000

and a way of holding very small numbers, such as:

$$1 \times 10^{-25}$$

that is, a decimal point followed by 24 zeros and a 1.

.0000000000000000000000001

Of course, we could represent the very large number by means of a suitably large numeric field. But in some sciences, such as astronomy, we use very large numbers such as these, but with relatively little accuracy. In order to measure the distance of a galaxy in light-years, an astronomer would rarely concern himself/herself with a precise large number such as:

129384757438547487485.1928345

and would probably accept:

$$1.294 \times 10^{20}$$

In such circumstances, we are concerned with the *size* but not the exact value of the numbers. The same argument applies to very small numbers such as a micro-biologist might encounter. A micro-biologist may accept:

$$1.486 \times 10^{-20}$$

as an approximation to an exact value of

0.0000000000000000000001485755627586

for the dimensions of a virus. Again, we are concerned with the *size* but not the exact value of the numbers.

Real numbers

Most programming languages allow us to meet all these requirements:

- fractions;
- large approximate numbers; and
- small approximate numbers.

Because this range of numbers is similar to those of the mathematical real numbers, such values are often referred to as **real** numbers to distinguish them from the integer numbers we met earlier.

Activity 1

List some situations – other than astronomy and micro-biology – in which you might need to hold very large numbers or very small numbers.

Floating point numbers

Many programming languages represent real values by means of **floating point numbers**. A floating point number such as:

$$1.294 \times 10^{20}$$

would be held internally as **two** parts:

1294 (this is called the **mantissa**)

and

20 (this is called the **exponent**)

like this:

$$\text{mantissa} \times 10^{\text{exponent}}$$

In this case, the number ten is known as the **base** or the **radix** for the representation.

So our number is represented by the mantissa and the exponent, and we may think of it as being held like this in memory:

$$\boxed{+1294 \ +20}$$

Similarly, the number:

$$1.4858 \times 10^{-20}$$

would be held like this:

+1486 –20

In practice, the numbers might be held in binary form and the value would be represented by the expression:

$$\text{mantissa} \times 2^{\text{exponent}}$$

using 2 instead of 10 as the base for the calculation. For the purposes of the present explanation, however, it will be convenient to think of our floating point numbers as being held as decimal values.

Normalized numbers

Each floating point number includes the sign of the mantissa (+ for positive values, – for negative values) and the sign of the exponent (+ for very large numbers, – for very small numbers). But you will see that we do not hold a decimal point with the number. The exponent is always an integer (we would, for example, never hold a number as 10 to the power 2.5), but there is a decimal point in the mantissa. So how are we to know whether:

+1486 –20

means 0.1486 times ten to the power –20, or 1.486 times ten to the power –20, or 14.86 times times ten to the power –20? The convention is that *the decimal point is assumed to come after the first digit of the mantissa*, so that this particular real number represents:

1.486

times ten to the power –20.

What would the number:

+0123 +20

represent? This would represent the value:

$$0.123 \times 10^{20}$$

as would

+1230 +19

Numbers in which the first digit of the mantissa is non-zero, as with:

+1486 –20
+1230 +19

are known as **normalized** or standard real numbers, and their mantissa always lies in the range 1.0 to 9.999. Numbers which have a zero as their first digit, as with

+0123 +20

are known as **unnormalized** real numbers. Most processing software works faster when the numbers are normalized than when they are not, and the machine language instruction sets of some computers include special arithmetic operations, one set for normalized real numbers and another for unnormalized real numbers.

Question

28 Write the mantissa and the exponent of the following real numbers in the same form as our examples above.

(a) −2807057248308.540840145
(b) 7303693043954437760.4
(c) 07879144595.99371328
(d) −943066597.39
(e) 36863257603
(f) .000006884504172768894
(g) 4675981592527.5912660
(h) 949243283689849.032
(i) −0.0000000009049871404
(j) 87637289648.2483392749

Real numbers in storage

Now let's look at the way in which bits and bytes can be used to store real numbers. There are a variety of different standards and methods available, depending upon the hardware and the software which is used. We shall consider a typical system of representing floating point numbers.

We have already seen that a real number is held in two parts, a mantissa and an exponent, and this is exactly the same way in which the numbers are held internally. The only difference between the examples shown above and the actual bit patterns held in computer storage is that we held decimal numbers whereas the computer holds the numbers as binary patterns. It is usual to employ four bytes (a word) to hold a real number, with the 32 bits being used as shown in Figure 3.8.

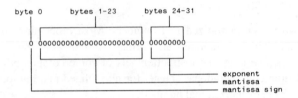

Figure 3.8 *Floating point numbers in storage*

The **mantissa sign** field indicates the sign of the number and will be either negative (1) or positive (0).

The **mantissa** represents a binary fraction in the range 1.0 to 1.11111111111111111111111, and the integer 1 is omitted, to save space. Thus, a mantissa of:

10000000000000000000000

represents the binary fraction:

0.10000000000000000000000

that is, 2 to power −1, which is:

0.5

in decimal. Adding the missing 1, we arrive at a value of:

1.5

for the mantissa. A mantissa of:

10100000000000000000000

represents the binary fraction:

0.10100000000000000000000

which is 2 to power −1 (0.5 in decimal) plus 2 to power −3 (0.125 in decimal), which gives us:

120

0.625

in decimal. Adding the missing 1, we arrive at a value of:

1.625

for the mantissa.

Binary	Decimal	Binary	Decimal
00000000	0	00111110	0.2421875
00000001	0.00390625	00111111	0.24609375
00000010	0.0078125	01000000	0.25
00000011	0.01171875	01110000	0.4375
00000100	0.015625	01111000	0.46875
00000111	0.02734375	01111100	0.484375
00001000	0.03125	01111110	0.4921875
00001110	0.0546875	01111111	0.49609375
00001111	0.05859375	10000000	0.5
00010000	0.0625	11000000	0.75
00011100	0.109375	11100000	0.875
00011110	0.1171875	11110000	0.9375
00011111	0.12109375	11111000	0.96875
00100000	0.125	11111100	0.984375
00111000	0.21875	11111110	0.9921875
00111100	0.234375	11111111	0.99609375

Figure 3.9   *Representing the mantissa*

The table in Figure 3.9 shows the decimal equivalents of some binary fractions. In the table, we have used only 8 bits to represent the binary fraction. This means that, when we convert an 8-bit binary fraction to its decimal equivalent, the smallest increment between one value and the next is:

00000001

which represents the binary fraction:

0.00000001

and which is equivalent to the decimal fraction:

0,00390625

so we can only show to this accuracy, that is, to an accuracy of about three or four places of decimals. But by using 23 bits, we can represent values correct to the binary fraction:

0.00000000000000000000001

which is equivalent to the decimal fraction:

0.00000011920928955078125

giving an accuracy of about seven places of decimals.

121

The **exponent** is held without an explicit sign. Instead, the possible range of values:

    00000000

to

    11111111

is used to represent the range −127 to 128. That is, an exponent of:

    −127

is represented by:

    00000000

and an exponent of:

    128

is represented by:

    11111111

In order to convert a particular representation to the equivalent floating point exponent, we convert the binary representation to the decimal equivalent and subtract 127. Some examples are shown in the table in Figure 3.10.

Binary Representation	Decimal equivalent	Exponent
00000000	0	−127
00000001	1	−126
00000010	2	−125
01111110	126	−1
01111111	127	0
10000000	128	1
10000001	129	2
10000010	130	3
10000011	131	4
11111101	253	126
11111110	254	127
11111111	255	128

Figure 3.10   *Representing the exponent*

We can observe how this works in practice by looking at a binary pattern to see what floating point number it represents. The four bytes:

    11111111 10000000 00000000 10000010

represent the binary pattern:

11111111100000000000000010000010

This is first broken into its component parts:

1 11111111000000000000000 10000010

The mantissa sign is 1 (negative).
The mantissa is represented by the pattern:

11111111000000000000000

which represents the fraction:

0.99609375

and adding the missing 1, we get a mantissa of:

1.99609375

The exponent is represented by the pattern:

10000010

which represents:

130

and subtracting 127, we get the exponent 3. So the floating point pattern:

11111111100000000000000010000010

represents the decimal number:

$$-1 \times 2^3 \times 1.99609375 = -15.96875$$

To convert a decimal number into its floating point representation, we carry out the same process in reverse. Thus, to convert the decimal number:

143.5

we can immediately write down the mantissa sign:

mantissa sign = positive = 0

We then repeatedly divide the number by 2 until we arrive at a value of the form 1.xxxxx to get the exponent:

$$143.5 = 2^7 \times 1.12109375$$

If the original value were less than 1, then we should repeatedly multiply the number by 2 to bring it into the range 1.0 to 1.9999, this would yield a negative exponent.

In this instance, the exponent is 7 and the mantissa is 1.12109375. Adding 127 to the exponent, we get:

134

which is represented by the 8-bit pattern:

exponent = 10000110

Finally, we subtract 1 from the mantissa 1.12109375 to get:

0.12109375

which is represented by the 23-bit pattern:

mantissa = 00011111000000000000000

Putting all these together, we get:

mantissa sign = positive = 0
mantissa = 00011111000000000000000
exponent = 10000110

which tells us that the floating point representation of the decimal number 143.5 is:

0 00011111000000000000000 10000110

or inside the computer, it would be held as four bytes:

00001111 10000000 00000000 10000110

Questions

29 The 32-bit patterns shown here represent floating point numbers. Following the procedure described in the text, convert the numbers to their decimal equivalent:

(a) 11000001011100000000000000000000
(b) 01000000010100000000000000000000
(c) 10111111101100000000000000000000
(d) 01000000010110000000000000000000
(e) 11000001001100000000000000000000

(f) 01000001000100000000000000000000
(g) 10111111110000000000000000000000
(h) 10111111111100000000000000000000
(i) 01000000110000000000000000000000
(j) 11000000001100000000000000000000

30 Following the procedure described in the text, convert these decimal values to the equivalent 32-bit floating point numbers:

(a) +1.25
(b) +4.5
(c) −2.5
(d) −2.25
(e) +1.125
(f) +3.0
(g) −10.0
(h) +12.0
(i) +7.5
(j) +3.75

Single-precision and double-precision

We have been using four bytes to hold our floating point numbers. Some computer systems have a facility for using 8 bytes to hold a floating point number. The further 32 bits (giving a total of 56 bits for the mantissa) are used to hold more digits of the mantissa. Because this gives greater accuracy, numbers which are held in 32 bits (4 bytes) are known as **single-precision** floating point numbers, and numbers represented by 64 bits (8 bytes) are known as **double-precision** floating point numbers. Using 56 bits to represent the mantissa, we can represent values correct to the binary fraction:

0.0000 0000 0000 0000 0000 0000 0000 0000 0000 0000 0000 0000 0000 0001

which is equivalent to the decimal fraction:

0.0000 0000 0000 0000 1387 7787 8078 1445 6755 2953 9585 1135 2539 062

giving an accuracy of about 17 places of decimals

E-notation

Just as integer values are used in Pascal expressions such as:

125

number := 36;

and the value written out exactly as an integer, so real numbers are written with a decimal point, like this:

price := 36.25;
value := quantity * 128.00;

For very large real numbers, the value may be specified in a form similar to the mantissa and exponent notation which we met above:

distance := 1.294 e 20;
diameter := 1.4858 e –20;

the *e* being read as **times ten to the power** . . . . Some languages allow you to specify double-precision values in the form:

distance := 1.294 d 20
diameter := 1.4858 d –20

This method of writing floating point numbers is known as **E-notation**.

Packed decimal

There is one type of data in which numeric fields are held in decimal form. This is known as **packed decimal** because the decimal digits are *packed* together, two to a byte, thereby taking up less space than if they were held as ASCII data or as binary numbers.

To see how this is done, let us consider the decimal value:

12345

This would be held in three bytes, as shown in Figure 3.11 (a). Each digit would then be encoded into its binary quivalent, as in diagram (b).

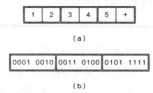

(a)

(b)

Figure 3.11   *Packed decimal numbers: 1*

Each packed decimal values occupies a whole number of bytes. If the value had an **even** number of digits then there would be four unused bits. For example,

−987654

would be converted as in Figure 3.12.

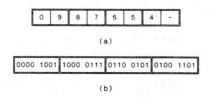

(a)

(b)

Figure 3.12 *Packed decimal numbers: 2*

The convention is to use hexadecimal F (1111) to represent the +
sign, and hexadecimal D (1101) to represent the − sign.

Since there is no facility for holding a decimal point, packed decimal
data always represent integer values. Where packed decimal is available, there will be some facility for implying the position of a decimal
point within a value. Cobol, for example, will allow you to describe a
packed decimal field by means of a statement such as:

02 AMOUNT PICTURE S9999V99 USAGE IS COMPUTATIONAL–3

indicating that AMOUNT is to hold a packed decimal number
(specified by the USAGE IS COMPUTATIONAL–3) with an arithmetic sign (specified by the S) and with a decimal point implied so that
the value represents two places of decimals specified by the V).

Questions

31 Convert the following decimal numbers to their packed decimal form, writing the answers as one-, two- or three-byte
binary patterns:

(a) 2
(b) +4567
(c) 12
(d) −453256
(e) 19
(f) −12
(g) −99

(h) 8745219

(i) 4345675

(j) −1234

32 The following binary patterns represented packed decimal numbers. Convert them to the *unpacked* form.

(a) 00010001 01111111

(b) 00110100 00010001 00110100 01111111

(c) 00000111 01001101

(d) 00000011 00111101

(e) 00000011 00000001 00010111 00011111

(f) 00000111 01000011 00001101

(g) 01111111

(h) 01000111 00000001 01000111 00111111

(i) 00010011 01000001 00011101

(j) 00000111 00111111

Boolean data type

There is a further type of data which has a far more narrow range than the numbers and characters which we have considered so far. For example, if we are processing a file of student information, we might wish to indicate whether or not a particular student is a member of the dramatic society. We could achieve this by means of a data field which will contain a letter Y if the student is a member of the dramatic society, or a letter N if the student is not a member of the dramatic society.

This situation may be handled more elegantly by means of a **Boolean** value which represents only one of two possible two states: *true* or *false*. We use Boolean values in situations where we only need to indicate whether something is *true* or *false*.

Whereas an integer value is assigned by statements such as:

```
total := 0;
total := 36;
```

where 0 and 36 are integer values, a Boolean field is assigned values by statements such as:

```
dram.mem := true;
dram.mem := false;
```

where *true* and *false* are (the only possible) Boolean values. Just as we have functions to handle numeric values,

> std.dev := sqrt (variance),

so there are functions to handle boolean values:

> over21 := *true*;
> under21 := not(over2l) and not(age=21);
> jnr.dram := under21 and dram.mem;

In all these cases, the boolean variables can take only one of the values *true* or *false*. A Boolean variable could not, for example, hold a value of 12345, and statements such as:

> over21 := 12345

are invalid and would be rejected by the Pascal compiler.

More importantly, it is possible to use these Boolean variables and values in making decisions in the program. For example:

> if over21 then writeln('NOT ELIGIBLE');
> if not over21 and not dram.mem then
> begin
> counter := counter + 1
> end

This makes the program much easier to read than otherwise.

Activity 2

We have seen that the condition:

> 'This student is a member of the dramatic society'

can be represented by a Boolean value of either *true* or *false*.

Write down ten other examples of data which can only be one of two possible values and which might be represented by Boolean values in this way.

We really only need the smallest possible unit of storage to hold a Boolean value. A single bit would be ideal, but many languages do not have a facility for handling individual bits, so it is not unusual to find that:

00000000

represents the Boolean value *false* and:

00000001

represents *true*.

Some languages, such as Fortran, have facilities for using each of the eight bits in a byte as Boolean values. This allows us to hold eight different Boolean values in one byte. Thus, if my program used Boolean variables to record information such as:

> dramsoc indicates whether a dramatic society member
> rugclub indicates whether a rugby club member
> chsclub indicates whether a chess club member
> socclub indicates whether a sports and social club member
> married indicates whether married
> livesin indicates whether living in hall of residence
> handicp indicates whether handicapped
> ownscar indicates whether owns a car

then I could use just one byte to record all these facts for each student. This obviously reduces the amount of space occupied by the data.

Question

33 I am using a single byte to record all the eight conditions shown above – reading from the left-most bit to the right-most bit, and using the fact that 0 means *false* and 1 means *true*. so that a 1 in the left-most bit means that this student is not a member of the dramatic society, and so on.
What do the following patterns represent?

(a) 00000111 for Mary Wilson.
(b) 00011100 for Ferid Alkarim.
(c) 11111110 for Michael Costas.
(d) 10000011 for Suraya Khan.
(e) 11100101 for Alan Parker.

Data types in programming languages

We have seen that there are a number of important data types which are commonly used in programming:

- integer numbers;
- real numbers
- characters and strings;
- Boolean values:

and, to a lesser extent,

- packed decimal;

and most programming languages have facilities for handling these **primitive data types**. Some languages, including Pascal, allow you to define *your own* data types.

To a certain extent, the compiler can recognize the type of data of a constant or a literal by its form. So a value such as

36

would be identified as an integer number. Similarly, the number

123.456

is a real number,

123e20

is a floating point number,

'A'

is a character,

"THE HORSE IS IN THE YARD"

is a string, and

true

is a Boolean value.

Question

34 Using the informal convention illustrated in the text, write down whether the following values are integer, real, floating point, character, string, or Boolean values.

(a) '?'
(b) 121.456

    (c)   "true"
    (d)   "D"
    (e)   16
    (f)   1e–10
    (g)   false
    (h)   2.
    (i)   "MARY WILSON"
    (j)   +99

Most programming languages only allow each variable to hold one type of data. Thus, a certain variable cannot hold a *string* value at one point in the processing and an *integer* value elsewhere in the program. We have seen that it can be relatively easy for the compiler to identify the data type of a constant, but it is less easy for the compiler to recognize the data type of a *variable*, that is, the data type of the data which can be held in a variable.

In order to avoid the confusion as to which type of data is held in each variable, it is the programmer's responsibility to declare the name of the variables which will be used in a program and, at the same time, to specify the type of data which each variable will hold.

How this is done depends upon the language which you are using.

Data types in Basic

In Basic, it is not necessary to declare variables before they are used. Indeed there is no formal way of specifying that you intend to use certain variable names. The best that you can do is to include a set of assignment statements such as:

    AMOUNT = 0
    NAME$ = ''

at the beginning of your program.

Most versions of Basic only distinguish between numeric values and string values, and use the convention that variable names which consist of just letters:

    A
    S
    VALUE
    AMOUNT

are numeric variables holding numeric values, whilst variable names which end in a $ sign:

A$
NAME$

are string variables holding string values.

In some of the early versions of Basic, variable names could only consist of a letter, a letter and a digit, or a letter and a dollar sign. Later versions allow longer names.

If Basic can get away with only two types of data – numeric and character strings – why do other programming languages offer so many, and why should a programming language concern itself with data types? The simplest answer is that the programming language must be able to supply and support the types of data and information which we need to handle in our programs. The more types there are, the more powerful the coding can be.

Microsoft Basic which is found on PC-compatible computers uses an extension of these conventions:

Variable names which end with a $ sign:

NAME$
DESCRIPTION$

are used to hold string values, as in standard Basic.

Variable names which end with a % sign:

DAYSDURATION%
QUANTITY%

are used to hold integer values.

Variable names consisting of just letters, or a string of letters followed by a ! sign:

INTERESTRATE
HOURSWORKED!

are used to hold single-precision values.

Variable names which end with a # sign:

DAYSDURATION#
SALARY#

are used to hold double-precision values.

There are certain other rules governing the names of your variables in Microsoft Basic: the name which is used to identify a variable must begin with a letter and may contain any combination of letters, digits and full stops; the name may be up to 40 characters in length.

Data types in Ada

In the programming language called Ada, there are only two types of numeric data: **universal integer** and **universal real**, and the programmer uses subtypes of these **parent types**. Each subtype represents a part of the parent type specified by minimum and maximum values. Any attempt to use a value outside the range which is permissible for that type will result in a *constraint error*. For convenience, most versions of Ada provide a package of standard subtypes:

```
INTEGER
SHORT_INTEGER
LONG_INTEGER
FLOAT
SHORT_FLOAT
LONG_FLOAT
CHARACTER
BOOLEAN
STRING
```

and these imply a range of values which are available on a particular machine. Other implementations on other machines may have different ranges.

The programmer may define his/her own data types. This is illustrated by the following statements:

type DAYOFYEAR is range 1. . 365

declares DAYOFYEAR as an integer lying in the specified range.

type VALUE is digits 10 range −1.0E20 . . +1.0E20

declares a floating point number, held with an accuracy of 10 digits lying in the specified range.

type VALUEFIX is delta 0.001 range −100.00 . . +100.00

declares a fixed point real number held with 3 places of decimals – as specified by the *delta* value – lying in the specified range.

type STATUS is (SINGLE, MARRIED, DIVORCED, WIDOWED)

declares an enumerated data type equivalent to those of Pascal.

Arrays are specified in the familiar manner:

SALES : array (1 . . 10, 1. . 20) of FLOAT

Data types in APL

The programming language APL began life as a mathematical notation and evolved into a very powerful language aimed at the mathematical user. For this reason, APL offers only one data type: numeric.

As in Basic, APL variables and numbers are not declared before use, and values may be written with or without a decimal point, so the type of the value – real or integer – is of no concern to the APL processor. Variable names may consist of any combination of letters and digits, and they may be up to 80 characters in length.

Some APL assignments and their results are shown in Figure 3.13.

```
4 + 7      1 1
7 - 2      5
2 - 7      ⁻ 5
3 x 4      1 2
3 * 3      2 7
3 ÷ 2      1 . 5
3 * ⁻ 2    0 . 1 1 1 1 1 1 1 1 1 1

VALUE←4 + 7
ROOT←(X - Y)* . 5
```

Figure 3.13   *APL assignments*

Note the way in which APL represents negative numbers (by means of a raised minus sign), subtraction (by means of a normal minus sign), multiplication (by means of the cross) and exponentiation (by means of the asterisk). It is interesting to note the way in which assignment statements are written:

destination ← source
VALUE ← 4 + 7

which is more explicit than the more familiar

135

> destination = source
> value = 4 + 7

or

> value := 4 + 7

of most other languages.

Data types in Cobol

In Cobol, the data types and also, in certain cases, the amount of storage which is to be allocated to each data field, must be specified in the preliminary WORKING STORAGE SECTION of the program.

A description such as:

> 02 NAME PICTURE X(20) USAGE IS DISPLAY.

would instruct the compiler to allocate 20 bytes (indicated by the picture X(20) clause) for holding ASCII data (indicated by the DISPLAY clause). Cobol has a number of assumptions and conventions which simplify the specification of your fields, and you will learn these if you proceed to study Cobol.

A description such as:

> 02 QUANTITY PICTURE 999 USAGE IS DISPLAY.

would instruct the compiler to allocate three bytes (indicated by the picture 999 clause) for holding ASCII data (indicated by the DISPLAY clause).

As you might expect, arithmetic cannot be performed on such DISPLAY fields. If you wish to hold numeric data which is to be used in calculations, then you must use the COMPUTATIONAL forms. A description such as:

> 02 COUNTER USAGE IS COMPUTATIONAL.

would allocate a fixed number of bytes to hold a binary (that is, an integer) number. The actual range of values which are available for a COMPUTATIONAL number depends upon the computer and the compiler which you are using.

A description such as:

> 02 SALARY USAGE IS COMPUTATIONAL–1.

would allocate storage to hold a single-precision floating point number, and a description such as:

02 ALLOWANCE USAGE IS COMPUTATIONAL–2.

would allocate storage to hold a double-precision floating point number.

A description such as:

02 FILE-SALARY USAGE IS COMPUTATIONAL–3.

would allocate storage to hold a packed decimal number.

We have already mentioned that Cobol has a facility for implying the position of a decimal point within a value. For example, the statement:

02 AMOUNT PICTURE S9999V99 USAGE IS COMPUTATIONAL–3.

indicates that the variable called AMOUNT is to hold a packed decimal number with an arithmetic sign (specified by the S) and with a decimal point implied to represent two places of decimals (specified by the V).

In Cobol, the name which is used to identify a variable (this is called a *label*) must begin with a letter and may contain any combination of letters, digits and hyphens. Some compilers regard only the first 8 characters of the name and ignore the rest.

Data types in Fortran

In Fortran, we could declare the data types of our variables *explicitly* with statements such as:

```
INTEGER AMOUNT, ORDER
REAL INTER, PRICE, VALUE
DOUBLE PRECISION VOLUME, RANGE
LOGICAL SOLD, READY
CHARACTER CODE
```

However, there is a convention in Fortran – known as **implicit naming** – which says that, unless the programmer declares them otherwise, all variable names beginning with one of the letters:

I, J, K, L, M, N

are integer variables holding integer values, whilst all others are real variables holding real numbers. This means that a variable with a name such as:

INT43
ITEMS

will hold *integer* values and such names may be used without being declared on an INTEGER statement, whilst a variable with a name such as:

AMOUNT
RATE90
VALUE

beginning with letters A to H or O to Z, indicates that the variable is to hold *real* values.

All other variables must be declared explicitly. Strings are declared as a number of characters, so that:

CHARACTER NAME*30

indicates that the variable called NAME is to hold a string of up to 30 characters. If this size specification is to apply to a number of variables, then the form:

CHARACTER*30 NAME, STREET, TOWN, COUNTY

may be used, and all the variables NAME, STREET, TOWN and COUNTY will be capable of holding up to 30 characters of data.

Some versions of Fortran extend the size specification to types of data other than characters. So you may come across declarations such as:

INTEGER*32 ASTRON
REAL*64 VALUE1, VALUE2, VALUE3,
COMPLEX*32 ROOTS

to specify the number of bytes of memory which are to be used to store each of the numbers.

Fortran has a further data type: COMPLEX. We have not encountered this before. Complex values are numeric and are used in mathematical and engineering work. Each complex number consists of two values; the first is the *real* part, the second is the *imaginary* part. Don't confuse the word *real* here with the real numbers we have used earlier. Thus, a complex constant such as:

(3,4)

represents the complex number:

3+2*i*

or some engineers may write this as:

3+2*j*

We need not go into the detail of complex numbers here, but we could just remind ourselves that *i* (or *j*) is used to represent the square root of −1. Thus, if we add two complex numbers together, for example,

(3,4) + (2,−7)

we are really adding:

$$= 3 + 4i + 2 - 7i$$
$$= 5 - 3i$$
$$= (5,-3)$$

There is nothing particular startling about this. But, if we *multiply* two complex numbers together, for example,

(3,4) ∗ (2,−7)

we are really multiplying:

$$(3+4i) * (2-7i)$$
$$= 3*2 + 4i*2 - 3*7i - 4i*7i$$
$$= 6 + 8i - 21i - 28i^2$$
$$= 6 - 13i + 28 \text{ (because } i^2 = -1\text{)}$$
$$= 34 - 13i$$
$$= (34,-13)$$

The complex arithmetic capabilities of Fortran will do this automatically for us. Figure 3.14 shows a fragment of a Fortran program which performs this calculation and then goes on to use two functions to display the real and the imaginary parts of the result. This program would display the numbers:

(34, −13)

as we should expect from the above calculation.

```
COMPLEX NUMBER1, NUMBER2, NUMBER3
NUMBER1 = (3,4)
NUMBER2 = (2,-7)
NUMBER3 = NUMBER1 * NUMBER2
PRINT *,NUMBER3
```

Figure 3.14   *Complex numbers in Fortran*

In Fortran, the name which is used to identify a variable must begin with a letter and may contain only letters and digits. Most compilers only permit names of six characters or less in length, whilst other allow longer names but regard only the first 6 characters of the name and ignore the rest. Thus, the names:

QUANTI
QUANTITY
QUANTITATIVE

would all refer to the same variable, and the last two variables may be rejected by some compilers.

Data types in Pascal

In Pascal, all variables and their type must be declared at the start of the program. This is done by statements of the form:

```
var value, distance: real;
    quantity, number. ordered: int;
    sold, out.of.stock: Boolean;
    code: char
```

Values may be assigned to each type of variable by an expression of the correct type. For example, using the variables declared above, we might use statements such as:

```
quantity := 36;
sold := true;
code : = 'Y';
value := 2.67;
distance := 2.5e–5; { = 0.000025 }
distance := 35.234e7; { = 352340000.0}
```

A real value such as 2.67 is said to be written in *fixed form*, whilst a value such as 2.5e6 is said to be written in *floating point form*.

Strictly speaking, statements such as:

```
quantity := 36.1;
quantity := 36.0;
```

are incorrect because they assign (what are clearly) real values to (what has been defined as) an integer variable. But, like many compilers, Pascal does not quibble about this conflict and converts the real value to the equivalent integer value (36 in both instances).

To hold a string of characters, we could define an array of characters:

name : array[1 . . 30] of char

and then assign values to this string by statements such as:

name : = "WILLIAM JOHNSON AND MARY SMITH"

In Pascal, the name which is used to identify a variable (its *identifier*) must begin with a letter and may contain only letters and digits. Some compilers regard only the first 8 characters of the name and ignore the rest.

Data types in PL/1

In the language PL/1, data types are specified by means of one or more **attributes**. These attributes are:

- FIXED or FLOAT or COMPLEX to specify the nature of the data,
- BINARY or DECIMAL to specify the way in which the data is to be held,
- the number of digits, and
- the location of the decimal point.

For example, the declaration:

FIXED DECIMAL (10,4)

would declare a fixed point decimal number accurate to 10 places of decimals and with four digits after the decimal point. So that an example of a value held in such a variable would be:

123456.0987

Data types in C

In the C language, the nature of the variables must be declared explicitly by means of statements of the form:

```
int standx, ItemCounter;
short value, TotalAmount;
long words;
float interest;
```

141

double distance;
char flag, name[30].

It is worth noting the following points:

- C does not have a facility to handle Boolean values. In practice, integers are used to represent logical values;
- *float* and *double* are used to declare single-precision real variables and double-precision real variables, respectively;
- *int* is used to declare an integer variable occupying one word of storage;
- *short* is used to declare an integer variable occupying two bytes of storage. This lets you save space on a computer which has a four-byte word;
- long is used to declare an integer variable occupying four bytes of storage.

This means that, depending upon the word length of the computer which you are using, *int* may be the same as *short* (as on the IBM-PC) or *int* may be the same as *long*.

Values may be assigned to each type of variable by an expression of the correct type. For example, using the variables declared above, we might use statements such as:

standx = 36;
TotalAmount = 52.55;
flag = 'Y';
name[30] = "WILHELMINA"

In C, the name which is used to identify a variable must begin with a letter and may contain any combination of upper-case letters, lower-case letters, digits and underscore characters. Some compilers regard only the first 8 characters of the name and ignore the rest.

Questions

I want to be able to use the names below for variables in a Fortran program. I have shown the type of data which the variable is to hold. For each variable, indicate whether or not I must use a type declaration statement and, if so, what this statement would be.

35 INTRST to hold a single-precision real value.
36 KOUNT to hold an integer value.

37 LIMIT to hold a double-precision real value.
38 NODE to hold to a single character.
39 QUANT to hold a single-precision real value.
40 SNO to hold an integer value.
41 VALID to hold a Boolean value.
42 COUNTED to hold a single-precision real value.
43 VALUE to hold a double-precision real value.
44 WORKEX to hold a text string of ten characters.

Activity 3

Repeat the previous questions for someone who is writing programs in:

(a) C.
(b) Pascal.
(c) Cobol.
(d) Microsoft Basic.
(e) Any other programming language which you have used.

Remember that you may have change the names to fit the rules of the individual languages.

Type checking

In those languages which require the programmer to declare the names and the types of the variables which will be used in a program, the compiler is able to check that the variables are used correctly. This is known as **type checking**. For example, if the variables:

```
code: char
amount, price, value: real
```

have been declared, then the compiler can reject any erroneous statements such as:

```
value ;= code * price
```

in which the programmer has accidentally used the variable **code** in the wrong context: a *character* string cannot be used in an *arithmetic* statement. By causing the error to show up at the compilation stage – that is, sooner rather than later – the language has helped us to avoid a situation in which the error may only appear when the program is being executed.

Because all variables must be defined before they are used, the compiler can also recognize errors in statements such as:

value := price * amooount

in which a typing mistake has resulted in an undefined variable (**amooount**) being used. Such errors will be detected as the program is being compiled and will save time when the program is being tested later. Even though it may seem an unnecessary chore when you have to define all your variables before you can use them, it does reduce the number of errors which can slip into your coding and thereby saves you time and trouble later. These are probably the most powerful justifications for the existence of program data types.

Activity 4

Make a list of the programming languages with which you are familiar.
For each language:

- list the data types which are available;
- write down examples of the statements and declarations which you might use to declare variables of each type;
- write down some examples of invalid uses of the data types in each language.

Draw up a table showing which data types are available in which languages.
Which data type(s) are most widely available?
Which data type(s) are least widely available?
If you are not familiar with any programming languages yet, use the languages which we have described in the text.

Besides the primitive data types which we have mentioned, there are a number of additional facilities to be found in the various programming languages. These may not be widely available. In some languages, you may have to construct your own versions of these facilities, if you need them, using the tools which the language offers. With some languages, they may regarded as *data structures*, rather than *data types*.

Arrays

Most programming languages have some facilities for handling an **array** of data. This is a sequence of contiguous storage locations. The array is identified by name, and each individual storage location – each **element** – within the array is identified by its numeric position within the array – its **subscript**.

Thus if we had an array called A comprising 10 elements, we could visualize the array as in Figure 3.15.

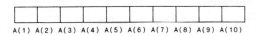

A(1) A(2) A(3) A(4) A(5) A(6) A(7) A(8) A(9) A(10)

Figure 3.15 *A simple array*

The first element would have the subscript 1 and would be identified by the reference:

A(1)

the second element would be identified by A(2) and so on.

The programmer must declare the amount of space required for the array. In Basic, this would be done by the statement:

DIMENSION A(10)

Obviously, the programmer must take care not to attempt to access invalid elements of the array by using statements such as:

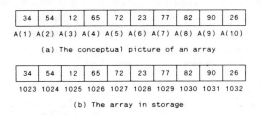

(a) The conceptual picture of an array

(b) The array in storage

Figure 3.16 *The physical picture of an array*

145

A(−123) = 43
PRINT A(11)

The physical representation of such an array is simple. All we need to know are the start address of the sequence, the size of each element and the number of elements. Thus, if we imagine that our array contained values as in Figure 3.16 (a), then this might be held in memory as a sequence of one-byte locations starting at address 1023, as in Figure 3.16 (b).

To tell us all we need to know about the location of the array and its elements, we need only store the following information:

start address:	1023
size of elements:	1 byte
number of elements:	10

Thus, to transform an array reference such as A(n) into a physical address, we would use the algorithm:

A(n) is at (n−1) * 1 + 1023

So A(3) is located at:

A(3) is at (3−1) * 1 + 1023

= 2 * 1 + 1023
= 2   + 1023
= 1025

The processor would also check that the subscript *n* is within the acceptable range.

The information which describes the array is held in a **dope vector**. In the case, the actual contents of the dope vector would be the three values illustrated in Figure 3.17.

The dope vector is created by the compiler and used by the run-time controlling processor whenever an attempt is made to access an element in the array. By comparing the subscript which the program is attempting to access with the information in the dope vector, the run-time processor is able to accept an identifier such as:

A(X)

when X has a value in the range 1 to 10, but it will reject an attempt to access the array when X has a value of, say, −123 or 11.

start address	1023
size of elements	1 byte
number of elements	10

(a)

1023	1	10

(b)

Figure 3.17 *A dope vector*

The dope vector which is created and used by one compiler/run-time processor might hold different information from the dope vector created and used by another compiler/run-time processor.

Question

45 Write down the contents of the dope vectors for each of the following arrays:

(a) An array of 30 elements starting at address 10012. Each element is to occupy 4 bytes.

(b) An array of 1000 one-byte elements starting at address 19001.

(c) An array starting at address 12345 whose subscripts run from 1 to 199 and which is to hold 8-byte floating point numbers.

Subscripts

Some programming languages have facilities to start the array at a subscript other than 1. For example, you might wish to process statistical data relating to the years 1980 to 1989 and choose to hold this in an array. If we were using Basic, two possibilities spring to mind. We could use:

• An array of 1989 elements, with the subscripts running from 1 to 1989 (and ignore the first 1979 elements). The program would include statements such as:

DIMENSION STATS(1989)
STATS(1982) = 4

147

This would waste a great deal of storage space.

- An array of 10 elements with the subscripts running from 1 to 10 (and subtract 1979 from each subscript before we use it).

DIMENSION STATS(10)
STATS(1982–1979) = 4

This would complicate the coding of the program unnecessarily.

It would be much more convenient to have the subscripts running just from 1980 to 1989, so that we could write explicit statements such as:

STATS(1982)=4

This would reduce the amount of storage used by the program and it would simplify the coding. Pascal, and some other languages, will allow us to achieve this by declaring an array like this:

STATS = array [1980 . . 1989] of integer

and the assignment statement would then be:

STATS[1982] := 4

We might visualize this array as in Figure 3.18.

In such circumstances, the dope vector needs to hold much more information, as shown in Figure 3.18 (b).

Year:	1980	1981	1982	1983	1984	1985	1986	1987	1988	1989
	44	31	4	0	72	23	11	10	9	2
Address:	3333	3334	3335	3336	3337	3338	3339	3340	3341	3342

(a) the array

```
start address:        3333
size of elements:     1 byte
lowest subscript:     1980
highest subscript:    1989
```

(b) the dope vector

Figure 3.18 *An array with specific subscripts*

We do not need to hold the number of elements in the dope vector since this can be calculated from the subscript range.

Just as it may be convenient for the programmer to use an array whose subscripts start at 1980 and go up to 1989, it may also be convenient to have an array with subscripts which start at, say, −30 and go up to 40; for example, we might be recording the temperatures at an Antarctic survey station.

Questions

46 Write down the contents of the dope vector which we might use to describe an array which would hold the Antarctic survey readings mentioned in the text. The readings are to be held as four-byte numbers starting at address 30476.

47 How can we calculate the number of elements in the array from the dope vector? How many elements are there?

48 How can we calculate the total storage space occupied by the array from the dope vector? What is the total storage space occupied by the array?

Working with arrays

All languages allow the elements of an array to be handled individually by means of the subscripts. The programmer may use explicit references, as in the Basic statements:

    PRINT A(3)
    TOTAL A(l) + A(2)
    INPUT A(10)

or indirectly, by using a variable or an arithmetic expression as a subscript:

    FOR X = 1 TO 10
       TOTAL = TOTAL + A(X)
    NEXT X

    PRINT A(X + Y – 32)

Some languages offer other, often much more powerful, ways of handling arrays. The more that the programming language will do for you, the fewer opportunities there are for you to make mistakes. Some dialects of Basic, for example, offer the:

    MAT INPUT

and

149

MAT PRINT

statements to enter data into an array and to display the contents of an array. A statement such as

MAT INPUT A

is obviously simpler than having to write an explicit piece of coding such as

    FOR X=1 TO 100
      INPUT A(X)
    NEXT X

Other dialects of Basic offer statements which will set all the elements of an array to a specific value:

    DIMENSION A(100)
    MAT A = 1

which would set all the 100 elements of array A to 1, or

    DIMENSION A(100), B(100)
    MAT A = MAT B

which would copy all the 100 elements of array B, one by one, into the corresponding elements of array A.

The APL language is exceptional in the way in which it handles arrays (which it calls *vectors*) and multi-dimensional arrays (or *matrices*). We can illustrate this by means of some simple examples. If an APL array A contains the values:

    1 2 3 4 5 6

and the array B contains the values:

    9 8 7 6 5 4

then the statement:

    C ← A × B

will produce a new array, called C, containing the *products* of the corresponding elements:

    9 16 21 24 25 24

The APL statement:

+ / A

will add up all the elements in array A and display the result:

21

and the even more powerful statement:

D ← + / A × B

will calculate the products of the corresponding elements and add them all up, and put the result:

119

into a variable called D.

Activity 5

Choose any language with which you are familiar and write a sequence of coding to reproduce the action of the three APL statements described above:

C ← A × B
+ /A
D ← + / A × B

What are the advantages of APL over the language which you chose? What are the advantages of your language over APL?

Homogeneous arrays

How do you think the compiler would handle the situation in which we wanted the various elements of the array to hold different types of data? For example, we might want to hold an integer in STATS(1), a character string in STATS(2), a floating point number in STATS(3), and so on.

An array such as those we have considered above, where all the elements are of the same type, is known as a **homogeneous array** and one in which the elements are of different types is known as a **heterogeneous array**. In general, it is not possible to hold mixed data types within one array and most compilers specify that heterogeneous arrays cannot be used.

As we shall see when we look at **pointers** later, a possible solution could be devised in which the elements of an array are pointers to variables of other data types. Figure 3.19 shows how such an array might be visualized.

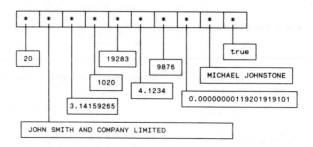

Figure 3.19   *A heterogenous array*

A solution along these lines is offered in the SNOBOL language.

We shall meet another one way around this problem when we look at the concept of records later.

Arrays with several dimensions

The arrays we have been looking at have consisted of just a single sequence of elements. However, most programming languages will also let you handle two-dimensional arrays – sometimes called matrices – which you can visualize as a set of pigeon-holes, as shown in Figure 3.20 (a). Some languages, such as Fortran, have facilities for three-dimensional arrays. No matter what facilities the language offers, an array is always stored as a sequence of storage locations.

We have seen how a one-dimensional array might be held. A two-dimensional array would be held in exactly the same manner, with the elements *stretched out* into a single sequence of storage locations. An array with five rows of four columns which we would define by a Basic statement such as:

DIMENSION B2(5,4)

might be visualized like the arrangement in Figure 3.20 (a). This could be transformed into a one-dimensional sequence row-by-row, starting at storage address 2345, as shown in Figure 3.20 (b), or it might be transformed column-by-column, starting at, say, location 3345, as shown in Figure 3.20 (c). Which of these two possibilities is used depends upon the particular compiler which you are using.

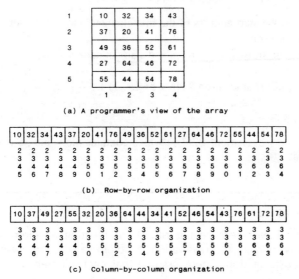

(a) A programmer's view of the array

(b) Row-by-row organization

(c) Column-by-column organization

Figure 3.20 *Arrays in storage*

This time, the algorithm for locating an array reference such as B2(2,1) is slightly more complicated. If we use the row-by-row transformation, the algorithm to convert a reference such as B2(x,y) into an actual address is:

B2(x,y) is at location $s + c*(x - 1) + y - 1$

where s is the start address of the first element, and c is the numbers of columns in the array.

Thus, our array has four columns and starts at address 2345, so array element:

B2(3,2) is at location $2345 + 4*(3 - 1) + 2 - 1$
$= 2345 + 8 + 1$
$= 2354$

153

and, as we see, element B2(3,1) which contains the value 36 is located at address 2354.

If we use the column-by-column transformation, the algorithm to convert a reference such as B2(x,y) into an actual address is:

$$B2(x,y) \text{ is at location } s + r*(y - 1) + x - 1$$

where s is the start address of the first element, and r is the numbers of rows in the array.

Thus, our array has five rows and starts at address 3345, so array element:

$$B2(3,2) \text{ is at location } 3345 + 5*(2 - 1) + 3 - 1$$
$$= 3345 + 5 + 2$$
$$= 3352$$

and, as we see, element B2(3,1) which contains the value 36 is located at address 3352.

Questions

49 We have seen the algorithms for locating an element in a row-by-row transformation, and in a column-by-column transformation. These assume that each element is just one byte in size.

Rewrite each of these algorithms for the situation in which the array B2 starts at storage address 40001 and each element of the array is 4 bytes in size.

Use the algorithms to find the addresses of these elements in the table in Figure 3.21.

	Row by row	Column by column
B2(1,1)		
B2(5,4)		
B2(1,4)		
B2(5,1)		
B2(3,1)		

Figure 3.21   *Element addresses*

Redraw the transformed diagrams showing the actual addresses for the elements of the array and use this to check your answers.

50 What information would the dope vector for a two dimensional array contain?

How does the information in the dope vector relate to the numbers in the algorithms in the previous question?

How would your solution change if you wished the range of subscripts for one of the dimensions to run from 1976 to 1980 instead of from 1 to 5?

51 How can the number of elements in the two-dimensional array be calculated from the dope vector?

52 How can the total storage space occupied by the two-dimensional array be calculated from the dope vector?

Activity 6

Draw an array with 7 columns and 5 rows. Put any numbers into each element of the array.

Draw a diagram to show how the array would be represented in a *column-by-column* transformation. The address of the first location is 8743 and each element is two bytes in size.

Write down what the dope vector should contain.

Write down the algorithm which would be used to locate the element ARRAY(x,y) in your transformation. Use your algorithm to find the address of the elements:

    ARRAY(1,1)
    ARRAY(7,5)
    ARRAY(1,5)
    ARRAY(7,1)
    ARRAY(3,3)

Check these with your *column-by-column* transformed diagram.

Draw a diagram to show how the array would be represented in a *row-by-row* transformation. The address of the first location is 1288 and each element is four bytes in size.

Write down the algorithm which would be used to locate the element ARRAY(x,y) in your transformation. Use your algorithm to find the address of the elements:

    ARRAY(1,1)
    ARRAY(7,5)
    ARRAY(1,5)

ARRAY(7,1)
ARRAY(3,3)

Check these with your *row-by-row* transformed diagram.

Records

We have mentioned that it is usual for an array to be homogeneous, that is, one in which all the elements are of the same type. There is one familiar data type which resembles an array but in which the elements may be of *different* types: this is a **record**.

In Pascal, we could define a record data type called STAFF like this:

```
Type STAFF = record
        NAME: string;
        AGE: integer;
        SALARY: real;
        MANAGER: Boolean;
    end;
```

and then use this data type to define other variables:

```
var EMPLOYEE: STAFF
```

which tells the compiler that the variable EMPLOYEE is of STAFF data type.

Each **field** of the EMPLOYEE record is identified by a reference made up of the name of the variable (EMPLOYEE in this instance), followed by a full-stop and the name of the field (NAME, AGE, SALARY or MANAGER in this instance). So our coding might include statements like:

```
EMPLOYEE.NAME := "Watkins";
EMPLOYEE.AGE := 42;
EMPLOYEE.SALARY := 320.75;
EMPLOYEE.MANAGER := true;
```

We might visualize the resultant EMPLOYEE variable as being like that in Figure 3.22.

Algol and Snobol use a similar notation and allow an entire record to be built up by means of a single statement of the form:

```
EMPLOYEE : ("Watkins", 42, 320.75, true)
```

Watkins	42	320.75	true

Figure 3.22 *EMPLOYEE variable of data type STAFF*

Note that by using the term *record*, we are not assuming that the data is going to be written to, or read from, an output device such as disk or tape.

Activity 7

(1) If you are familiar with a language, such as Cobol, which allows you to define records, rewrite the above EMPLOYEE record declaration and the statements which would create the record shown in Figure 3.22 in that language.

(2) Of the programming languages which you have used, choose one which offers the concept of records and write the declarations and the statements which would create the records shown in Figure 3.23.

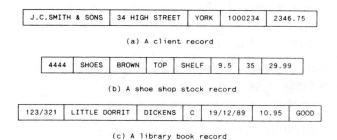

(a) A client record

(b) A shoe shop stock record

(c) A library book record

Figure 3.23 *Some records*

You may make any assumptions about the nature of the data.

Enumerated data types

When we were looking at arrays, we considered a situation in which we needed to hold statistics for the years 1980 to 1989 and we saw how convenient it would be to have an array whose subscripts run from

1980 to 1990. We found a solution in Pascal which allowed us to define an array by means of a statement of the form:

STATS = array [1980 . . 1989] of integer;

The first element of the array would be STATS[1980] and the final element would be STATS[1989], ten elements in all.

Now let us suppose that, in another situation, we wished to record the number of people who visited the college library each day. We could define an array:

VISITS = array [1 . . 7] of integer;

and then, by deciding that day 1 is Monday, day 2 is Tuesday and so on, we could record a *Monday* visit as:

VISITS[l] := VISITS[1] + 1;

a *Sunday* visit as:

VISITS[7] := VISITS[7] + 1;

and so on. When we wish to print a list of the visits made on each day, we could use a loop of the form:

for D := 1 to 7
   do writeln (VISITS[D]);

However, it would make the coding easier to read if we were able to use statements of the form:

VISITS[Monday] := VISITS[Monday] + 1;

VISITS[Sunday] : = VISITS[Sunday] + 1;

and even:

for D : Monday to Sunday
   do writeln (VISITS[D]);

We could solve this problem simply by assigning constant values (1 to a constant called Monday, 2 to a constant called Tuesday, and so on). But Pascal will allow us to produce the same effect by means of an **enumerated** data type or an **ordinal** data type. We must first define the data type:

type DAYS (Monday, Tuesday, Wednesday, Thursday,
Friday, Saturday, Sunday);

and then we can use the names *Monday* through to *Sunday* exactly as required.

It is possible to have a sub-range taken from the list of DAYS:

WEEKDAYS = (Monday . . Friday);

There are also facilities for finding the *predecessor* for any day (that is, the day before), and the *successor* for any day (that is the day after), and the ordinal position of any day (that is the position within the range). Thus, the function

pred(Wednesday)

would return *Tuesday*; the function

succ(Wednesday)

would return *Thursday*; the function

ord(Wednesday)

would return 3.

The requirements of the values listed for an enumerated data type are:

- there must be a finite number of values;
- the values must be ordered (the order in which they are specified is important);
- the values must be unique (we could not have two Mondays, for example);
- the values must be discrete (you cannot have any notion such as Monday-and-a-half);
- the values must be contiguous (there must be no gaps between the values).

It is these requirements which permits the individual values of an enumerated data type to be represented by the integers from 1 upwards.

Question

53 Use the list of requirements given in the text to decide which of the following are acceptable ranges (and sub-ranges) for enumerated (or ordinal) data types:

(a)   (Jan, Feb, Mar, Apr, May, Jun, Jul, Aug)

    (b)   (Jun . . Aug)
    (c)   (Spring, Summer, Winter, Autumn)
    (d)   (Man, Woman, Child)
    (e)   (Baby, Child, Child, Adult)
    (f)   (Silk, Wool, Satin, Wool)
    (g)   (yes, no, maybe, sometimes, unknown)
    (h)   (once, twice, thrice, fourtimes, fivetimes)

Implementing enumerated data types

Most compilers implement enumerated data types by giving each name a numeric value. So, if we defined a data type as:

> type DAYS (Monday, Tuesday, Wednesday, Thursday,
> Friday, Saturday, Sunday);

then Monday would be assigned an integer value of 1, Tuesday 2, and so on. Therefore, in processing terms, two sets of statements:

> VISITS[1] := VISITS[1] + 1;

and

> VISITS[Monday] := VISITS[Monday] + 1;

would have exactly the same effect, although the use of an enumerated data type in the second statement simplifies the coding. Each particular compiler may represent this type of data in a different manner, so the internal form is of no concern to us and changing it would disturb the run-time processor. For this reason, it is not possible to output (or input) a value held in, say, the storage location identified by *Monday* and the other names in the above examples.

Activity 8

Earlier, we gave a list of requirements of the values declared in an enumerated data type. Look at this list and state why each of these requirements is necessary for this compiler.

Let us imagine that a particular Pascal compiler represents each of the names in an enumerated data type by an integer 1, 2, 3, and so on.

Indicate how each of the valid ranges shown in the Question 47 would be represented by this compiler.

Pointers

By now, you should feel quite comfortable with the concept of the computer's memory as being made up of a sequence of bytes, and of these bytes being grouped together into blocks of 2 or more bytes to represent the storage locations, and of the storage locations being used to hold the data assigned to the variables used in the program. It is convenient to think of the Basic program shown in Figure 3.24 (a) or the Pascal program shown in Figure 3.24 (b) as using the memory locations shown in Figure 3.24 (c). The contents shown in diagram (c) will be loaded into the storage locations, one at a time, as each of the three assignment statements is executed.

```
A=12
B=56
C=A+B
PRINT C
END
```

(a)   A Basic program

```
var A, B, C: integer;
begin
      A := 12;
      B := 56;
      C := A+B;
      writeln (C)
end.
```

(b)   A Pascal program

A	B	C
12	56	67

(c)   The storage locations

Figure 3.24   *Variables and storage*

The storage locations are laid out, or **allocated**, when the program is loaded for execution and is based upon information about the nature and memory requirements which are mapped out in the **symbol table** produced by the compiler. We shall discuss this further when we look at the task of compiling a program.

In general, this means that the amount of data that we can handle is limited by the number of variables which we have declared or used in the program. However, there are situations in which we do not know – when we write the program – how much data will have to be processed. For example, we might need to process a list of the figures about the number of books which the students have borrowed from the college library. We want to hold our data like the lists shown in Figure 3.25, but we do not know exactly how long the list will be.

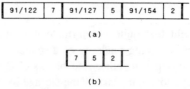

(a)

(b)

Figure 3.25 *Dynamic lists*

During the college vacation there may be only a few, if any, figures, at other times there may be several hundred figures, and during the examinations there may be several thousand figures. What we need is a system which will allow us to have just as many variables as we need; not too few, otherwise the program would abort because we have run out of space at busy times, and not too many (as we might have if we declared a huge array to hold the data), otherwise we are wasting storage space and causing the program to be slow in loading and execution.

Programming languages such as Pascal allow us to overcome this problem by the use of **pointers**. A pointer is a variable which does not contain *data* but contains the *actual address of a storage location where the data is to be found*. By using pointers, we can create new variables **dynamically**, as the program is executing.

We shall introduce the nature of pointers by looking at an intermediate solution to the above problem. To simplify the explanation, let us ignore the students' registration numbers and imagine that we just need to hold the numbers of books which are out on loan, as shown in Figure 3.25 (b). We could specify that we wish to use pointers by means of a definition like this:

type BOOK: ^ integer;

The vertical arrow identifies this as a pointer data type. We can read this as saying that *BOOK is not a memory location but a pointer to a memory location which holds an integer*. In order to use a variable of the type BOOK, we would then issue declarations of the form:

var STUDENT1, STUDENT2, STUDENT3: BOOK;

When the program is loaded into memory, the three variables would be allocated storage as shown in Figure 3.26 (a), but their contents will be undefined at this stage.

Before we can use these variables in our program, we must ask for

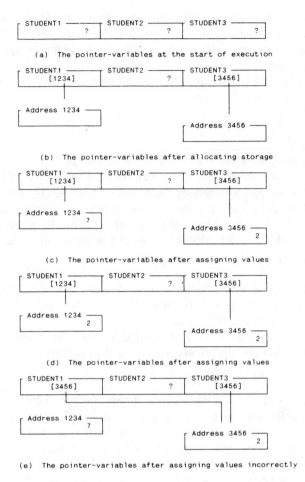

(a) The pointer-variables at the start of execution

(b) The pointer-variables after allocating storage

(c) The pointer-variables after assigning values

(d) The pointer-variables after assigning values

(e) The pointer-variables after assigning values incorrectly

Figure 3.26 *Pointer variables*

storage to be allocated to the variables. We would do this by means of a statement of the form:

```
new(STUDENT1);
new(STUDENT3);
```

The Pascal processor would then look around memory for two free memory locations in which integers can be stored. Let us imagine that we find two unused areas of memory at addresses 1234 and 3456. The addresses of these memory locations would then be held in the pointer variables. The resulting situation would then be as shown in Figure 3.26 (b). For our explanation, we have shown the address enclosed in square brackets.

To assign values into these storage locations, we would then use Pascal statements of the form:

```
STUDENT1^ := 7;
STUDENT3^ := 2;
```

The resulting situation would then be as shown in Figure 3.26 (c). Notice that we use the identifiers STUDENT1^ and STUDENT3^ to show that we are not handling the variables STUDENT1 and STU-DENT3 but the storage locations *to which they point*. So if we wished to move the 2 from address 3456 (where STUDENT3 points) into address 1234 (where STUDENT1 points), we would use the statement:

```
STUDENT1^ : = STUDENT3^;
```

with the results shown in Figure 3.26 (d). We can read this statement as 'move the data in the location to which STUDENT3 points into the location to which STUDENT1 points'.

Note that if (by accident or by design) we omit the vertical arrow which identifies this as a pointer, as in a statement such as:

```
STUDENT1 := STUDENT3;
```

then we should arrive at the situation shown in Figure 3.26 (e) where both variables point to the same storage location. After this statement has been executed, the number 7 which is stored at address 1234 has been lost and its location cannot be reused by the computer.

When a storage location is no longer required, it can be released by means of the Pascal statement:

```
dispose(STUDENT1)
```

The area of memory to which STUDENT1 previously pointed will then be available for use by any further:

```
new(pointervariable)
```

statements.

Linked lists

The illustration which we used to introduce pointers is a fairly trivial one, and using pointers has no real advantage in this particular situation; we can still only use three variables. In order to solve the college library problem, we can apply pointers in a much more useful way by using a **record** instead of a simple integer to hold the data. Each record will contain:

(1)   the student's registration number;
(2)   the number of books borrowed; and
(3)   a pointer to the next record in the list.

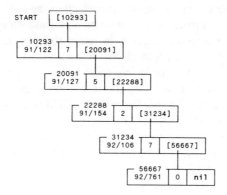

Figure 3.27   *A linked list*

We can visualize the **linked-list** of records like the elements shown in Figure 3.27. There are only five records in the list at this stage and we want to hold these in order of student registration number. In this diagram, we have shown the pointers as pointing to actual addresses. The addresses are enclosed in square brackets. Here we see that the first record in the list contains two pieces of data:

- 91/122 (the student's registration number) and
- 7 (the number of books out on loan)

and a pointer which directs us to the memory location – 10293 – where the next record is held; in turn, the next record contains its pieces of data and a pointer to the next record, and so on to the end of the list. The final record contains the special indicator:

nil

to show that it is the end of the chain.

We also need another pointer variable – I've called mine START – to show us where the first record in the chain is to be found. Notice that the memory locations 10293, 20091 and so on are not in any particular sequence. These actual addresses in START and in the list are allocated to us when we use the *new* statement to grab a new memory location.

Holding our data in this manner has several advantages:

• we can hold as few or as many records as we like;
• the list can grow virtually indefinitely (in fact, until we have used up all the available memory);
• we can delete records from any point within the list, as shown in Figure 3.28. Compare this with the previous illustration. We should use the Pascal *dispose* statement to return the storage used by the deleted record and make it available for use again, if we need it;
• we can insert new records at any point within the list, as shown in Figure 3.29. This will allow us to control the sequence in which the records are held in the list. Compare this diagram with the earlier illustrations.

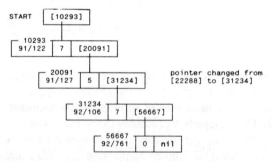

Figure 3.28   *Deleting the record for student 91/154*

Question

54 Describe how the diagram in Figure 3.29 would change if we made the following five alterations to that linked list. Assume that all five changes are made in the sequence shown.

Draw your own diagrams to show the linked list at each stage.

(a) Add a record for student 91/999.
(b) Add a record for student 92/999.
(c) Add a record for student 90/100.
(d) Delete the record for student 91/125.
(e) Delete record 90/100, the first record in the list.
(f) Delete record 92/999, the last record in the list.

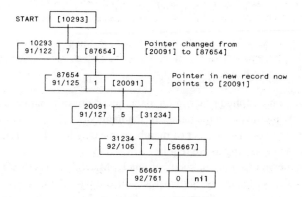

Figure 3.29 *Inserting the record for student 91/125*

Set types

A **set** is an unordered collection of unique values. The individual values in a set are called **members**. The members of a set are all of the same type. Sets are widely used in mathematics and can be applied to commercial data processing in situations where:

- we need to collect data values together without duplication; or
- we are not concerned with the order in which the data values are held; or
- we need to know if a particular value is a member of a given set; or
- we need to add two or more sets together to produce a new single set; or
- we need to find the difference between two sets; or
- we need to find values which are in one or more sets.

For example, we may be processing information about the college athletics club. We could use a set to hold the names of the people who

```
┌─ Squash Club ──────┐
│ Mary Wilkinson     │
│ Marc Rodgers       │
│ Peter Radcliffe    │
│ Alison Steetley    │
│ Peter Jones        │
│ Michael Anderson   │
│ Pauline Smith      │
│ Chris Marlowe      │
│ Iris Docherty      │
│ Stanley Siddons    │
│ Ferid Bzeouich     │
└────────────────────┘
```

Figure 3.30   *The college squash club set*

are members of the squash club. We might visualize the set as shown in
Figure 3.30.

A set is suitable for processing such data because:

- There is no implied order in the data, and it doesn't matter in which
  order we write down the names of the members.
- There may be any number of members in each club: the list of members can be as long as we require.
- Each person is only a member once: MARY WILKINSON, for
  example, will only be shown once in the list of members of the
  squash club (unless there are two different Mary Wilkinsons at the
  college).

Pascal is one of the few languages which offers us an in-built facility
for handling sets. In this situation, we must first define our set. We
might do this by a fragment such as:

```
type
        Name = array [1 . . 30] of char;
        SquashClub = set of Name;
var
        Student: Name;
```

which first defines the type *Name* as an array of up to 30 characters, and
then goes on to use this to define *SquashClub* as a set of such names.
We also declare *Student* to be a variable of type *Name*.

A section of code to add a student's name to the *SquashClub* set
might look like this:

```
Student := 'George Eliot';
SquashClub := SquashClub + [Student];
```

We enclose the *Student* in square brackets to make it a set (with only
one member) because Pascal will only allow us to add two sets together

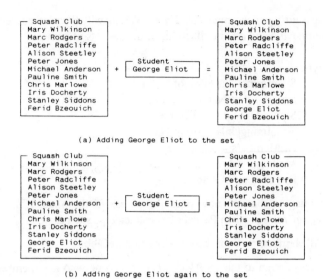

(a) Adding George Eliot to the set

(b) Adding George Eliot again to the set

Figure 3.31 *Adding members to a set*

in this manner. An important feature of sets is maintained when we add a student's name to the *SquashClub* set: if the name is already present, then no action is taken. This is illustrated in Figure 3.31, where we add George Eliot to the *SquashClub* and then attempt to add the same name again. The diagram also reminds us that the set is unordered and the true location of the new member is unpredictable.

We could use another set to hold the names of the people who are members of the college swimming club. This is illustrated in Figure 3.32.

Figure 3.32 *The college swimming club*

Having said what we mean by *Name*, Pascal will then let us declare *SwimmingClub* and other collections of data as sets of names:

```
type
      SwimmingClub = set of Name;
      Both = set of Name;
      SquashOnly = set of Name;
      SwimmingOnly = set of Name;
      AllMembers = set of Name;
      Mailing = set of Name;
      Rugby = set of Name;
```

If we imagine that we now hold the names in the *SquashClub* and *SwimmingClub* sets, then Pascal offers statements such as:

AllMembers := SquashClub + SwimmingClub;

which will assign to the set *AllMembers* everyone who is a member of either or both of the clubs. In the language of sets, the sign represents the **union** operation.

The statement:

Both :+ SquashClub * SwimmingClub;

will assign to the set *AllMembers* everyone who is a member of both of the clubs. In the language of sets, the * sign represents the **intersection** operation.

The statement:

SquashOnly := SquashClub – SwimmingClub;

will assign to the set *AllMembers* everyone who is a member of the Squash Club but not a member of the Swimming Club. In the language of sets, the – sign represents the **difference** operation.

Questions

Use the sets SquashClub and SwimmingClub, as shown in the diagrams (where George Eliot is now a member of the Squash Club) above to write down the members of the sets which are produced by the following Pascal statements. You may assume that all the statements are correct and that all the sets have been properly declared.

```
55    AllMembers := SquashClub + SwimmingClub;
56    Both := SquashClub * SwimmingClub;
57    SquashOnly := SquashClub – SwimmingClub;
58    Swimmingonly := SwimmingClub – SquashClub;
59    SquashClub := SquashClub + ['William Brown']
60    SquashOnly := SquashOnly + ['Ferid Bzeouich']
61    Mailing := SquashOnly * SwimmingOnly;
```

In addition to the union, intersection and difference operations, Pascal has facilites for testing the contents of sets. Thus, we are able to write a program to ask, for example, whether George Eliot is a member of the Squash Club. This is done by means of statements such as:

IF 'George Eliot' IN SquashClub THEN . . .

and allows us to take some appropriate action according to whether the result of this test is true or false.

Other operations are illustrated by these statements:

IF SquashOnly = Mailing THEN . . .

to test whether the two sets contain exactly the same members, no more and no fewer. The order of the members of the two sets has no effect on the results.

IF SquashOnly < > Rugby THEN . . .

to test whether the two sets do not contain exactly the same members.

IF SquashOnly <= MasterClass THEN . . .

to test whether all the members of the SquashOnly set are also members of the MasterClass set, that is, whether SquashOnly is a subset of MasterClass. The MasterClass set may well contain many more members than the SquashOnly set.

IF MasterClass >= Rugby THEN . . .

to test whether the MasterClass set is a superset of all the Rugby set, that is, whether MasterClass contains all the members of Rugby. The MasterClass set may well contain many more members than the Rugby set.

171

IF ['Mary Brown'] <= Rugby THEN . . .
IF 'Mary Brown' IN Rugby THEN . . .

will both test whether the value 'Mary Brown' is a member of the Rugby set. The IN operation differs from the <= (is a subset of) operation in that it operates upon a value and a set, whereas <= operates upon two sets.

Questions

Complete these sentences:

62 'A set SET1 is a subset of another set SET2 if . . .' Give some examples to illustrate a subset.

63 'A set SET1 is a superset of another set SET2 if . . .' Give some examples to illustrate a superset.

In your own words, write down the question which each of the following IF statements is asking, and state whether the statements would return the value *true* or the value *false*. Base your answers upon the sets which you produced as your solutions to the previous Questions.

64 IF SquashOnly = SquashClub THEN . . .
65 IF SquashOnly<= SquashClub THEN
66 IF AllMembers <= SquashClub THEN
67 IF 'Marc Jones' IN SquashOnly THEN . . .
68 IF SquashOnly <= AllMembers THEN . . .
69 IF AllMembers >= SquashClub THEN . . .
70 IF SquashOnly >= SquashClub THEN . . .
71 IF 'John Smith' IN Both THEN . . .
72 IF SquashOnly < > SquashClub THEN . . .

Recap

- A computer program has a need to handle various types of data: an integer number, a real number (with a decimal fraction), a floating point number (for a very large or a very small value), a character, a Boolean value (of *true* or *false*).
- All data is held inside the computer as a sequence of binary patterns. Each binary pattern is stored in one or more contiguous bytes of memory.

- In order to let the processor know how the binary pattern in a particular storage area is to be interpreted, the programmer must specify the *data type* of that storage area.
- Most program languages allow a wide range of data types to be handled. The elementary data types correspond to the common data processing requirements of programs: integer, real, character, string, Boolean, packed decimal, arrays, records, enumerated, pointers and sets. Some languages offer more data types and others allow the programmer to define his/her own data types.
- In some languages the data type of a variable must be specified explicitly, others impose specific conventions which use the name of a program variable to determine its data type.
- By demanding to know the data type of each variable (and literals), the compiler is able to carry out type checking and thereby identify many programming errors which might otherwise go undetected.

Answers to questions

1 00000100
00000101
00000110
00000111
00001000
00001001
00001010
00001011
00001100
00001101
00001110
00001111

2 11110100
11110101
11110110
11110111
11111000
11111001
11111010
11111011
11111100
11111101

```
  11111110
  11111111
3 00000100 4
  00000101 5
  00000110 6
  00000111 7
  00001000 8
  00001001 9
  00001010 10
  00001011 11
  00001100 12
  00001101 13
  00001110 14
  00001111 15
  11110000 240
  11110001 241

  11110100 244
  11110101 245
  11110110 246
  11110111 247
  11111000 248
  11111001 249
  11111010 250
  11111011 251
  11111100 252
  11111101 253
  11111110 254
  11111111 255
```

4 (a)   203 (decimal) = 11001011 (binary)
  (b)   244 (decimal) = 11110100 (binary)
  (c)   11 (decimal) = 00001011 (binary)
  (d)   115 (decimal) = 01110011 (binary)
  (e)   1010 (decimal) = 11110010 (binary)
  (f)   15 (decimal) = 00001111 (binary)
  (g)   127 (decimal) = 01111111 (binary)
  (h)   217 (decimal) = 11011001 (binary)

5 There would be 100 rules:

```
0 + 0 = 0
1 + 0 = 1
2 + 0 = 2
:
9 + 0 = 9
```

```
1 + 1 = 2
2 + 1 = 3
3 + 1 = 4
:
9 + 9 = 8 carry 1
```

6 01001101 (binary) = 77 (decimal)
00100110 (binary) = 38 (decimal)
01110011 (binary) = 115 (decimal)
We can confirm that the answer is correct by checking the decimal addition:
     77 + 38 = 115 (decimal)

7 (a)   00000110   + 10100011   = 10101001
        6   + 163   = 169
  (b)   01000001   + 10001001   = 11001010
        65   + 137   = 202
  (c)   00010110   + 11011010   = 11110000
        22   + 218   = 240
  (d)   00000011   + 11101010   = 11101101
        3   + 234   = 237
  (e)   01101000   + 10010011   = 11111011
        104   + 147 = 251
  (f)   00100110   + 10000100   = 10101010
        38   + 132   = 170
  (g)   00000101   + 11010010   = 11010111
        5   + 210   = 215
  (h)   01010000   + 10000000   = 11010000
        80   + 28   = 208

8 0

9 255

10 There are 256 different patterns, so a byte can represent any one of 256 different values.

11 The = character

12 The / character

13 The lower-case letter z

14 The letter A

15 106

16 00100100

17 108

18 The number of boxes could be written as:

  (a)   10 or decimal(10) or dec(10)
  (b)   1010 or binary(1010) or bin(1010)

(c) A or hexadecimal(A) or hex(A)

or you might have written them with subscripts to indicate the form in which they are written:

(a) 10   or   10
    10   decimal
(b) 1010 or (1010) or 1010 or (1010)
    2   2   binary   binary
(c) A   or (A)   or A   or   (A)
    16   16   hexadecimal   hexadecimal

19 (a) OB
   (b) 04
   (c) 73
   (d) 7F
   (e) CB
   (f) D9
   (g) FO
   (h) F2
   (i) F4
   (j) FF

20 You should have included the following in your answer:
- Punctuation marks and symbols: . , ? ! ' "
- Special characters: £ $ % & * ( ) [ ] { }
- Arithmetic signs: + – = /
- Special forms of the ordinary letters, such as italics, bold face, and so on.
- Foreign language letters and punctuation:

  Ç ü é â ä à å ç ê ë è ï î ì Ä Å É æ Æ ô ö ò û ù ÿ ö ü ¢ £ ¥ Pt ƒ á í ó ú ñ Ñ a̲ o̲ ¿ ¡ « »

- Graphics symbols and shapes, such as lines and corners for drawing boxes and shading:

- Special mathematical symbols:

  α π Σ σ μ τ θ Ω δ φ ∈ ∩ ± ≥ ≤ ÷ ≈ °

You might also have suggested sounds and colours, but these are held as binary patterns, in exactly the same way as all other data, and when these patterns are sent to the required device, they generate the sounds and images required.

21 0101011101010101 (binary) 22357 (decimal)
22 1111111111111111 (binary) 65535 (decimal)
23 16777215
24 4294967295
25 (a) 9913
    (b) 9856
    (c) 9745
    (d) 9610
    (e) 9507
    (f) 9470
    (g) 9374
    (h) 9234
    (i) 9117
    (j) 9058
26 (a) 1110101011000001
    (b) 1111101100010000
    (c) 1110111101100111
    (d) 1111101000011000
    (e) 1110101100000010
    (f) 1111111111010111
    (g) 1111100100010010
    (h) 1111001010010010
    (i) 1110100011101010
    (j) 1111010011010011
27 Your solutions should include:

    (a) decimal numbers (such as 123456), large numbers (987654321), negative numbers (–12345, –10);
    (b) fractions (such as 3.14159 or 123456.7890988765) or numbers between 0 and 1 or numbers between 0 and –1 (0.0001, –0.05, 0.000000000000001).
28 (a) –280706+12
    (b) +730369+18
    (c) +078791+10
    (d) –943067+08
    (e) +368633+10
    (f) +688450–07
    (g) +467598+12
    (h) +949243+14
    (i) –904987–10

   (j) +876373+10
29 (a) −15.0
   (b) +5.0
   (c) −1.375
   (d) +5.5
   (e) −11.0
   (f) +9.0
   (g) −1.5
   (h) −1.875
   (i) +6.0
   (j) −2.75
30 (a) 00111111101000000000000000000000
   (b) 01000000100100000000000000000000
   (c) 11000000001000000000000000000000
   (d) 11000000000100000000000000000000
   (e) 00111111100100000000000000000000
   (f) 01000000010000000000000000000000
   (g) 11000001001000000000000000000000
   (h) 01000001010000000000000000000000
   (i) 01000000111000000000000000000000
   (j) 01000000011100000000000000000000
31 (a) 00101111
   (b) 00000100 01010110 01111111
   (c) 00000001 00101111
   (d) 00000100 01010011 00100101 01101101
   (e) 00000001 10011111
   (f) 00000001 00101101
   (g) 00001001 10011101
   (h) 10000111 01000101 00100001 10011111
   (i) 01000011 01000101 01100111 01011111
   (j) 00000001 00100011 01001101
32 (a) 117
   (b) 3411347
   (c) −74
   (d) −33
   (e) 301171
   (f) −7430
   (g) 7
   (h) 4701473
   (i) −13411
   (j) 73

33 (a) Mary Wilson is not a member of the dramatic society, she is not a member of the rugby club, she is not a member of the chess club, she is not a member of the sports and social club, she is not married, she lives in the hall of residence, she is handicapped, she is a car owner.

    (b) Ferid Alkarim is not a member of the dramatic society, he is not a member of the rugby club, he is not a member of the chess club, he is a member of the sports and social club, he is married, he lives in the hall of residence, he is not handicapped, he is not a car owner.

    (c) Michael Costas is a member of the dramatic society, he is a member of the rugby club, he is a member of the chess club, he is a member of the sports and social club, he is married, he lives in the hall of residence, he is handicapped, he is not a car owner.

    (d) Suraya Khan is a member of the dramatic society, she is not a member of the rugby club, she is not a member of the chess club, she is not a member of the sports and social club, she is not married, she lives in the hall of residence, she is handicapped, she is a car owner.

    (e) Alan Parker is a member of the dramatic society, he is a member of the rugby club, he is a member of the chess club, he is not a member of the sports and social club, he is not married, he lives in the hall of residence, he is not handicapped, he is a car owner.

34 (a) character
    (b) real
    (c) string
    (d) string (one character in length)
    (e) integer
    (f) floating point
    (g) Boolean
    (h) real
    (i) string
    (j) integer

35 REAL INTRST

36 I could use the statement:

INTEGER KOUNT

but because of the implicit naming convention, it is assumed to be of integer type since it begins with K and I need not declare KOUNT explicitly.

37 DOUBLE PRECISION LIMIT

38 CHARACTER NODE

39 I could use the statement:

REAL QUANT

but because of the implicit naming convention, it is assumed to be of single-precision real type since it begins with Q and I need not declare QUANT explicitly.

40 INTEGER SNO

41 LOGICAL VALID

42 COUNTED is more than six characters in length and is too long a name for Fortran. If I try to use the name COUNTED, Fortran will use only COUNTE and this may be confused with other names, such as COUNTER, which would also be truncated to six characters. A better plan is to change it to something like:

REAL CNTD

but because of the implicit naming convention, it is assumed to be of single-precision real type since it begins with C and I need not declare CNTD explicitly.

43 DOUBLE PRECISION VALUE

44 I could use either of these statements:

CHARACTER*10 WORKEX
CHARACTER WORKEX*10

Figure 3.33 *A dope vector: solution*

45 The dope vectors might be as shown in Figure 3.33.

46 The dope vector could be:

start address: 30476
size of elements: 4
lowest subscript: −30
highest subscript: 40

47 The total number of elements can be calculated by the formula:

number of elements = highest – lowest + 1

In this case, we find that there are:

number of elements = 40 – (–30) +1

that is, 71 elements in the array.

48 To calculate the total storage space occupied by the array, we multiply the number of elements by the size of the elements.
In this case, the total storage space would be:

total space = 71 times 4 = 284 bytes

49 For the row-by-row transformation, the general algorithm is:

B2(x,y) is at location s + 4*(c*(x–1) + y–1)

or, in this particular instance:

B2(x,y) is at location 40001 + 4*(4*(x–1) + y–1)

and for the column-by-column transformation, the algorithm is:

B2(x,y) is at location s + 4*(r*(y–1) + x – 1)

or

B2(x,y) is at location 40001 + 4*(5*(y–1) + x – 1)

The table in Figure 3.34 shows the solution.

	Row by row	Column by column
B2(1,1)	40001	40001
B2(5,4)	40077	40077
B2(1,4)	40013	40061
B2(5,1)	40065	40017
B2(3,1)	40033	40009

Figure 3.34   *Element addresses: solution*

50 The dope vector might contain the information shown in Figure 3.35 (a).
This will enable us to handle the problem described in the question. But if we wished to start at subscripts other than 1, a more general set of information might be held in a dope vector such as that shown in Figure 3.35 (b).

51 The total number of elements can be calculated by adding up the number of elements in each dimension. In the case of the dope vector shown here, this would be:

number of elements = (5–1)+1 + (4–1)+1
= 9 elements

```
start address:                          40001
size of elements:                       4
number of elements in 1st dimension:    5
number of elements in 2nd dimension:    4
```

(a)

```
start address:                          40001
size of elements:                       4
number of dimensions:                   2
lowest subscript for 1st:               1
highest subscript for 1st:              5
lowest subscript for 2nd:               1
highest subscript for 2nd:              4
```

(b)

Figure 3.35   *Some possible dope vectors*

52   To calculate the total space occupied by the array, we multiply the number of elements by the size of the elements.

In this case, this would be:

total space = 9 times 4 = 36 bytes.

53   You should have given the following answers:

(a)   Acceptable.

(b)   Acceptable, provided that the range *Jun* to *Aug* has already been defined.

(c)   Acceptable. The fact that *Autumn* and *Winter* seem to be in the wrong order is not important.

(d)   Acceptable.

(e)   Not acceptable because *child* is specified twice.

(f)   Not acceptable because *wool* is specified twice.

(g)   Acceptable.

(h)   Acceptable.

54   The following action would take place:

(a)   The new record must fall between records 91/129 and 92/106. We should first obtain a new storage location for the new record. Then we should change the pointer held in record 91/129 to point to the new memory location. The pointer in the new record should point to memory location 31234 where the following record, 92/106, is to be found.

(b)   The new record must come after record 92/761, the last record in the list. We should first obtain a new storage location for the new record. Then we should change the pointer held in record 92/761 to point to the new memory location. The pointer in the new record should then be set to *nil* to show that it is the end of the list.

(c)   The new record must fall before record 91/122, the first in the list. We should first obtain a new storage location for the new record. Then we should change the pointer held in the START variable to point to the new memory location. The pointer in the new record should point to memory location 10293 where the following record, 91/122, is to be found.

(d)   This record comes between records 91/122 and 91/127. We should first change the pointer in record 91/122 so that it points to memory location 20091 where record 91/127 is to be found. Then we should use the Pascal *dispose* statement to return the storage used by the deleted record 91/125.

(e)   This record comes between the START variable and record 91/122. We should change the pointer held in the START variable to point to memory location 10293 where the following record, 91/122, is to be found. Then we should use the Pascal *dispose* statement to return the storage used by the deleted record 90/100.

(f)   The record comes after record 92/761. We should change the pointer held record 92/761 to **nil** to show that it is now at the end of the list. Then we should use the Pascal *dispose* statement to return the storage used by the deleted record 92/999.

55   AllMembers now contains the members: Alison Steetley; Chris Marlowe; Chris Simpson; David Simpson; Ferid Bzeouich; George Eliot; Iris Docherty; Marc Rodgers; Mary Wilkinson; Michael Anderson; Pauline Smith; Peter Johnstone; Peter Jones; Peter Radcliffe; Richard Pearson; Stanley Siddons.

56   Both now contains the members: Alison Steetley; Ferid Bzeouich; Iris Docherty; Mary Wilkinson; Pauline Smith; Peter Jones.

57   SquashOnly now contains the members: Chris Marlowe; George Eliot; Marc Rodgers; Michael Anderson; Peter Radcliffe; Stanley Siddons.

58   SwimmingOnly now contains the members: Chris Simpson; David Simpson; Peter Johnstone; Richard Pearson.

59   SquashClub now contains the members: Alison Steetley; Chris Marlowe; Ferid Bzeouich; George Eliot; Iris Docherty; Marc Rodgers; Mary Wilkinson; Michael Anderson; Pauline Smith; Peter Jones; Peter Radcliffe; Stanley Siddons; William Brown.

60 There is no change since Ferid Bzeouich is not a member of the Squash Club. SquashOnly still contains the members: Chris Marlowe; George Eliot; Marc Rodgers; Michael Anderson; Peter Radcliffe; Stanley Siddons.

61 Mailing is an empty set since there is no one who is a member of the SquashOnly set and also a member of the SwimmingOnly set. We could represent the empty set in Pascal by [ ].

62 'A set SET1 is a subset of another set SET2 if all the members of SET1 are also present in SET2.' The SquashOnly set is a subset of the SquashClub set; the Both set is a subset of the SwimmingClub set and also a subset of the SquashClub set.

63 'A set SET1 is a superset of another set SET2 if SET1 contains all the members of SET2.' The SquashClub set is a superset of the SquashOnly ; the AllMembers set is a superset of the SwimmingClub set and all the other sets in our examples.

64 'Does the SquashOnly set contain exactly the same members as the SquashClub set?' The result is *false.*

65 'Is the SquashOnly set a subset of the SquashClub set?' The result is *true.*

66 'Is the AllMembers set a subset of the SquashClub set?' The result is *false.*

67 'Is Marc Jones a member of the SquashOnly set?' The result is *true.*

68 'Is the SquashOnly set a subset of the AllMembers set?' The result is *true.*

69 'Is the AllMembers set a superset of the SquashClub set?' The result is *true.*

70 'Is the SquashOnly set a superset of the SquashClub set?' The result is *false.*

71 'Is John Smith a member of the Both set?' The result is *false.*

72 'Is the SquashOnly set different from the SquashClub set?' The result is *true.*

4: Abstract data types – ADTs

Objectives

After reading this chapter, you should be able to:

- Produce a formal specification of a data type.
- Describe the operations which form a part of a specification of a data type.
- Describe the nature and use of an **abstract data type.**
- Produce a specification for an abstract data type.
- Name and describe some frequently-encountered abstract data types.
- Distinguish between the **specification** and the **implementation** of an abstract data type.
- Define the terms **syntax** and **semantics** as they are used in a specification.
- Describe and produce a **pre-condition** and a **post-condition**.
- Describe the meaning of **information hiding** and say why it is important and how it can be achieved.

After working through the previous chapter, you should have an intuitive idea of what we mean by a data type. Now we must extend this and produce a more formal definition.

What do we mean by a data type?

There are several possible answers to this question.

We might say that *a data type is a way of interpreting the value which is represented by a sequence of bytes and words in the computer's memory*. Thus, if we were to look at a specific part of memory and find that a particular 4 byte word contained the binary pattern:

01000110010100100100010101000100

then this could be interpreted in different ways. If we knew that the storage location represented a binary integer data type, and therefore held a binary integer value, it would represent the number:

1179796804

If we knew that the storage location held a floating point number, then it would represent the value:

+13457.31640625

If it was to be interpreted as a string of characters, it would represent the word:

FRED

The compiler and the run-time processor must know the format of the data in order to know how to react if we try to add a value of, say, 100 to the value in that storage location. The result would be quite different in each of these three situations.

So it is essential that we and the compiler agree upon what each storage location is to represent and how it is to be interpreted.

Another definition might be that *a data type is a set of values* which are permissible for that data type. Using this definition, we could specify that, for example, a value of the *integer* data type is any value in the range:

−32767 to +32768

or we could write this as the set:

{−32767 −32766 −32765 . . . 32766 32767 32768}

More precisely, we could say that a value of the *Boolean* data type was either of the values:

{true false}

This definition fits in well with Pascal statements such as:

```
type SMALLINT: 0 . . 999;
type LARGEINT : 10000 . . 99999
var Xrange, Yrange : SMALLINT;
var LargeOne : LARGEINT;
```

which allow us to indicate that variables of the type SMALLINT, such as Xrange and Yrange, may only take values in the range 0 up to 999, and variables of the type LARGEINT, such as LargeOne, may only take values in the range 10000 up to 99999. Any attempts to assign a value outside the specified range, such as:

Xrange := 32 – 400;
Xrange := 1000;
LargeOne := 2;
Yrange := LargeOne;

will be rejected by the compiler or the run-time processor. Even inconsistent use of the simple types – integer and real – in a context such as:

var VALUE: real;

will cause the compiler to reject a statement such as:

for VALUE = 1 to 20 do writeln(VALUE);

because the *for* statement can only use an *integer* variable to control the loop, but VALUE has been declared as a real variable.

This leads us on to a further feature of data types: *a data type is a means of checking the validity of an operation*. Sometimes, this **type-checking** can be performed by the compiler (as with the use of a real number in a *for* loop), and at other times the run-time processor may perform the checking (as when we assigned a large value to Yrange).

The more the compiler, and/or the run-time processor can authenticate each operation, the more errors will be detected and the fewer bugs will get into the program.

We can go even further by prescribing that certain operations can only be performed on certain types of data. For example, Pascal uses the / operator to divide one real number by another to get a real result, and the *div* operator to divide one integer number by another to get an integer result. Thus, the statements:

var Real1, Real2: real;
var Int1, Int2: integer;
var Switch: Boolean;

then the statements:

Real1 := Real1 / Real2;
Real2 := 123.456 / 2.5
Int1 := Int1 div Int2;
Int2 := 123 / 5

187

would be valid, but the statements:

> Real1 := Real1 div Real2;
> Int1 := Int1 / Int2;
> Int2 := Switch / Int1;

would be invalid. Having said that, we should point out that most compilers will, in fact, accept the first two of these invalid statements but will change the numbers to the required (real or integer) form. It will, however, be quite ruthless in rejecting the final example.

This leads us on to yet another feature of data types: *a data type implies a specific set of operations which may be performed upon that data type*.

Combining these various notions, we are able to produce the following definition for a data type. A data type is:

(a) a set of values; and
(b) a set of operations which can be performed upon those values.

Let us consider the *integer* data type:

(a) We cannot list all the possible values, but we can say that the values are taken from the set of integer numbers. Most compilers do specify a precise range for the values which an integer may take; typically this range will be:

$\{-32767\ -32766\ -32765 \ldots 32766\ 32767\ 32768\}$

(b) The operations which are available for use with integers are those expressed by the following symbols:

+	addition of integers;
−	subtraction of integers;
*	multiplication of integers;
/	division of integers;
<=	testing whether one integer is less than or equal to another;
< >	testing whether two integers are not equal;
<	testing whether one integer is less than another;
=	testing whether two integers are equal;
>=	testing whether one integer is greater than or equal to another;
>	testing whether one integer is greater than another.

We are assuming that anyone reading this list knows what we mean by the terms *addition, division, greater than, equal to.* For example, what does *division* mean when applied to integer numbers and an integer result? The answer would probably be something like:

If we divide an integer *I* by another integer *J*, the result is an integer *K* such that

$$K * J <= I$$

As we shall see later, it is not unusual for a definition of one operation to use another of the operations for the data type.

We shall not define the operations for the primitive data types. The intuitive meanings of these symbols will suffice for our purposes.

Such a list of values and operations allows us to handle any values of the *integer* data type.

The software engineering technique known as *VDM*, the Vienna Development Method, would represent this information about the integer data type by the diagram shown in Figure 4.1.

```
values:
   {-32768, ...32767}

operations:
   +, -, *, /, <=, <>, <, =, >=, >
```

Figure 4.1 *VDM notation for data type **integer***

We could possibly shorten this list by omitting those operators which represent a combination of other operators. This would leave us with:

+   addition of integers;
−   subtraction of integers;
*   multiplication of integers;
/   division of integers;
=   testing whether two integers are equal;
<   testing whether one integer is less than another;
>   testing whether one integer is greater than another.

Two of the other primitive data types which we met in Chapter 3 were *real, character* and *string.*

Activity

(1) Define the *real* data type in the manner used in the text to define the *integer* data type.
Draw a VDM box diagram to represent the *real* data type.
(2) Repeat this for the *character* data type.

To distinquish between the characters and strings, we shall use the convention of writing characters in the style:

'A'

enclosed in single quotes, and strings in the style:

"ABCDE"

enclosed in double quotes. This helps us recognize that the value:

"A"

is a *string* of length 1 and not a character.

Questions

We wish to produce a definition for the *string* data type.

1 Can we list, all the possible strings? If so, list them. If not, suggest an alternative solution.
2 Write down a list of the operations which you might wish to perform on a string.
3 Write down a list of the operations which you might wish to perform on a string and a character.
4 Using the list of operations which you produced, or using those in the model answers, write down some examples of the use to suggest some appropriate operators for these operations and to illustrate what they would do.

There will be occasions when you need to be able use a certain data type in your program design, but that data type is not available in the language which you are using. What can you do?

An abstract data type

An **abstract data type** (usually abbreviated to ADT) is a data type which is required by the analyst but which may not be supported by the particular programming language which is to be used; indeed, it may not be supported by *any* programming language.

A simple abstract data type

For example, we know that the Basic language uses simple data types such as numbers and strings, and data structures such as arrays to hold data. However, an analyst may need to handle data to represent the Boolean values, *true* or *false*. The range of values for this data type is

{true, false}

and we need to have operations which would include:

(a) to set a variable to true or to false;
(b) to test whether a variable is true or false;
(c) to test whether either of two variables is true;
(d) to test whether both of two variables are true.

We could simulate this – or **implement** the data type – by using two strings "TRUE" and "FALSE", and the four operations might then be coded as:

(a) VARIABLE1 = "TRUE"; VARIABLE2= "FALSE"
(b) IF VARIABLE1="TRUE" THEN . . .
(c) IF VARIABLE1="TRUE" OR VARIABLE2="TRUE" THEN
     . . .
(d) IF VARIABLE1="TRUE" AND VARIABLE2="TRUE"
     THEN . . .

This is one way in which we might implement Boolean data type using only the strings which are available in Basic. The abstract data type required by the analyst has been implemented by means of strings in the Basic program written by the programmer.

Assignment 1

A system analyst has asked you to write a program which will handle sets of numbers.

Describe how you would implement a set of numbers using one of the languages with which you are familiar. Remember the features of sets which we discussed earlier:

- there may be any number of members in the set;
- the members are not held in any particular sequence;
- each member is only present once in the set.

Write down the coding which you would use to perform the following operations:

(a) Clear the contents of a set.
(b) Perform the union of two sets to produce a third set.
(c) Perform the difference (or subtraction) of two sets to produce a third set.
(d) Perform the intersection of two sets to produce a third set.
(e) Test whether two sets are equal. Remember that the set

  [a, b, z, c]

is equal to the set

  [c, b, z, a]

(f) Test whether one set is a subset of another.
(g) Test whether a given number is in a set.
(h) Test whether one set is a superset of another.

Make a note of any restrictions, such as the size of the set, which are imposed by your solution.

ADT: queue

In another, more complex situation, the analyst may need to handle data as if it were held in a **queue**. The data in the queue is to behave exactly like a (well-mannered!) queue at a bus stop, as illustrated in Figure 4.2.

The analyst needs to know that:

- When a new piece of data is added to the structure, it will be added to the *end* of the queue. A new piece of data cannot be added to any other point in the queue.
- When a piece of data is extracted from the structure, it will be taken from the *head* of the queue. An existing piece of data cannot be extracted from any point in the queue.

If the analyst can assume that such a data structure is available, then he/she can proceed to design the system which uses that structure. In

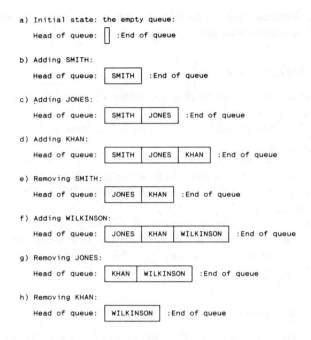

a) Initial state: the empty queue:

   Head of queue: ⬚ :End of queue

b) Adding SMITH:

   Head of queue: | SMITH | :End of queue

c) Adding JONES:

   Head of queue: | SMITH | JONES | :End of queue

d) Adding KHAN:

   Head of queue: | SMITH | JONES | KHAN | :End of queue

e) Removing SMITH:

   Head of queue: | JONES | KHAN | :End of queue

f) Adding WILKINSON:

   Head of queue: | JONES | KHAN | WILKINSON | :End of queue

g) Removing JONES:

   Head of queue: | KHAN | WILKINSON | :End of queue

h) Removing KHAN:

   Head of queue: | WILKINSON | :End of queue

Figure 4.2   *The analyst's view of a queue*

designing the system and using this abstract data structure, the analyst is not concerned with the **implementation** of the queue, that is, the way in which the program is made to behave like a queue. The analyst needs to be able to visualize a situation where the operation

   queue + new.member

will result in *new.member* being added to the *tail* of the queue, and the operation

   queue – member

will result in the member being dropped (or extracted) from the *head* of the queue. Compare the behaviour of a queue with, for example, that of a set such as we discussed in Chapter 3.

   The analyst is simply concerned with the *behaviour* of the data structure. What is required is a new type of data – a queue – which behaves in a certain way; just as integers behave in one way, real numbers in

193

another, Boolean values in another, so our queue behaves in yet another way. This is an abstract data type.

A possible implementation: 1

The queue may be implemented in any one of several possible ways. For example, one programmer may decide to hold the data in an array, using a variable to indicate the number of students in the queue, as shown in Figure 4.3.

When a new student is added to the queue, the *Next-student* indicator shows where the new student is to be added and this will be updated as the new student is added to the end of the queue. This is illustrated in diagrams (a) to (d) of Figure 4.3.

When a student is removed from the queue, the student at the head of the queue may be deleted and all the following students will be moved up, and the indicator reset accordingly. This is illustrated in diagrams (e) to (h) of Figure 4.3.

A possible implementation: 2

As an alternative, another programmer may use an array and two indicators: the *Head-of-queue* indicator to show where the head of the queue is and the *Next-student* indicator to show where the next student will be added. These two pointers gradually move down the queue as students are added and deleted from the queue. This is illustrated in Figure 4.4.

A possible implementation: 3

A third programmer may decide an entirely different implementation, using **pointers** instead of an array. A possible visualization of this is shown in Figure 4.5 (page 198). In this implementation, we use two pointers which contain actual storage addresses which will be used to locate the head of the queue and the address at which the next addition to the queue will be placed. The queue itself is represented by means of a series of pointers, each one containing the name of the student and the address of the following student. Initially, the queue consists of one empty storage location; in this particular case, the queue starts at storage address 29384. If these is no student or no pointer, then the special value **nil** is used. When a new student is added to the queue, the name

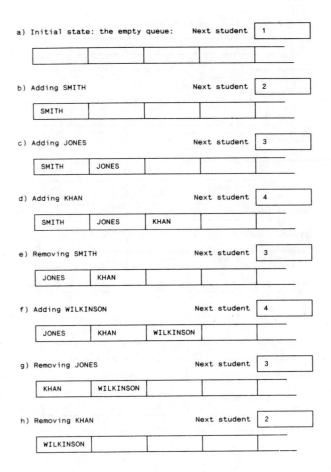

Figure 4.3 *A queue: implementation 1*

is placed in the location indicated by the *Next-student* pointer, and a new storage location is found for the next student in the queue; then the new student pointer and the *Next-student* pointer are set to point to this next empty location. When a student is removed from the head of the queue, the *Head-of-queue* pointer is used to locate the head of the queue, then this storage location is released and the *Head-of-queue* pointer is set to point to the new head of the queue.

195

a) Initial state: the empty queue:

Head of queue `1`   Next student `1`

b) Adding SMITH:

SMITH				

Head of queue `1`   Next student `2`

c) Adding JONES:

SMITH	JONES			

Head of queue `1`   Next student `3`

d) Adding KHAN:

SMITH	JONES	KHAN		

Head of queue `1`   Next student `4`

e) Removing SMITH:

SMITH	JONES	KHAN		

Head of queue `2`   Next student `4`

f) Adding WILKINSON:

SMITH	JONES	KHAN	WILKINSON	

Head of queue `2`   Next student `5`

g) Removing JONES:

SMITH	JONES	KHAN	WILKINSON	

Head of queue `3`   Next student `5`

h) Removing KHAN:

SMITH	JONES	KHAN	WILKINSON	

Head of queue `4`   Next student `5`

Figure 4.4 *A queue: implementation 2*

Assignment 2

What do we mean by the implementation of an abstract data type?

What is the difference between an abstract data type and the *implementation* of an abstract data type?

Look at the three implementations of the abstract data type *queue* which we illustrated above and write down:

(a) some advantages of each implementation,
(b) some disadvantages of each implementation.
(c) any restrictions which each implementation imposes.

Suggest some other ways in which it might be possible to implement a queue.

Specifying an ADT

In order to communicate his/her requirements to a programmer, the analyst must specify (or describe) the ADT, its range of acceptable values and the operations which are expected of it. Using this specification, the programmer can then select some suitable physical data types (or data structures) by which he/she can implement the ADT. Strictly speaking, it does not matter *how* the programmer implements the ADT, provided that it meets the analyst's specification. In practice, however, there may be other criteria which guide the programmer into choosing one of several possible alternative ways of implementing an ADT. You probably mentioned some of these in your answers to the previous assignment. For, example, it may be very time-consuming to remove a student from the queue when we implement version 1 of our queue, or there may not be sufficient space to hold a very large queue when we implement version 2 of our queue.

Since the ADT only exists in the mind of the analyst, it is important to remember that *the behaviour of.the ADT can only be observed by the effect and the results of the operations.*

In the case of our queue, each queue is a sequence of students and some of the operations which the analyst might wish to perform upon the queue might be:

(1) to add a new student to the end of the queue;
(2) to find out which student is at the head of the queue without changing the queue;

197

(3)   to remove the student at the head of the queue;

(4)   to find out how many students there are in the queue;

(5)   to create a new and empty queue.

If we were designing a completely new computer language which would allow us to handle queues, then we might define our data type by means of statements such as:

CLASSLIST is of type queue;

and to add a new student to the end of the queue we might have a new form of the + statement:

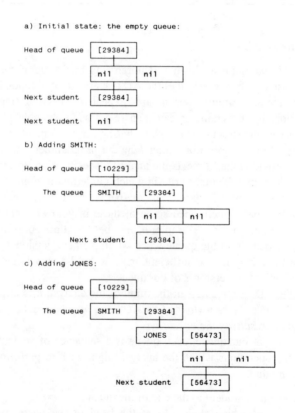

a) Initial state: the empty queue:

Head of queue   [29384]

nil   nil

Next student   [29384]

Next student   nil

b) Adding SMITH:

Head of queue   [10229]

The queue   SMITH   [29384]

nil   nil

Next student   [29384]

c) Adding JONES:

Head of queue   [10229]

The queue   SMITH   [29384]

JONES   [56473]

nil   nil

Next student   [56473]

Figure 4.5 (and opposite) *A queue: implementation 3*

d) Adding KHAN:

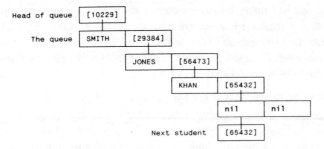

e) Removing SMITH:

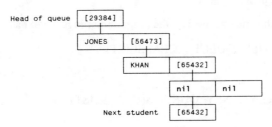

f) Adding WILKINSON:

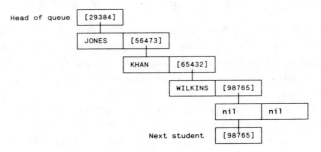

g) Removing JONES:

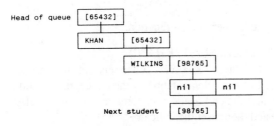

CLASSLIST = CLASSLIST + 'SMITH'

and so on. But many languages do not allow us to invent new operations in this manner. Instead, we have to use the existing forms of the language and adapt them to our needs.

In our case, the analyst might indicate that the five proposed operations are to be used in situations such as:

CREATE.NEW.QUEUE(CLASSLIST)

to create a new and empty queue called CLASSLIST. In an implementation such as our arrays, this operation would probably initialize the contents of the array and the indicators which point to the various parts of the queue.

In practice, this may be used by the programmer in a context as:

CREATE.NEW.QUEUE.P(CLASSLIST)

or

CALL CREATE.NEW.QUEUE.S(CLASSLIST)

or

CLASSLIST = CREATE.NEW.QUEUE.F(CLASSLIST)

The choice from these possibilities may depend upon the programming language which is being used. Some languages may only allow the programmer to use *procedures* (like CREATE.NEW.CREATE.P in Pascal or BBC Basic), or *subroutines* (like CREATE.NEW.QUEUE.S) whilst others may allow you to use *functions* (like CREATE. NEW.QUEUE.F). Since we are concerned with the abstract definition, we shall simply define the operation and not the way in which it is to be implemented. However, the general discussion will assume that a reference such as:

CREATE.NEW.QUEUE(CLASSLIST)

returns a value and is, therefore, a function.

ADD.TO.QUEUE(CLASSLIST,'KHAN')

to add a new student 'KHAN' to the end of the queue called CLASSLIST. In the implementation of the queue, this would use the indicators to find the end of the queue, move the value 'KHAN' into this position and then reset the indicator.

HEAD.OF.QUEUE(CLASSLIST,HEADNAME)
   to find the student which is at the head of the queue called
   CLASSLIST and load this into the variable HEADNAME without
   changing the queue.

DELETE.FROM.QUEUE(CLASSLIST)
   to remove the student at the head of the queue called CLASSLIST

COUNT.QUEUE(CLASSLIST,HEADCOUNT)
   to put a count of the number of students in the queue called
   CLASSLIST into the variable HEADCOUNT without changing the
   queue.

Question

5   In Figure 4.2, we saw the analyst's view of a queue. Imagine
    that these are the names of students who have applied to be
    referees of the college Soccer Club. Using the operations:

   ADD.TO.QUEUE
   HEAD.OF.QUEUE
   DELETE.FROM.QUEUE
   COUNT.QUEUE
   CREAT.NEW.QUEUE

   as described in the text, write down the operations which
   would be used to put the queue called REFEREES in the states
   shown in diagrams (a) to (h) of Figure 4.2.

Specifying an operation

We could specify our HEAD.OF.QUEUE operation informally, like
this:

(a) | HEAD.OF.QUEUE : queue $\longrightarrow$ string
(b) | $x \longmapsto y$
(c) | **pre-condition:** x is not empty
(d) | **post-condition:** y is the head of queue x

The line:

   HEAD.OF.QUEUE : queue $\longrightarrow$ string

tells us the *name* of the operation (HEAD.OF.QUEUE in this instance)
and the *data types* which it uses. In this case, we see that the input data

201

is a queue and the output data is a string; the string being a student's name. If the final implementation of the operation were to be used with any input value which is not a queue, then the result would be unpredictable.

This line is called the **syntax** of the operation. That is, the grammar, or the rules, which must be obeyed by anyone who will use this operation. They must write down the name HEAD.OF.QUEUE, they must provide a queue as input, and they will receive a string as the output from the operation.

The line:

$$x \longmapsto y$$

shows the names of the corresonding input value and output value, telling us that each value of x *maps to* a corresponding value of y. The names x and y are chosen quite arbitrarily and we shall use x and y as *dummy names* when we describe the action of the operation in a moment.

The line:

pre-condition: x is not empty

shows the *pre-condition*, that is, the condition (or conditions) which must be true when the program is about to use the operation. If the operation is used and this condition is not true (in this case, if the queue *is* empty), then the output result will be unpredictable. If there are no special conditions imposed by the operation, then this will conventionally be written as:

pre-condition: true

The word **pre-condition** is shown in bold face type or underlined in handwritten work.

Finally, the line:

post-condition: y is the head of queue x

shows the *post-condition*, that is, the condition (or conditions) which must be true when the operation has been used. This line describes the *action* of the operation, and may indicate how the output value (y) is to be derived from the input value (x). The word **post-condition** is shown in bold face type or underlined in handwritten work.

This line is called the **semantics**, or the meaning, of the operation.

Question

6 Using the sets *queue, string, Boolean* and *integer*, write informal specifications, based on the examples used in the text, for the operations illustrated by these examples:

(a) ADD.TO.QUEUE(CLASSLIST,'KHAN')
(b) DELETE.FROM.QUEUE(CLASSLIST)
(c) COUNT.QUEUE(CLASSLIST)
(d) CREATE.NEW.QUEUE(CLASSLIST)
(e) IS.QUEUE.EMPTY(CLASSLIST) which will return a true or false value according to whether the queue is empty or not.

Formal specifications

Specifications such as these are said to be *informal* because we use English-language text to describe the pre-condition and the post-condition. Unless the operation is relatively simple, or the text description is lengthy, the specification may be imprecise or ambiguous. A *formal* specification uses only mathematical language to describe the conditions. The mathematical language which is available for describing such operations includes the operations themselves.

To specify the IS.QUEUE.EMPTY operation, we could use the fact that a new queue (created by the CREATE.NEW.QUEUE operation) is empty. So the informal specification:

> **post-condition**: y is true if queue is empty,
> otherwise y is false

could be written in the language of the queue operations as:

> **post-condition**: y is true if x = CREATE.NEW.QUEUE(x)
> otherwise y is false

but if we realize that this means:

> **post-condition**: y is true if (x = CREATE.NEW.QUEUE(x) is true)
> otherwise y is false

we can write this more simply as:

> **post-condition**: y = (x = CREATE.NEW.QUEUE(x))

Note that we have introduced another operation (that of *queue equality*) here. This might have been more obvious if we had written:

post-condition: y = (x EQ CREATE.NEW.QUEUE(x))

and allows us to see whether or not two queues are identical in both size, content and order.

It may even be useful to introduce other operations to help us to write our specifications. Thus, we might have a new operation:

TAIL.OF.QUEUE(CLASSLIST,TAIL.QUEUE)

which puts all but the head of the CLASSLIST queue into another queue called TAIL.QUEUE.

We could then use this new operation to specify the:

DELETE.FROM.QUEUE(CLASSLIST)

operation which we defined informally as:

DELETE.FROM.QUEUE : queue $\longrightarrow$ queue
$\qquad$ x $\longmapsto$ y
pre-condition: x is not empty
post-condition: y is x with head removed

We would first think about the DELETE.FROM.QUEUE operation in terms of what it does:

when we delete the head of the CLASSLIST queue, we produce a new queue which consists of the tail of the original CLASSLIST.

Writing this using only the queue operations, we get the formal post-condition for the DELETE.FROM.QUEUE operation:

post-condition: y = TAIL.OF.QUEUE(x)

We can use the TAIL.OF.QUEUE operation again to specify the COUNT.QUEUE operation:

COUNT.QUEUE(CLASSLIST)

which we defined informally as:

COUNT.QUEUE : queue $\longrightarrow$ integer
$\qquad$ x $\longmapsto$ y
pre-condition: true
post-condition: y is the number of strings in x

We could use the fact that:

> the length of a queue is 1 more than the length of the tail of the queue.

That is:

COUNT.QUEUE(x) = 1 + COUNT.QUEUE(TAIL.OF.QUEUE(x))

except when x is empty, in which case:

COUNT.QUEUE = 0

giving us the formal post-condition for the COUNT.QUEUE operation:

post-condition: y = 0 if x= CREATE.NEW.QUEUE(x)
>>otherwise
>>y = 1 + COUNT.QUEUE(TAIL.OF.QUEUE(x))

This idea of using a function to define itself is known as **recursion** and we shall mention it again when we look at functions.

We use the same language to specify the pre-conditions of our operations. Thus, we could write the pre-condition:

pre-condition: x is not empty

using the operations specified above as:

pre-condition: x < > CREATE.NEW.QUEUE(x)

Assignment 3

The analyst requires the following new operations:

(1) To convert a string value into a queue of one string.
(2) To add one queue to the end of another queue.
(3) To compare two queues to see whether they are identical.

Produce formal specifications for these operations.

Produce formal specifications for all the remaining operations described in the text.

The specification of the ADT: queue

Summarizing all that has gone before, we would finally specify our ADT by means of these four parts:

(1)   The name of the ADT. In our case, this is:

QUEUE(string)

(2)   The sets used. In our case, these are:

strings
queues
Boolean values
integer values

(3)   The syntax of the associated operations. In our case, this is:

HEAD.OF.QUEUE : queue → string
ADD.TO.QUEUE : queue, string → queue
DELETE.FROM.QUEUE : queue → queue
COUNT.QUEUE : queue → integer
CREATE.NEW.QUEUE : → queue
IS.QUEUE.EMPTY : queue → Boolean

(4)   The semantics of the operations.

Assignment 4

An analyst has a requirement to handle data as if it were held in a stack. A familiar example of a stack is a pile of trays in a self-service restaurant: a customer takes a tray from the top of the pile; the assistant replaces a used tray on the top of the pile. The behaviour of a stack which is used to hold students' names is shown in Figure 4.6.

The analyst needs to know that:

• when a new piece of data is added to the structure, it will be added to the *top* of the stack; and
• when a piece of data is extracted from the structure, it will be taken from the *top* of the stack.

Produce a list of the operations which might be needed to handle the stack.

Write a formal specification for the ADT stack.

Assignment 5

Using a language of your own choice and any implementation

which is appropriate to that language, write a module to implement each of the operations required to support the ADT stack. Depending upon which language you use, each module may be a subroutine, a procedure or a function.

---

a) Initial state: the empty stack:

Top of stack: ⬚ :Bottom of stack

b) Adding SMITH:

Top of stack: | SMITH | :Bottom of stack

c) Adding JONES:

Top of stack: | JONES | SMITH | :Bottom of stack

d) Adding KHAN:

Top of stack: | KHAN | JONES | SMITH | :Bottom of stack

e) Removing KHAN:

Top of stack: | JONES | SMITH | :Bottom of stack

f) Adding WILKINSON:

Top of stack: | WILKINSON | JONES | SMITH | :Bottom of stack

Figure 4.6 *The analysts's view of a stack*

Implementing an ADT

The ADTs required by an analyst are almost unlimited in their nature. We have already met sets, queues and stacks, and we could conceive further examples:

- A **sequence** or a **list** or a **dynamic array** in which the elements are held in a certain order. New elements are added so that the list remains in the correct order and they may be deleted from any position within the list. An example is shown in Figure 4.7.
- A **bag** or a **heap** in which the contents are held in no specific order and any number of occurrences of each value is allowed. A bag is similar to a set, except that a bag may contain duplicate values.
- A **tree** such as might be used to represent the structure of a business organization, with the managing director at the top of the tree, then the various managers who report directly to the managing director, then the various supervisors who report to these managers, then the

207

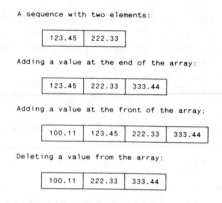

Figure 4.7 *A sequence / list / dynamic array*

employees who report to these supervisors, and so on. An example is shown in Figure 4.8.

- A **graph** or a **network** such as might be used to represent the distances between towns. An example is shown in Figure 4.9.

By definition, an abstract data type is a *fictitious* concept dreamed up by an analyst in order to be able to design a computer system. When the programmer comes to implement the ADT, he/she must live in the real world and they must face the realities of the programming language and the operating system which is being used.

Whatever the nature of the ADT, the analyst's specification will be sufficient to enable the programmer to devise some means of implementation. The programmer has a limited number of physical data types and data structures at his/her disposal to implement the ADT. The

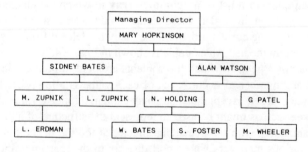

Figure 4.8 *A tree structure*

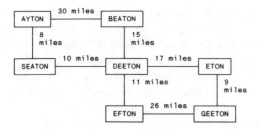

Figure 4.9   *A graph / network*

actual range of these will depend upon the language which is being used to write the program, and will normally include:

- simple variables,
- strings, and
- arrays.

Languages such as Pascal have a greater number of predefined data types, such as:

- sets,
- records, and
- pointers,

which can be used in the implementation of the ADT, and there may be facilities for user-defined types. The programmer must always know exactly what data types and data structures are available for use within the languages. If he/she does not know what tools are available, the implementation of ADTs (and other processing) will suffer.

Constraints during implementation

The analyst's specification for each operation of the ADT will specify the action which is required of that operation. Thus, the specification for the ADD.TO.QUEUE operation looked like this:

> ADD.TO.QUEUE : queue, string $\longrightarrow$ queue
>   x,s $\longmapsto$ y
> **pre-condition:** true
> **post-condition:** y is x with s added at the end

However, the pre-condition completely ignores the real-world situation.

The abstract queue is unlimited in size. The real implementation will have a finite size. We saw this whilst working through Assignment 2 earlier in this chapter. If the programmer chose to use an array to implement the queue, then the maximum number of entries in the queue will be fixed by the size of the array. If the queue was implemented by means of pointers, then the size of the queue will be limited by the amount of free storage which is available.

The analyst may have overcome this by specifying:

pre-condition: the queue is not full

but this is not the analyst's responsibility. There is no reason why the abstract queue should have a limit to the number of entries which are allowed. This is purely a practical **constraint** imposed by the real-world implementation.

If the analyst had chosen to address the problem of the queue being full, he/she might have used another convention, that of including error messages in the sets used by the operations. In this situation, the specification may look like this:

ADD.TO.QUEUE : queue, string $\longrightarrow$ queue UNION errors
  x,s $\longmapsto$ y UNION e
pre-condition: true
post-condition: if x is full
           then
                e = 'the queue is full'
           else
                y is x with s added at the end

and the message:

'the queue is full'

is a member of a new set, the *set of error messages,* which now forms a part of our specification. The syntax:

ADD.TO.QUEUE : queue, string $\longrightarrow$ queue UNION errors

now shows that the information returned by the operation is:

queue UNION errors

that is, it is either a *queue* or an *error message.*

Assignment 6

For each of the ADTs mentioned above:

> sequence / list / dynamic array
> bag
> tree
> graph / network

- Write down a list of operations which you would use to specify the ADT.
- Produce formal specifications for the operations.
- Produce a formal specification for the ADT.
- Give a practical situation in which the ADT might be used.
- Devise a suitable implementation of the ADT in a language of your choice.

Information hiding

The actual way in which an ADT is implemented is of no concern to the analyst, as we have reiterated many times, nor is it any real concern of the programmer who will subsequently use the ADT and the associated operations in his/her programs. They are not concerned whether, say, a queue is implemented as an array or by means of a set of pointers. Indeed, after it has been used for some time, it may be found that a certain implementation is slow and inefficient and the actual implementation may be completely changed without affecting the programs which use the ADT.

The fact that the programmer who writes programs to handle the ADT does not know how the data type is implemented is a desirable feature. If he/she knows that a certain implementation uses, say, an array, then a programmer may be influenced by this when writing a program; he/she may try to take advantage of the situation, they may even try to amend the implementation. This is overcome by a technique known as **information hiding** in which as many details as possible about the implementation are hidden from the programmer who will use the ADT. This can be achieved to a greater or lesser extent, depending upon which programming language is being used. An implementation in which the programmer is able to see what is going on is said to be **transparent**, and an implementation which is completely hidden from the programmer is said to be **opaque**.

211

Some languages do not have any real facilities for information hiding; if a certain set of operations are implemented as modules such as:

- subroutines,
- functions, and/or
- procedures,

the language may only allow these to be used transparently, in full sight of the programmer. Some languages allow the modules to be written and compiled separately and only the (unreadable) object versions available to the programmer.

Assignment 7

Consider the language which you chose to implement the abstract data structures from the previous assignments.

What facilities does the language offer for information hiding?

Is the coding of your implementation transparent or opaque to the programmer who uses your operations?

Can a programmer who is using the operations detect how the abstract data structure is implemented?

Could a programmer change your implementation by any means?

How good is the language at information hiding?

Recap

- All programming languages have some concept of data types.
  These typically include numbers and strings, and are extended to include Boolean values, characters, pointers, sets and many more in some languages.
- A systems analyst frequently needs to be able to imagine his/her data being handled in some other way: as a queue, a stack, a bag, a tree, a network. Where the language is not able to support such data, the analyst must resort to an abstract data type, ADT.
- The specification of an ADT consists of a set of values which the data of that type can take, together with a set of operations which can be performed upon the data values. The specification of the operation includes the syntax, details of the input

and output values, the pre-condition(s) and the semantics, the post-condition(s) for that operation.

- The way in which the ADT is actually implemented in the final program depends upon the resources of the language being used. But provided that it performs the required operations and handles data of the specified nature, the implementation will be deemed appropriate.

- The concept of information hiding allows the implementation to be concealed from the programs and the programmers who will use the operations.

Answers to questions

1 There is an unlimited number of possible strings, so we could not list them all. We could define a string in words, such as: *a string is a sequence of zero to 32768 ASCII characters.*

2 Your list may include the following:

(a) test whether or not a string is empty;
(b) build a string from two other strings;
(c) find the length of the string;
(d) delete the first character from the string, leaving the rest;
(e) pick off the first character of a string. You may have included this in your answer to the next question;
(f) test whether two strings are equal;
(g) test whether one string comes before the other when they are sorted in alphabetic order.

3 Your list may include the following:

(h) build a string by adding a character to a string;
(i) convert a string of length 1 to a character;
(j) convert a character to a string of length 1.

4 Your list may include the following:

(a) ISEMPTY("*AAAA*") would return the value *false*
(b) "ABC" + "XYZ" would return the value "ABCXYZ"
(c) LENGTH("abc") would return the value 3
(d) TAIL("*ABC*") would return the value "BC"
(e) HEAD("*ABC*") would return the value 'B'
(f) test, whether two strings are equal. For example, the two strings:

213

"CAT" and "CAT"
are equal, but the strings:
"Cat" and "CAT"
are not.

(g) test whether one string comes before the other. For example, the string:
"cat"
comes before the string:
"dog"
in a dictionary which is sorted in the ASCII sequence. Therefore,
"cat" < "dog"
would be *true*, whilst:
"DOG" < "CAT"
would be *false*.

(h) PREFIX('A',"bcde") would return the value "Abcde"

(i) STRINGCHAR("A") would return the value 'A'

(j) CHARSTRING('A') would return the value "A"

5 The following operations would be used:

(a) CREATE.NEW.QUEUE(REFEREES)

(b) ADD.TO.QUEUE(REFEREES,'SMITH')

(c) ADD.TO.QUEUE(REFEREES,'JONES')

(d) ADD.TO.QUEUE(REFEREES,'KHAN')

(e) DELETE.FROM.QUEUE(REFEREES)

(f) ADD.TO.QUEUE(REFEREES,'WILKINSON')

(g) DELETE.FROM.QUEUE(REFEREES)

(h) DELETE.FROM.QUEUE(REFEREES)

6 Your solutions should be something like these:

(a) ADD.TO.QUEUE : queue, string $\longrightarrow$ queue

$x, s \longmapsto y$

pre-condition: true
post-condition: y is x with s added at the end

(b) DELETE.FROM.QUEUE : queue $\longrightarrow$ queue

$x \longmapsto y$

pre-condition: x is not empty
post-condition: y is x with head removed

(c) COUNT.QUEUE : queue $\longrightarrow$ integer

$x \longmapsto y$

pre-condition: true

post-condition: y is the number of strings in x

(d) CREATE.NEW.QUEUE: $\longrightarrow$ queue
$\quad\qquad\qquad\longmapsto$ y
pre-condition: true
post-condition: y is an empty queue

(e) IS.QUEUE.EMPTY : queue $\longrightarrow$ Boolean
$\qquad\qquad\quad$ x $\longmapsto$ y
pre-condition: true
post-condition: y is true if queue x is empty,
$\qquad\qquad\qquad\qquad$ otherwise y is false.

5: Programming structure and structures

Objectives

After reading this chapter, you should be able to:

- Describe the physical construction of a program and the concept of **structured programming**.
- Name the basic constructions which are used in an **imperative programming language**.
- Describe the **surface structures** by which the underlying constructions are implemented in specific languages.
- Describe an **exception condition**.
- Draw a **tree diagram** or a **Jackson diagram** to represent the structure of a program.
- Describe the concept of **modular programming**.
- Describe how **functions**, **procedures** and/or **subroutines** are used to construct a program.
- Describe some ways in which data can be passed between a program and its subprograms.
- Distinguish between local variables and **global variables.**
- Describe the concept of **scope**.
- Distinguish between **calling by value** and **calling by reference**.
- Describe the concept of common data.

In the preceding chapters, we have seen how data is used and how special data types can be specified. Now we need to look at the processing aspects of a programming language. Throughout this discussion, we shall concern ourselves with **imperative** programming languages, that is, those languages such as C, Cobol, Basic, Fortran, Pascal and the other third generation languages, where a program represents a set of *do this, do that* instructions to the computer. The discussion does not apply to other language models, such as enquiry languages, logic-oriented programming languages and others which we shall meet later.

Structured programming

In order to see the basic processes which go on inside a program, let us start by looking at the subject of **structured programming**.

Structured programming is a well-known technique for developing computer programs. A structured program is one which is composed of a set of discrete **units**. The processing path flows from one unit to the next, each unit having a single entry point and a single exit point. This is shown in Figure 5.1.

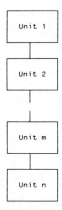

Figure 5.1   *A structured program*

Compare this with the **spaghetti coding** of the **non-structured** program shown in Figure 5.2. It is obvious that the flow of control in such a non-structured program is difficult to follow. If a problem occurs within such a program at, say, statement 1001, then it will be a very tedious process to unravel the maze in order to discover the path by which the processing reached that particular point. It will be an equally difficult task to try to correct the problem. In the structured program, on the other hand, we know that statement 1001 can only have been reached by the gradual flow of processing down from the top of the program, and any error can be much more easily located and corrected.

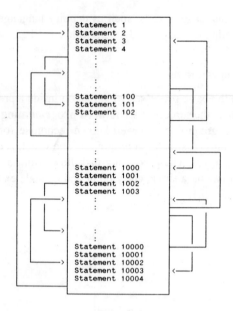

```
Statement 1
Statement 2
Statement 3
Statement 4
     :
     :
     :
Statement 100
Statement 101
Statement 102
     :
     :
     :
     :
Statement 1000
Statement 1001
Statement 1002
Statement 1003
     :
     :
     :
Statement 10000
Statement 10001
Statement 10002
Statement 10003
Statement 10004
```

Figure 5.2   *A non-structured program*

Program structures

In the context of Figure 5.1, we could define a **unit** as:

A sequence of one or more structures in which there is only one entry point to the sequence and one exit point from the sequence.

The structures in such a unit will comprise elements from one or more of the categories:

- sequence – where the actions take place one after another;
- selection – where a test is made to determine which of several possible actions is taken;
- iteration – where the action is carried out repeatedly until a certain condition is found.

Although the **surface structures** – the coding – by which these processes are represented will depend upon the language which you are using, the following structures are frequently encountered in current third generation programming languages.

218

Sequence

A **sequence** is a single unit which performs its work, and then passes control to the next physical unit in the program.

  (a) A simple statement, such as input / output statements and assignment statements, as shown in Figure 5.3 (a)
  (b) A call to an internal subroutine, such as GOSUB, as shown in Figure 5.3 (b)
  (c) A call to an external routine, procedure or function, by means of statements such as CALL, PROC or PROCEDURE. Since such a call implies that the processing returns to the unit, it does not conflict with our definition.

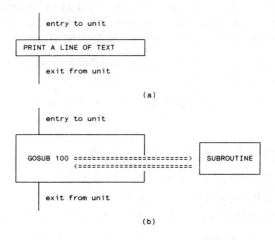

Figure 5.3 *A sequence structure*

Assignment statements

The assignment statement is probably the simplest of all sequential program operations. Its essential action is that of taking a piece of data from one location and copying it into another location. For the task of:

  take the data held in location A and copy it into location B,

most languages use the (slightly anomalous) notation:

  B = A

as in Basic and Fortran, or:

    B := A

as in Algol, Pascal and C.

Although the significance is slightly different, APL and Smalltalk use the more explicit notation:

    B   A

and Cobol uses the most explicit form:

    MOVE A TO B.

Arithmetic calculations

The assignment statement is extended to the task of performing calculations in most languages. The action here is to perform a calculation and then assign the result to a specific variable. For the task of:

take the data held in location A and the data held in location B and add them together and put the result into location C,

most languages use the (slightly anomalous) notation:

    C = A + B

as in Basic and Fortran, or:

    C := A + B

as in Algol, Pascal and C.

Smalltalk uses the more explicit notation:

    C   A + B

and Cobol uses the most explicit form:

    ADD A TO B GIVING C.

Most languages have some means of performing standard calculations such as taking square roots, finding the sine, cosines and tangents of angles, and taking logarithms and antilogarithms. These are usually provided in the form of **functions**, as we shall see later, and are incorporated into the assignment statement in contexts such as:

    A = SQRT(B)
    SINAB = COS(A)*SIN(B) + SIN(A)*COS(B)

Activity 1

For any of the languages with which you are familiar, write down the format of the assignment statements and the way in which calculations such as those mentioned in the text might be written.

Selection

A **selection** is a unit which tests for one or more conditions and according to the result(s) of the test takes one or more courses of action, and then passes out of the unit.

(a) An IF structure with one of two possible choices returning to a common flow on leaving the unit, as shown in Figure 5.4. This is sometimes called a **simple selection**.

(b) A CASE structure with two or more possible choices returning to a common flow on leaving the unit. This is sometimes called a **multiple selection** because there are several possible choices. The structure shown in Figure 5.5 consists of tests but, in practice, any number of tests may take place. The IF structure is really a special instance of the CASE with one or two choices.

Most languages place an important restriction upon the CASE structure: the various conditions can only be dependent upon the value of a

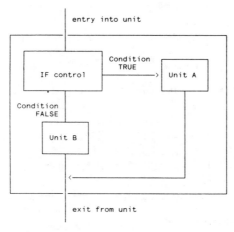

Figure 5.4   *A select structure: IF*

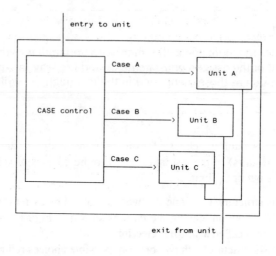

Figure 5.5   *A select structure: CASE*

```
case depending upon code letter:
     case A
          action = add
     case D
          action = delete
     case C
          action = change
     case X
          stop
     otherwise
          print error message 33
end case
```

(a) CASE with a single discriminant: **code letter**

```
begin case
     case age>65 and sex is male
          status=retired
     case age>60 and sex is female
          status=retired
     case age<18
          status=juvenile
     otherwise
          status=standard
end case
```

(b) CASE with multiple discriminants

Figure 5.6   *CASE structures*

single variable, the **discriminant**. This is illustrated in Figure 5.6 (a). Such languages do not allow the programmer to implement a design such as that shown in Figure 5.6 (b). Furthermore, some languages, including Pascal, do not have an *otherwise* facility to catch the situation when all the previous cases fail.

Activity 2

For any of the languages with which you are familiar, write down the format of the simple selection structure and the multiple selection structure. How would your language handle the designs shown in Figure 5.6?

Logical expressions

Logical expressions are encountered in the context of selection and also in the control of iteration which we shall discuss in a moment. A logical expression returns a value of *true* or *false*, according to some condition specified in the expression. The languages differ in the ways in which they express logical expressions and compound conditions. Some typical examples, shown as a part of an IF statement, are illustrated in Figure 5.7.

Those languages which offer Boolean data types, allow Boolean values true and false to be set and tested in such logical expressions. This improves the legibility in a context such as:

retired := ((age > 65) and (sex = 'm'))
      or
      ((age > 60) and (sex = 'f'))

```
Fortran:   IF(A.EQ.B)
           IF(A.GT.B.OR.C.LT.D)
           IF(A.EQ.B.AND.C.EQ.D)

C:         if (a == b)
           if (a > b || c < d)
           if (a == b && c == d)

Pascal:    if a = b
           if (a > b) or (c < d)
           if (a = b) and (c = d)

Basic:     IF A > B
           IF A > B OR C < D
           IF A = B AND C = D
```

Figure 5.7 *Logical expressions*

and the use of this Boolean variable *retired* in a subsequent logical expression:

> if retired then . . .

makes it clear to the reader what is happening.

Activity 3

For any of the languages with which you are familiar, write down the format of the logical expressions which would be used in IF structures and other statements.

Iteration

An **iteration** is a unit which performs a certain process repeatedly until a specified condition is reached. When this condition is reached, control passes out of the unit. The testing of the condition and the control of the iteration is handled entirely by the programming language.

- (a) A FOR structure. Figure 5.8 shows a FOR structure in which Unit A is repeated whilst a control variable takes all values in a specified range. When the control variable attains the value at the end of the range, the iteration stops and control passes out of the unit.
- (b) A LOOP UNTIL structure. Figure 5.9 shows a LOOP UNTIL structure, in which Unit A is repeatedly executed until a specified condition is true. When the condition is satisfied, control passes out of the unit.
- (c) A LOOP WHILE structure. Figure 5.10 shows a LOOP WHILE structure, in which Unit A is repeatedly executed while a specified condition is true. When the condition is no longer satisfied, control is passed out of the unit.

In general, it is unnecessary to have both the LOOP UNTIL and the LOOP WHILE, because logically, the LOOP UNTIL and LOOP WHILE are very similar; the difference being that one tests for the **reverse** of the condition tested by the other. If both are available, their use does avoid the circumlocution which is sometimes required to code and test for certain conditions. Even the FOR structure could be coded in terms of either the LOOP WHILE or the LOOP UNTIL structure.

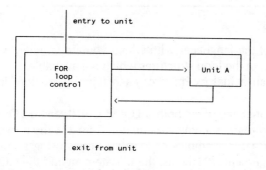

Figure 5.8   *An iteration structure: FOR loop*

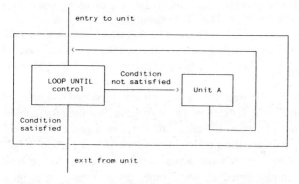

Figure 5.9   *An iteration structure: LOOP UNTIL*

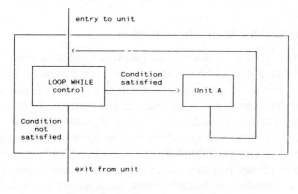

Figure 5.10   *An iteration structure: LOOP WHILE*

Activity 4

For any of the languages with which you are familiar, write down the format of the loop structures which are available.

Write an actual example of each type of structure in the language.

If the language offers both a LOOP UNTIL and a LOOP WHILE structure, are the statements similar in format? Why is this so?

Rewrite your examples of loop structures using a control variable, assignment statements, the IF statement and the GOTO statement instead of the loop structure provided by the language.

What are the advantages and disadvantages of using the language's own loop control statements?

What are the advantages and disadvantages of using your own loop control with the IF and GOTO statements?

Surface structures

In the activities of this chapter, you have already produced examples of the way in which some programming languages allow the programmer to implement the sequence, selection and iteration aspects of the program design. These are the **surface structures** of that particular language. Now let us look at some actual surface structures to see how these may be implemented in some other programming languages, looking first at the underlying designs behind the surface structures.

Surface structures in structured English

Some analysts use a tool known as **structured English** or **pseudo-code** to develop their designs for a piece of processing. Structured English is a stylized version of ordinary English which can be used to make the transition from the design to the final coding much easier than if the coding were to be expressed in, say, a piece of written narrative.

Figure 5.11 shows some examples of how these structures might be represented in structured English. As you see, the coding is laid out rather like ordinary program code; the main difference is that the processing is described in English. There are few – if any – technical expressions used. Even the simple total = 0

statement could be rephrased in English as

    set the total to zero

Structured English has another advantage in that it is fairly easy for a non-technical user to read and comprehend the design, thereby checking that the processing meets his/her requirements.

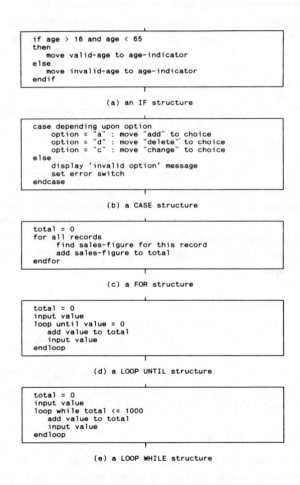

```
if age > 16 and age < 65
then
    move valid-age to age-indicator
else
    move invalid-age to age-indicator
endif
```

(a) an IF structure

```
case depending upon option
    option = "a" : move "add" to choice
    option = "d" : move "delete" to choice
    option = "c" : move "change" to choice
else
    display 'invalid option' message
    set error switch
endcase
```

(b) a CASE structure

```
total = 0
for all records
    find sales-figure for this record
    add sales-figure to total
endfor
```

(c) a FOR structure

```
total = 0
input value
loop until value = 0
    add value to total
    input value
endloop
```

(d) a LOOP UNTIL structure

```
total = 0
input value
loop while total <= 1000
    add value to total
    input value
endloop
```

(e) a LOOP WHILE structure

Figure 5.11 *Surface structures in structured English*

227

We shall use structured English informally for many of the processing descriptions which we use in this book.

Surface structures in C

Some typical surface structures for the C language are shown in Figure 5.12.

C implements the CASE structure by means of the *switch* statement. This offers a *default* as a means of handling the situation in which none of the case selections is satisfied.

C offers an alternative structure for the CASE structure which is also offered in other languages and is sometimes known as an **if-else ladder**.

Surface structures in Cobol

Figure 5.13 shows some examples of how these structures might be represented in standard Cobol 1974.

Until recently, Cobol made very few concessions to some of the structures which we have been looking at. However, the Draft Proposed Revised X3.23 American National Standard Programming Language COBOL, puts forward a number of changes which, amongst other things, provide for an EVALUATE statement to represent the CASE structure. This is illustrated in Figure 5.14. The new proposals also include a large number of END- statements which terminate the various structures more clearly than does the full-stop. Some of these are also shown in Figure 5.14

Surface structures in Fortran

The logical IF statement which is available on Fortran (Figure 5.15(a)) offers a form virtually identical to those of other languages which offer a multi-line structure.

Fortran has no facility for implementing a case structure, other than as an *if-else ladder* (Figure 5.15(b)), and there is no surface structure equivalent to the LOOP WHILE or LOOP UNTIL structure.

Surface structures in Pascal

Figure 5.16 shows some examples of these structures in Pascal. Pascal was specially designed to allow structured principles to be put into practice.

228

```
if (a > b)
    {
    x := a
    }
else
    {
    x := b;
    }
```

(a) an IF structure

```
switch(code)
{
    case '+' : total := total + value;
    case '-' : total := total - value;
    case '=' :
        printf(total);
        total := 0
    default : writeln('invalid code')
}
```

(b) a CASE structure

```
if (code == '+')
    {
    total := total + value;
    }
else if (code == '-')
    {
    total := total - value;
    }
else if (code == '=')
    {
    printf(total);
    total := 0
    }
else
    {
    writeln('invalid code')
    }
```

(c) an IF-ELSE ladder

```
total = 0;
scanf(%c,&value);
while (total <= 1000)
    {
    total = total + value;
    scanf(%c,&value);
    }
```

(d) a LOOP WHILE structure

Figure 5.12   *Surface structures in C*

Activity 5

Make notes about the ways in which the surface structures for simple selection differ in the languages illustrated in the text. Include any other languages which you have used.

Make notes about the ways in which the surface structures for

```
IF AGE > 16 AND AGE < 65
    MOVE VALID-AGE TO AGE-INDICATOR
ELSE
    MOVE INVALID-AGE TO AGE-INDICATOR .
```

(a) an IF structure

```
IF OPTION = "A"
    MOVE "ADD" TO CHOICE
    ELSE
        IF OPTION = "D"
            MOVE "DELETE" TO CHOICE
            ELSE
            IF OPTION = "C"
                MOVE "CHANGE" TO CHOICE .
```

(b) a CASE structure

```
PERFORM VARYING COUNT FROM 1 BY 1 UNTIL COUNT=10
    ADD SALES-FIGURES(COUNT) TO TOTAL .
```

(c) a FOR and LOOP UNTIL structure

Figure 5.13   *Surface structures in Cobol: 1*

```
EVALUATE OPTION
    WHEN "A"
        MOVE "ADD" TO CHOICE
    WHEN "D"
        MOVE "DELETE" TO CHOICE
    WHEN "C"
        MOVE "CHANGE" TO CHOICE
    WHEN-OTHER
        GO TO ENTER-OPTION .
```

The EVALUATE structure

Proposed Cobol statements having a closing END- element:

```
ADD       ...    END-ADD
COMPUTE   ...        END-COMPUTE
DIVIDE    ...    END-DIVIDE
EVALUATE  ...        END-EVALUATE
IF        ...    END-IF
IF        ...  ELSE ... END-IF
MULTIPLY  ...        END-MULTIPLY
PERFORM   ...    END-PERFORM
SEARCH    ...    END-SEARCH
SUBTRACT  ...        END-SUBTRACT
UNSTRING  ...        END-UNSTRING
```

Figure 5.14   *Surface structures in Cobol: 2*

multiple selection differ in the languages illustrated in the text. Include any other languages which you have used. Which languages include an *otherwise* facility to catch the situation where all the preceding tests fail?

```
IF(A.GT.B) THEN
     X=A
ELSE
     X=B
END IF
```

(a) an IF structure

```
IF (CODE.EQ.'+') THEN
     TOTAL = TOTAL + VALUE
ELSE IF (CODE.EQ.'-') THEN
     TOTAL = TOTAL - VALUE
ELSE IF (CODE.EQ.'=') THEN
     WRITE *,TOTAL
     TOTAL = 0
ELSE
     WRITE *,'INVALID CODE'
END IF
```

(b) an IF-ELSE ladder

```
     DO 100 COUNT = 1, 100
     FCALC = FCALC * COUNT
100 CONTINUE
```

(c) a FOR structure

Figure 5.15   *Surface structures in Fortran*

Make notes about the ways in which the surface structures for loop control differ in the languages illustrated in the text. Include any other languages which you have used.

Exception conditions

There is one occasion on which the rule of *one entry-one exit to each unit* may be broken. That is when we detect an **exception condition** which may affect further processing. An exception condition may be any of:

● an error in the data which means that the program cannot proceed: a piece of data accepted by the program may be an account code which should be one of A or C or X. The identification of an invalid account code such as W would generate an exception condition, since we are unable to proceed with that set of data.
● a request from the user to abandon the process. A user may be entering the name, age, address, telephone number and other details about a client, and when he/she has entered the address may choose to abandon this particular client to perform some other work. We do

231

```
IF ClientBalance < ClientLimit
THEN
    WRITE (ClientAccountNumber,' is overdrawn')
ELSE
    WRITE (ClientAccountNumber,' is in the black')
```

(a) an IF structure

```
CASE Number OF
    1:2:3: WRITE (Number,' is 1 or 2 or 3');
    4:5:6: WRITE (Number,' is 4 or 5 or 6');
    7:8: WRITE (Number,' is 7 or 8')
END
```

(b) a CASE structure

```
FOR Counter := 1 TO 100 DO
    Total := Total + Value[Counter]
```

(c) a FOR structure

```
REPEAT
    BEGIN
        Total:=Total+Value[Counter];
        Counter:=Counter+1
    END
UNTIL (Value[Counter] = 0) OR (Counter > 99)
```

(d) a LOOP UNTIL structure

```
WHILE (Value[Counter] <> 0) AND (Counter < 100) DO
    BEGIN
        Total:=Total+Value[Counter];
        Counter:=Counter+1
    END
```

(e) a LOOP WHILE structure

Figure 5.16 *Surface structures in Pascal*

not want to force the user to enter all the remaining data before terminating the task, If we check each piece of data entered by the user to see if it is, say, STOP, then we could generate an exception condition and go on to terminate the program, ignoring the partial data about the client.

Note that an exception condition is not necessarily an error.

Activity 6

Describe some other situations in which an exception condition may be required.

Handling exception conditions

If we adhere strictly to structured programming principles, on detection of an exception condition we should have to set a switch and only complete the processing of subsequent units according to the setting of this switch. As a result, the coding could become very messy and the execution time unnecessarily protracted. Such exceptions may be handled more neatly by leaving the main processing flow completely, as shown in Figure 5.17.

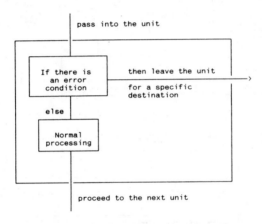

Figure 5.17 *Exception conditions: 1*

An exception condition will normally be handled by the use of a GO TO statement, the much maligned *bête noire* of structured programming, but a boon in such instances. The destination on leaving the unit depends upon the logic of the program. Processing may pass to some **standard** exception-handling unit within the program, as shown in Figure 5.18 (a). Alternatively, the processing may return to the start of the program, as shown in Figure 5.18 (b).

Tree diagrams

It is often convenient to think of a program and its subroutines being organized as a **tree diagram**.

233

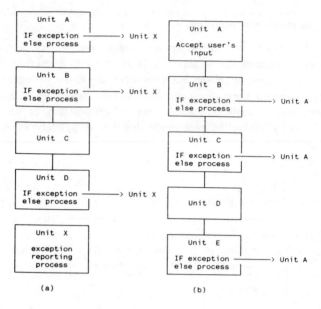

Figure 5.18 *Exception conditions: 2*

```
10    REM INITIALIZATION
20    REM OPEN FILES
30    REM CONSTANTS
40    REM SET TOTALS
      :
50    GOSUB 140: REM GET CUSTOMER DETAILS
60    GOSUB 160: REM GET CUSTOMER RECORD
70    GOSUB 180: REM GENERATE INVOICE
80    GOSUB 200: REM PRINT INVOICE
      :
100   STOP
120   REM SUBROUTINES
140   REM GET CUSTOMER DETAILS
      :
150   RETURN
160   REM GET CUSTOMER RECORD
      :
170   RETURN
180   REM GENERATE INVOICE
      :
190   RETURN
200   REM PRINT INVOICE
      :
210   RETURN
220   END
```

Figure 5.19 *A sequence of coding*

For example, let us consider a sequence of Basic coding which is shown in Figure 5.19. We have omitted some sections of the program and shown them as dots.

Activity 7

In your own words, describe the action of the Basic program in Figure 5.19.

We might depict the processing as a tree diagram with the various subroutines *hanging* from the main body of the coding, as in Figure 5.20.

An even better representation might be that shown in Figure 5.21. In this diagram, we have introduced a new **control routine** which now calls the initialization process as a subroutine and then each of the original subroutines in turn. The control routine will consist of just a set of:

GOSUB

statements calling the subroutines in turn. Such a tree diagram is a useful way of showing how the program is constructed and what subroutines are required by the program.

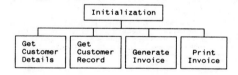

Figure 5.20   *Tree diagram: 1*

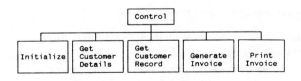

Figure 5.21   *Tree diagram: 2 – using a control routine*

235

Question

1 The coding in Figure 5.19 is represented by the tree diagram in Figure 5.20.

Rewrite the coding shown in Figure 5.19 so that it is reprsented by the tree diagram in Figure 5.21.

Draw a box around the Basic coding which represents each of the boxes on the tree diagram.

A tree diagram such as that shown in Figure 5.21 is sometimes called a **Jackson diagram**, after the American computer scientist Michael Jackson who introduced the technique.

In a great many situations, it may be required for a subroutine to call other subroutines. For example, the subroutine which we use to:

GET CUSTOMER DETAILS

may call another subroutine which checks whether or not the customer is on the file. If the customer is not on the file, then the subroutine may call another subroutine which displays an error message. We would represent this by the tree diagram shown in Figure 5.22.

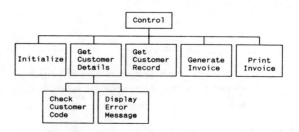

Figure 5.22   *Tree diagram: 3*

The tree diagram does not attempt to show:

- the data which passes between the various subroutines;
- the sequence in which the subroutines are called;
- whether a particular subroutine is called more than once;
- whether a subroutine is called every time the program is executed. In the program shown here, if there are no errors, then the:

236

DISPLAY ERROR MESSAGE

subroutine will never be called.

There might even be situations in which a particular subroutine may be called by several subroutines. In this program, the:

DISPLAY ERROR MESSAGE

subroutine may be called by the other subroutines, displaying a different error message each time. We could represent this by the tree diagram shown in Figure 5.23.

Later, we shall consider the ways in which data may be passed from one part of the program to another.

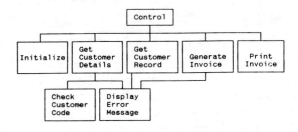

Figure 5.23 *Tree diagram: 4*

Activity 8

Obtain a copy of the listing of a program which you have written.
Draw boxes around the various coding units.
Draw a tree diagram for the processing.

Modular programming

Modular programming is the technique of writing a program as a series of independent units or **modules**, passing control from one to another to perform the overall task of the program. This is not quite the same as structured programming, although it is possible to write each structure (or **unit** in our earlier discussion) – or group of contiguous structures – as a separate program module, as we saw when we discussed the

237

Jackson methodology. The separate modules can then be invoked in turn from a main controlling program, as illustrated in Figure 5.24. Here we see how the control program passes control to Module 1. When the processing within Module 1 is complete, control is returned back to the main program. From here, control is passed to Module 2, then back to the main program . . . and so on. In practical terms, these modules are usually implemented as external subroutines and procedures. Only when a module is called will it be loaded into memory by the run-time processor.

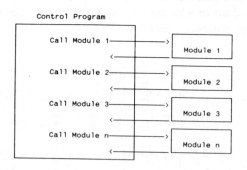

Figure 5.24 *Modular programming*

In this case, the main control program would consist simply of a set of call statements:

    Call module 1
    Call module 2
    Call module 3
         :
    Call module n

The separate modules may in turn pass control to other (lower-level) modules, as we saw earlier.

Constructing the main program as a series of modules has several important advantages:

(1) The structure of the main processing can be seen more clearly, and is therefore more understandable, than with a large monolithic program.

(2) The task of writing the separate modules can be allocated to a number of programmers.

(3)   Complex routines, or those whose efficiency is important to the total processing, can be written by experienced programmers, leaving the simpler routines to trainee and junior staff.

(4)   The programmers need only concern themselves with one module at a time, and can concentrate their attentions on the input data to that module, the processing done by that module, and the output results produced by that module.

(5)   Each module can be designed, written, compiled (or generated) and tested separately.

(6)   During testing of the module, a simple harness can be constructed which will provide test input values to the module, call the module, and then verify the output results produced.

(7)   During testing of the system, a dummy module can be constructed – returning valid results – until such time as the real module is ready for use.

(8)   Maintenance of the overall program is more easily carried out. Modification or enhancement of a single module does not affect the rest of the system, any amended module can be amended and tested in isolation.

(9)   The control and monitoring of the development of the system is simplified, since the time and resources required to produce the individual modules can be more easily estimated and scheduled.

(10) Economic benefits can be had if a module can be used in more than one part of the system.

During the design stage, it is the analyst's responsibility to identify and specify the action of the various modules which make up the entire system.

Activity 9

Consider a large computer project which you have worked on or which you have read about.

Write down a brief description of what the project is intended to do.

Describe why it would be important to apply modular programming techniques in the development of the project.

Functions or subroutines?

Now we shall look at the ways in which we might implement these modules which are such an important part of modular programming. Most programming languages have some means of incorporating additional pieces of coding – the processing modules – into a program. A language may offer one, or all, of:

- An internal processing module, such as a Pascal procedure, a Basic GOSUB subroutine.
- An external processing module.
- A function.

Each is an independent piece of processing, out of the main program flow and called into play when and if required.

Internal processing modules

An **internal processing module** is held within the program which uses it and compiled with that program. In Basic, **internal subroutines** are accessed by means of statements such as:

GOSUB 100

which will branch to the statement label 100 and continue processing from there. When a RETURN statement is encountered, the processing will return to the statement immediately after the GOSUB statement. This is illustrated in Figure 5.25 (a). I've enclosed the coding of the subroutine in a box.

Because the subroutine is held within that program and compiled with it, the subroutine cannot be used by another program.

A similar effect can be achieved by the means of a Pascal **procedure**. Here, control is passed to the procedure simply by using its name:

displayline

The processing jumps from the procedure back to the main program when the end of the procedure is reached. This is illustrated by the program in Figure 5.25 (b). The variables *limit* and *number* are within the *scope* of the procedure and the main program and are, as we saw earlier, accessible from either part of the coding.

```
PRINT 'Enter the upper limit: ';
INPUT LIMIT
FOR X=1 TO LIMIT
    GOSUB 100
NEXT X
STOP
```

```
100  REM DISPLAY LINE FOR VALUE X
     PRINT X, SQRT(X), X*X, X*X*X
     RETURN
```

```
END
```

(a) Internal subroutines in Basic

```
program numericvalues;
var limit : integer;
    number : real;
```

```
procedure displayline;
    var root, square, cube : real
    begin
        root := sqrt(number);
        square := number * number;
        cube := number * square;
        writeln(number:7:2,
                root:7:2,
                square:7:2,
                cube:7:2)
    end;
```

```
begin
    writeln('Enter the upper limit: ');
    readln(limit);
    for x := 1 to limit
        do
            begin
                number := x;
                displayline;
            end {of for loop}
end.
```

(b) Procedures in Pascal

Figure 5.25   *Internal processing routines*

The data used by the program and the processing module may be handled in several ways:

- the module may accept data from the main program, as with the Pascal variable *number* in Figure 5.25 and the variable *Inputvalue* in Figure 5.26;
- the module may generate its own data and pass this back to the main program;
- the module may do both of these, taking data from the main program and using this to calculate new results which are then passed back to the program;
- the module may do neither and simply perform some action using no data or generate its own data.

With Basic internal subroutines, there is no problem concerning the data parameters which are to pass between the subroutine and the main

241

program; the same variables and variable names are used throughout the program. In Pascal, there is no problem if the variables are in scope. But if the module is to process different variables at different points in the program, it is necessary to declare the parameters which are to be used to pass data across to the module. This is illustrated in Figure 5.26. Here the value of the variable *number* in the main program will be transferred to the variable *Inputvalue* in the procedure, and then back when the processing of the procedure terminates. Later, the same action takes place using the variable *InputNumber*.

```
program numericvalues;
var limit : integer;
    InputNumber, number : real;

    procedure displayline (Inputvalue : real)
        var root, square, cube : real
        begin
            root := sqrt(Inputvalue);
            square := Inputvalue * Inputvalue;
            cube := Inputvalue * square;
            writeln(Inputvalue:7:2,
                    root:7:2,
                    square:7:2,
                    cube:7:2)
        end;

begin
    writeln('Enter the upper limit: ');
    readln(limit);
    for x := 1 to limit do
        begin
            number := x;
            displayline(number);
        end {of for loop} ;
    writeln('Enter a number to be processed: ');
    readln(InputNumber);
    while Inputnumber > 0 do
        begin
            displayline(InputNumber);
            writeln('Enter a number to be processed: ');
            readln(InputNumber)
        end {of while loop}
end.
```

Figure 5.26   *Parameters in a Pascal procedure*

The precise way in which the data is passed to and from the procedure depends upon the operating system which is being used. Some move the actual contents of the variable *number* into the variable *Inputvalue* and then back before returning the main program, others simply move a pointer which indicates the location of *number* so that the processing within the procedure uses (and possibly changes) the true contents of the variable *number* throughout. We'll look at this in more detail later.

External processing modules

If you have written a particularly useful procedure, it may be of interest to other programmers. If other programs need to use your procedures, then – in Pascal – they must include the coding of the procedure in every program which is to use that procedure. We have already seen that this can be a great disadvantage as regards **information hiding**, which tells us that the actual way in which a procedure works should be transparent (and also inaccessible) to the user.

Some languages have facilities for calling up such procedures from a library of general procedures, subroutines and functions. Standard Pascal does not have such a facility, although some implementations do offer library facilities.

Fortran and certain other languages do have facilities for the main program and the subroutine to be written (and compiled) as separate program units. Control is passed to a subroutine by means of a CALL statement and is returned to the calling program by means of the RETURN statement. This is illustrated in Figure 5.27. The two sections of coding (a) and (b) are created and compiled quite separately. When this subroutine DLINE has been added to the module library, it may be used by any program (including, of course, the program PTABLE shown here).

```
      PROGRAM PTABLE
      INTEGER X
      PRINT *,'Enter the upper limit: '
      READ *,LIMIT
      DO 100 X = 1, LIMIT, 1
         CALL DLINE(X)
 100  CONTINUE
      END
```

(a)   The main program

```
      SUBROUTINE DLINE(VALUE)
      INTEGER VALUE
      ROOT = SQRT(VALUE)
      SQUARE = VALUE * VALUE
      CUBE = SQUARE * VALUE
      PRINT *, VALUE, ROOT, SQUARE, CUBE
      RETURN
      END
```

(b)   The subroutine

Figure 5.27   *External subroutine in Fortran*

243

Activity 10

Think about the languages which you have used. Do they have facilities for:

- internal subroutines;
- external subroutines.

How is control passed from the main program to a subroutine?

How is control passed back from the subroutine to the calling program?

How are data values passed from the main program to the subroutines?

Functions

Another type of processing module is the **function**. The main difference between a function and the processing routines which we have considered so far is that a function returns a single value, it does not perform any other processing such as input or output.

The examples shown in Figure 5.25 use the square root function to perform the task of finding the square root of a number. The Basic program uses the statement:

    PRINT SQRT(X)

whilst the Pascal program uses a function in the statement:

    ROOT := sqrt(number)

In both cases, the identifiers *SQRT(X)* and *sqrt(number)* behave and are used rather like a number. It may be convenient to think of the name of the function as representing a variable.

Most languages have a standard set of such functions. These are known as **intrinsic functions** because they are automatically recognized by the compiler and are not declared or defined in the program. Typically, the list of intrinsic functions will include:

    square root
    natural logarithms
    trigonometric sines
    trigonometric cosines
    trigonometric tangents

trigonometric arctangents (the reverse of tangents)
exponentiation (the reverse of natural logarithms)

and will be used by writing references such as:

A = SQRT(B.)
N = LOG(34*B)
ANS = SIN(D)
ANS = COS(A)*COS(B) – SIN(A)*SIN(B)

Not all functions are arithmetic or mathemetical in nature. There may be functions for handling strings of data, for handling Boolean data and for converting data from one type to another.

Activity 11

Think about the languages which you have used. Draw up a table showing the names of the intrinsic functions which are available in each of the languages and the ways in which the functions are referenced.

The nature of functions enables them to be handled and used in arithmetic expressions just like any other value. Thus, a statement such as:

A = SQRT(B) * SIN(D)

is virtually identical in form to:

A = B + C

The references SQRT(B) and SIN(D) both represent a numeric value. You can even have *nested* references such as:

NTH = EXP(LOG(NUMB)/N)
A = SQRT(SQRT(SQRT(SQRT(XYZ))))

It is important for the programmer to distinguish between subroutine and procedure calls such as:

CALL DISPLAYLINE(X)
displayline(InputNumber)

and function references such as:

A = SQRT(B)
root := sqrt(number)

Whilst the function reference:

A = SQRT(SQRT(SQRT(SQRT(XYZ))))

is acceptable, in this case, finding the 16th root of a value. It would, however, be nonsense to write:

CALL DISPLAYLINE(DISPLAYLINE(X))

As a general rule,

a *function* accepts one or more pieces of data, performs a calculation using these pieces of data and returns a specific value to the calling program,

whereas:

a *subroutine* (or *procedure* or *subprogram* or whatever construction the language uses) may or may not accept one or more pieces of data, carry out some processing (including calculation, input and output) and may or may not return pieces of data to the calling program.

Since the function name represents a value, those languages which allow you to define your own functions may also require you to specify the type of data which the name of that function returns. A Fortran example of such a function is shown in Figure 5.28. An example using Pascal is shown in Figure 5.29. Observe how the name of the function, SQSUM, is used in both instances just as if it were a variable.

```
      INTEGER FUNCTION SQSUM(VALUE)
      INTEGER VALUE, NUMBER
      SQSUM = 0
      IF VALUE >= 0 THEN
          DO 100 NUMBER = 1,VALUE,1
              SQSUM = SQSUM + NUMBER * NUMBER
100       CONTINUE
      END IF
      END
```

(a)   The function

```
PROGRAM DSQSUM
PRINT *,'Enter an integer'
READ *,N
PRINT *,'The sum of the squares up to ',N,' is ',SQSUM(N))
END
```

(b) Using the function

Figure 5.28   *A Fortran function*

246

```
program dsqsum;
    var n : integer;
```

```
        function sqsum(value : integer) : integer;
        var number : integer;
        begin
            sqsum := 0;
            if value >= 1 then
                for number := 1 to value
                do
                        sqsum := sqsum + number * number
        end {of function};
```

```
begin {main program}
    writeln('enter an integer');
    readln(n);
    writeln ('the sum of the squares up to ',n,' is '
            sqsum(n))
end {of main program}.
```

Figure 5.29 *A Pascal function*

Basic offers **user-defined** functions. These must be defined in each program where they are to be used and – on most versions of Basic, including that of the PC – they are written on one line, as illustrated in Figure 5.30 where we define and use a function called FNCALCA. This means that the action of the function is generally limited to a single assignment statement.

```
100 PRINT "THIS PROGRAM CALCULATES X*(X+1)/2 FOR ANY X"
```

```
200 DEF FNCALCA(X) = X * (X+1) / 2
```

```
300 FOR Y=1 TO 20
310 PRINT Y, FNCALCA(Y)
320 NEXT Y
330 PRINT "Enter a number: ";
340 INPUT VALUE
350 IF VALUE = 0 THEN STOP
360 PRINT VALUE, FNCALCA(VALUE)
370 GO 330
380 END
```

Figure 5.30 *User-defined function in Basic*

The C language behaves slightly differently, as illustrated by the function definition in Figure 5.31. Here, the value to be returned is held in the variable *b* and the programmer indicates this by specifying the name of the variable on the *return* statement.

```
int sqsum(v);
    int v;
{
    int a, b;
    b = 0;
    for (a=1; a<=n; a=a+1)
        b=b+a*a;
    return b;
}
```

Figure 5.31 *Defining a C function*

Activity 12

Modify the Fortran, Pascal and C functions shown in the text so that they will calculate and return the sum of the squares of the integers within a specific range. Thus, the reference:

sqrang(num1, num2)

will return the sum of the squares of all the integers in the range *num1* to *num2* inclusive.

Think about the languages which you have used. Do they allow you to define your own functions? If so, how is this done?

Rewrite the SQSUM function in each of your languages.

Arguments

As our examples have illustrated, data may be passed between the main program and any modules (functions, subroutines, procedures) by means of **arguments** or **parameters**. The coding of the module uses **dummy arguments** or **formal parameters** and these represent the actual values which will be used when the module is called. In the Pascal statement:

procedure displayline (Inputvalue : real)

and the Fortran statement:

SUBROUTINE DLINE(VALUE)

the names Inputvalue and VALUE are the **formal parameters** which will be used in the coding of the module. In the program which uses these modules, any name may be used for each of the formal parameters. Thus, we might encounter Pascal statements such as:

displayline(number);
displayline(34.56);

and Fortran statements:

CALL DLINE(NUMBER)
CALL DLINE(12.345)

The only points which must be observed unfailingly are:

- the number of arguments,
- the type of arguments, and
- if there is more than one argument, the sequence of the arguments

248

specified by the calling program must be the same as those of the dummy parameters in the module. Thus, since the procedure *displayline* has been written to accept a single real number as its argument, it would be wrong to write statements such as:

displayline(valuel,value20);

which passes two arguments to the module, or:

displayline(100);

which passes an integer argument to the module.

Scope

In some circumstances, it may not be necessary to pass data to the module in this way. For example, we did not have to pass any data to the Basic internal subroutine. This is because the variables which we used in the main program were still **within the scope** of the coding in the subroutine. This is how the value held in the variable *X* was available to the statement of the subroutine. We say that in a Basic program and its internal subroutines all the variables are **global variables,** that is, they can be used to carry values throughout the entire processing unit.

In contrast, if we consider the Fortran subroutine DLINE shown in Figure 5.27, the variables ROOT, SQUARE and CUBE are **local variables** – local to the subroutine DLINE – and their contents are inaccessible outside that subroutine.

The scope of a variable is important. It can be used to simplify the task of passing data to a module, and, if ignored, it may result in one module inadvertently upsetting the contents of a variable used by another module.

Besides affecting the range of the program's variables, the concept of scope also applies in relation to the range over which a procedure is accessible in the various parts of a Pascal program. This is illustrated in Figure 5.32. Here we see a program which uses three procedures, BB, EE and FF. In turn, procedure BB uses two of its own procedures, CC and DD; procedure FF uses its own procedure GG. The variable AA1 which is defined in the main program is accessible in every procedure – AA1 is a global variable. On the other hand, CC1, for example, is defined in procedure CC and is a local variable which is only accessible within procedure CC. Any references to CC1 in, say, the coding of procedure EE or in the coding of the main program (at the very foot of the diagram) would be unrecognized and would be rejected by the compiler.

```
program AA;
   var AA1: real;

   procedure BB;
      var BB1: real;

      procedure CC;
         var CC1: integer;
      begin
      : {AA1 BB1 CC1 accessible here}
      end {of procedure CC};

      procedure DD;
         var DD1: integer;
      begin
      : {AA1 BB1 DD1 accessible here}
      end {of procedure DD};

   begin
   : {AA1 BB1 accessible here}
   end {of procedure BB};

   procedure EE;
      var EE1: real;
   begin
   : {AA1 EE1 accessible here}
   end {of procedure EE};

   procedure FF;
      var FF1: integer;

      procedure GG;
         var GG1: real;
      begin
      : {AA1 FF1 GG1 accessible here}
      end {of procedure GG};

   begin
   : {AA1 FF1 accessible here}
   end {of procedure FF};

begin
: {AA1 accessible here}
end. {of program AA}
```

Figure 5.32 *Variable scope in a Pascal program*

We can summarize this by saying that:

the scope of a variable is restricted to the **block,** that is, the program (or procedure) in which it is defined and in any procedures *within* that program (or procedure).

Thus, the variable AA1 can be used to pass a value into any one of the procedures in this program.

If there is a potential conflict between identifiers, such as might arise if we had defined a variable called ZZ1 both in the main program and in, say, procedure EE, then any references such as:

ZZ1 := 0;

within procedure EE would use the **local** variable defined in procedure EE and not the global variable.

We shall mention this topic again when we discuss the way in which the compiler carries out its scope checking in a language such as Algol and Pascal.

Similarly, procedures are only accessible within the limits of their scope. Thus, in Figure 5.32, procedures BB, EE and FF may be called from within the coding of the main program, but procedures CC, DD and GG cannot be called from the main program becaue they are local procedures. Similarly, the procedures CC and DD may be called from procedure BB, and procedure GG may be called from procedure FF. The procedures BB, EE and FF may refer to each other since they are declared at the same *level of scope*. Procedures CC and DD may refer to each other for the same reason. However, whilst procedure GG can make use of procedure EE, procedure GG is inaccessible to procedure EE.

We can summarize this by saying that:

one procedure may call any procedures which are defined with the procedure itself, and it may call another procedure which is declared before it in the same block.

There is a slight complication when we attempt to access procedure EE from procedure BB. Since the Pascal compiler does not know about the existence of procedure EE as it is compiling procedure BB, there must be some way of telling it to anticipate the procedure EE. This would be done by means of the statement:

procedure EE; forward;

which would be placed before the definition of procedure BB.

Languages which control the scope of their variables and procedures in this manner are known as **block structured** languages. Algol, Pascal and PL/1 are block structured languages.

We discuss the scope checking process which Pascal performs when we look at compiling in Chapter 8.

251

Activity 13

Redraw the diagram in Figure 5.32 to show the names of the procedures which are accessible within the coding of the procedures and the main program.

Redraw the diagram in Figure 5.33 to show the names of the varibles and the procedures which are accessible within the coding of the procedures and the main program.

```
program MAIN;
    var MAIN1: real;

    procedure AA;
        var AA1: real;
    begin
    : { Variables:                                          }
    : { Procedures:                                         }
    end;

    procedure BB;
        var BB1: real;

        procedure CC;
            var CC1: real;
        begin
        : { Variables:                                      }
        : { Procedures:                                     }
        end;

    begin
    : { Variables:                                          }
    : { Procedures:                                         }
    end;

    procedure DD;
        var DD1: real;

        procedure EE;
            var EE1: real;

            procedure FF;
                var FF1: real;
            begin
            : { Variables:                                  }
            : { Procedures:                                 }
            end;

        begin
        : { Variables:                                      }
        : { Procedures:                                     }
        end;

        procedure GG;
            var AA1, DD1, GG1, MAIN1: real;
        begin
        : { Variables:                                      }
        : { Procedures:                                     }
        end;

    begin
    : { Variables:                                          }
    : { Procedures:                                         }
    end;

begin
: { Variables:                                              }
: { Procedures:                                             }
end.
```

Figure 5.33   *Procedure and variable scope in Pascal*

Calling a module

Let us now consider what happens when an external module is called in for execution. The run-time processor first goes to the appropriate library to find the module, and then the machine code instructions for the module are loaded into memory and storage space is allocated for the local variables belonging to that module.

The way in which data is passed into the module depends upon the operating system which is being used. Let us consider the Fortran DROOTS program and the RTSUB1 subroutine shown in Figure 5.34. The action of this program is to accept two real numbers from the user and then use these in a simple calculation, returning the answer to the calling program.

When the main program is executed, the contents of the computer's memory will be as shown in diagram (b). The three boxes represent the storage allocated to the three variables used by the program, and the shaded area represents the machine code instructions of the main program. The processing will then commence with the execution of the code in the shaded area in diagram (b). When the:

CALL RTSUB1

statement is executed, the run-time processor will retrieve the object code for the subroutine, as shown in diagram (d) and load this into memory, with the computer memory now looking like diagram (e). Then the transfer of control will take place. The contents of the storage location of NUMBER will be copied into the storage location for VALUE1 in the subroutine, ROOT into VALUE2, and ANSWER into VALUE3. A jump will then be made to the object code of the subroutine and the processing there will be act upon the contents of VALUE1, VALUE2 and VALUE3. Then, when the RETURN statement is encountered in the subroutine, the contents of the storage location of VALUE1 will be copied into the storage location of NUMBER, VALUE2 into ROOT, and VALUE3 into ANSWER. When this has been done, a jump will be made back to the instruction immediately following the CALL statement in the main program.

An operating environment where the actual contents of the variables are moved between the main program and the subroutine in this manner, is known as **call by value** or **pass by value**.

In a similar manner, the Pascal procedure declared by the statement:

```
PROGRAM DROOTS
REAL NUMBER, ROOT, RESULT
PRINT *, 'Enter the number: '
READ *, NUMBER
PRINT *, 'Enter the root: '
READ *, ROOT
CALL RTSUB1(NUMBER, ROOT, RESULT)
PRINT *, RESULT
END
```

(a) the coding for the main program

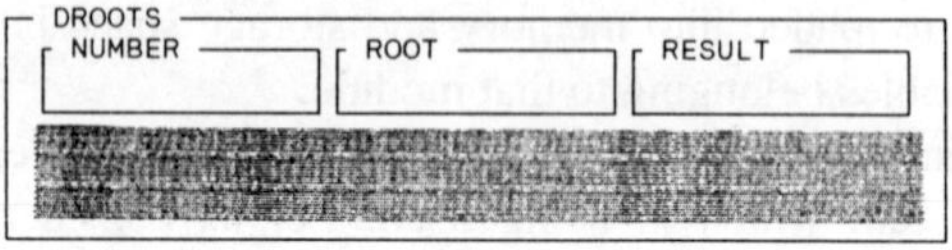

(b) storage used by the main program

```
SUBROUTINE RTSUB1(VALUE1, VALUE2, VALUE3)
WORK1 = ALOG(VALUE1)
WORK2 = WORK1 / VALUE2
VALUE3 = EXP(WORK2)
RETURN
END
```

(c) the coding for the subroutine

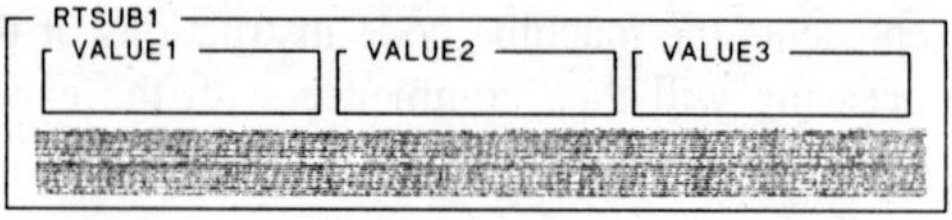

(d) the storage used by the subroutine

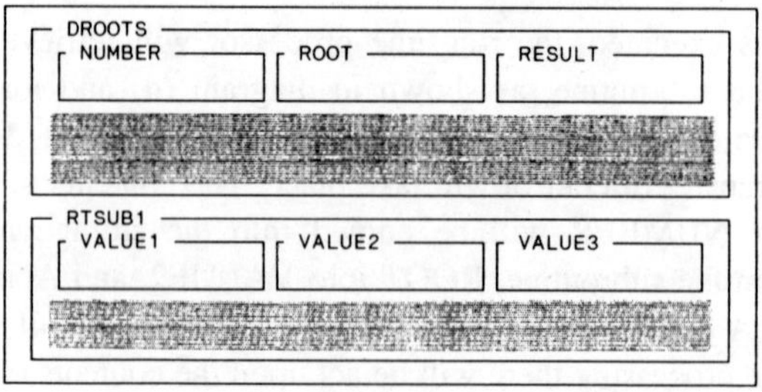

(e) the computer memory at runtime

Figure 5.34 *Fortran external subroutine in storage*

procedure displayline (Inputvalue : real)

and used in a program by means of the statement:

displayline(MyNumber)

will be called by value, with only the contents of the variable

254

MyNumber being passed into the procedure, just as we have described. Pascal calls this a *value parameter*. But any changes made to the variable *Inputvalue* inside the procedure will not affect the contents of *MyNumber* in the main program. The value is not put back into *MyNumber* when the processing returns to the main program.

For situations where we *need* the procedure to change the value of one (or more) of the input parameters, Pascal allows another means of passing data to a procedure – **call by reference** or **pass by reference**. The statement:

procedure displayline (var Inputvalue : real)

indicates that Inputvalue is a *variable parameter*. Now, when we pass control to the procedure, by means of a statement such as:

displayline(MyNumber)

the address of the variable *MyNumber* is taken across. Any changes made to *Inputvalue* in the procedure will act immediately upon the variable *MyNumber* in the main program. Transferring control between the main program and the procedure, and then back to the main program, is obviously much faster when this *call by reference* facility is used.

If some of the data arguments are to be changed and others are not, then this will be indicated on the procedure statement:

procedure calculate (val1, val2 : real;
            var val3 : real;
            val 4 : integer;
            var val5 : char);

with *var* indicating the arguments which are to be changed by the procedure. A typical use of this procedure might look like:

calculate(rep, datax, no3, said, code);

The Ada language takes a slightly more precise attitude to passing data. Each data name is preceded by one of:

in if that variable is to pass data into the subroutine,
out if that variable is to be changed to pass data out of the module, or
in out if that variable is to pass data into the module and to be changed to pass data out of the module.

So the *calculate* procedure in Ada might look like this:

procedure calculate (val1, val2 : in float;

val3 : in out float;
val4 : in integer;
val5 : in out char);

Activity 14

Modify the Fortran and Pascal functions which you wrote earlier to calculate and return the sum of the squares of the integers in a specific range and rewrite these as a subroutine and a procedure, respectively. Thus, the Fortran statement:

CALL SBRANG(NUM1, NUM2, RESULT)

and the Pascal statement:

PRRANG(NUM1, NUM2, RESULT);

will return with RESULT containing the sum of the squares of all the integers in the range *NUM1* to *NUM2* inclusive.

COMMON data

Some languages, such as Fortran, offer an alternative means of passing data from the main program to the subroutines: global variables held in a **COMMON data** block.

Look at the modified version of DROOTS and RTSUB2 shown in Figure 5.35. Here, the variables are declared by means of a COMMON statement. This tells the compiler that these variables are to be *global variables* and not local to the DROOTS program. The global variables will then be loaded into an area of memory – known as the COMMON data block – outside the coding of the main program, as shown in diagram (b). The size of the COMMON block is determined by the main program (three storage locations, in this instance). To the main DROOTS program, these three storage locations will be known as NUMBER, ROOT and RESULT respectively. Any changes which DROOTS makes to the variable which it knows as NUMBER will be made to the first COMMON variable. To the subroutine, the same three storage locations will be known as VALUE1, VALUE2 and VALUE3 respectively. So the main program and the subroutine can both handle exactly the same storage locations.

```
PROGRAM DROOTS
COMMON NUMBER, ROOT, RESULT
PRINT *, 'Enter the number: '
READ *,  NUMBER
PRINT *, 'Enter the root: '
READ *,  ROOT
CALL RTSUB2
PRINT *, RESULT
END
```
(a) the coding for the main program

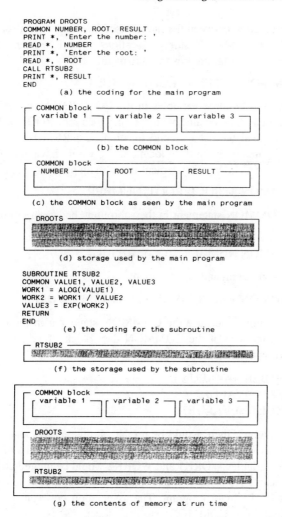

(b) the COMMON block

(c) the COMMON block as seen by the main program

(d) storage used by the main program

```
SUBROUTINE RTSUB2
COMMON VALUE1, VALUE2, VALUE3
WORK1 = ALOG(VALUE1)
WORK2 = WORK1 / VALUE2
VALUE3 = EXP(WORK2)
RETURN
END
```
(e) the coding for the subroutine

(f) the storage used by the subroutine

(g) the contents of memory at run time

Figure 5.35 *Fortran external subroutine in storage: COMMON*

Note that the CALL RTSUB2 statement and the SUBROUTINE RTSUB2 statement do not now need to communicate the data between the program and the subroutine, so there are no parameters specified on either the SUBROUTINE statement or the CALL statement. The same arrangement could be used for two or more subroutines which are to be called from the main program and/or the subroutines themselves.

257

The association between the names used by the program (or subroutine) and the COMMON storage locations is *positional*. By this, we mean that, if the program uses the statement:

COMMON NUMBER, ROOT, RESULT

then there will be three variables in the COMMON block; NUMBER will be the name associated with the first location, ROOT will be the name associated with the second location, and RESULT will be the name associated with the third location. We would have got the wrong answers if the COMMON statement in the main program had been:

COMMON RESULT, ROOT, NUMBER

and the COMMON statement in the subroutine had been left as it was. It would also have been wrong to have had the statement:

COMMON NUMBER, ROOT, RESULT

in the main program and the statement:

COMMON VALUE1, VALUE2, VALUE3, WORK1, WORK2

in the subroutine. Because the COMMON statement in the main program fixes the size of the COMMON data block (three storage locations) and whilst the associations:

NUMBER → VALUE 1
ROOT → VALUE2
RESULT → VALUE3

would be correct, there would be no data storage corresponding to the names WORK1 and WORK2 in the subroutine. The results of attempting to use variables WORK1 and WORK2 would be unpredictable.

It is possible for the COMMON block in the subroutine to be *shorter* than that of the main program. The association between the variable names and the COMMON storage locations is, however, still positional. So, if we had another subroutine which needed just the value of NUMBER from the main program, this subroutine might include the statement:

COMMON FIRST1

and a subroutine which needed just the values of NUMBER and ROOT from the main program might include the statement:

COMMON PART1, PART2

It is not possible to define, say, just the second COMMON variable. If a subroutine is only interested in the value of ROOT from the main program, then it cannot use the statement:

    COMMON SECOND1

since this would be associated with NUMBER, the first COMMON storage location, and the statement:

    COMMON , SECOND1

would be rejected by the compiler. In this case, a dummy name must be supplied so that SECOND1 is in the correct position:

    COMMON IGNORE, SECOND1

This difficulty can be overcome by the use of *labelled COMMON*, as we shall see in a moment.

Activity 15

Look at the Fortran program and subroutines shown in Figure 5.36. Draw a diagram similar to those in Figure 5.35 to show the contents of memory at run time when the main program and the subroutines are being used.

Now rewrite the coding so that all data is passed between the program and the subroutines by means of a COMMON data block.

Draw a new diagram showing the contents of memory at run time when the main program and the subroutines are being used.

Labelled COMMON

Fortran has facilities for using several **labelled COMMON** blocks, each one identified by name. In this case, a program need only include names for the COMMON block which it uses. When this feature is used, the COMMON statements have forms such as:

    COMMON /CHUNK1/ VALUE1, VALUE2, VALUE3
    COMMON /PERSON/ NAME, AGE, ADDRESS

and a subroutine which use just one of these blocks might then contain the statement:

```
PROGRAM MAIN1
*  PROGRAM TO PRINT THE SQUARE ROOT AND CUBE ROOT
*  OF THE NUMBERS 1 TO 10
      INTEGER I
      REAL ANSWER1, ANSWER2
      DO 12 I=1, 10, 1
          CALL SUB1(I, ANSWER1, ANSWER2)
          PRINT *, I, ANSWER1, ANSWER2)
12    CONTINUE
      END
```

```
SUBROUTINE SUB1(INT1, ROOT2, ROOT3)
*    PUT THE SQUARE ROOT OF INT1 INTO ROOT2
*    PUT THE CUBE ROOT OF INT1 INTO ROOT3
     INTEGER INT1
     REAL ROOT2, ROOT3
     ROOT2 = SQRT(INT1)
     CALL CUBERT(INT1,ROOT3)
     RETURN
     END
```

```
SUBROUTINE CUBERT(INTEG, ROOT3)
*    PUT THE CUBE ROOT OF INTEG INTO ROOT3
*    CONVERT INTEG TO A REAL NUMBER
     INTEGER INTEG, REALINTEG, REALOG, WORK1
     REAL ROOT3,
     REALINTEG = INTEG
     REALOG = ALOG(REALINTEG)
     WORK1 = REALOG / 3.0
     ROOT3 = EXP(WORK1)
     RETURN
     END
```

Figure 5.36 *COMMON data in a Fortran Program and subroutines*

COMMON /PERSON/ WHOM, WHEN, WHERE

Since this subroutine does not use labelled COMMON block CHUNK1, there is no need to include definitions for CHUNK1 in the subroutine.

Using COMMON data

A COMMON data block can only be used where its layout is known and is the same in all the programs and subroutines which use that COMMON block. This makes it inconvenient to use existing subroutines which use COMMON data. For a subroutine to be truly independent and, therefore, usable in a greater number of programs and appropriate to a greater number of users, a list of parameters forms a better means of communicating with the programs and subprograms which use that subroutine.

Recap

- Most large programs are built according to structured programming techniques where the processing is performed by an assembly of program structures. These structures fall into three main groups: sequence, selection and iteration.
- Although the same structures are used in most imperative programming languages, the surface structures of the actual program statements may differ slightly.
- An exception condition is an unusual or unexpected condition which causes the processing flow to divert from the linear flow through the program.
- A program can be constructed and depicted as a tree structure, wherein one module invokes one or more other modules, and these, in turn, invoke other modules.
- The construction of a program as a series of independent processing modules is known as modular programming. The application of modular programming techniques to program development improves the efficiency of the design, coding and testing of the modules.
- The separate modules may represent functions, internal processing routines and external processing routines.
- Data may be passed to the external modules as a series of parameters when the transfer of processing takes place, or by means of global variables.

Answer to question

Figure 5.37 shows a possible solution to this question.

Your answer may use different line-numbers, but this does not matter.

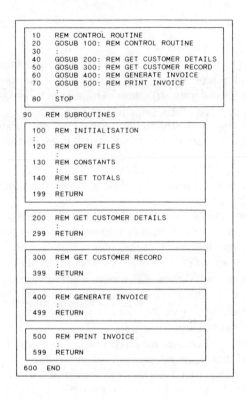

```
10    REM CONTROL ROUTINE
20    GOSUB 100: REM CONTROL ROUTINE
30    :
40    GOSUB 200: REM GET CUSTOMER DETAILS
50    GOSUB 300: REM GET CUSTOMER RECORD
60    GOSUB 400: REM GENERATE INVOICE
70    GOSUB 500: REM PRINT INVOICE
      :
80    STOP

90    REM SUBROUTINES

100   REM INITIALISATION
      :
120   REM OPEN FILES
      :
130   REM CONSTANTS
      :
140   REM SET TOTALS
      :
199   RETURN


200   REM GET CUSTOMER DETAILS
      :
299   RETURN


300   REM GET CUSTOMER RECORD
      :
399   RETURN


400   REM GENERATE INVOICE
      :
499   RETURN


500   REM PRINT INVOICE
      :
599   RETURN

600   END
```

Figure 5.37   *Coding with a control routine*

6: Specifying a programming language

Objectives

After reading this chapter, you should be able to:

- Recognize and use the terms: **grammar, production, terminal symbol, non-terminal symbol, start symbol, goal symbol, sentence, metalanguage, metasymbol,** and **language**.
- Distinguish between the **syntax** and **semantics** of a grammar.
- Use and describe some of the ways in which the syntax of a language may be defined: **Backus-Naur form; extended Backus-Naur form; syntax diagrams**.
- Derive valid sentences from a grammar.
- Describe and apply the concept of **parsing**.
- Use the terms **context-free** and **context-sensitive** grammars.

Specifying a language

If we were to invent a new programming language, there are two main points which we must tell a programmer who is going to use that language: the first point is how the statements of the language are constructed and how they are written by a programmer when he/she is writing a program in that language (this is the **syntax** of the language); the second point is what the statements do and what their action is when each statement is executed as the program is running (this is the **semantics** of the language).

A language is specified by writing down the syntax and the semantics of each statement which is acceptable in that language.

Activity 1

As we saw in Chapter 5, most languages have statements which will allow iteration.

Thus, if we wanted to find the sum of the numbers 1 to 5, we might use a Pascal statement which looks like this:

    for x := 1 to 5 do sum := sum + x;

or the corresponding Basic structure:

```
FOR X = 1 TO 5
  SUM= SUM + X
NEXT X
```

(a) Compare and contrast the syntax of the loop structure in the two languages.
(b) Compare and contrast the semantics of the loop structure in the two languages.
(c) Look at the two examples shown here and compare the syntax and the semantics of the statements which add the value of the variable X (or x) into the variable SUM (or sum).
(d) How do other languages perform this same addition operation? Comment on the syntax of the statements in those languages.

Let us consider these two aspects one at a time.

How do we describe the syntax of the language? What must we specify in order to make it clear exactly how the statements of a programming language must be written? To answer this question, let us ask the same question about a human language, say, English or French. In the case of the English language, we must specify the vocabulary and the grammar. We must specify the words (the building blocks of the languages) and the rules by which these words are joined together to make accurate and intelligible sentences.

Let us suppose that we wish to specify a set of rules which will allow us to construct simple English sentences such as:

    the man sees the boy
    a boy hits a girl
    a girl hits the man

We could describe the construction – the syntax – of the sentences by means of a narrative such as:

A sentence consists of the word **the** or the word **a**
followed by one of the words **man, boy** or **girl**
followed by either of the words **sees** or **hits**
followed by either of the words **the** or **a**
followed by one of the words **boy, girl** or **man**.

Unfortunately, this is not a very clear description. Any such description is particularly ambiguous when we use the word *or*. It is frequently very difficult (particularly in the spoken language) to indicate the range of action of the word *or*. For instance, are we to read the first part of this description like this:

A sentence consists of the word **the** or (the word **a**
followed by one of the words **man, boy** or **girl**),
followed by either of the words **sees** or **hits**
followed by either of the words **the** or **a** . . .

so that the sentence:

the sees the . . .

would be acceptable? Or are we to read it as:

A sentence starts with (the word **the** or the word
a) followed by (one of the words **man, boy** or **girl**)
followed by (either of the words **sees** or **hits**)
followed by (either of the words **the** or **a**) ...

so that sentence such as:

the man sees the . . .
a girl hits a . . .

would be acceptable? The latter case is probably the one that we intended, but it would be very dangerous if we expected the reader to guess what we meant.

We can specify the structure of the sentences much more precisely by using a mathematical pattern such as:

<sentence> ::= <subject> <verb> <object>

This tells us that a valid sentence consists of:

- a subject, followed by

- a verb, followed by
- an object.

It also indicates that all three parts must be present in the specified order in order to build an acceptable sentence.

We must then define the various parts <subject>, <verb> and <object>. So we could then define <subject> as:

<subject> ::= <article> <noun>

and this would then require us to define:

<article> ::= **a** | **the**
<noun> ::= **boy** | **girl** | **man**

These last two definitions list the valid examples of articles and verbs. The vertical bar | has the meaning of *or*, so the last definition tells us that a noun may be any one of **boy** or **girl** or **man**.

Such a set of rules is called a **grammar**.

Questions

1 Write down suitable definitions for:

<verb>
<object>

Add any further definitions which you need.

2 It is now required to accept the sentences:

the girl hits me
the man sees him

Modify your definitions for <object> and add any further definitions which you need.

3 We now require there to be a full stop at the end of the sentence. Modify your definitions to reflect this change.

4 Which of the following sentences are acceptable to the grammar which we have defined? Give the reasons why any invalid sentences would be unacceptable.

(a) the man hits a girl.
(b) a girl sees the man.
(c) the girl sees the girl.
(d) a man sees her.
(e) a man hits a man.

    (f)   the boy hits me
    (g) the man sees a man.
    (h) she sees the man.
    (i)   a boy sees me.
    (j)   the girl sees me.
    (k) I see me.

5 Modify the definitions so that they will accept the sentences:

> the small man hits the big boy.
> the English girl sees me.

Add any further definitions which you need.

6 Modify the definitions so that they will accept the sentences:

> the small, English girl hits the big, French boy.
> the English girl sees me.

Add any further definitions which you need.

Recursive rules

In the answers to the last questions, we produced the definitions:

> \<adjective> ::= \<adjword> | \<adjword> , \<adjective
> \<adjword> ::= **big** | **small** | **English** | **French**

These two rules tell us that an adjective may be any one of the words:

> big
> small
> English
> French

or one of these words followed by a comma and another adjective.
    A rule such as:

> \<adjective> ::= \<adjword> | \<adjword>, \<adjective>

in which the same symbol:

> \<adjective>

in this instance appears on both sides of the ::= symbol is called a
recursive rule.

The adjectives generated by this particular recursive rule are valid within the grammar which we have defined, although in human English, these would, of course, be unacceptable examples of adjectives. These rules would, for example, allow us to generate valid sentences which included adjectives such as:

> big, small
> English, French
> big, big, big, big, big, small
> big, big, big, French
> French, English
> French, small

A solution which avoids this situation might be to create the rules:

> <adjective> ::= <sizeword> | <nationality> | <sizeword>
> , <nationality>
> <sizeword> ::= **big** | **small**
> <nationality> ::= **English** | **French**

The grammatical rules for English – and indeed, for any foreign language – are very complicated. It would, for example, be a very complex set of rules which could accept phrases such as:

> red, wooden, kitchen door

but reject:

> kitchen, wooden, red door.

Can you say why the second phrase is not acceptable in ordinary English speech?

It would, in fact, be a very large and complex set of rules which we would have to write down for the construction of English and which could be used to test the accuracy of every possible acceptable English sentence. Changing fashions in the spoken language complicate the matter further. Some of the syntax checking tools which you might find on a word-processing system use such rules to determine whether or not a sentence is acceptable.

A programming language, however, is far simpler and the rules far fewer. This is one reason why a programming language is so stylized and unnatural. Using our grammar, it is quite easy to check whether or not a given sentence is acceptable or not. This is one reason why

English or Chinese, for example, are unsuitable tools for writing computer programs.

BNF : Backus-Naur form

The formal language which we used to specify the form and grammar of our simple English sentences is known as a **metalanguage**. A metalanguage is an artificial language constructed specially for the purpose of specifying a programming language precisely and exactly. We shall use the metalanguage known as **Backus-Naur form** – BNF for short – with some additional features in the version known as **EBNF – Extended Backus-Naur form.** The rules which we derived for the grammar of our simplified version of the English language are some simple instances of the BNF language.

BNF can be used for defining both the vocabulary and the grammar of a programming language.

Before we start, we must introduce some of the jargon which BNF uses.

A **production** is a definition (we used the word *rule* earlier) which describes how the element of grammar is to be derived. Thus:

    <noun> ::= **boy** | **girl** | **man**

is an example of a production which states that (in our particular subset of the English language) a noun is defined as any one of the words **boy**, **girl** or **man**.

Terminal symbols are the parts of a production which are used to build up and construct the **non-terminal symbols**. Thus, in the production:

    <noun> ::= **boy** | **girl** | **man**

we see that:

    <noun>

is a non-terminal symbol, and:

    boy
    girl
    man

are terminal symbols. A non-terminal symbol must appear on the right of ::= sign in at least one production. A terminal symbol is one of the basic building blocks and is not used on the left of the ::= sign. In this book, we shall show terminal symbols in **bold face** type.

In the production

<noun phrase> ::= <article> <adjective> <noun>

all of <noun phrase>, <article>, <adjective> and <noun> are non-terminal symbols. In the production:

<sentence> ::= <subject> <verb> <object>

the symbol <sentence> is not used in any other productions and is called a **start symbol**. A start symbol cannot appear on the right of the ::= sign in any production. Because the start symbol is the main product of the grammar, some writers use the term **goal symbol** instead of start symbol. Every correct form derived for the start symbol is known as a **sentence** of that grammar.

The special symbols such as ::= and I and <and> and others which we shall meet later, are known as **metasymbols**.

The set of all the sentences which can be generated by means of the grammar is known as the **language** of that grammar.

Activity 2

(1)   In your own words, write down the meaning of the terms:

    (a)   grammar,
    (b)   production,
    (c)   terminal symbol,
    (d)   non-terminal symbol,
    (e)   start symbol,
    (f)   goal symbol,
    (g)   sentence,
    (h)   metalanguage,
    (i)   metasymbol,
    (j)   language,

and give some examples of each drawn from the material used in the text.

(2)   You have been asked to establish a set of rules for constructing dates. The rules are to be used to generate all acceptable dates of the form:

31/12/1990

31 January 1991
1 December 1991

for all the dates of this century.

Create a grammar to generate such dates. The grammar should not generate dates such as

33 December 1949
29 February 1991

Indicate the start symbol, the terminal symbols, the non-terminal symbols.

How many valid sentences are there in the language of your grammar?

Assignment 1

The statements shown in Figure 6.1 are valid for a certain dialect of the Basic language. Construct a set of rules to define each type of statement.

Note the following points about these statements:

(1)   The colon is used to separate several statements which are written on one line of the program.

(2)   The names of string variables end with a dollar sign.

Statement	Note
`A = 32`	
`LET A = 32`	
`A = 32 / B`	
`A = 123.456`	
`X = 0: B = 0: C = 32`	1
`A$ = "YES"`	2
`MESSAGE$ = "THIS IS THE END OF THE PROGRAM"`	3
`B$ = A$ ; "NO"`	4
`GO 100`	
`GO TO 2000`	
`IF A<>B THEN A=0: B=0`	
`IF A=B THEN A=0: B=0 ELSE A=HIGHEST: B=LOWEST`	
`IF A=B THEN GO 100`	
`PRINT A`	
`PRINT MESSAGE$`	
`PRINT A, B, C`	
`PRINT A; B; C`	5
`PRINT B / 32`	
`PRINT MESSAGE1:`	
`DIMENSION ARRAY1(10)`	
`DIMENSION ARRAY2(5,7)`	
`DIMENSION ARRAY3(13), ARRAY4(3,5), ARRAY5(7)`	
`DIM ARRAY1(10)`	

Figure 6.1   *Basic statements*

(3) Variable names may be any length but consist only of letters and numbers.

(4) The semi-colon is used to concatenate strings to build a single string.

(5) The semi-colon is used to concatenate output in the PRINT statement.

The rules of standard Basic apply in other situations.

Deriving a sentence from a grammar

Let us consider the set of productions:

> <sentence> ::= <subject> <verb> <object>.
> <subject> ::= <article> <noun> | <subject pronoun>
> <verb> ::= **sees** | **hits**
> <object> ::= <article> <noun> | <object pronoun>
> <article> ::= **a** | **the**
> <noun> ::= **boy** | **girl** | **man**

In order to derive a sentence from this grammar, we would begin with the start symbol:

> <sentence>

From this, we should then produce:

> <subject> <verb> <object>.

Then, using the production for <subject> we should produce:

> <article> <noun> <verb> <object>.

Then, using the production for <object> we could produce:

> <article> <noun> <verb> <article> <noun>.

Then, using the production for <article> we could produce:

> a <noun> <verb> <article> <noun>.

Then, using the production for <noun> we could choose any of the terminal symbols to produce:

> a boy <verb> <article> <noun>.

Then, using the production for <verb> we could choose any of the terminal symbols to produce:

>a boy hits <article> <noun>.

Then, using the production for <article> we could choose any of terminal symbols to produce:

>a boy hits the <noun>.

Then, using the production for <noun> we could choose any of the terminal symbols to produce:

>a boy hits the man.

This, then, is a valid sentence derived from our grammar.

It will be obvious that, once the grammar has been specificed, it is a fairly routine matter to generate valid sentences in the language.

Assignment 2

Using only the grammar which you derived for the Basic statements in the last assignment (or, better still, borrowing the grammar produced by one of your colleagues), and ignoring any previous knowledge about the Basic language, derive two valid forms of each statement.

Parsing

When we have defined a grammar, besides using it to *derive* accceptable sentences as we did in the previous section, we are also able to use the grammar to *recognize* acceptable sentences. This process is called **parsing** and allows us to determine whether or not a particular sentence is valid within the grammar.

Let us parse the particular sentence:

>he sees a man.

to see whether or not it is a valid sentence of the grammar:

>   <sentence> ::= <subject> <verb> <object> .
>   <subject> ::= <article> <noun> I <subject pronoun>
>   <article> ::= **a** I **the**

273

```
<noun> ::= boy | girl | man
<verb> ::= sees | hits
<subject pronoun> ::= he | she
<object> ::= <article> <noun> | <object pronoun>
<object pronoun> ::= him | her
```

Commencing with the start symbol, the grammar tells us that a <sentence> is a <subject> followed by a <verb> followed by an <object> followed by a full stop. We can represent this by a **parsing tree**, as shown in Figure 6.2.

Figure 6.2   *A parsing tree: 1*

We now start to traverse the tree, starting at the left-most branch which, in this case, is for the <subject>. A <subject> may consist of either:

<article> <noun>

or

<subject pronoun>

This allows two possibilities. The first possibility, shown in Figure 6.3 (a) requires that the sentence should begin with an <article>:

a

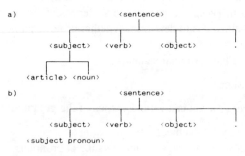

Figure 6.3   *A parsing tree: 2*

274

or

the

Our sentence:

he sees him.

does not begin with either, so this possibility can be ruled out. The second possibility, shown in Figure 6.3 (b), requires that the sentence should begin with a subject pronoun:

he

or

she

Our sentence begins with the word **he**, which is a valid , so this branch of the tree is satisfied, as shown in Figure 6.4 (a).

The next step is to follow the next branch of the tree to see if the <verb> is satisfied. Using the production for <verb>, we see that the word **sees** is a verb, so this branch of the tree is satisfied, as shown in Figure 6.4 (b)

Following the next branch of the tree, we see that there are two possibilities for <object>. The first, Figure 6.4 (c), requires that the next word is an <article>. The next word **a** is indeed an article, so this branch of the tree is satisfied, so we arrive at Figure 6.4 (d).

Going along the next branch, we see that the next word must be a <noun>, and **man** is acceptable, so this branch of the tree is satisfied, bringing us to Figure 6.4 (e).

Finally, we see that the last element must be a full stop. There is a full stop at the end of the sentence, so the sentence:

he sees a man.

parses correctly according to our grammar, as in Figure 6.4(f).

Activity 3

Following the steps described above, parse these sentences using the same grammar to check that the sentences are valid:

(1)   a man hits him.

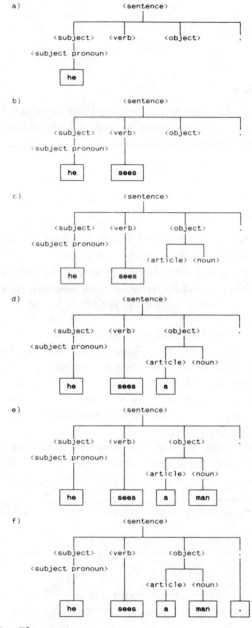

Figure 6.4   *The parsing tree in practice*

276

(2)   he sees he.

Draw the final tree structure in each case.

Question

7   You have been asked to define the grammar for a programming language which might be used for a pocket calculator. This will accept the following statements:

    1+2=
    2.5*3.5=
    −2.545*−3.555=
    2+3−4=
    +3++4=

There may be any number of values in the statement, these may be positive or negative numbers, they may be specified with or without a decimal point, and they will be connected by one of the arithmetic operators:

    *
    +
    −
    /

Define a production for the start symbol:

    <sentence> ::=

Define the other productions.
Test your productions on the statements shown above.

EBNF: Extended Backus-Naur form

When a production includes a choice of several possible terminal or non-terminal symbols, this can make the notation less easy to read. For example, in the solution to the last question, we used the production:

    <string> ::= <digit> | <digit> <string>

meaning that a <string> could consist of one or more digits.

The BNF notation has been extended to the EBNF (extended Backus-Naur form) and simplifies this by using braces symbols:

{ }

in a production such as:

<string> ::= <digit> { <digit> }

to indicate that a string is made up of a digit followed by 0, 1 or more digits.

Questions

8 Using the EBNF notation, would the following productions be correct for the grammar of the pocket calculator? Justify your answers.

(a) <expression> ::= <number> { <operator> <expression> }
(b) <sentence> ::= <number> { <operator> <sentence> } =
(c) <number> ::= { <sign> } <unsigned>

The EBNF uses square brackets to indicate that a part of the production is **optional** and may be included or may be omitted. We could use this to modify our production for changing it from:

<number> ::= <sign> <unsigned> I <unsigned>

to:

<number> ::= [<sign>] <unsigned>

We could also rewrite the production:

<unsigned> ::= <string> I <string> . <string>

as:

<unsigned> ::= <string> [. <string>]

These extensions make the productions easier to read.

Questions

9 Would the productions:

<unsigned> ::= <string> [. <string>]
<string> ::= <digits> { <digit> }
<digit> ::= 0 | 1 | 2 | 3 | 4 | 5 | 6 | 7 | 8 | 9

accept these unsigned numbers:

(a) 1
(b) 1.
(c) 1.1
(d) .1
(e) 12.34

as valid or not?

10 The production:

<unsigned> ::= [<string>] [. <string>]

would be acceptable for the above unsigned numbers. Why would it not be suitable for our grammar?

11 Derive a production which would be valid for all the above unsigned numbers and for the requirements of our pocket calculator grammar.

12 In a certain oriental language, a word may be constructed in several ways:

(a) A word may consist of a consonant followed by a vowel followed by a sound **n** or **ng**. For example:

man
pang
kan
fang

(b) A word may consist of vowel followed by a sound **n** or **ng**. for example:

an
ang
un
ung

(c) A word may consist of a consonant followed by just a vowel. For example:

279

ma
pa
ku
fu

(d) A word may consist of just a vowel. For example:

a
u
i

(e) A word may consist of a double vowel. For example:

aa
uu
ii

The language has only three vowels (a, i, u) and seven consonants (b, f, k, m, n, p, t).

Write a set of productions which will allow valid words to be derived and parsed.

More EBNF symbols

There are several other symbols used in EBNF notation. The asterisk may be used instead of the braces to indicate that a symbol may be used 0 or more times. For example, the production:

    \<string\> = \<digit\> \<digit\>*

is equivalent to the form:

    \<string\> ::= \<digit\> { \<digit\> }

which we introduced earlier.

The dagger may be used to indicate that a symbol may be used 1 or more times. So we could have expressed the production for \<string\> by:

    \<string\> ::= \<digit\>†

One problem with any such notation is that you must be very careful not to confuse the metasymbols (which are a part of the notation) with the terminal symbols (which are a part of the generated sentences). Thus, if we wanted to write down a production to generate sentences such as:

<a>
<aaaa>
<bbbb>
<cccc>

which include the characters <and>, then we could not write:

<token> ::= < <letter> { <letter> } >

as this would be ambiguous and does not allow us to distinguish between the <and> which are required in the token and the metasymbols which enclose the symbol *letter*. One convention to overcome this is to underline the terminal symbols or, in handwritten work, to highlight the terminal symbols in some manner. In this case, we might write:

<token> ::= <u><</u> <letter> { <letter> } <u>></u>

An alternative would be to establish two new terminal symbols:

<opener> ::= <
<closer> ::= >

and then use these in the production:

<token> ::= <opener> <letter> { <letter> } <closer>

The same technique could be used to indicate any spaces which must appear within the production.

Questions

13   In a certain grammar, we encounter the production:

<string1> = <digit> <digit>*

where the asterisk is a metasymbol. In another production:

<string2> = <digit> <digit><u>*</u>

the asterisk is a terminal symbol.
   Give some examples of valid instances and some invalid instances of <string1> and <string2>.

Activity 4

The purpose of this activity is to summarize what we have said about EBNF and the metasymbols which are used.

Write down the EBNF notation which you will use to show that a certain part of a specification is to be used in the following manner:

(a) Essential and unchanged. This part *must* be specified exactly as shown. For example, the word PRINT in a statement such as:

   PRINT A+B

(b) Optional. This part may be omitted or included. For example, the expression in a PRINT statement may be omitted or included, so that:

   PRINT
   PRINT A

are both acceptable.

(c) Optional and unchanged. This part may be omitted or included, but if it is included, it must be specified exactly as shown. For example the word LET may be omitted from an assignment statement:

   LET A=B
   A=B

are both acceptable, but:

   let A+B

is not acceptable.

(d) One of several possibilities. For example, the expressions in a PRINT statement may be separated by a comma or a colon:

   PRINT A,B
   PRINT A:B

(e) None or more repetitions. This part may be omitted or it may be repeated as many times as necessary. For example, a literal string may consists of none, one or many characters enclosed in " signs:

"THIS IS A !£$%^&*( )_@ LITERAL STRING"
"A"
""

(f)   One occurrence followed by none or more repetitions. For example, a positive integer number is made up of one or more digits.

Assignment 3

Modify your solution to the earlier BNF assignment and produce a set of EBNF rules to define each type of statement shown in Figure 6.1.

Syntax diagrams

The syntax of a language may also be specified graphically by means of diagrams known as **syntax diagrams** or **railroad diagrams**, such as those in Figure 6.5. These are often used to describe the syntax of Pascal statements.

By starting at the left and following the permitted routes through the diagram, you will be able to derive valid sentences from the grammar.

Let us look at the use of syntax diagrams to present the grammar for the pocket calculator which we met earlier. Using BNF and EBNF, the productions were:

```
<sentence> ::= <expression> =
<expression> ::= <number> [ <operator> <expression> ]
<number> ::= [ <sign> ] <unsigned>
<operator> ::= * | + | - | /
<sign> ::= + | -
<unsigned> ::= <string> [ . <string> ] | . <string>
<string> ::= <digit> { <digit> }
<digit> ::= 0 | 1 | 2 | 3 | 4 | 5 | 6 | 7 | 8 | 9
```

The syntax diagrams for <sentence> and <digit> are shown in Figure 6.5.

The syntax diagram for <sentence> is fairly simple and tells us that, starting at the top left, we must have an <expression> followed by an equal sign.

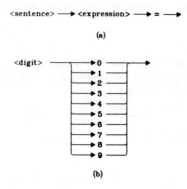

Figure 6.5   *Syntax diagrams*

The syntax diagram for <digit> tells us that, starting from the top left, we may proceed along any of the lines in the direction of the arrows, and select any one of the digits 0 through to 9. We leave the diagram at the top right.

Note that this technique overcomes the ambiguity of the word *or* and the I symbol

---

Questions

14   Draw the syntax diagram for <operator>

15   Draw a syntax diagram for <adjword> which you defined in your answer to Question (6).

16   Produce a new syntax diagram for <adjective> which will only allow adjectives such as

> big
> small
> English
> French
> big, English
> big, French
> small, English
> small, French

or no adjective at all, and which will reject adjectives such as:

> French, small

big, big, big, small, French, English, big
French, French
English,,,,,,, small
small,,,,,,, English

Recursion in syntax diagrams

We can show recursion quite clearly by sending the route back on itself. So we could define <string> like this:

Notice how the central path allows us to select just the first digit and then leave without generating any further digits.

Questions

17 Draw the syntax diagram for <number> to show that the sign is optional.

18 Draw the syntax diagram for <expression> to show that this may include an unlimited sequence of numbers separated by operators.

Assignment 4

Construct railroad diagrams to define each type of Basic statement shown in Figure 6.1.

Context-free grammars

We should run into difficulties if we were to use BNF or EBNF or syntax diagrams to check the syntax of all the statements of a programming language. One reason is that they do not offer any facility for cross-checking the various parts of the sentences. For example, if we had productions such as:

<sentence> ::= **the** <subject> <verb>
<subject> ::= **boy | girl | boys | girls**
<verb> ::= **sing | sings | shout | shouts**

we should not be able to check that the singular or plural subject agrees with the singular or plural verb. This would allow us to generate sentences such as:

the girl sing
the boys shouts

We could, of course, include many more alternatives:

<sentence> ::= <singular> | <plural>
<singular> ::= **the** <subject1> <verb1>
<plural> ::= **the** <subject2> <verb2>
<subject1> ::= **boy | girl**
<verb1> ::= **sings | shouts**
<subject2> ::= **boys | girls**
<verb2> ::= **sing | shout**

but this would make our grammar more complicated. A grammar such as this, which derives each sentence without any concern for the conditions or the **context** in which the sentence is being derived and used, is known as a **context-free grammar**.

A **context-sensitive grammar** does much more than this, modifying each production according to conditions which have, or which have not, been detected earlier. For example, let us imagine that we wanted a grammar to parse the Pascal statement:

for counter := 1 to 20 do lista[counter] := 0;

then, in order for this to be correct, the variable called *counter* must have already been declared as an integer, and an array called *lista* must have been declared. This means that, in order to be able to check whether the statement is entirely acceptable, we must use other information about *counter* and *lista* which should have been given earlier. If *counter* and *lista* have not been declared, or if they are of the wrong data types, then the statement will be invalid.

Because they are so complicated, context-sensitive grammars are not widely used in the specification of programming languages. In general, context-free methods (such as EBNF and syntax diagrams) are used where appropriate and the context-sensitive parts of the grammar are expressed in English or by some other means.

Assignment 5

For the grammars which you have produced to validate the Basic statements in Figure 6.1, which parts of the grammar should be context-sensitive?

Semantics

We have seen that in order to specify a programming language, we must specify the syntax; this tells us how the statements of the language are constructed and how the programmer should write acceptable statements in that language. Now we need to see how we specify the **semantics** of the language. The semantics tells us what the statements of the language do.

There are three principal methods which are used for specifying the semantics of a language:

- by means of an English narrative description;
- by means of an example:
- by means of substitution.

Let's see how we do this.

Specification by narrative description

To use the first of these methods to define the IF statement whose syntax we have defined as:

    IF <condition> THEN <statement> ELSE <statement>

we might write an English narrative description like that shown in Figure 6.6.

```
The IF statement has the form:

    IF condition THEN label1 ELSE label2

where condition is any logical expression
resulting in a boolean value of true or
false, and label1 and label2 are statement
labels which have been declared in the
program.

If the condition evaluates to true, then the
processing will jump to the statement at
label label1 and continue from that
statement.  If the condition evaluates to
false, then the processing will jump to the
statement at label label2 and continue from
that statement.
```

Figure 6.6   *Semantics: by narrative description*

Assignment 6

Use the method of *specification by narrative description* to define any three of the Basic statements shown in Figure 6.1.

Specification by example

If we were to define the same statement by example, we would provide a real illustration of the statement with an English language explanation. If we were defining the semantics of the Pascal IF statement, we might produce the definition shown in Figure 6.7. Our specification might also include some incorrect examples of the statement, indicating why they are incorrect. This might also describe the action which the compiler is to take when such an incorrect statement is found.

```
When the statements:

    int1 = 1;
    int2 = 2;
    IF int1 > int2 THEN d99 ELSE d77

are executed, the processing will jump to the
statement at label d77.  When the statements:

    int1 = 1;
    int2 = 2;
    IF int1 < int2 THEN d99 ELSE d77

are executed, the processing will jump to the
statement at label d99.
```

Figure 6.7   *Semantics: by example*

Assignment 7

Use the method of *specification by example* to define any three of the Basic statements shown in Figure 6.1.

Specification by substitution

If we chose to define a statement by substitution, we would provide an alternative piece of coding which would produce the same effect as the statement. To illustrate this, let us consider the FOR ... NEXT loop structure. We might define this as illustrated in Figure 6.8.

```
The FOR ... NEXT structure:

      FOR X=1 TO 10
            PRINT X
      NEXT X

has the same effect as the sequence:

      X=1
111   PRINT X
      X=X+1
      IF X<10 THEN 111 ELSE 999
999   REM CONTINUE
```

Figure 6.8 *Semantics: by substitution*

This method assumes that the programmer is familiar with the action of the IF statement and other statements and the various program elements which are used in the substitution, and that these have been defined earlier in the specification of the language. We encountered this concept when we were looking at the operations associated with abstract data types in Chapter 4.

Assignment 8

Use the method of *specification by substitution* to define any three of the Basic statements shown in Figure 6.1.

It is not unusual to find all three types of definition in the specification of a particular language.

Activity 5

Go to the library and look at the reference manual for a programming language which you have not used before.

Which method(s) are used to define the semantics of the language?

Which method do you personally find easiest to understand?

We have seen how the syntax and the semantics may be defined for a language. This information will be needed when the compiler is written for that language. We shall look at this in Chapter 8.

Recap

- The specification for a computer language comprises two parts: the syntax, which describes the form of the statements; the semantics, which describe the meaning and action of the statements.
- The syntax can be specified by means of a notation such as the Backus-Naur form (BNF), the extended Backus-Naur form (EBNF), or syntax diagrams.
- EBNF and similar notations are metalanguages which define the syntax of the language by means of a grammar consisting of a set of productions. There is one production for each part of the language. Each production is built up from start symbols, goal symbols, terminal symbols and non-terminal symbols. They are linked together using the metasymbols of the metalanguage.
- The set of productions for the grammar allow valid sentences to be derived for the language, and they allow sentences to be parsed to check that they are valid sentences of the language.
- A context-free grammar checks each sentence only to see that it is a production in its own right and independent of all the other sentences used. A context-sensitive grammar checks each sentence to see that it is a valid production and that it is also consistent with all the other sentences used in the language.

Answers to questions

1   <verb> ::= **sees** | **hits**
    <object> ::= <article> <noun>
2   <object> ::= <article> <noun> | <object pronoun>
    <object pronoun> ::= **me** | **him**
3   <sentence> ::= <subject> <verb> <object>.
4   (a), (b), (c), (e), (g), (i), (j) are acceptable. The following are unacceptable:

   (d)   **her** is not acceptable.
   (f)   The full stop is missing.
   (h)   **she** is not acceptable.
   (k)   **I** is not acceptable and **see** is not acceptable.

5   <subject> ::= <article> <noun> | <article> <adjective> <noun>

   <object> ::= <article> <noun> | <article> <adjective> <noun> | <object pronoun>

   <adjective> ::= **big** | **small** | **English** | **French**
6   <adjective> ::= <adjword> | <adjword> , <adjective>
    <adjword> ::= **big** | **small** | **English** | **French**
7   Your productions could be something like these:

   <sentence> ::= <expression> =
   <expression> ::= <number> | <number> <operator> <expression>
   <number> ::= <sign> <unsigned> | <unsigned>
   <operator> ::= * | + | _ | /
   <sign> ::= + | _
   <unsigned> ::= <string> | <string> . <string>
   <string> ::= <digit> | <digit> <string>
   <digit> ::= 0 | 1 | 2 | 3 | 4 | 5 | 6 | 7 | 9
8   (a)   Yes.
   (b)   No. Because <sentence> is the start symbol and cannot appear on the right of any production. Also, the = cannot be repeated as this production would allow.
   (c)   No, because only one <sign> may be used.
9   (a)   Valid.
   (b)   Invalid.
   (c)   Valid.
   (d)   Invalid.
   (e)   Valid.
10   The production would accept a null unsigned number and it would also accept just a decimal point. As a result, a sentence such as:

+3–+3=

which we should expect to give the answer 0, could be interpreted as:

+3–<null>+3 =

which we might expect to give the answer 6.

11 We could use the BNF productions:

<unsigned> ::= . <string> | <string> | <string> . <string>

or we could extend this to:

<unsigned> ::= . <string> | <string> [. <string>)

12 <word> ::= [<consonant>] <vowel> [<ending>] | <double>
<consonant> ::= **b** | **f** | **k** | **m** | **n** | **p** | **t**
<vowel> ::= **a** | **u** | **i**
<ending> ::= **n** | **ng**
<double> ::= **aa** | **uu** | **ii**

13 Valid instances of <string1> would include:

123
12
123456789012345

and invalid instances would include:

11*

Valid instances of <string2> would include:

1
11*
12*
99*

and invalid instances would include:

1234
12345*

14 See Figure 6.9 (a).
15 See Figure 6.9 (b).
16 See Figure 6.9 (c).
17 See Figure 6.9 (d).
18 See Figure 6.9 (e).

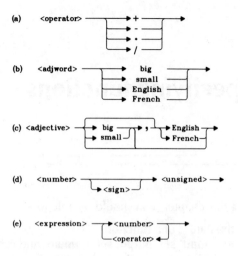

Figure 6.9 *Syntax diagrams: solutions*

7: Specifying functions

Objectives

After reading this chapter, you should be able to:

- Describe the nature of a **function**.
- Use the terms **input set**, **output set**, **domain**, and **range**.
- Distinguish between an **informal description** and a **formal description** of a function.
- Distinguish between a **partial function** and a **total function**.
- Write an informal description and a formal description for a function.
- Describe and apply the technique of **recursion** in functions.

We have seen how the format and action of the statements of a language can be specified. Now we must see how the functions of a language are defined.

Specifying functions

A function is any process which transforms data from one value to another. Thus, the square root function on your calculator will take one piece of data, called the **input**, and use this to produce another piece of data, called the **output**.

A more complicated example might be a function to perform a calculation such as:

$$y = 4x^2 - \sqrt{x}$$

Let us call this function CALC.

To evaluate the CALC function by hand, we would take a value of x, square it and multiply this by 4, and then subtract the square root of x from the result.

If we were thinking of a **computer** function to perform the same task, we might visualize it like this:

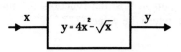

The box represents a function which accepts from us a number (x), uses this to perform a calculation to produce a number (y) and passes the value of y back to us. It is quite convenient for the programmer to think of a function as a **black box** which takes the input and uses this to produce the necessary output. This concept of *information hiding* which we met earlier applies to almost all the standard functions which you will use.

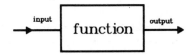

The programmers who will subsequently use this CALC function are not concerned with the manner in which the function achieves its results. We merely wish to describe a tool which the programmer can call upon when he/she needs to perform a particular action when writing his/her programs.

For example, if I asked my programming team to implement the CALC function, then I might find that one programmer had chosen to write a piece of code as:

$$y = 4 * x * x - \sqrt{x}$$

whilst another might have chosen:

$$y = 2*x$$
$$y = y*y - \sqrt{x}$$

The two are equivalent: they both meet the requirements and they both do what is wanted. When I wish to use this function in my program, I will write down the name of the function and the argument, that is, the value of x, which is to be used. For example, a reference such as:

CALC(9)

will submit the argument 9 to the function, the function will perform the calculation and return the value 321.

Question

1 What values are represented by each of these references? Give your answer to four places of decimals.

(a) CALC(1)
(b) CALC(1.5)
(c) CALC(15)
(d) CALC(0)
(e) CALC(2)
(f) CALC(2.5)
(g) CALC(27)
(h) CALC(3)
(i) CALC(36)
(j) CALC(4.5)
(k) CALC(49)
(l) CALC(5)

As someone using this function, I am not particularly interested in how the result is produced, and I may not even be concerned whether one method is faster or more efficient than the other. Provided that:

CALC(4)

gives me the result 62, then I am content with the function, instead of writing down the original piece of coding every time I wish to perform the action.

In order to specify this function rigorously, as I must do if am describing the function for the programmer who will implement it for me, I must also indicate any restrictions on the data which will be used with the function.

Activity 1

Give some values of *x* for which the CALC function would not be suitable.

How would you describe the values of *x* which could be handled by the function?

The value of x must be a real number and it must be greater than, or equal to 1. We could not use the function if x had a value of –56, or if x had a value of "YES" or "WESLEY".

The data which the computer handles – both in the specific case of the CALC function and generally – falls into one or more **sets**. It is therefore necessary for us to remind ourselves of some of the basic features of sets.

Sets

If you are already familiar with the concept of sets and the notation used with sets, you may skim the next few sections.

A **set** is a collection of objects which have some features in common. For example, the set called **rainbow** which comprises all the colours of the rainbow might be written as:

   rainbow = {red, orange, yellow, blue, green, indigo, violet}

The set is given a **name** (rainbow) and the various **members** which make up the set are enclosed in braces { and }.

Two important features of sets are:

(1)   The members of the set may be written in any order.
(2)   Each member is only present once in the set.

The first point tells us that the two sets:

   {red, blue, green, white}

and

   {red, white, green, blue}

are equivalent sets, because the order in which members are written is not important.

The second point tells us that, if we have a set:

   FIRST5 = {A, B, C, D, E}

which is the set of the first five letters of the alphabet, and we have another set:

VOWELS {A, E, I, O, U}

which is the set of English vowels, then, if we add these two sets together to form a single set, the result will be:

{A, B, C, D, E, I, O, U}

where each member is only present once.

Because the order in which the members are held is of no importance, the three sets:

{A, B, C, D, E, I, O, U}
{U, O, I, E, D, C, D, E}
{I, B, C, E, D, A, O, U}

are considered to be identical sets.

Questions

Using the brace notation illustrated in the text to declare the sets FIRST5 and VOWELS, write down the following sets:

2 The set DAYS which consists of all the days of the week.
3 The set TDAYS which consists of the names of all the days of the week which contains the letter T.
4 The set MMONTHS which consists of the names of all the months of the year which contain the letter M.

Is a member of ...

We use the symbol ∈ to express the idea that a certain element is a member of a set. So, the statement:

TUESDAY ∈ DAYS

tells us that TUESDAY is a member of the set DAYS.

We put a line through the ∈ sign to indicate that a certain element is *not* a member of a set. So the statement:

TUESDAY ∉ MONTHS

tells us that TUESDAY is not a member of the set MONTHS.

Operations on sets

There are a number of operations which we can perform on sets.

Union – represented by the symbol $\cup$ – has the effect of adding two sets together and producing a single set consisting of all the members of *either* or *both* sets. We would use the notation:

SET1 = FIRST5 $\cup$ VOWELS

to indicate that a new set SET1 is produced by the union of the two sets FIRST5 and VOWELS together. SET1 would therefore consist of:

SET1 = {A, B, C, D, E, I, O, U}

Difference – represented by the minus sign – has the effect of subtracting one set from another. We would use the notation:

SET2 = FIRST5 – VOWELS

to indicate that a new set SET2 is produced by the subtraction of the set VOWELS and FIRST5. SET2 would therefore consist of:

SET2 = {A, B, C, D}

Intersection – represented by the symbol $\cap$ – has the effect of overlapping two sets and producing a single set consisting of all members which are found in *both* sets. We would use the notation:

SET3 = FIRST5 $\cap$ VOWELS

to indicate that a new set SET3 is produced by intersecting the two sets FIRST5 and VOWELS together. SET3 would therefore consist of:

SET3 = {A, E}

If we take the intersection of two sets which have no common members, such as:

SET3 = {A, B, C, D} $\cap$ {X, Y, Z}

then the result will be the *empty set*. This can be written as:

ϕ (which is the Greek letter *phi*)

or

{ }

Question

5   Write down the contents of the sets produced by the following operations.

   (a)   SETA = {yes, no, maybe, never, sometimes} ∪ {ever, never}
   (b)   SETB = {1, 2, 3, 4, 5, 6} ∪ {0, 1, 2, 11}
   (c)   SETC = {yes, no, maybe, never, sometimes} ∩ {ever, never}
   (d)   SETD = {John, Michael, Peter} ∩ {Peter, John}
   (e)   SETE = {Carol, Alison, Mary} ∩ {Lesley, Sharon, Tracey}
   (f)   SETF = {red, orange, yellow, green, blue, indigo, violet} − {red, white, blue}

Writing the members of a set

In many cases, it is possible for us to write down all the members of each set explicitly. In some situations, however, it is not possible to do this. How could we write down the set which consists of all the even whole numbers? We have seen that we could use a statement such as:

$$\text{EVENS} = \{.\,.\,-10, -8, -6, -4, -2, 0, 2, 4, 6, 8, 10, \ldots\}$$

An alternative shorthand way of doing this is to write:

$$\text{EVENS} = \{x \in \text{integers} : x = 2n, n \in \text{integers}\}$$

or

$$\text{EVENS} = \{x \in \mathbb{Z} : x = 2n, n \in \mathbb{Z}\}$$

which we read as 'the set EVENS consists of all the values called x which are members of the set of integers, such that x is equal to 2 times some other number n and n is a member of the set of integers.

   If we wanted a more specific range of even numbers, such as the eleven values:

$$\text{EVENSX} = \{-10, -8, -6, -4, -2, 0, 2, 4, 6, 8, 10\}$$

We could write this in any of the forms:

$$\text{EVENSX} = \{x \in \text{integers} : x = 2n, n \in \text{integers}, n \leq 5, n \geq -5\}$$
$$\text{EVENSX} = \{x \in \mathbb{Z} : x = 2n, n \in \mathbb{Z}, n \leq 5, n \geq -5\}$$
$$\text{EVENSX} = \{x \in \mathbb{Z} : x = 2n, n \in \mathbb{Z}, -6 < n < 6\}$$
$$\text{EVENSX} = \{n \in \mathbb{Z} : n = 2x, x \in \mathbb{Z}, x \leq 5, x \geq -5\}$$

EVENSX = [x ∈ ℤ : x = 2y, y ∈ ℤ, y ≤ 5, y ≥ –5}

The names x, *y*, *n* are chosen arbitrarily.

Questions

6 How would we read these declarations?

   (a) EVENSA = {y ∈ ℤ : y = 2n, n ∈ Z, n ≤ –10}
   (b) EVENSB = {x ∈ ℤ : x = 2n, n ∈ Z, –6 < n < 6}

7 Using the ∈ notation, write down a declaration for each of the following sets:

   (a) The infinite set of integers:

> VALUESA = {. . –11, –9, –7, –5, –3, –1, 1, 3, 5, 7, 9, 11, . . .}

   (b) The finite set of integers:

> VALUESB = {–11, –9, –7, –5, –3, –1, 1, 3, 5, 7, 9, 11}

   (c) The infinite set of integers:

> VALUESC = {27, 28, 29, 30, 31, . .}

   (d) The infinite set of integers:

> VALUESD = {28, 30, 32, 34, 36, 38, . .}

Activity 2

Using the sets which were derived in Question (5), write down the results of the following expressions:

   (a) SETA + SETC
   (b) SETA – SETC
   (c) SETC – SETA
   (d) SETD + SETE
   (e) SETF – {red}
   (f) SETB – {2, 4, 5}
   (g) {x ∈ ℤ : x > 50} – {y ∈ ℤ : y < 60}

Primitive types in formal specifications

Data types are important to the systems analyst when he/she is producing specifications for the functions and processing which are to be used in a computer system. In our discussion of data types in Chapter 4, we used a notation which allows us to specify our syntax in a form such as:

HEAD.OF.QUEUE : queue → string

The notation which the analyst uses to identify the data types formally is an alternative to the forms we used earlier and is a shorthand notation very similar to that of pure mathematics. A detailed discussion need not concern us here, but the following will be useful for our present purposes.

In this notation, the sets of natural numbers is usually represented by the symbol $\mathbb{N}$ or the name *naturals*. This denotes the complete set of natural, whole numbers. Using the notation of sets, we can say that:

$\mathbb{N}$ = { the integers 0, 1, 2, 3, 4, and so on}

If it is necessary to restrict the range of natural numbers for a particular reason, then you may use the notation:

$\mathbb{N}_{50}$

which is the set of natural, whole numbers which are less than or equal to 50. That is:

$\mathbb{N}_{50}$ = { 0, 1, 2, 3, 4, . . . 48, 49, 50}

The set $\mathbb{Z}$ or *integers* comprises all the positive and negative integers and zero. That is:

$\mathbb{Z}$ = {. . . –9999, –9998, . . –3, –2, –1, 0, 1, 2, 3, . . 9999 . . .}

So *naturals* is a subset of *integers*.

The set $\mathbb{R}$ or *reals* denotes all the real numbers. It is impossible to list all the possible real values. Here are just a few instances:

$\mathbb{R}$ = {–99999999999.99999999, –9999.9998, –9999.9997, –2, –1.9, –1.8, 0, 1, 1.2, 2, 3, 3.14159, 5678, 9999 . .}

The set $\mathbb{Q}$ or *rationals* denotes all the rational numbers, that is, those which are the quotient of two integers. That is:

$\mathbb{Q}$ = { 0.25, 0.5, 0.3333. . , 0.4, 0.6666 . . , 1.2 . . .}

The set $\mathbb{B}$ or *Booleans* denotes all the possible Boolean values. That is:

$\mathbb{B} = \{\text{true, false}\}$

The set $\mathbb{C}$ or *characters* denotes the set of characters which are valid for the particular computing environment in which we are working. That is:

$\mathbb{C} = \{ A, B, C, .. , 1, 2, 3, .. /, !, @, £, \$, ...\}$

The set $\mathbb{S}$ or *strings* denotes the set of strings of all characters which are members of the set *characters*. We have already noted that it is impossible to list all the possible strings. Here are just a few instances:

$\mathbb{S} = \{ \text{CAT, MAT, AAA, AAAAA, BAAA, CAPABLE}, ...\}$

The use of the special symbols $\mathbb{Z}$, $\mathbb{N}$, $\mathbb{R}$, $\mathbb{Q}$, $\mathbb{B}$, $\mathbb{C}$, and $\mathbb{S}$, is merely a shorthand method for writing the function specifications which we shall discuss later. You could also use this notation for the operations which we specified in Chapter 4.

Questions

8 To which of the sets *Booleans, characters, naturals, rationals, reals* and/or *integers* (as we described them above) do the following values belong?
   Some values may belong to more than one set.

   (a) 0.5
   (b) 123
   (c) 1.456
   (d) A
   (e) 0
   (f) 3.14159... (the mathematical constant π)
   (g) true
   (h) f
   (i) –123
   (j) PROGRAM

9 Write the valid arguments of the CALC function using the set notation which we have discussed.

Now let's return to our discussion of CALC and functions.

The input set and the domain

We are making a number of restrictions and assumptions about the value of x in describing the CALC function. Your answers to the previous questions suggest that we are assuming:

(a)   That x is a number. Otherwise we could not use it in an arithmetic calculation.

(b)   That x is not negative. Otherwise we could not take the square root.

We could say that x must be a member of the set of real numbers and x must be greater than or equal to 0, or using our notation, x is a member of the set

$$\{x \in \mathbb{R}, x \geq 0\}$$

The set values of x from which the values of x are drawn is known as the **input set** of that function. So the input set for the CALC function is:

$$\{x \in \mathbb{R}\}$$

The set of values of x for which the function is valid is known as the **domain** of that function. So the domain for the CALC function is:

$$\{x \in \mathbb{R}, x \geq 0\}$$

In this case, the domain is a subset of the input set, because not all real numbers are acceptable (a value of -123.456 would be a valid member of the input set, but not a valid member for the domain of the function).

Mapping

For each value of x there is a corresponding value of y which is returned by the function. For those of the above values of x which are valid, we find that (to four decimal places), we can represent the corresponding values of y like this:

$$1 \longmapsto 3$$
$$1.2 \longmapsto 4.6646$$
$$2 \longmapsto 14.5858$$
$$3 \longmapsto 34.268$$

The symbol $\longmapsto$ is read as **maps to** so we can read

$1 \longmapsto 3$

as '1 maps to 3', and we can read the general expression:

CALC: $x \longmapsto y$

as 'the function CALC maps x to y'.

The names x and y are arbitrary names which we shall use to describe the action of the function later.

The output set and the range

The set from which the values of y are drawn is known as the **output set** of that function. The set values of y for which the function is valid is known as the **range** of that function.

We can picture the domain and the range as shown in Figure 7.1. Here we see the two sets of data, the domain and the range; the members of the two sets are linked by arrows representing the mapping described above.

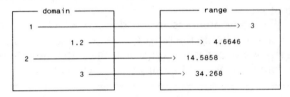

Figure 7.1   *CALC: mapping the domain to the range*

Questions

10   Amend the diagram in Figure 7.1 by adding the following values to the domain set:

3.142
5678
0.01
0.351
−1
99
0

and write the corresponding mappings to numbers in the range. You may have to use your calculator for this question. Use an accuracy of no more than three places of decimals.

11 Amend the diagram in Figure 7.1 by adding the following values to the range set:

> 3.142
> 62
> −1
> 321
> 1020
> 0

and write the corresponding mappings from numbers in the domain. You will have to use your calculator for this question.

12 Give some values of *x* which are in the input set but not in the domain of the function.

13 Give some values of *x* which are in the domain of the function but not in the input set.

14 Give some values of *y* which are in the output set, but not in the range.

15 Give some values of *y* which are in the range but not in the output set.

16 Are there any numbers in the domain which map to more than one number in the range?

17 Are there any occasions on which more than one number in the domain may map to a single number in the range?

Each number in the domain has one and only one corresponding number in the range.

Our function is called CALC, and we use this name in expressions such as:

> CALC(5)

to represent the output value from the function CALC when 5 is used as the input value. This would be: 97.764.

We can even use more complicated expressions, such as:

> CALC(CALC(5))

In such cases, we *work outwards* starting at the innermost function:

> CALC(5)

which is evaluated first and returns the value 97.764, as before. This result is then used with the next function:

CALC(97.764)

which returns the value 38221.311. You may nest such functions to almost any depth, and you may mix the functions:

FUNC23(FUNC1(CALC(O)))
CALC(CALC(FUNC32(CALC(43))))

provided that the output from one function is suitable input to the next, that is, the range of one function must be within the domain of the next.

Activity 3

Draw a map like that in Figure 7.1 for about 20 values of the function QUAD1 which performs the action:

$$y = x^2 - 7x + 3$$

What restrictions, if any, must we place on the values of x? What is the domain? What is the range?

Questions

18 Does the expression

CALC(QUAD1(x))

always have the same value as

QUAD1(CALC(x))

for all values of x? Give your reasons.

19 Use the functions described in the text to write down the values of the following expressions:

(a) QUAD1(–3)
(b) QUAD1(3)
(c) QUAD1(2.5)
(d) QUAD1(6.5)
(e) QUAD1(13)
(f) QUAD1(13.5)
(g) QUAD1(18)
(h) QUAD1(21.5)
(i) QUAD1(25)

(j)   QUAD1(27.5)
(k)   QUAD1(0)
(l)   QUAD1(QUAD1(0))
(m) CALC(QUAD1(–3))
(n)   QUAD1(CALC(–3))

As we have seen, there may be two numbers in the domain set which yield the same result in the range. For example, with an input value of 5, the SQUARE function would return an output value of 25 and an input value of –5 would also return an output value of 25. There can be several members of the domain which produce the same result in the range. *There can never be a function for which one input value produces two different output values.*

There may also be some numbers in the output set which do not fall within the range of the function.

Describing a function

A function is described in a manner very similar to that for the operations which we used with abstract data types earlier. It is quite possible to use the notation which we introduced for specifying ADT operations to specify a function. We introduce this second notation to equip you to understand this if you encounter it in your later studies.

We could describe our FUNC1 function like this:

(a)
(b
(c)
(d)

$$\text{FUNC1} : \mathbb{R} \longrightarrow \mathbb{R}$$
$$x \longmapsto y$$
domain $x \geq 0$
where $y = 4x^2 - \sqrt{x}$

The line:

$$\text{FUNC1} : \mathbb{R} \longrightarrow \mathbb{R}$$

tells us the *name* of the function (FUNC1, in this instance) and the *data types* which it uses. In this case, we see that a real input value produces a real output value. If the function is used with any input value which is not a real number (such as "XYZ"), then the output result will be unpredictable.

This line specifies the **syntax** of the function. Anyone who uses this function must write down the name FUNC1, they must provide a real number as input, and they will receive a real number as the output from the function.

It is possible to have functions in which any input data type produces any other output data type, such as:

$$\mathbb{R} \longrightarrow \mathbb{B}$$
$$\mathbb{Z} \longrightarrow \mathbb{Z}$$
$$\mathbb{Z} \longrightarrow \mathbb{R}$$
$$\mathbb{R} \longrightarrow \mathbb{Z}$$

and many more.

The line:

$$x \longmapsto y$$

shows the *names* of the corresponding input value and output value, telling us that each value of x maps to a corresponding value of y. The names x and y are chosen quite arbitrarily and we shall use x and y as *dummy names* when we describe the action of the function.

The line:

domain $x \geq 0$

shows the domain, that is, the input values which (together with the input set specified on the syntax line) are acceptable for the function. In this instance, we see that the x must have a value of 0 or greater than 0. If the function is used with any other input values (such as -3.5), then the output result will be unpredictable. The word **domain** is shown in bold face type or underlined in handwritten work.

If the domain is the same as the input set, then the domain line may be omitted.

Finally, the line:

where $y = 4x^2 - \sqrt{x}$

describes the *action* of the function, and indicates how the output value (y) is to be derived from the input value (x). The word **where** is shown in bold face type or underlined in handwritten work.

This line specifies the **semantics**, or the meaning, of the function. That is, the action by which the output value is derived from the input value.

It may not always be possible to use a mathematical expression in the semantics. For example, if I were asked to write a description of the function called INITIAL which takes a string of data as input and returns a single character (the first character of the input string), I might write a narrative description like this:

FUNC6 : $\mathbb{S} \longrightarrow \mathbb{C}$
s $\longmapsto$ c
domain s $<>$ " "
where c is the first character of s

Notice that we have used the domain to impose a condition upon the input value that it is not an empty string.

Questions

Write a description for each of the following functions. Give your function a suitable name and pay particular attention to the domain.

20 Write a description of the function:

$$y = x^2$$

21 Write a description of the function:

$$y = 2x$$

22 Write a description of the function:

$$y = 3x^3 - \sqrt[3]{x}$$

23 Write a description of the function:

$$y = \left(\frac{x}{2} \right)$$

in which x must be an integer.

24 Write a description of the function:

$$y = \left(\frac{2}{x} \right)$$

in which x must be an integer.

25 Write a description of the function which will return the largest integer which is less than or equal to the real number input value.

26 Write a description of a function which will return the value −1 if the input real number is less than zero, the value 0 if the input value is equal to zero, or the value 1 if the input value is greater than zero.

Partial functions and total functions

Functions such as CALC and FUNC6 are known as **partial functions** because they are not valid for the whole of the input set. Functions such as TWICE and FUNC4 are called **total functions** because they are valid for all values of x which lie within the input set.

If we required to make FUNC6 a total function so that it would accept an empty input string, then we might have used this definition instead:

> FUNC61 : $\mathbb{S} \longrightarrow \mathbb{C}$
> $\qquad$ s $\longmapsto$ c
> **where** c = '' if s = " ";

otherwise c is the first character of s.

In practice, most functions are implemented as partial functions, since they are easier to write if they do not have to check the validity of each piece of input data. Although, from the programmer's point of view, total functions are often preferable to partial functions because they will accept any input value (provided that it lies within the valid input set) and they do not require the programmer to check that the input value lies within the acceptable domain.

Questions

Indicate whether the following statements are true or false:

27 For a partial function, the input set is the same as the domain.
28 For a total function, the input set is the same as the domain.
29 A total function will have no **domain** in the description.

Indicate which of these functions are partial and which are total.

30 $y = \sqrt[5]{x}$
31 $y = \sqrt{\sqrt{x}}$
32 $y = 1/x$

Functions with other types of data

A function may act upon data other than real numbers. The function HALF, which you produced as your solution to Question (23), acts upon integer input to produce a real number as the output. In this case, the function description had the syntax:

$$\text{HALF} : \mathbb{Z} \longrightarrow \mathbb{R}$$

There can be almost any combination of data, including abstract data types and the basic sets:

integer
real
character
string
Boolean

in function descriptions.

Questions

33 Look at these narrative descriptions of certain functions [A to K] and match them up with one of the lines (a to k) in this list:

(a) $\text{FUNCZ} : \mathbb{S} \longrightarrow \mathbb{Z}$
(b) $\text{FUNCZ} : \mathbb{Z} \longrightarrow \mathbb{R}$
(c) $\text{FUNCZ} : \mathbb{Z} \longrightarrow \mathbb{C}$
(d) $\text{FUNCZ} : \mathbb{R} \longrightarrow \mathbb{Z}$
(e) $\text{FUNCZ} : \mathbb{S} \longrightarrow \mathbb{B}$
(f) $\text{FUNCZ} : \mathbb{C} \longrightarrow \mathbb{Z}$
(g) $\text{FUNCZ} : \mathbb{S} \longrightarrow \mathbb{C}$
(h) $\text{FUNCZ} : \mathbb{R} \longrightarrow \mathbb{S}$
(i) $\text{FUNCZ} : \mathbb{R} \longrightarrow \mathbb{B}$
(j) $\text{FUNCZ} : \mathbb{C} \longrightarrow \mathbb{S}$
(k) $\text{FUNCZ} : \mathbb{Z} \longrightarrow \mathbb{S}$

which describes a suitable input set and output set for that function.

[A]   To return the square root of an integer, so that:

FUNCA(5) would return the value 2.23606798

[B]   To return a string of spaces of a specified length, so that:

FUNCB(5) would return the value " "

[C]   To convert a number into a string of words, so that:

FUNCC(12.34) would return "twelve point three four"

[D]   To return the first character from a string of characters, so that:

FUNCD("MY NAME IS ALISON") would return 'A'

[E]   To return the character for any integer ASCII code, so that:

FUNCE(65) would return the value 'A'

[F]   To return a string of 10 occurrences of a specified character, so that:

FUNCF('A') would return the value "AAAAAAAAAA"

[G]   To return a number showing the number of characters in the input string, that is, the length of the input string, so that:

FUNCG("TODAY") would return the value 5
FUNCG(" ") would return the value 0

[H]   To return the ASCII numeric code for any character, so that:

FUNCH('A') would return the value 65

[I]   To return an indication of whether a specified number is zero or not, so that:

FUNCI(123.456) would return the value false, and
FUNCI(0.0) would return the value true.

[J]   To return an indication of whether a string is empty or not, so that:

FUNCJ("ABC") would return the value false, and
FUNCJ(" ") would return the value true.

[K]   To return a number truncated to the nearest integer, so that:

FUNCK(12.99) would return the value 12

34   Suggest suitable names for the functions described in the previous question. The names should be more meaningful than FUNCA or FUNCB and would remind the programmer of the action of the functions.

Activity 4

Write a description for each of the functions used in the preceding questions.

More than one input value

It is possible for a function to use more than one input value in order to produce a single output value. Let us imagine that we need to describe a function – we'll call it ADD2 – which will add two real numbers together and return the sum. Thus, the expression:

ADD2(1.2,2.3)

will return the value 3.5. We could describe our ADD2 function like this:

ADD2 : $\mathbb{R} \times \mathbb{R} \longrightarrow \mathbb{R}$
$(x,y) \longmapsto z$
where $z = x + y$

Since the function is total, there is no **domain**. The important differences between this description and that for the function FUNC1 which we met earlier are:

the line:

ADD2 : $\mathbb{R} \times \mathbb{R} \longrightarrow \mathbb{R}$

tells us that there are two real input numbers. The symbol X is conventionally used to separate the two input values and reminds us that we are concerned not with the arithmetic product of the two input values, but with the **Cartesian product**, that is every possible combination of two real numbers. If we had to describe a more complicated function, we might have lines such as:

FUNC12 : $\mathbb{R} \times \mathbb{Z} \longrightarrow \mathbb{R}$
FUNC13 : $\mathbb{R} \times \mathbb{Z} \times \mathbb{R} \longrightarrow \mathbb{R}$
FUNC14 : $\mathbb{S} \times \mathbb{R} \times \mathbb{Z} \longrightarrow \mathbb{B}$

The line:

$(x,y) \longmapsto z$

shows the *names* of the corresponding input values and output value.

Questions

35 Write a description for a partial function called STRING which will return a string made up of a number of occurrences of a specific character. Thus,

STRING(10,'A') will return the value "AAAAAAAAAA"

Pay particular attention to the **domain** for the input values. The function is not to handle expressions such as:

STRING(O,'A')
STRING(–99,'B')
STRING(4,'')

36 Change the description for the STRING function so that it is a total function.

37 Write a description for a partial function called SUBSTRING which will return a string of characters taken from a specific string. Thus,

SUBSTRING("ABCDE",1,1) will return the value "B"
SUBSTRING("ABCDE",2,3) will return the value "BCD"
SUBSTRING("ABCDE",3,2) will return the value "CD"

that is, the programmer specifies the start position and the length of the substring which is to be extracted from the input string.

Pay particular attention to the **domain** for the input values. Think about the relationship between the length of the string and the start and length values. The function is not to handle expressions such as:

SUBSTRING("",1,2)
SUBSTRING("ABCDE", –9,3)
SUBSTRING("ABCDE",3,999)

In your description, you may use the LEN function (or the FUNCG function) which we met earlier; this returns the length of the input string.

38 Change the description for the SUBSTRING function so that it is a total function. The function is now to produce results such as these:

SUBSTRING(" ",1,2) will return the value ""
SUBSTRING("ABCDE",–9,3) will return the value ""
SUBSTRING("ABCDE",3,999) will return the value ""

SUBSTRING("ABCDE",0,3) will return the value ""
SUBSTRING("ABCDE",999,2) will return the value ""
SUJBSTRING("ABCDE",3,0) will return the value ""

Other data types

You may include other data types, including ADTs, in your syntax, provided these have been properly defined. For example, we may have a need to handle data types such as *names* and *addresses*. We could then produce a description such as:

FIND: name ⟶ address

n ⟼ a

where a is the address of the employee identified by the name n.

It is important for you remember that when we describe a function we are simply indicating what the function is to do. Subsequently, when we are writing a program which needs that function, we can call upon the function and trust that it will do what we want of it. We are not concerned with the way in which the function achieves our requirements: that is up to the programmer who will implement the function.

Assignment 1

In this activity, you will use the primitive data types which we used earlier, together with a new data type: **dates**. A systems analyst is designing a piece of software in which it is necessary to be able to handle such dates. The provision of a set of functions to handle these dates will greatly simplify the task of writing the programs for the new software. You may assume that the ADT *date* has already been defined.

A *date* is a sequence of information of the form:

dd/mm/yy

representing a calendar date in the British format. In such a date, *dd* is an integer representing the day of the month, *mm* is an integer representing the month, and *yy* is an integer representing the year.

(1)   Write a description for a function called BUILD which will return a date constructed from three input integers. Thus,

BUILD(31,12,99) will return the date 31/12/99
BUILD(31,12,1995) will return the date 31/12/95

(2) Write a description for a function called PERIOD which will return the number of days between two given dates. Thus

PERIOD(1/12/93,13/12/93) will return the value 12

(3) Write a description for a function called BEFORE which will return an indication of whether one date is before another. Thus,

BEFORE(1/12/93,13/12/93) will return the value *true*,
BEFORE(1/12/93,1/11/93) will return the value *false*.

(4) Write a description for a function called VALID which will return an indication of whether a date is valid. Thus,

VALID(13/12/93) will return the value *true*,
VALID(41/11/93) will return the value *false*.

(5) Write a description for a function called SELECTD which will return the day-number of a specific date. Thus,

SELECTD(31/12/93) will return the value 31

Describe two similar functions which will return the month-number and the year.

Formal descriptions

We have seen that the semantics of a function description describe the action of the function. The semantics will be used by the programmer who will subsequently have to write a piece of coding to implement the function. According to which language the programmer uses to write the function, it may be implemented by means of a subroutine, a procedure, a function, a module, or whatever term is used in the chosen language. The syntax and the semantics merely tell him/her about the external features of the *black box*: what the input is to be, what the action is to be, and what the corresponding output will be. They do not describe the way in which the calculation is to be performed, that is up to the analyst or the programmer who will implement the function.

We have seen that the semantics can be presented as an informal written narrative:

s = " " if t = 0, otherwise
s = t

or as a more formal mathematical expression:

317

$$y = 2x$$

Obviously, the mathematical way is the most precise and the less likely to have any flaws or omissions. In order to achieve the greatest clarity in their definitions, some analysts use only the fundamental operations and functions which are available for the data types which are used in the syntax of the function description.

Thus, if we were using a function which was informally described as:

> TWICE : $\mathbb{Z} \longrightarrow \mathbb{Z}$
> $\qquad x \longmapsto y$
> **where** y is twice the value of x

then the fundamental operations for integers are:

+   addition of integers,
−   subtraction of integers,
*   multiplication of integers,
=   equality of two integers,
≥   greater than or equality of two integers,
< >   inequality of two integers,
≤   less than or equality of two integers.

and a formal description would use only these operations.

Using these operations, we should present our definition as:

> TWICE : $\mathbb{Z} \longrightarrow \mathbb{Z}$
> $\qquad x \longmapsto y$
> **where** $\quad y = 2 * x$

If we wished to insist that the input values are drawn from a certain domain, then we would also use these same operations to define the domain:

> TWICE : $\mathbb{Z} \longrightarrow \mathbb{Z}$
> $\qquad x \longmapsto y$
> **domain** $\quad x \geq 0$
> **where** $\quad y = 2 * x$

As another example, let us consider the mathematical function:

$$y = x^2$$

then the formal semantics would not allow us to write:

where $y = x^2$

or

where $y = x$ squared

because our list of operations does not include any for taking squares or for raising a number to a power. Instead, we must write:

where y = x * x

Similarly, if we consider the mathematical function:

$$y = \sqrt{x}$$

then the formal semantics could not be:

where y = √x

or

where y = the square root of x

because our list of operations does not include one for taking roots. Instead, we must write:

where y * y = x

In computer terms, this may not make sense, but it does precisely describe what we want of our function.

It may even be convenient to introduce *working* values. Suppose that we wish to evaluate the function:

$$y = 4x + \sqrt{x}$$

then we could write the semantics for this as:

where y = 4 * x + t
      t * t = x
      t ≥ 0

using *t* as an intermediate working value.

In some situations, it may be necessary to clarify that we are using the operators as they apply to integers. For example, let, us suppose that we had a **divide** operation, the division of integers to produce an integer result is a different operation from the division of two reals to produce a real result. In such circumstances, a subscript word (or letter) will be written after the operator.

$/_{\text{integer}}$ division of integer numbers
$/_{\text{real}}$ division of real numbers

Questions

Using only the operations shown above, and not including a division operator, produce formal descriptions for the following functions. All input and output values are to be real numbers. You may assume that the operations for real numbers are the same as those for integers, as described above.

39 Write a description for the function:

$$y = x^4$$

40 Write a description for a function which returns the cube root of the input value.

41 Write a description for the function:

$$y = 3x^3 - \sqrt[3]{x}$$

42 Write a description for the function:

$$y = \left(\frac{x}{2} \right)$$

in which *x* must be real.

43 Write a description for the function:

$$y = \left(\frac{2}{x} \right)$$

Activity 5

(1) Write a description of a function which will return the largest integer whose square is less than or equal to the input value. Thus,

func(10)
> would return the value 3 (because the square of 3 is less than or equal to 10),

func(9)
> would return the value 3 (because the square of 3 is less than or equal to 9),

func(8)
> would return the value 2 (because the square of 2 is less

than or equal to 8).

(2) Write a description of a function which will return the value
−1 if the input integer number is less than zero, the value 0 if
the input value is equal to zero, or the value 1 if the input
value is greater than zero.

Assignment 2

Write descriptions for the following functions. You may make your
own assumptions about any points which are not clear from the
narrative here. You may also use these functions in describing any
of the other functions.

(1) A function called DECAP is required is to remove the first
character of a string. Thus,

  DECAP("ABCDE") will return "BCDE"

(2) A function called TAIL is required to return all but the first
character of a string. Thus,

  TAIL("ABCDEF") will return "BCDEF"

(3) A function called TAIL1 is required to return the last character of a string. Thus,

  TAIL1("ABCDEF") will return "F"

(4) A function called JOINS to return a string which consists of
two input strings joined together. Thus,

  JOINS("ABCDE","XYZ") will return "ABCDEXYZ"

(5) A function called JOINC to return a string which consists of
an input character and an input string joined together. Thus,

  JOINC('A',"XYZ") will return "AXYZ"

(6) A function called ISIN to return a *true* or *false* indication as to
whether a specific character is found in a specific string.
Thus,

  ISIN("ABCDEF",'A') will return *true*
  ISIN("ABCDEF",'X') will return *false*

(7) A function called ISNULL to return a *true* or *false* indication
as to whether a specific string is empty. Thus,

      ISNULL(" ") will return *true*
      ISNULL("ABCDEF") will return *false*

(8)   A function called NEXT1 to return the character which follows a specific character in the alphabet.. Thus,

      NEXT1('A') will return 'B'
      NEXT1('P') will return 'Q'
      NEXT1('Z') will return 'A'
      NEXT1('!') will return ''

(9)   A function called SAME to return a *true* or *false* indication as to whether two strings are identical. Thus,

      SAME("ABCDEF","ABCDEF") will return *true*
      SAME("ABCDEF","ABCDEFIJ") will return *false*
      SAME("ABCDEF","ABCDEFGHIJK") will return *false*
      SAME("ABCDEF","ABCD") will return *false*

(10) A function called REVERSE to return a string which consists of the contents of the input string in the reverse order. Thus,

      REVERSE("ABCDE") will return "EDCBA"

(11) A function called INT.STRING to return the string equivalent of an integer input number. Thus,

      INST.STRING(1234) will return "1234"

(12) A function called SHIFTN to return an integer number which is derived from the input integer number by shifting the right-most digit to the left of the number. Thus,

      SHIFTN(1234567) will return 7123456

(13) A function called SHIFTS to return a string which is derived from the input string by shifting the right-most character to the left of the string. Thus,

      SHIFTS("ABCDEFGHI") will return "HABCDEFG"

Recursion

We have encountered the concept of recursion earlier. This is a valuable tool for designing and writing programs and involves the repeated use of a certain feature until a terminating condition is used. Recursion can be recognized in situations where the result of an operation performed on one piece of data is derived from a certain fixed value and the same operation performed on a part of the data.

For example, when we were looking at the operation to find the number of students in a queue, we used the fact that:

the length of a queue is 1 more than the length of the tail of the queue.

That is:

COUNT.QUEUE.B(x) = 1 + COUNT.QUEUE.B(TAIL.OF.QUEUE(x))

except when x is empty, in which case:

COUNT.QUEUE.B = 0

and this gave us the formal post-condition for the COUNT.QUEUE.B operation:

post-condition: y = 0 if x = CREATE.NEW.QUEUE(x)
          otherwise
          y = 1 + COUNT.QUEUE.B(TAIL.OF.QUEUE(x))

If we use the operation to find the length of the queue called STUDENTQUEUE which has the contents:

WATKINS	ATKINS	SIMPKINS

then the operation:

COUNT.QUEUE.B(STUDENTQUEUE)

which we can visualize as meaning:

COUNT.QUEUE.B(| WATKINS | ATKINS | SIMPKINS |)

will look at the first part of the post-condition:

y = 0 if x = CREATE.NEW.QUEUE(x)

and test whether the queue is empty. This is not true, so the next part of the post-condition is performed:

y = 1 + COUNT.QUEUE.B(TAIL.OF.QUEUE(x))

323

or, diagrammatically,

1 + COUNT.QUEUE.B(| ATKINS | SIMPKINS |)

This requires us to find the tail of the queue, which is:

| ATKINS | SIMPKINS |

and find the length of this by carrying out the operation which we can visualize as:

COUNT.QUEUE.B(| ATKINS | SIMPKINS |)

This is not empty, so the length of this is:

COUNT.QUEUE.B(| SIMPKINS |)

When we evaluate this, we must find the tail of the queue, which is:

the empty queue, and find the length of this by carrying out the operation which we can visualize as:

COUNT.QUEUE.B(| |)

This *is* empty, so the length is 0. We can now go back through the operations carrying our results with us. This is illustrated in Figure 7.2.

This example illustrates the two important features of recursion:

- The operation uses itself to evaluate the results.
- There must be some terminating condition (or conditions) which are used for special (terminal) values during the elaboration of the operation.

A typical recursion is represented by the coding:

```
functionR(value1)
    if
        terminating.condition
    then
        terminating.action
    else
        functionR(value2)
    endif
```

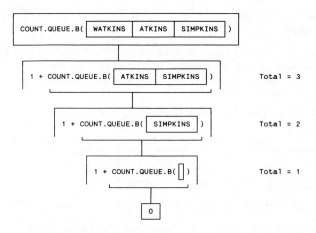

Figure 7.2   *Recursion with COUNT.QUEUE.B*

Questions

Factorials are commonly encountered in mathematics (and invariably in computer textbooks which discuss recursion).

You may know that the factorial of the number 9, for example, is the product of all the integers:

Factorial 9 = 9 × 8 × 7 × 6 × 5 × 4 × 3 × 2 × 1

44 Write an English sentence which suggests how you may use recursion to evaluate the factorial of a number.

45 What is the terminating condition?

46 Write the routine in the style shown for function ℝ above.

47 Write down a formal or an informal description of the operation which will find the factorial of any number.

We shall see some implementations of the factorial operation when we look at the Prolog and the Lisp languages.

Activity 6

In your owns words, write down some examples of other processing which might be performed by means of a recursive function.

Assignment 3

Choose any programming language with which you are familiar.

How would you implement the functions in Assignment 2 in that language? How would the functions be called by a program which uses them?

Write the coding for each of the functions in your programming language.

Write a demonstration program to test the action of each function:

DECAP("ABCDE") should return "BCDE"

TAIL("ABCDEF") should return "BCDEF"

TAIL1("ABCDEF") should return "F"

JOINS("ABCDE","XYZ") should return "ABCDEXYZ"

JOINC('A',"XYZ") should return "AXYZ"

ISIN("ABCDEF",'A') should return *true*
ISIN("ABCDEF",'X') should return *false*
ISNULL(" ") should return *true*
ISNULL"ABCDEF") should return *false*

NEXT1('A') should return 'B'
NEXT1('P') should return 'Q'
NEXT1('Z') should return 'A'
NEXT1('!') should return ''

SAME("ABCDEF","ABCDEF") should return *true*
SAME("ABCDEF","ABCDEFHIJ") should return *false*
SAME("ABCDEF","ABCDEFHIJK") should return *false*
SAME("ABCDEF","ABCD") should return *false*.

REVERSE("ABCDE") should return "EDCBA"

INST.STRING(1234) should return "1234"

SHIFTN(1234567) should return 7123456

SHIFTS("ABCDEFGH") should return "HABCDEFG"

Recap

- Functions are widely used in computer programming and offer a means of deriving a specific output value from one or more input values.

- The input value(s) are drawn from specific sets of data, possibly restricted by imposing a domain on the data. The output values lie within a specific set of data and are derived from the input value(s) according to the semantics specified for that function. A total function is valid for all data values in the input set, a partial function is only valid for data values within the domain specified for the function.
- According to the requirements of the users, the semantics of a function may be described informally using conventional English narrative, or a more formal mathematical description may be given using only the logical/mathematical operations which are available for the data sets concerned.
- Recursion is a technique which can be used to simplify the description of a function by using the function itself within the semantics.

Answers to questions

1   (a)   3
    (b)   7.7753
    (c)   896.1271
    (d)   0
    (e)   14.5858
    (f)   23.4189
    (g)   2910.8039
    (h)   34.268
    (i)   5469.9173
    (j)   78.8787
    (k)   9597
    (l)   97.764
2   DAYS = {MONDAY, TUESDAY, WEDNESDAY, THURSDAY, FRIDAY, SATURDAY, SUNDAY}
3   TDAYS = {TUESDAY, THURSDAY, SATURDAY}
4   MMTHS = {MARCH, MAY, SEPTEMBER, NOVEMBER, DECEMBER}
5   You should have produced the following answers. Remember that the *order* of the elements is not important.

    (a)   SETA = {yes, no, maybe, never, sometimes, ever}
    (b)   SETB = {1, 2, 3, 4, 5, 6, 0, 11}
    (c)   SETC = {never}
          The answer:

              Never

or

SETC = Never

is incorrect because *never* is an element (or member) of a set and not a set. The results of union and intersection are always sets, and sets are always shown in braces.

(d)   SETD = {Peter, John}
(e)   SETE is empty and would be written either as:

SETE = φ

or

SETE = {}

(f)   SETF = [orange, yellow, green, indigo, violet]

6 (a)   The set EVENSA consists of all the values called y which are members of the set of integers, such that y is equal to 2 times some other number n which is a member of the set of integers and n is less than or equal to –10.

(b)   The set EVENSB consists of all the values called y which are members of the set of integers, such that y is equal to 2 times some other number n which is a member of the set of integers and n lies between –6 and 6.

7   There is often more than one way of declaring such a set. Your answers should look something like these:

(a)   VALUESA = $\{x \in \mathbb{Z} : x = 2n+1, n \in \mathbb{Z}]$
(b)   VALUESB = $\{x \in \mathbb{Z} : x = 2n+1, n \in \mathbb{Z}, n \le 5, n \ge -6\}$
(c)   VALUESC = $\{x \in \mathbb{Z} : x \ge 27\}$
(d)   VALUESD = $\{x \in \mathbb{Z} : x = 2n, n \in \mathbb{Z}, n \ge 14\}$

8 (a)   reals, rationals or $\mathbb{R}$, $\mathbb{Q}$
(b)   naturals, integers or $\mathbb{N}$, $\mathbb{Z}$
(c)   reals, rationals or $\mathbb{R}$, $\mathbb{Q}$
(d)   characters, strings or $\mathbb{C}$, $\mathbb{S}$
(e)   reals, integers or $\mathbb{R}$, $\mathbb{Z}$
(f)   reals or $\mathbb{R}$
(g)   Booleans or $\mathbb{B}$
(h)   characters, strings or $\mathbb{C}$, $\mathbb{S}$
(i)   integers or $\mathbb{Z}$
(j)   strings or $\mathbb{S}$

9   The arguments of CALC are members of the set

argument $\in \{x \in \mathbb{R}, x \ge 0\}$

10 You should have added these to your diagram. It does not matter where you wrote the numbers or drew the mapping arrows.

$3.147 \longmapsto 37.716$
$5678 \longmapsto 128958660.600$
$0.01 \longmapsto -0.1$
$0.351 \longmapsto -0.1$
$99 \longmapsto 39194.05$
$0 \longmapsto 0$

Notice that the two input values 0.001 and 0.351 both produce the same output value. So there should be two arrows mapping to the single number 0.1 in the output set.

There is no mapping for the input value 1 since it is not in the domain set.

11 You should have added these to your diagram. It does not matter where you wrote the numbers or drew the mapping arrows.

$1.0187 \longmapsto 3.142$
$4 \longmapsto 62$
$9 \longmapsto 321$
$16 \longmapsto 1020$
$0 \longmapsto 0$

There is no mapping which produces the output value -1 since it is not in the range set.

12 If x has any value 0 or less, then this is in the input set (real numbers) but not in the domain.

13 All numbers in the domain must also be in the input set.

14 The value -30 is in the output set (or real numbers) but not in the range since there is no value for x which would give an output value of -30. The smallest possible value for y is about 0.297 (when x has an input value of 0.157), so any value lower than -0.297 is in the output set, but not the domain.

15 All numbers in the range must also be in the output set.

16 No. There must only be one number in the range for each number in the domain.

17 Yes. The numbers 0.01 and 0.351 in the domain both map to -0.1 in the range.

18 No.

19 (a) 33.

(b) -9.

(c) -8.25.

    (d)   –0.25.

    (e)   81.

    (f)   90.75.

    (g)   201.

    (h)   314.75.

    (i)   453.

    (j)   566.75.

    (k)   3.

    (l)   –9.

    In evaluating this expression, we first evaluate QUAD1(0) and this returns the value 3; then we use this value with the outer brackets (and the first QUAD1), to get QUAD1(3) which returns the value –9.

    (m) 4350.256. The innermost function, QUAD1 (–3) is evaluated first, to return a value of 33, then this is used in the function CALC(33) which returns the value 4350.256.

    (n) QUAD1(CALC(–3)) is invalid. An attempt is first made to evaluate the inner-most function CALC(–3), but this is invalid, so the entire function is invalid and cannot be evaluated.

20 SQUARE : $\mathbb{R} \longrightarrow \mathbb{R}$

                $x \longmapsto y$

    domain $x \geq 0$

    where $y = x^2$

21 TWICE : $\mathbb{R} \longrightarrow \mathbb{R}$

              $x \longmapsto y$

    where $y = 2x$

Note that there are no restrictions on the range of x; it may be a positive number, zero or a negative number. Therefore, we need not specify a domain.

22 FUNC4 : $\mathbb{R} \longrightarrow \mathbb{R}$

              $x \longmapsto y$

    where $y = 3x^3 - \sqrt[3]{x}$

23 HALF : $\mathbb{Z} \longrightarrow \mathbb{R}$

             $x \longmapsto y$

    where $y = \left(\dfrac{x}{2} \right)$

24 RECIP2 : $\mathbb{Z} \longrightarrow \mathbb{R})$

          $x \longmapsto y$

    domain $x <> 0$

    where $y = \dfrac{2}{x}$

Note that x cannot have the value 0, so we must provide a domain in our description.

25 INT : $\mathbb{R} \longrightarrow \mathbb{Z}$

$x \longmapsto y$

where y is the largest integer which is less than or equal to x.

Note that x may have any value, although it must be a real number.

26 SIGN : $\mathbb{R} \longrightarrow \mathbb{Z}$

$x \longmapsto y$

where $y = -1$ if $x < 0$

$y = 0$ if $x = 0$

$y = 1$ if $x > 0$

27 False.

28 True.

29 True.

30 Total.

31 Partial. Negative values are not allowed.

32 Partial. The input x cannot take a value of 0.

33 You should have produced the following answers:

Function [A] would use the sets shown on line (b).
Function [B] would use the sets shown on line (k).
Function [C] would use the sets shown on line (h).
Function [D] would use the sets shown on line (g).
Function [E] would use the sets shown on line (c).
Function [F] would use the sets shown on line (j).
Function [G] would use the sets shown on line (a).
Function [H] would use the sets shown on line (f).
Function [I] would use the sets shown on line (i).
Function [J] would use the sets shown on line (e).
Function [K] would use the sets shown on line (d).

34 These names are more meaningful than FUNCA, FUNCB and so on. It does not matter if yours are not exactly the same as my answers. The language which you will be using may restrict the use of names such CHAR or INTEGER for the functions.

[A] IROOT or ISQRT would remind the programmer that the input number is to be an integer.

[B] SPACES or SPACE.

[C] WORDS or RWORDS (to remind the programmer that the input number is to be a real).

[D] FIRST or INITIAL. This is the same function that we introduced in the text.

[E] CHARACTER or CHAR.
[F] STRING or STRING10.
[G] LEN or LENGTH.
[H] SEQ or SEQUENCE or VALUE.
[I] RZERO or ZERO.
[J] ISEMPTY or EMPTY.
[K] INT or INTEGER.

35 Your solution may have imposed different conditions on the domain.

$$STRING : \mathbb{Z} \times \mathbb{C} \longrightarrow \mathbb{S}$$
$$(i,c) \longmapsto s$$

domain $i \geq 0$, $c <> $ ''

where s = a string of repetitions of c of length i

36 $STRING : \mathbb{Z} \times \mathbb{C} \longrightarrow \mathbb{S}$
$$(i,c) \longmapsto s$$

where s = " " if $i \leq 0$;
s = " " if c = ' '

otherwise s = a string of repetitions of c of length i

37 The sum of the start and the length values must not be more than 1 greater than the length of the string.

$$SUBSTRING : \mathbb{S} \times \mathbb{Z} \times \mathbb{Z} \longrightarrow \mathbb{S}$$
$$(s,i,j) \longmapsto t$$

domain s <> " ", $i > 0$, $i + j \leq LEN(s) + 1$

where t = string starting at the i th character of s and LEN(t) = j.

38 You may have written the semantics of your description slightly differently from mine.

$$SUBSTRING : \mathbb{S} \times \mathbb{Z} \times \mathbb{Z} \longrightarrow \mathbb{S}$$
$$(s,i,j,) \longmapsto t$$

where t = " " if LEN(s) = 0;
t = " " if $i > LEN(s)$;
t = " " if $i \leq 0$;
t = " " if $j \leq 0$;
t = " " if $i + j > LEN(s) + 1$

otherwise t = string starting at the i th character of s and LEN(t) = j.

39 $FOURTH : \mathbb{R} \longrightarrow \mathbb{R}$
$$x \longmapsto y$$

where $y = x * x * x * x$

In these solutions, we have not used subscripted operators. The nature of the operators is clear from the context.

40 $CUBEROOT : \mathbb{R} \longrightarrow \mathbb{R}$

$$x \longmapsto y$$

where $y * y * y = x$

41 FUNC4 : $\mathbb{R} \longrightarrow \mathbb{R}$

$$x \longmapsto y$$

where $y = 3 * x * x * x - t$

$$t * t * t = x$$

42 HALF ; $\mathbb{R} \longrightarrow \mathbb{R}$

$$x \longmapsto y$$

where $2 * y = x$

43 RECIP2 : $\mathbb{R} \longrightarrow \mathbb{R}$

$$x \longmapsto y$$

domain $x <> 0$

where $y * x = 2$

44 The factorial of any number, x, is x times the factorial of the number $(x–1)$.

45 The factorial of 1 is 1 (or you may have chosen to say that the factorial of 0 is 1).

46 Your coding should look something like this:

```
factorial(value1)
    if
        value ≤ 1
    then
        answer = 1
    else
        answer = value1 * factorial(value1 – 1)
    endif
```

47 You could have specified the function (or the operation) in either of these two forms:

FACTORIAL : $\mathbb{Z} \longrightarrow \mathbb{Z}$

$$x \longmapsto y$$

domain $x \geq 0$

where $y = 1$ if $x \leq 1$

otherwise

$$y = x * \text{FACTORIAL}(x–1)$$

FACTORIAL : $\mathbb{Z} \longrightarrow \mathbb{Z}$

$$x \longmapsto y$$

pre-condition $x \geq 0$

post-condition $y = 1$ if $x \leq 1$

otherwise

$$y = x * \text{FACTORIAL}(x–1)$$

8: Compilers and compiling

Objectives

After reading this chapter, you should be able to:

- Describe the tasks performed by a compiler: **lexical analysis**, and **syntax analysis**.
- Describe the contents and the use of a **symbol table**, the **array table**, the **constant table**.
- Produce a symbol table and a **storage map**.
- Construct and evaluate a **reverse Polish** or **post-fix expression**.
- Convert **in-fix expressions** to post-fix form, and vice versa.
- Describe the nature of **scope checking** and **optimization** as they are performed by a compiler.
- Produce an outline design for a compiler.

A compiler

The fundamental tasks of a compiler are:

- To read the source program from a disk or tape file.
- To report any syntax errors in the source program.
- To produce an object version of the program.
- To write the object version of the program to disk or tape file.

If we were to design a compiler, then our top-level design might look like this:

- Compiler : version 1
- Read the source program from backing storage
- Report any syntax errors
- Produce the object program
- Write the object program to backing storage

Assignment 1

(1) Make a copy of the top-level design for a compiler shown in the text.

(2) To this design add more detail, so that if there are any errors the compiler will not write the object program to backing storage.

A suggested solution to this assignment is given at the end of this chapter.

In the assignments in this chapter, you will develop a design for your own compiler. We shall assume that this will be for a dialect of Basic, but you may prefer to produce a compiler for a completely new language of your own design.

At each stage, you may make the design as detailed as you wish. It should be possible to implement the compiler in a language with which you are familiar.

The most important of the compiler's tasks – those of reporting any syntax errors and producing the object program – require the compiler to:

- Identify the various words and elements used by the programmer; and from these

- Distinguish the keywords of the language from the identifiers used by the programmer.

- Distinguish the data elements of the program from the processing elements.

- Produce a storage map for the data elements.

- Convert the processing elements into equivalent pieces of object code.

- Reject as errors any elements which cannot be successfully converted into data or object code.

Let us consider the short Pascal program shown in Figure 8.1. This may be written in the indented format shown in diagram (a). This is easier for the programmer to read, but to the compiler it is equivalent to the version shown in diagram (b).

There are certain **delimiting characters** which the programmer must use to separate one word or one statement from another. These are important because they enable the compiler to break down the contents of the program and then to be able to understand and interpret the source program.

```
program tentimes;
const
      factor = 10;
var
      a, b: integer;
begin
      a := 123;
      b := a * factor
end.
```

(a) the indented layout

```
program tentimes; const factor = 10; var a, b: integer; begin
a := 123; b := a * factor end.
```

(b) a sequence of characters

Figure 8.1 *A Pascal program*

Question

1 Write down some of the delimiting characters in the Pascal program shown in Figure 8.1 and indicate what they tell the compiler.

Lexical analysis

The compiler breaks the text of the program down into units of information separated by these delimiting characters and produces a list such as that shown in Figure 8.2. The entries in this list are known as **symbols**. This stage of the compilation is known as the **lexical analysis**.

Activity 1

Get a printed copy of a small program written in a language with which you are familiar and make a list of the separator characters which are used there.

Produce a list of the symbols for the program.

Assignment 2

To your design for a compiler add the refinements which will allow it to:

● analyse the source program according to the delimiting symbols; and

- break the program down into a set of symbols.

A suggested solution to this assignment is given at the end of this chapter.

```
program
tentimes
;
const
factor
=
10
;
var
a
,
b
:
integer
;
begin
a
:
=
123
;
b
:
=
a
*
factor
end
.
```

Figure 8.2 *The list of symbols*

The symbol table

In performing the lexical analysis and breaking down the program in this way, the compiler produces the **symbol table**. The symbol table is not the list of symbols shown in Figure 8.2, but is almost like a *map* which the compiler builds up to show the data – the *constants* and the *variables* – which are used by the program. For each data item, the information held in the symbol table shows:

- The name which the programmer has used to identify the constant or the variable.
- The class of the item (indicating whether this is a constant or a variable). This may depend upon the language in which the program is written, since not every language has a facility to declare constants. The compiler may also include function and procedure names here.
- The type of the item; this indicates whether it is *integer, real, character, Boolean* and so on. Again, the various possibilities will

depend upon the language in which the program is written. If an array is used, this will be specified as the type of the item.

This information will be used for type checking. This would enable the compiler to identify and take the appropriate action if there is any invalid usage of the variables such as an attempt to use a string variable in an arithmetic expression.

- The amount of storage space occupied by this item. This will normally depend upon the type of the item.
- The detail. This gives more information about the symbol and will be one of:

  - The value, if the item is a constant.
    Some compilers use a **constant table** to hold details of the constants which are used.
  - A reference to another table – known as the **array table** – if the item is an array.

- The start address. This is the address at which that variable (or constant) is to be found in memory. This will be 0 for the first variable, and each successive variable will be placed in the next available location in memory. This is illustrated by the symbol table shown in Figure 8.3.

Name	Type	Class	Detail	Address
factor	integer	constant	10	0
a	integer	variable		4
b	integer	variable		8

(a) the symbol table

Address	Contents
0 1 2 3	factor
4 5 6 7	a
8 9 10 11	b

(b) the storage map

Figure 8.3 *The* tentimes *program*

The symbol table for the *tentimes* program is shown in Figure 8.3(a). This enables us to draw a **storage map** of the area which will be occupied by each variable in the program, as shown in diagram (b).

With most programming languages, all constants and variables must be declared at the start of the program and before they are used. This makes it easy for the compiler to build the symbol table; it also makes it easier for the compiler to reject undefined variables as these are encountered later during the compilation.

With languages such as Basic, which do not require variables to be declared before use, the compiler must read through the entire program, building the symbol table as it goes. When a constant is encountered in Basic statements such as:

    MSG$ = 'END OF JOB'
    PRINT 'THANK YOU'
    FOR X=Y TO 100

then the constants

    'END OF JOB'
    'THANK YOU'
    100

will be added to the symbol table.

Some compilers construct another table – the **constant table** – to hold all the constants. A constant table is illustrated in Figure 8.4. By doing this, the compiler is able to reduce the storage space used by using the same constant if these are encountered elsewhere in the program. For example, if the same program had a statement such as

    X = Y/100

Name	Type	Class	Detail	Address
	string	constant	1	100
	string	constant	2	110
	number	constant	3	119

(a) the symbol table

Ref	Type	Length	Value
1	string	10	END OF JOB
2	string	9	THANK YOU
3	number	4	100

(b) the constant table

Figure 8.4 *Symbol table and constant table*

339

or

IF VALUE > 100 THEN STOP

then the compiler would find that the constant 100 had already been entered into the constant table. The original constant 100 will then be referenced once more.

Constants and variables

You should be careful to distinguish between *constants* and *variables*. Pascal identifies constants and variables quite clearly by means of statements such as:

const pi = 3.14159;
vat = 17.5;

var Price, TotalPrice : real;
Quantity : integer;

In the Pascal program, we can assign any values to the variables Price, TotalPrice and Quantity, but it would be wrong to write a statement such as:

vat: = 0;

The compiler would reject such statements.

With Basic, the distinction is less obvious. In a statement such as:

MSG$ = 'END OF JOB'

you may think of MSG$ as being a constant (since it may never change in this particular program); it is nevertheless a *variable*, since it would be perfectly feasible to have another statement

MSG$ = 'YES'

later in the program. The term *constant* is used for those elements which cannot be assigned values as the program executes, such as strings:

'END OF JOB'
'THANK YOU'
100
'YES'

340

and numbers:

100

It would be wrong to write statements such as:

'END OF JOB' = 'FINISHED'
100 = 0

Some dialects of Basic do offer a facility for declaring constants by means of statements of the form:

EQUATE PI TO 3.14159

In addition to the constants and variables used by the program, the compiler may add other items to the symbol table, such as the names of any procedures, subroutines and functions which are used by the program.

Questions

2 How does the compiler know how much storage space to allocate for each constant and variable?
3 Produce the symbol table and the storage map for the Pascal *multiply* program shown in Figure 8.5.

```
program multiply;
const
      multiplier = 10.5;
      pi = 3.14159;
   var
      result, first, second : real;
      counter, counter2 : integer;
      flag, finished : boolean;
```

Figure 8.5   *A Pascal fragment*

4 Produce the symbol table, the constant table and the storage map for the Basic program shown in Figure 8.6. This uses numeric values only.
5 Produce the symbol table and the constant table for the Basic program shown in Figure 8.7. This uses numbers and strings.

341

```
         FOR  X=1  TO  10
             SQUARE=X*X
             CUBE=X*X*X
             PRINT  X,SQUARE,CUBE
         NEXT  X
         END
```

Figure 8.6   *A Basic program: 1*

```
         MSG$='What  is  your  name'
         PRINT  MSG$;
         INPUT  NAME$
    100  FOR  X=1  TO  10
             ROOT=SQRT(X)
             SQUARE=X*X
             CUBE=X*X*X
             PRINT  X,ROOT,SQUARE,CUBE
         NEXT  X
         MSG2$='Any  more,  ';NAME$;'?  '
    200  PRINT  MSG2$;
         INPUT  RESP$
         IF  RESP$='Y'  THEN  GO  100
         IF  RESP$  <>  'N'  THEN  GO  200
         END
```

Figure 8.7   *A Basic program: 2*

Arrays and the symbol table

If a variable is declared to be an array by means of a statement such as:

var values : array[1 . . 10] of integer;

or

DIMENSION VALUES(10)

then the entry in the symbol table will be as shown in Figure 8.8 (a).
The number 1 in the *detail* column refers to an entry in another table,

Name	Type	Class	Detail	Address
values	array	variable	1	0

(a) symbol table entry for an array

Ref	Index type	Element type	Lower subscript	Upper subscript
1	integer	integer	1	10

(b) the array table

Figure 8.8   *An array in the symbol table*

the **array table,** which holds the *dope vector* information for the array. You will recall from Chapter 3 that the dope vector describes the array and its subscripts.

In some languages, where the subscripts need not be numeric and the number of elements cannot therefore be calculated arithmetically from the range of subscripts, it may be necessary to hold the number of elements in the array table.

In Pascal and other languages it is possible to have *an array of arrays.* Such an array would be defined by a statement such as:

var stats : array [–5 . . 5] of array [3 . . 10] of real;

and the appropriate entries in the symbol table and the array table would be as shown in Figure 8.9. This time, we need a further reference in the array table to show where the secondary array is defined.

Name	Type	Class	Detail	Address
stats	array	variable	1	0

(a) symbol table entry for an array

Ref	Index type	Element type	Ref	Lower subscript	Upper subscript
1	integer	array	2	-5	5
2	integer	integer		3	10

(b) the array table

Figure 8.9 *A multi-dimensional array in the symbol table*

Questions

6 How does the compiler know how much storage space to allocate for an array?

7 Produce the symbol table and the array table for the Basic program shown in Figure 8.10 which uses numbers, strings and arrays.

8 Produce the symbol table, the constant table and the array table for the fragment of a Basic program shown in Figure 8.11 which uses multi-dimensional arrays.

```
          DIM VALUES(10)
100   FOR  X=1 TO 10
              VALUES(X)=X*X
      NEXT X
      FOR Y=1 TO 10
              PRINT Y,VALUES(Y)
      NEXT Y
      MSG2$='Any more, ';NAME$;'? '
200   PRINT MSG2$;
      INPUT RESP$
      IF RESP$='Y' THEN GO 100
      IF RESP$ <> 'N' THEN GO 200
      END
```

Figure 8.10   *A Basic program: 3*

```
          DIM VALUES(10)
          DIM NAMES$(5,20)
          MSG1$='Enter name of student '
          MSG2$='Enter details for student '
          MSG3$=' for subject '
100   FOR X=1 TO 10
              VALUES(X)=X*X
      NEXT X
      FOR X=1 TO 5
              PRINT MSG1$;X;
              INPUT NAMES$(X,1)
              FOR Y=2 TO 20
                      PRINT MSG2$;X;MSG3$;Y;
                      INPUT NAME$(X,Y)
              NEXT Y
      NEXT X
```

Figure 8.11   *A Basic program: 4*

Activity 2

Produce the symbol table, the constant table and the array table, as required, for a short program written in a language with which you are familiar.

Assignment 3

To your design for a compiler add the refinements which will allow it to use the symbols to create the symbol table and the other tables which are built at this stage.

A suggested solution to this assignment is given at the end of this chapter.

Syntax analysis

When the source program has been analysed into symbols and the symbols used to construct the various tables, the compiler will begin to check the syntax – the grammar – of the program. This is the **syntax analysis** stage of compilation. To do this, the compiler must use, directly or indirectly, the specification of the language. This specification will be presented as a set of BNF or EBNF rules or as a set of railroad diagrams such as we saw in Chapter 6. Look back at your solutions to the assignments there in which you produced a set of BNF, EBNF and railroad diagrams specifying the syntax of a set of Basic statements.

For Pascal, the overall fomat of a program is defined by:

    \<program> ::= **program** \<identifier> ; \<block> .

with a \<block> being defined to include one or more of the:

    const
    type
    var
    procedure
    function

and

    begin . . . end
    \<statement>

components of a program.

For Basic, a program could be defined by a set of productions which might include those shown in Figure 8.12.

Assignment 4

Amend the list of productions shown in Figure 8.12 so that it includes all the statements which are available in the version of Basic which your compiler will handle.

From your knowledge of programs written in the Basic language – or indeed programs in any other language – you will realize that each type of statement is identifiable by the first symbol. This will be either:

```
<program> ::= {<statement> <delimiter>} END

<delimiter> ::= newline | :

<statement> ::= <assignment-statement>    |
                <input-statement>    |
                <if-statement>    |
                <print-statement>    |
                <goto-statement>    |
                <dimension-declaration>    |
                <gosub-statement    |
                <return-statement    |
                <for-statement>

<assignment-statement> ::= <string-assignment>    |
                           <numeric-assignment>

<string-assignment> ::= [LET] <string-identifier> =
                        <string-expression>

<numeric-assignment> ::= [LET] <numeric-identifier> =
                         <numeric-expression>

<input-statement> ::= INPUT <identifier> {, <identifier>}

<if-statement> ::= IF <condition> THEN <statement> [ELSE
                   <statement>]

<condition> ::= <expression> <relational-operator> <expression>

<relational-operator> ::= = | < | > | <> | <= | >=

<goto-statement> ::= <goto-word> <label>

<goto-word> ::= GO | GOTO | GO TO
```

Figure 8.12   *Some EBNF productions for Basic*

- a special symbol, such as IF, INPUT, PRINT, LET or DIMEN-SION; or
- an identifier (this is really a LET statement without the word LET); or
- a label.

A statement which starts with a label, such as:

    10 PRINT 'END OF JOB'

is simply a special case of the PRINT statement. We can ignore the label during the syntax analysis.

So, in general, we are able to say that a print statement begins with the symbol PRINT, an input statement begins with the symbol INPUT, and so on. An assignment statement, however, may begin with either an identifier or the symbol LET. Thus, when the compiler encounters a new statement and this statement begins with, say, the symbol PRINT, it can jump to a routine which will analyse the following symbols in that statement to check that they represent a valid PRINT statement.

Syntax checking in general

Once you have produced a set of specifications for each type of statement, it is a fairly simple matter to transform these into designs for coding. For example, the assignment statement has the form:

<assignment-statement> ::= [**LET**] <identifier> = <expression>

made up of a specified *sequence* of symbols, so a design for the routine to validate the syntax of this statement might be as shown in Figure 8.13 (a).

The relational operator is specified as:

<relational-operator> ::= = | < | > | < > | <= | >=

and will be one of the *range* of possible characters, so a design for the routine to validate the relational operator might be as shown in Figure 8.13 (b).

```
*     Get the next symbol and check that this is an
      identifier.

*     Get the next symbol and check that this is an equal
      sign.

*     Get the next symbol and check that this is an
      expression.

            (a) checking the assignment statement

*     Get the next symbol
      case depending upon the current symbol
          if it is =
          if it is >
          if it is <=
          if it is <>
          if it is <=
          if it is >=
      end case

            (b) checking the relational operator
```

Figure 8.13 *Designs for syntax checking: assignment statement*

In the case of the input statement,

<input-statement> ::= **INPUT** <identifier> {, <identifier>}

we must check for *repetitions* of a part of the statement, so a design for the routine to validate the syntax of this statement might be as shown in Figure 8.14.

```
    *    Get the next symbol and check that this is an identifier
    *    Get next symbol
         loop until the current symbol is end-of-statement
    *         check that this is a comma
    *         get next symbol and check that this is an identifier
         end loop
```

Figure 8.14   *Design for syntax checking: input statement*

Syntax checking in action

When the appropriate routine has been called to check the remaining sequence of symbols in, say, an input statement, the compiler will verify that the symbols conform to the syntax for that statement and it will continue to check the symbols until the end of that statement it encountered.

If we were to consider the routine which checks the format of an input statement, we would first look at the specification for that statement:

<input-statement> ::= **INPUT** <identifier> {, <identifier>}

and use this to build a design for the routine.

We have already used the fact that the first symbol is INPUT to decide which routine to use, so, based upon the general designs shown above, the INPUT-checking routine might look like that shown in Figure 8.15.

In this illustration, we have used the programming concept of *gosub*, but you could just as easily use a notation such as

jump to the routine which . . .

Assignment 5

(1)   In the text, we have seen three processing routines: checking a sequence of symbols; checking for one of a range of symbols; checking for repetitions of a symbol.

Using the language which you will use to implement your compiler, write suitable coding for each of these three routines.

(2)   To your design for a compiler add the refinements which will allow it to:

- check whether or not a symbol indicates the start of a new statement;

- take appropriate action to check the syntax of the statement which is indicated by the symbol;
- add designs for each of the routines which validate each type of statement.

```
gosub 100:      ** get the next symbol and check that
                this
                is an identifier
get the next symbol
loop until this symbol is end-of-statement
     gosub 100: ** check that this is a comma
     get the next symbol
     gosub 100:      ** get the next symbol and check
                     that
                     this is an identifier
end loop
terminate routine with no errors

100  * Subroutine to check that next symbol is an identifier
get the next symbol
if this symbol is not an identifier
then
     report error 'AN IDENTIFIER EXPECTED'
     gosub 999
     return
end if

200  * Subroutine to check that this symbol is a comma
if this symbol is not a comma
then
     report error 'COMMA OR END-OF-STATEMENT EXPECTED'
     gosub 999
     return
end if
return

999  * Subroutine to skip this statement
skip until end-of-statement encountered
return
```

Figure 8.15   *Syntax check for INPUT statement*

Syntax errors

Note that, when it detects an error, this compiler only discards the offending statement (by skipping to the end of that statement), and it does not abandon the entire compilation. By doing this, you can save the programmer a lot of time by reporting as many errors as possible during each compilation. Obviously, an error in one statement (such as a DIMENSION statement) may mean that many subsequent statements (those which use the array) cannot correctly be compiled.

In some situations, it may possible to recover from the error before the end of the statement. For example, in our syntax check for the INPUT statement, we looked to see if the first symbol was an identifier: if it was not, then we printed an error message and skipped the rest of that statement. An alternative action might be to report the error but then assume that the symbol *had been* an identifier and carry on with the checking the rest of the statement.

In some situations, it may be possible to recover from an error by taking some specific action, for example, if a programmer had written a Basic statement such as:

RESP$ = TOTAL

in which a numeric value (held in TOTAL) is assigned to a string variable (RESP$). You may decide to reject the statement and print an error-message, or you may arrange for the program to convert the numeric value into the equivalent string and assign this to RESP$.

Assignment 6

(1) Look at your set BNF or EBNF productions and/or railroad diagrams for the Basic statements. Select one of your sets of specifications for use in this and the subsequent assignments.
    Complete your set of specifications to include:

- checking identifiers,
- checking string-expressions and numeric-expressions,

and any other specifications which you might need as you proceed.

(2) To your design for a compiler add designs for the routines which will allow it to:

- check the syntax of each type of statement according to your specifications;
- check the format of the identifiers used in the program;
- create the appropriate entries in the symbol table.

Make your own decisions as to what action you will take when an error is found.

Arithmetic expressions

Now we must see how our compiler is to handle arithmetic expressions. When we encounter Basic statements such as:

LET A = B + C

we can convert these directly into machine code instructions: we know the storage addresses of A, B, and C from the symbol table; we know the sequence of machine code instructions which will take the contents of two storage areas, add them together and put the result into a third storage area. But what about more complicated statements such as:

LET A = 2 * B – 3 * C

or

LET X = (2*B)/(3*C)+32

How are these to be transformed? We obviously need a more general way of transforming any arithmetic expression into a manageable form.

Reverse Polish notation

In ordinary algebra and arithmetic, we are used to writing expressions in forms such as:

1 + 2
3 * 4
5 – 6
7 / 8

Most arithmetic operations are **dyadic operations** such as these, that is, they process just *two* operands at a time. In order that we are able to perform more complex operations, such as:

2 * 3 * 4 / 5 * 6 – 7 + 8
(1 + 2) * (3 / 4)

we must break these down into a simpler form which allows the dyadic operations to be carried out. This is done by rewriting the expressions using a notation which is known by the names **post-fix notation** or **reverse Polish notation**. In this post-fix notation, the operands come first and then the operators.

Let us look at a simple post-fix expression. The conventional (or **infix**) expression:

1 + 2

would be written as the *post-fix* expression:

1 2 +

We simply move the arithmetic sign into position *after* the second operand; hence the name *post-fix* notation. This expression can be interpreted as:

take the number 1, then the number 2, then add them together.

As another example, consider the in-fix expression:

77 / 11

which would be written as the *post-fix* expression:

77 11 /

Again, we move the arithmetic sign into position *after* the second operand. This expression can be interpreted as:

take the number 77, then the number 11, then divide the first by the second.

A more complicated expression such as:

2 * 3 * 4

would be written as:

2 3 * 4 *

which can be interpreted as:

take the number 2, then the number 3, then multiply them together, then get the result (6), then take the number 4, then multiply them together.

Some further examples are shown in Figure 8.16.

In-fix notation	Post-fix notation
1 + 2	1 2 +
3 * 4	3 4 *
5 - 6	5 6 -
7 / 8	7 8 /
1 * 2 - 3	1 2 * 3 -
1 + (2 * 3)	1 2 3 * +
(1 + 2) * (3 - 4)	1 2 + 3 4 - *
1 + 2 / 3	1 2 3 / +

Figure 8.16   *Some examples of post-fix notation*

The main steps in taking an expression written in the in-fix notation and transforming this into post-fix notation are:

(1)   Write down the expression in the ordinary (in-fix) manner. Let us take this expression as an example:

$$\frac{(3*4)}{(5-2*7)}$$

(2)   Write the expression on one line (without numerators and denominators), adding any brackets to clarify the expression, so that the expression becomes:

    $(3*4)/(5-2*7)$

(3)   Reading from left to right, add brackets to indicate the precedence: the * and / operators and their operands are bracketed first; the + and – operators and their operands are bracketed next.

    Thus, an expression such as:

    $11 + 22 * 33$ becomes $11 + (22 * 33)$

and

    $11 + 22 * 33 / 44$ becomes $11+ ((22 * 33) / 44)$

Our expression becomes:

    $(3*4)/(5-(2*7))$

(4)   Consider any bracketed expressions (3*4) and (5-(2*7)) as simple operands, and move the operator (/ in this case) to the right of the second operand:

    $(3*4)(5-(2*7))/$

(5)   For the contents of each bracketed expression, repeat the basic operation of moving the operator into position behind the second operand, and remove that set of brackets:

    $3\;4*(5-(2*7))/$

and then:

    $3\;4*5\;(2*7)-/$

and finally:

    $3\;4*5\;2\;7*-/$

(6)   Write down the final post-fix expression:

$$3\ 4*5\ 2\ 7*-/$$

An even more complicated expression:

$$\frac{1+2}{3*4} - \frac{5/6}{7-8}$$

could be transposed by means of the sequence illustrated in Figure 8.17.

$$\frac{1+2}{3*4} - \frac{5/6}{7-8}$$

```
Step 1: ((1 + 2) / (3 * 4)) - ((5 / 6) / (7 - 8))
Step 2: ((1 + 2) / (3 * 4))   ((5 / 6) / (7 - 8)) -
Step 3: ((1 + 2)   (3 * 4) /) ((5 / 6) / (7 - 8)) -
Step 4: ((1 + 2)   (3 * 4) /) ((5 / 6)   (7 - 8) /) -
Step 5: ( 1 2 +    (3 * 4) /) ((5 / 6)   (7 - 8) /) -
Step 6: ( 1 2 +    3 4 *   /) ((5 / 6)   (7 - 8) /) -
Step 7: ( 1 2 +    3 4 *   /) ( 5 6 /    (7 - 8) /) -
Step 8: ( 1 2 +    3 4 *   /) ( 5 6 /    7 8 -   /) -
Step 9:   1 2 +    3 4 *   /   5 6 /     7 8 -   /   -
Final expression:

        1 2 + 3 4 * / 5 6 / 7 8 - / -
```

Figure 8.17   *Writing a post-fixed expression*

Questions

Write the following in-fix expressions using the post-fix notation:

9 $23 * 34 + 56$
10 $12 * 34 + 56 - 78$
11 $98 * (87 + 76) - 65$
12 $\dfrac{12 + 34}{87 - 6\,5} * \dfrac{45 * 56}{98 - 11}$

Evaluate the expressions. We shall use these results to check your solutions to the assignments later in this chapter.

An algorithm to convert in-fix expressions to post-fix

This means that our compiler must convert each in-fix expression into a post-fix expression. An algorithm for doing this is shown in Figure 8.18. In this design, we assume that the expression is entered in a form such as:

(1+3) * (4–5)

This is then handled as a string of elements:

(1 + 3) * (4 – 5)

and these are interpreted by the main loop in the algorithm. We use a

```
operators  = '*/-+()'
priorities = '332211'
input the expression
for each element of the expression
        if element is in list of operators
        then
                loop while the priority of this element is <=
                that of the element at the the top of the stack
                        output the element at the the top of the
                        stack
                        pop the stack
                end loop
                push this element on to the stack
        else
                case depending upon this element
                        case element = (
                                push this element on to the stack
                        case element = )
                                loop while the top of the stack is not (
                                        output the top of the stack
                                        pop the stack
                                endloop
                                pop the stack
                        otherwise
                                output this element
                end case
        end if
end for
```

(a) the algorithm

Symbol	Stack	Output	Postfix
(	(		
1	(	1	1
+	(+		1
2	(+	2	1 2
)		+	1 2 +
/	/		1 2 +
(	/ (		1 2 +
3	/ (	3	1 2 + 3
–	/ (–		1 2 + 3
4	/ (–	4	1 2 + 3 4
)	/	–	1 2 + 3 4 –
finish		/	1 2 + 3 4 – /

(b) Transforming (1+2)/(3-4) ——> 1 2 + 3 4 - /

Figure 8.18 *Converting in-fix to post-fix notation*

355

stack to store the operators. The elements in the expression are processed from left to right. When an operand is encountered, it is sent for output by the routine. When an operator is encountered, its priority is compared with that of the operator at the top of the stack. The priority of the operators is represented by the variables called *operators* and *priorities*.

* and /	highest
+ and –	next highest
(and)	next highest

If the priority of the current element is lower than or the same as that of the operator at the top of the stack, then that at the top of the stack is sent for output and then removed from the stack; the new operator is then pushed on to the top of the stack.

If the element is an open bracket, then this is pushed on to the stack. If the element is a closing bracket, then the operators on the stack are output and popped, one by one, until a matching (is found.

Figure 8.18 (b) shows the step by step elaboration of the in-fix expression:

$$(1 + 2) / (3 - 4)$$

Assignment 7

(1) Using the programming language in which you will implement your compiler, write a program to convert in-fix notation expressions to post-fix notation expressions.

Use your program to check your answers to the questions which were asked earlier in this section.

(2) Modify the design for your compiler so that arithmetic expressions are first converted into post-fix expressions.

Evaluating a post-fix expression

Most processing routines use a stack to store the operators, the operands and the results as a post-fix expression is evaluated. The post-fix expression is examined, element by element, from left to right. When a data value is encountered, this is placed at (or *pushed on to*) the top of the stack, and when an operator is encountered, the processor will perform the appropriate action on the elements at the top of the stack. The processed elements will then be removed (or *popped*) from the stack and the result pushed on the stack for further processing.

The fact that the data is in a stack implies that, as with any stack, the last piece of data in is the first piece of data out.

We can illustrate this by looking at the elaboration of the post-fix expression:

   1 2 +

This is shown in Figure 8.19 (a). As the expression is evaluated from left to right

- The processor will first encounter the data value 1 and push this on to the top of the stack.
- When the next processing element (the value 2) is encountered, the top element (the value 1) will be pushed down and the number 2 will be pushed on the stack.
- The next element is the arithmetic operator + (addition). Because this is an operator (and not a data value) the processor will retrieve the top two elements from the stack, add them together and push the result pushed on the stack.

Since there are no further elements in the expression, the process stops and the value 3 is output from the top of the stack.

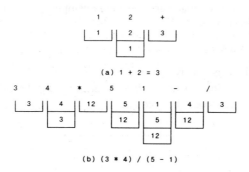

(a) 1 + 2 = 3

(b) (3 * 4) / (5 - 1)

Figure 8.19 *Evaluating post-fix expressions*

A more complicated expression such as:

   (3 * 4) / (5 - 1)

would be transformed into:

$$3\ 4 * 5\ 1 - /$$

Figure 8.19 (b) shows the successive contents of the stack as the expression is elaborated. As each element is encountered in the stack:

- The first data element, 3, is pushed on the stack.
- The next data element, 4, is pushed on the stack.
- The next element * indicates multiplication and multiplies together the top two elements (3 and 4, returning a result of 12). The two (used) values are then popped from the stack and the result is pushed on the stack.
- The next data element, 5, is pushed on the stack.
- The next data element, 1, is pushed on the stack.
- The next element – indicates subtractions and subtracts the next to the top element from the top element (1 from 5, returning a result of 4). The two (used) values are then popped from the stack and the result is pushed on the stack.
- The next element / indicates division and divides the next to the top element by the top element (12 by 4, returning a result of 3). The two (used) values are then popped from the stack and the result (3) is pushed on the stack.
- Since there are no further elements in the expression, the process stops and the value 3 is output from the top of the stack.

If a mistake had been made and we were attempting to evaluate a post-fix expression such as

$$1\ 2\ 3\ 4\ 5\ 6 +$$

and had pushed too many elements on to the stack, then only the top element (11, the final result of 5 6 +) would be used; the values 4, 3, 2, 1 still on the stack would be ignored.

Questions

Evaluate the following post-fix expressions using a stack. Draw the state of the stack as each operand and each operator is encountered. Check your results with those from the previous questions.

13   11 22 33 + –
14   11 22 * 33 /

15 11 22 33 44 + – *
16 11 22 33 + – 2 *

An algorithm to evaluate post-fix expressions

Using a stack to handle the data, it is a fairly straightforward matter to write a program to evaluate post-fix expressions. A suggested algorithm is shown in Figure 8.20. As we have seen, the operands are held in the stack, and each operation is performed upon the top two elements in the stack; these two elements are then popped (removed) from the stack and the result pushed on to the top of the stack. The final result is the number which is left at the top of the stack.

```
for each element in the expression
    case depending upon the current element
        case the element is an operand
            push the element on to the stack
        case the element is an operator
            get operand1, the top element from the stack
            pop the stack
            get operand2, the top element from the stack
            pop the stack
            case depending upon the operator
                case operator = +
                    result = operand2 + operand1
                case operator = -
                    result = operand2 - operand1
                case operator = *
                    result = operand2 * operand1
                case operator = /
                    result = operand2 / operand1
            end case
            push the result on to the stack
    end case
end for
output the top element on the stack
```

Figure 8.20   *Evaluating a post-fix expression: an algorithm*

Assignment 8

(1) Using the programming language in which you will implement your compiler, write a program to evaluate post-fix expressions.
Use your program to check your answers to the Questions (9) to (12) earlier in this chapter.

(2) Using this program as a basis, write a routine for your compiler which will evaluate post-fix expressions.

(3) Modify the design for your compiler so that a standard routine for evaluating post-fix expressions is called each time an arithmetic expression is to be evaluated.

Producing the object code

The most significant part of the compiler's work is that of producing object code from the information gathered during the syntax analysis.

If you look back at the work which we did on macros, you will have realized that the task of generating a piece of object code from a string of parameters is fairly straightforward.

For example, you wrote a macro called FETCH which allowed an assembly language programmer writing programs for the SGO1 processor to write a statement such as:

FETCH 5

and the assembler would convert this macro to the assembly language instructions:

INPUT
IN 5

with the effect of accepting a value into the input register and then moving this to storage address 5. When we look at a Basic statement such as:

INPUT FRED

we can find the address at which the variable FRED is stored (let us call this address ffff) and immediately generate the assembly language instructions:

INPUT
IN ffff

Questions

17 Transform the following Basic statements into sequences of assembly language statements and macro statements for the SG01 (or the SG02) processor. You can ignore the restrictions imposed by the processors, such as the fact that there are only five data stores and we can only handle integers.

Assume that A is held in data store 1, B in data store 2, and C in data store 3.

(a) LET A = B
(b) A = B * C

(c) A = A * B * C
(d) INPUT A, B, C
(e) PRINT A

18 Transform the following Basic statements into sequences of assembly language statements and macro statements for the SG01 (or the SG02) processor, and then transform these into machine code instructions. As before, you can ignore the restrictions imposed by the processors, such as the fact that there are only five data stores and we can only handle integers.

Assume that A is held in data store 1, B in data store 2, and C in data store 3.

(a) IF A = B THEN A = 0
(b) IF B > C THEN STOP
(c) GO 20
(d) INPUT A,B
     IF B = C THEN PRINT B
     STOP

A better solution would be for the Basic compiler to produce a set of *machine language* instructions, op-codes and operands, so that the Basic statement, the source code:

INPUT A

would be transformed into the object code:

P
Q 1

One reason for this is that if our compiler produced an assembly language program, this would have to be assembled into machine code before it could be used.

Assignment 9

(1) Produce a set of transformations by which each basic sequence shown in Questions 17 and 18 can be converted into machine code for the SG01 processor.
(2) Produce a similar set of transformations by which the

statements of your language can be converted into the correct object code for your compiler.

Labels

We have completely ignored the use of statement labels in the Basic program and the previous solutions left the destinations of any jump statements unresolved. In order to handle explicit statement labels, such as those of statements such as:

GO 200

and the internal labels which we needed to use in order to handle comparisons and which we showed as:

JUMPGT [4]

the compiler must construct a program map which is built up – byte by byte – as each Basic statement is transformed. But in order to be able to do this, our compiler must transform the Basic statements into *object code* instructions, op-codes and operands.

Thus, the Basic program:

INPUT A,B
IF A = B THEN PRINT B
STOP

which we transformed into the macro/assembly language sequence:

        FETCH 1
        FETCH 2
        COMPARE 1 2
        JUMPEQ [6]
        JUMP [7]
    [6] WRITE 2
    [7] STOP

would be finally transformed into the machine code sequence:

        P
        Q 1
        P
        Q 2
        A 2 A

```
      A 3 B
      I
      K [6]    we do not yet know the address [6]
      M [7]    we do not yet know the address [7]
 [6]  N 2
      O
 [7]  R
```

Now that we know the actual contents of the program, we could use this information to produce a program map. This is done in very much the same way that we produced a storage map by considering the variables. When all the machine code instruction have been laid out, one op-code per byte and one operand per byte, it is a simple matter to resolve the addresses [6] and [7], replacing the dummy values by the actual storage address. The resulting program map is shown in Figure 8.21.

Assignment 10

(1) You should now have a fairly detailed design for your compiler. You should refine your design, imposing (and documenting) any restrictions on the format of the source language statements.

(2) If you have access to the machine code (or even the assembly language or any other language) of a real computer, then you should attempt to implement all or a part of your compiler there. If there is no such machine available to you, then assume that your programs are going to be compiled for use on the SG02 processor.

   If you intend to implement the evaluation of arithmetic expressions on the SG02 processor, you may simplify your task by assuming that the processor has machine code instructions which will perform addition, subtraction, multiplication and division.

Scope-checking

Depending upon the source language which it will handle, the compiler may have to make other checks. Typical of these is the task of checking the **scope** of variables. In Chapter 5, we mentioned the subject of scope

Address	Contents
0	P
1	Q
2	1
3	P
4	Q
5	2
6	A
7	2
8	A
9	A
10	3
11	B
12	I
13	K
14	to [6]
15	M
16	to [7]
17	[6] N
18	2
19	O
20	[7] R

(a) before resolving the addresses

Address	Contents
0	P
1	Q
2	1
3	P
4	Q
5	2
6	A
7	2
8	A
9	A
10	3
11	B
12	I
13	K
14	17
15	M
16	20
17	N
18	2
19	O
20	R

(b) after resolving the addresses

Figure 8.21   *Program map*

in block-structured languages such as Algol and Pascal. As a consequence of the scope, the compiler must also check that each variable used in the program is *in scope* and can be accessed from the block where it is used. In practice, this is done by building up a stack of the variables which are declared. As a new variable is declared, it is added to the top of the stack and when the block comes to an end, the local variables are popped from the stack. If there is a conflict between a local variable and a global variable, then the most recent one (the local variable) will be nearer to the top of the stack and this will be used when required in the processing.

This is illustrated in Figure 8.22 where we show the contents of the scope stack for a Pascal program. We have only shown the *var* statements which declare the variables. To the right of the diagram, we

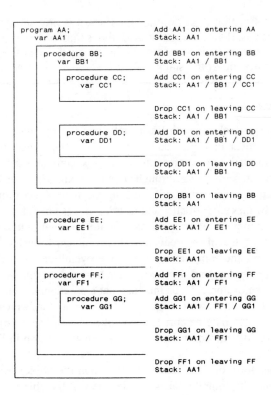

Figure 8.22 *Scope checking in a Pascal program*

show the progress of the scope stack. We imagine that the top of the stack is to the right of the diagram.

You may be interested to compare this illustration with that in Figure 5.32 which shows the same program AA and the variables which are in scope at each point in the program. You will observe that the contents of the scope stack (Figure 8.22) and the list of variables which are in scope at each point in the program are the same.

Activity 3

Look at the program MAIN which is shown in Figure 5.33 (page 252) and produce a diagram similar to that in Figure 8.22 which indicates the progress of the scope stack as MAIN is compiled.

Remember that the compiler must resolve any situations where a variable is defined locally and the same name is used for a global variable. This is achieved by using the variable which is nearer to the top of the stack.

Optimization

Our compiler looks at each Basic statement in turn and translates this into a fragment of object code. Finally, the fragments are collected together to produce the object program. Most commercial compilers do more than this by going through a process known as **optimization**. Optimization is concerned with making the final object program more efficient by making it smaller and faster, if this is possible.

Some compilers attempt to modify the original **source program** statements so that they produce a more efficient form for translation. This requires the compiler to look at the overall effect of a particular piece of processing and then reorganize this into a form which is more efficient. For example, let us imagine that a programmer has written the fragment of code shown in Figure 8.23 (a). A compiler which optimizes the source code may be able to recognize what is happening and reorganize this into the equivalent source statements shown in Figure 8.23 (b).

Another form of optimization works upon the **object code**. As this takes place, the compiler takes a wider view of the object program and looks at the fragments produced by the translation process to see how they fit together as a whole.

```
PRINT "START OF PROGRAM"
X=0
Y=0
X=1
Y=10
FOR K = X TO Y
        PRINT K
NEXT K
X=0
Y=999
```

(a) The original source statements

```
PRINT "START OF PROGRAM"
FOR K = 1 TO 10
        PRINT K
NEXT K
X=0
Y=999
```

(b) the optimized source statements

Figure 8.23 *Optimization of the source code*

Recap

- The main functions of a compiler are to read the statements of an object program and use these to produce an equivalent set of statements for the object program.
- The first stage of compilation is the lexical analysis where the individual symbols of the program are identified. These are used to construct a number of tables for use by the compiler: the symbol table, showing the name, type and storage address of each variable and constant in the program; the constant table, showing the nature and contents of the constants used in the program; the array table, showing the nature and size of the arrays used in the program.
- The next stage is the syntax analysis when the program instructions are converted into object code. This uses the information held in the compiler's tables.
- Arithmetic expressions written in conventional in-fix notation are converted to post-fix notation for ease of processing by the operations which are available on most processors.
- Some compilers perform an optimization phase, during which the final fragments of object code for the source language statements are assembled into the object program. This attempts to produce a more efficient version of the object code.

Answers to assignments

Suggested solution to Assignment 1

- Compiler : version 2
- Read the source program from backing storage
- Report any syntax errors
- Generate the object program
  if there are no errors
  then
- write the object program to backing storage
  end if

Suggested solution to Assignment 2

- Compiler : version 3
- Read the source program from backing storage

- Analyse the source code according to delimiting symbols
- Produce list of symbols used
- Report any syntax errors
- Generate the object program
  if there are no errors
  then
- write the object program to backing storage
  end if

Suggested solution to Assignment 3

- Compiler : version 4
- Read the source program from backing storage
- Analyse the source code according to delimiting symbols
- Produce list of symbols used
  for each symbol
- Create an entry in the symbol table
- Create an entry in the constant table
- Create an entry in the array table
  end for
- Report any syntax errors
- Generate the object program
  if there are no errors
  then
- write the object program to backing storage
  end if

Answers to questions

1 The space, the comma, the colon, the semi-colon and the full-stop. They indicate the end of words (the space and the comma), the end of statements (the semi-colon), and the end of the program (the full-stop). You might also have said that:

    =
    :=
    *

were delimiters since they separate one symbol from another.

2 The type tells the compiler indirectly how much space to allocate: an integer occupies four bytes, a real number occupies four bytes, a long floating point number occupies 8 bytes, and so on. As we saw in Chapter 3, the ways in which strings are

held depends upon the language, the compiler and the run-time processor. We shall assume that strings are held as a four-byte field and that the run-time processor handles the situation when a string is longer than four bytes.

3 See Figure 8.24. Note that we have assumed that a Boolean variable occupies just one byte.

4 See Figure 8.25.

Name	Type	Class	Detail	Address
multiplier	real	constant	10.5	0
pi	real	constant	3.14159	4
result	real	variable		8
first	real	variable		12
second	real	variable		16
counter	integer	variable		20
counter2	integer	variable		24
flag	boolean	variable		28
finished	boolean	variable		29

(a) the symbol table

Address	Contents
0 1 2 3	multiplier
4 5 6 7	pi
8 9 10 11	result
12 13 14 15	first
16 17 18 19	second
20 21 22 23	counter
24 25 26 27	counter2
28	flag
28	finished

(b) the storage map

Figure 8.24 *Symbol and constant tables for multiply*

369

Name	Type	Class	Detail	Address
X	number	variable		0
	number	constant	1	4
	number	constant	2	8
SQUARE	number	variable		12
CUBE	number	variable		16

(a) the symbol table

Ref	Type	Length	Value
1	number	4	1
2	number	4	10

(b) the constant table

Address	Contents
0 1 2 3	X
4 5 6 7	constant
8 9 10 11	constant
12 13 14 15	SQUARE
16 17 18 19	CUBE

(c) the storage map

Figure 8.25 *Tables and map for Basic program 1*

5 See Figure 8.26. We leave you to draw your own version of the storage map.

In this solution, each variable occupies four bytes; each string constant occupies as much space as it needs (I've represented a space by the _ character); the reference to the SQRT function occupies four bytes.

6 The number of elements in shown in the array table, and the type indicates the length of each element.

7 See Figure 8.27.

8 See Figure 8.28. We have not shown the entire string for the MSG$ variables.

9 23 * 34 + 56

(23 * 34) + 56

Name	Type	Class	Detail	Address
MSG$	string	variable		0
	string	constant	1	4
NAME$	string	variable		21
	string	constant	2	25
X	number	variable		26
	string	constant	3	30
	string	constant	4	34
ROOT	number	variable		38
SQRT	number	function		42
SQUARE	number	variable		46
CUBE	number	variable		50
MSG2$	string	variable		54
	string	constant	5	58
	string	constant	6	68
RESP$	string	variable		70
	string	constant	7	74

(a) the symbol table

Ref	Type	Length	Value
1	string	17	What_is_your_name
2	string	1	N
3	number	4	1
4	number	4	10
5	string	10	Any_more,_
6	string	2	?_
7	string	1	Y

(b) the constant table

Figure 8.26   *Tables for Basic program 2*

$(23 * 34) 56 +$
$23\ 34 * 56 +$
Result: 838

10 $12 * 34 + 56 - 78$
$((12 * 34) + 56) - 78$
$((12 * 34) + 56)\ 78 -$
$((12 * 34)\ 56 + 78 -$
$12\ 34 * 56 + 78 -$
Result: 386

11 $98 * (87 + 76) - 65$
$(98 * (87 + 76)) - 65$
$(98 * (87 + 76))\ 65 -$
$98\ (87 + 76) * 65 -$
$96\ 87\ 76 + * 65 -$
Result: 15909

12 $12 + 34 \qquad 45 * 56$

$$\frac{}{87 - 65}\ *\ \frac{}{98 - 11}$$

$((12 + 34) / (87 - 65)) * ((45 * 56) / (98 - 11))$

371

Name	Type	Class	Detail	Address
VALUES	array	variable	1	0
X	number	variable		40
Y	number	variable		44
MSG2$	string	variable		48
RESP$	string	·variable		52

(a) the symbol table

Ref	Index type	Element type	Ref	Lower subscript	Upper subscript
1	number	array		1	10

(b) the array table

Figure 8.27 Tables for Basic program 3

Name	Type	Class	Detail	Address
VALUES	array	variable	1	0
NAMES$	array	variable	2	40
MSG1$	string	variable		440
	string	constant	1	444
MSG2$	string	variable		466
	string	constant	2	470
MSG3$	string	variable		496
	string	constant	3	500
X	number	variable		513
	string	constant	4	517
	string	constant	5	521
	string	constant	6	525
Y	number	variable		529
	string	constant	7	533
	string	constant	8	537

(a) symbol table entry for an array

Ref	Type	Length	Value
1	string	22	Enter name of student_
2	string	26	Enter details for student_
3	string	13	_ for student
4	number	4	1
5	number	4	10
6	number	4	5
7	number	4	2
8	number	4	20

(b) the constant table

Ref	Index type	Element type	Ref	Lower subscript	Upper subscript
1	number	number		1	10
2	number	array	3	1	5
3	number	number		1	20

(c) the array table

Figure 8.28 Tables for Basic program 4

```
((12 + 34) / (87 − 65))    ((45 * 56) / (98 − 11)) *
((12 + 34)    (87 − 65) / ) ((45 * 56) / (98 − 11)) *
((12 + 34)    (87 − 65) / ) ((45 * 56)    (98 − 11) / ) *
(12 34 +      (87 − 65) / )  ((45 * 56)    (98 − 11) / ) *
(12 34 +      87 65 / )      ((45 * 56)    (98 − 11) / ) *
(12 34 +      87 65 − / )    (45 56 *      −98 11 − / ) *
12 34 +       87 65 − /      45 56 *       98 11 −   / *
12 34 +       87 65 − /      45 56 * 98 11 − / *
```
Result: 60.564

13 See Figure 8.29 (a).
14 See Figure 8.29 (b).
15 See Figure 8.29 (c).
16 See Figure 8.29 (d).

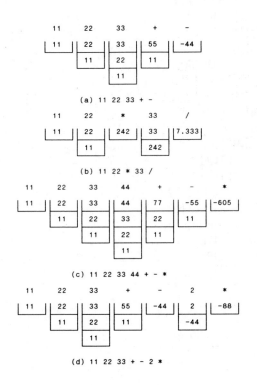

Figure 8.29 *Elaboration of post-fix expressions*

17   Your answers should be:

    (a) MOVE 1 2

    (b) MULTIPLY 2 3 1

    (c) MULTIPLY 1 2 99

        MULTIPLY 3 99 99

        MOVE 99 1

    (d) FETCH 1

        FETCH 2

        FETCH 3

    (e) WRITE 1

18   In these solutions we have not yet resolved the addresses which are to be the destination of the jump statements.

    (a)   COMPARE 1 2

            JUMPEQ [4]

            JUMP [5]

       [4] PUT 0 1

       [5]

    (b)   COMPARE 2 3

            JUMPGT [4]

            JUMP [5]

       [4] STOP

       [5]

    (c) JUMP [20]

    (d)   FETCH 1

            FETCH 2

            COMPARE 23

            JUMPEQ [6]

            JUMP [7]

       [6] WRITE 2

       [7] STOP

9:   Applying languages: commercial

Objectives

After reading this chapter, you should be able to:

- Distinguish between a **procedural** and a **non-procedural** language.
- Describe the features of a **report program generator**.
- Describe the features of a **program generator**.
- Distinguish between **data manipulation language, data description language**, and **data control language**.
- Describe the general features, the advantages and disadvantages of **enquiry languages**.
- Describe the principal features of some of the languages which are associated with databases: SQL; dBASE; QBE.
- Write the instructions necessary to handle data and produce reports in these enquiry languages.
- Describe some of the features of a **fourth generation language**.
- Describe the concept of **prototyping**.

A friend has just telephoned to ask how she can reach your house. You tell her:

(1)   Go along the M62 until you reach junction 24.
(2)   Turn off on to the A644 and follow the signs for Bingford.
(3)   At the second roundabout, take the first exit on to the A6401.
(4)   Take the second turning on the right into Wishley Avenue.
(5)   My house is the third on the left.

But the directions need not be given in this imperative manner. You could tell your friend your address, send her a map of the area and let her work out her own way to your house.

The first set of directions is called a **procedural** description, the second is a **non-procedural** description.

Activity 1

Describe some advantages of the map, as compared with the specific directions.
Describe some disadvantages of the map, as compared with the specific directions.

Procedural or non-procedural languages?

The non-procedural description has certain advantages: your friend might not have a car and she can easily work out (or ask about) the bus routes to reach your house, or find a route on her bicycle; she may have a car but she might not like driving on the motorway, so the map will show her the alternative routes; the M62 may be closed at junction 24, again the map will show her any alternative routes.

The non-procedural description has certain disadvantages: you cannot get a map to your friend immediately (unless she has a fax or her own map); your friend may not be very good at following maps, whereas she might easily follow your procedural directions.

All the programming languages that we have considered up to this point have been procedural languages or **imperative languages**. To write a program in an imperative language, the programmer presents a series of instructions to the computer and these are executed one by one. But it is now being increasingly more common to meet non-procedural programming languages.

When she is using a (non-procedural) map, your friend may reach a T-junction in the road; she will then look to see whether your house is to the left or to the right and then turn the car in that direction. In the same way, a non-procedural programming language can realize that if you want to update a record then it must first read the record from the file; if you have created a new record, then it will realize that you will want to write the record away to the file.

In this chapter, we shall look at some of the non-procedural languages which are available, paying particular attention to the needs of the ordinary commercial organization. Most of these languages allow facilities for the programmer to include procedural sections, for those special pieces of processing that the computer cannot guess.

We shall start by looking at the development of software tools beyond the third generation languages that we met back in Chapter 2. In the following chapter, we shall look at some non-procedural languages which are available for specialized applications. In the final chapter, we shall look at other models which can be used a basis for the design of a computer language.

Even before software

Report production is probably a most common requirement of any commercial computer application. In the late 1950s there were a great many pieces of equipment which were specially designed to handle and produce reports about data held on *punched cards*. These machines included:

- **Sorters** which sorted a deck of punched cards into sequence. The operator usually set a number of switches to indicate which column of the cards was to be used for each sort. For example, if we wished to sort a deck of cards according to the name which is punched in columns 5 to 25, the cards would first be sorted by the character in each column in turn.
- **Tabulators** which read a deck of punched cards and produced a printed report showing the contents of the cards. Tabulators were controlled by a **plug board**; this had a set of holes along the top, one hole for each of the columns in the card, and a row of holes down the side, one hole for each column of the printer. The operator moved around a large number of wires to connect the appropriate holes to indicate which column of each card was to be shown in which column of the printed report. Some tabulation equipment had facilities for accumulating and printing totals as the report was produced.

These pieces of equipment were **off-line**, that is, they were not connected to a computer but were controlled electro-mechanically by the operator. In fact, many companies did not use a computer at all, but simply punched their data into cards and then used a range of off-line equipment to handle the data.

Report program generators

In the early 1960s, when the move was made to electronic computers controlled by stored programs, many businesses still required the computer to produce the same sorts of reports that they had used and were familiar with before the computer arrived. For this reason, **report generators** and **report program generators** were amongst the first utility software to appear. The eponymous RPG (Report Program Generator) itself was developed by IBM in 1964, and went through several generations RPG II (in the mid-1960s) and RPG III (in 1980). It is now available on many ranges of computers (including desktop and PC systems) from a variety of manufacturers. The current version RPG/400 was introduced in 1989 for use on the IBM AS/400 computer system. This latest version finally broke away from the traditional punched card orientation which has always been a part of the RPG philosophy.

Report generators accept the analyst's specifications, and use these to produce a printed report. The RPG programmer uses a set of up to seven **specification sheets** to define a report. Each sheet may contain one or more lines of information, and the lines on each sheet are identified by a letter in column 6 which indicates the **form type**. Some simplified examples are shown in Figure 9.1.

The purpose of this RPG program is to take a series of disk records of the format shown in Figure 9.2 (a) and produce a printed report of the format shown in Figure 9.2 (b).

The following specifications are used to produce this report:

(1) In diagram (a), the first sheet contains the control specifications (identified by the *form type* H in column 6) and provides general information about the program and the computer system on which it is to run. We have omitted all the information and taken the defaults which the RPG system offers.

   The first four columns contain a sequence number for that part of the specification. This is a relic of the days when decks of punched cards were occasionally dropped and mixed up.

(2) In diagram (b), the file description specifications (form type F) describe each file which is used in the program, the format and size of the physical records, and the input/output device where the file is to be used.

   Our example illustrates how an asterisk in column 7 marks a line as a comment.

(3) The extension specifications (form type E) describe any data structures – such as arrays and tables – which are to be used in the program. Our example does not use any extension specifications.

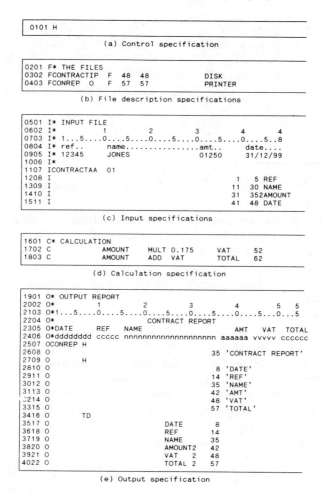

```
  0101 H
```
(a) Control specification

```
  0201 F* THE FILES
  0302 FCONTRACTIP  F  48  48           DISK
  0403 FCONREP   O  F  57  57           PRINTER
```
(b) File description specifications

```
  0501 I* INPUT FILE
  0602 I*        1        2        3        4        4
  0703 I* 1...5....0....5....0....5....0....5....0....5..8
  0804 I* ref..     name...............amt..     date....
  0905 I* 12345     JONES              01250      31/12/99
  1006 I*
  1107 ICONTRACTAA  01
  1208 I                                   1    5 REF
  1309 I                                  11   30 NAME
  1410 I                                  31  352AMOUNT
  1511 I                                  41   48 DATE
```
(c) Input specifications

```
  1601 C* CALCULATION
  1702 C          AMOUNT    MULT 0.175   VAT    52
  1803 C          AMOUNT    ADD  VAT     TOTAL  62
```
(d) Calculation specification

```
  1901 O* OUTPUT REPORT
  2002 O*        1        2        3        4      5    5
  2103 O*1...5....0....5....0....5....0....5....0....5...5
  2204 O*              CONTRACT REPORT
  2305 O*DATE   REF   NAME              AMT   VAT  TOTAL
  2406 O*dddddddd ccccc nnnnnnnnnnnnnnnnnnnnn aaaaaa vvvvv cccccc
  2507 OCONREP H
  2608 O                             35 'CONTRACT REPORT'
  2709 O        H
  2810 O                              8 'DATE'
  2911 O                             14 'REF'
  3012 O                             35 'NAME'
  3113 O                             42 'AMT'
  3214 O                             48 'VAT'
  3315 O                             57 'TOTAL'
  3416 O        TD
  3517 O              DATE           8
  3618 O              REF           14
  3719 O              NAME          35
  3820 O              AMOUNT2       42
  3921 O              VAT    2      48
  4022 O              TOTAL  2      57
```
(e) Output specification

Figure 9.1 *An RPG program*

(4) The line counter specification (form type L) is used if a printed report is to be produced on stationery of a special size or format. Our example is to produce its report on standard paper and does not use any line counter specification.

(5) In diagram (c), the input specifications (form type I) describes the records of each input file which is used by the program. For each field of the record, there will be a line indicating the position of that field within the record (shown as the start and end positions of

379

```
  12345      JONES            01250    31/12/99
  34567      WILKINSON        10075    01/12/99
  19283      HARRISON         05500    02/12/99
```

(a) the input disk records

```
                    CONTRACT REPORT
  DATE      REF   NAME                   AMT     VAT    TOTAL

  31/12/99 12345 JONES                  12.50   2.19   14.69
  01/12/99 34567 WILKINSON             100.75  17.63  118.38
  02/12/99 19283 HARRISON               55.00   9.63   64.63
```

(b) the printed report

Figure 9.2   *An RPG program in action*

that piece of data), the number of decimal places (2 places of decimals for the AMOUNT) and a field name which is used to identify
that field in the RPG program.

   We have added comments to show the format of the input
records. Only those fields which are used by the program need be
defined.

(6) In diagram (d), the calculation specification (form type C)
     describes the processing which is to be performed upon the data.
     This includes all totals, calculations, logic and data movement.
     The final element on each line shows the width of each field and
     the number of decimal places (2 in every case).

(7) In diagram (e), the output specification (form type O) describes the
     layout of the output report which is to be produced by the pro-
     gram. The programmer declares the (left-most) positions of the
     fields and text which are to appear on the report.

These parameters may then be saved and submitted to the report generator whenever the report is required.

Activity 2

Compare the use of RPG to produce the report shown in Figure
9.2 with the use of a language such as Cobol or Basic to perform
the same task.

   The RPG specification takes about 300 characters of information. Which requires more information, RPG or your program?

   The user wishes to change the system handled by the RPG
report shown here. A new field, the credit limit, has been added;
this is to have two places of decimals and starts in position 49 of

the disk records, as illustrated in Figure 9.3 (a). The format of the report is to be changed so that it looks like that in Figure 9.3 (b).

```
12345      JONES              01250      31/12/99100000
34567      WILKINSON          10075      01/12/99150000
19283      HARRISON           05500      02/12/99075000
```

(a) the input disk records

```
                    CONTRACT REPORT
\RULER            L
DATE      REF     NAME                 AMT    VAT   TOTAL   CREDIT
                                                            LIMIT
31/12/99 12345 JONES                 12.50   2.19  14.69  1000.00
01/12/99 34567 WILKINSON            100.75  17.63 118.38  1500.00
02/12/99 19283 HARRISON             55.00   9.63  64.63   750.00
```

(b) the printed report

Figure 9.3 *An RPG program in change*

Modify the RPG specification to do this. Make reasonable guesses as to which parts of the specification should be changed, and how.

Which is more flexible and easier to change, RPG or your program?

A system such as RPG avoids the need for the programmer to write his/her programs in a language such as Cobol or Pascal. All the processing is done by the RPG processor; whenever this particular report is to be produced, the RPG processor reads the set of specifications and uses these to produce the required output. There is no intermediate code produced, such as a Cobol or assembler version of a program.

Obviously, the main concern of RPG is in the production of printed reports. It is much more difficult to perform complicated processing and file updates using such a medium.

Program generators

In contrast, a **program generator** – or a **code generator** – is a software package which will accept the analyst's specifications written in some simplified intermediate language and then use these to produce a Cobol source program (or some other language) which will meet those specifications. The advantage of using a program generator is that it allows the flexibility of a normal programming language, but it removes much of the tedious part of program coding.

Any typical commercial application contains a similar set of OPEN, READ, WRITE and CLOSE statements, and a programmer spends a considerable amount of his/her time in writing statements which are similar, if not identical, to those which he/she has written earlier. For example, Fortran statements such as:

    WRITE(6,100) GROSS,NETT,TAX
 100 FORMAT(F10.2)

could be used to display the contents of the three variables on the screen and a sequence such as this will occur many times in a typical program. The WRITE statement specifies the variables whose contents are to be displayed and the FORMAT statement specifies the manner in which each numbers is to be displayed. The programmer has to concentrate carefully upon the syntax, and any missing commas or brackets will cause the compilation to fail. It would be much easier for the programmer to write a statement such as:

    PRINT 100 GROSS NETT TAX

which we might call a **meta-statement**, and submit this to a preprocessing program, or a program generator. Another program generator might be more powerful and able to transform the meta-statement:

    $WRITE GROSS NETT TAX 10.2

into the Fortran statements:

    WRITE(6,100) GROSS,NETT,TAX
 100 FORMAT(F10.2)

or it might transform the more complicated meta-statement:

    $WRITE GROSS 10.2 NETT 9.2 TAX 8.2

into the Fortran statements:

    WRITE(6,200) GROSS,NETT,TAX
 200 FORMAT(F10.2, F9.2, F8.2)

A typical program generator will accept a sequence of these meta-statements and use these to generate the equivalent statements in a third generation language, Fortran in our example. The resultant Fortran

382

source program can then be compiled, tested and debugged in the traditional manner.

Activity 3

(1) Compare and contrast the action of a program generator, such as we have outlined here, with the work done by a compiler.

(2) I want you to consider any of the programming languages which you have used and write down some of the statements which cause you most trouble when you are writing a program. For example, you should include statements where you:

- frequently forget to put commas and other punctuation;
- frequently forget to put brackets.

For each of these statements, write down a meta-statement which a program generator could transform into a valid statement.

In your own words, write down the rules for transforming your meta-statements into the correct form.

Partial action of a program generator

Some program generators are able to remove much of the programming effort and create a program from the analyst's program specification and allow the programmer to concentrate upon the more complicated logic and the calculations of the program. This speeds up program development. In most cases, the generated code may well be more efficient than equivalent coding produced by a programmer. This is particularly true if the programmer is inexperienced.

Some generators take just a part of the application – specific statements, the screen formats or the file input-output – and produce a set of source language statements or a routine to perform that specific task. The programmer can then **fill in the gaps** to produce the required program.

As these generators become more elaborate and more powerful and cater more to the needs of the final application program, they enter the grey area between simple utility software and fourth generation languages.

Activity 4

(1) Draw a box diagram showing the various steps which are taken when you create, amend, compile, test and execute a Basic program.

(2) Amend the diagram to show how a program generator might be used to generate the Basic program from a set of specifications produced by the programmer.

(3) In your own words, write down some of the advantages and some of the disadvantages of using a tool such as a program generator to produce programs, as compared to the use of a third generation language like Cobol or Pascal, when you are producing a computer program. Who gains from the advantages? Who loses as a result of the disadvantages?

As more and more data is held on computers, and more and more people need to be able to enquire and produce reports about such data, there has grown up a need for non-technical people to be able to produce their own reports . . . and with a minimum of effort.

RPG, Cobol, Basic, program generators and the other tools are satisfactory for trained and skilled programmers, but what about clerks, managers, accountants . . . people whose main concern is analysing statistics, producing reports and figures? They are not trained, nor do they have the time to train, as specialist computer programmers. How can they make use of the database?

Databases

As we discuss in the companion Students' Guide To Data-bases, a database can be defined as a collection of data which is organized such that each piece of data is accessible to those users who need it, inaccessible (or invisible) to those who do not need it, and such that each piece of data is held with minimal duplication. This last point really means that each piece of data is held in only one place; if this is not so, then there will be problems in ensuring the accuracy and integrity of the data held on the database. For example, what happens if an employee's address is held on several files? If the employee moves house, can we be sure that all the occurrences of his/her address are amended correctly?

There are many ways of organizing a database, and there is a corresponding variety of ways of handling the data and many languages for talking to and interrogating the database.

Database languages

We should first point out that most software for handling databases are divided into three parts: a **data manipulation language** (usually abbreviated to **DML**) which contains all the components which are necessary for manipulating the data on the database; a **data description language** or **data definition language** (the **DDL**) which the database administrator and the systems analysts use to declare the structure of the data within the database and to control access to the data; and finally, an **enquiry language** or a **query language** which is the means whereby the end-user is able to produce reports and handle enquiries about the database. There may even be a further **data control language** (the **DCL**) to allow the security features of the database, such as passwords and access permission, to be set and controlled.

Enquiry languages

In the following sections, we shall look at some of the most popular enquiry languages: SQL, dBASE and QBE.

Whatever the precise nature of the enquiry language, in general, they offer a realistic and cost-effective way of producing reports and making enquiries.

A number of common features are offered by the various enquiry languages which are available:

- They will produce printed or displayed reports. Some even offer facilities for producing spreadsheets and graphical output such as graphs and charts.
- You may specify which fields of the records are to appear on each report: one user may want a staff report showing the name and the telephone number; another user may want a report showing the department, name, salary and holiday allowance.
- The information in a report can be sorted into a specified order: the information in a staff report may be sorted into departments, then within the each department, the report may be sorted into order of

385

the employees' surnames, then, if there are several employees with the same name, these may be further sorted by initials.

- You may request that only specific values are to be included within the report: you may want a staff report for only those people who work in the RESEARCH department; you may want to know the names and details of all employees who earn more than £30,000 per year.
- Totals, averages, maximum and minimum values for numeric fields may be calculated and output in the report.
- Information in the report can be derived from one or more pieces of data on the file: the weekly pay can be derived from the annual salary by dividing by 52; the selling price of a stock item may be calculated by adding a standard 17.5% to the cost which is held on the file.

Indeed, in some environments, the enquiry language may be sufficiently powerful that an application programmer need never again write a report program.

For any special requirements which cannot be handled by the enquiry language, it may be worth the system analyst's talking the user into accepting something which can be produced much more easily and more cheaply by the standard enquiry language software, rather than going to all the time and expense of specifying, writing and testing a bespoke program in a language such as Cobol or Basic.

So let us have a look at some of the pros and cons of enquiry languages.

- In general, enquiry languages are quick and simple to use.
- They provide a facility whereby the end-user may interrogate the database directly.
- They can be learned quickly by anyone who is familiar with the sort of business problems to which they offer solutions.

This is an important point: the end-users can produce their own results without any dilution of ideas as they would be if the requirements had to be specified and interpreted by intermediate analysts and programmers.

The languages offer a number of advantages:

- They are flexible in the layout and content of the reports.
- They may be appropriate for both *ad hoc* enquiries and longer regular reports.

- They allow enquiries to be developed and made more quickly and without the long gestation period which is necessary when writing a standard program in a language such as Cobol or Basic.
- They are easier to use than a report generator or a third generation language, such as Cobol or Basic. A typical enquiry can often be specified in one line of typed input.
- If a user makes a mistake in the syntax or the logic of an enquiry, the error will be detected and immediately rejected by the processor.
- They allow a process of trial and error in the enquiry. If a user finds that a particular enquiry produces a large volume of output, then it may be reworded to reduce the size of the report.

A further advantage is that an enquiry language may be used as a **prototyping tool** for developing a standard report program. The users can play around with the language until they have derived the sort of report which they want and this can then be used as a model – the **prototype** – to specify their requirements and be rewritten as a Basic or Cobol program. If the language itself is suitably efficient, then the enquiry can be included as a standard part of the application system. We can discuss the technique of prototyping later when we look at fourth generation programming languages.

However, there may be some drawbacks in using certain enquiry languages:

- In some cases, enquiry languages are used only for making enquiries on the contents of the database – for data retrieval. Standard programs still have to be provided to update and maintain the data. The languages which shall consider here **do** offer facilities for creating, changing and deleting data from the files.
- They may make considerable demands on the design of the database, imposing constraints upon the nature and the relationships within the data which they will handle.
- They may demand that data be held in certain formats. For example, a date which is to be accessible by means of an enquiry language may have to be held in a meaningful form such as 01/12/91 or 011291 or 911201 instead of a more efficient internal or compacted form. In turn, this restriction will impose constraints upon the ways in which the data can be used and presented on the output reports.
- They may require considerable support from the standard programs which are written to update the database, requiring the programs to

387

establish and maintain entry points and other links within the database.

- If users are unfamiliar with the structure of the data, they may make inappropriate demands with their enquiries, causing the language to be inefficient when answering the enquiry, thereby wasting time, degrading the performance of the system and incurring expense.

- They may jeopardize the integrity of the database and put the security of the data at risk or demand additional security checks to be provided and maintained as the data is accessed.

As enquiry languages continue to increase in popularity, it is likely that many of these shortcomings will be removed.

Activity 5

Make a list of the sort of businesses which could benefit from the use of an enquiry language on their computer system.

Describe the sort of reports that they may wish to produce.

Would there be any disadvantages in using an enquiry language?

What would they be?

SQL

SQL was originally designed and implemented by IBM under the name SEQUEL – Structured English QUEry Language – and variations of SQL are now available on many commercial database management systems.

It is possible to use SQL as an enquiry language in its own right, and it is also possible to embed SQL commands within a **host language** such as C, Cobol, Pascal or PL/1. The SQL commands are usually distinguished from the statements of the host language by preceding them with some identifier, such as a special character or a keyword.

SQL allows us to visualize the data of our database as if it were held in a set of tables or columnar reports: data which can be thought of like this is known as a **relational database**. SQL uses the terms **table, row** and **column** where other data processing environments use the terms file, record and field.

To illustrate the use of SQL, let us start by creating a table with the name FURNITURE. To do this, we use the SQL CREATE TABLE command, as shown in Figure 9.4 (a). Imagine that the data in the table relates to the furniture which is currently sold by a chain of furniture retailers and shows the details of the stock at the various stores throughout the country. The CREATE TABLE command describes the nature and the format of the columns of our table. The names, such as FURNITURE, CODE and DESCRIPTION, are defined here and they then be used in SQL enquiries. It doesn't matter how you arrange an SQL command when you type it in. For clarity, we have laid out our examples with the various parts on separate lines.

```
CREATE TABLE FURNITURE (
    CODE CHAR(4) NOT NULL,
    DESCRIPTION CHAR(11),
    STOCK INTEGER,
    LOCATION CHAR(10),
    PRICE DECIMAL(6,2),
    MINIMUM INTEGER,
    MOVED CHAR(6) )

          (a) creating an SQL table

INSERT INTO FURNITURE (
    '4567',
    'BOOKCASE',
    '25',
    'SWINDON'
    '250.00',
    '10',
    '910729' )

      (b) inserting a row into a table

UPDATE FURNITURE
    SET PRICE = PRICE * 1.2

     (c) changing the price of all rows

UPDATE FURNITURE
    SET PRICE = PRICE * 1.2
    WHERE CODE = '4567'

    (d) changing the price of just one row

UPDATE FURNITURE
    SET PRICE = PRICE * 1.2
    WHERE LOCATION = 'SWINDON' AND PRICE < '200.00'

   (e) changing the price of selected rows

DELETE FROM FURNITURE
    WHERE CODE = '1234'

        (f) deleting a specific row
```

Figure 9.4   *SQL: manipulating a table*

Having created the table, SQL lets us use INSERT, UPDATE and DELETE commands for data manipulation. For example, to add a new row to the FURNITURE table, we would issue the command shown in Figure 9.4 (b). Note the form in which the date, the 29th July 1991, is entered.

To update *all* the FURNITURE rows, increasing the price by 20%, we could issue the command shown in Figure 9.4 (c), or we could update specific rows by commands such as those shown in Figure 9.4 (d) and (e).

Similarly, to delete a specific row from the table, we could issue a command such as that shown in Figure 9.4 (f).

If we required a report showing the entire contents of the table, as shown in Figure 9.5 (a), we could issue the enquiry:

SELECT * FROM FURNITURE

or, to display just selected columns, as shown in Figure 9.5 (b), we could issue the enquiry:

SELECT DESCRIPTION, STOCK, LOCATION FROM
FURNITURE

CODE	DESCRIPTION	STOCK	LOCATION	PRICE	MINIMUM	MOVED
8888	DESK	64	LONDON	56.00	30	930128
2222	DESK	98	MANCHESTER	56.00	30	930125
7777	STOOL	25	SWINDON	17.75	60	930119
1111	STOOLS	63	DONCASTER	20.00	60	930105
5500	TABLE	15	LONDON	50.00	25	930106
2200	SETTEE	36	SWINDON	10.00	30	921228
1500	CHAIR	33	MANCHESTER	25.00	60	921231
7000	DESK	70	DONCASTER	56.00	10	921220
5000	SETTEE	24	SWINDON	10.00	30	921223
8763	SIDEBOARD	10	LONDON	130.00	15	921225
3000	SIDEBOARD	58	MANCHESTER	130.00	15	921225
8500	TABLE		LONDON	50.00	25	921217
7500	CHAIR	85	LONDON	25.00	60	921214
6500	STOOL	93	DONCASTER	17.75	60	930123
3200	SIDEBOARD	15	MANCHESTER	130.00	15	930130

(b) All the columns of the table

SELECT DESCRIPTION, STOCK, LOCATION FROM FURNITURE

DESCRIPTION	STOCK	LOCATION
DESK	64	LONDON
DESK	98	MANCHESTER
STOOL	25	SWINDON
STOOLS	63	DONCASTER
TABLE	15	LONDON
SETTEE	36	SWINDON
CHAIR	33	MANCHESTER
DESK	70	DONCASTER
SETTEE	24	SWINDON
SIDEBOARD	10	LONDON
SIDEBOARD	58	MANCHESTER
TABLE		LONDON
CHAIR	85	LONDON
STOOL	93	DONCASTER
SIDEBOARD	15	MANCHESTER

(b) Selected columns

Figure 9.5 *An SQL report*

using the column names which we declared in the CREATE TABLE command.

Sorting

Notice that the rows in the report do not appear in any particular order; they are simply shown in the sequence in which they are held in the table. If required, we could supply sort specifications to request that the rows in the report be arranged in a specific sequence:

SELECT DESCRIPTION, STOCK, LOCATION, PRICE FROM
   FURNITURE
   ORDER BY PRICE

and we could add a GROUP specification to produce a visual control break (skipping a blank line) whenever the price of the items changes:

SELECT DESCRIPTION, PRICE, STOCK FROM
FURNITURE

   ORDER BY PRICE
   GROUP BY PRICE

We could use the SUM function, in an enquiry such as:

SELECT DESCRIPTION, STOCK, PRICE, SUM(STOCK)
FROM FURNITURE ORDER BY PRICE

to output the total value of the STOCK column on the report.

Selecting specific items

If we do not want all the rows of the table to appear on the report, we may specify selection criteria in an enquiry such as:

SELECT DESCRIPTION, STOCK, PRICE, SUM(STOCK)
FROM FURNITURE ORDER BY PRICE
   WHERE PRICE < '100.00'
   AND
   LOCATION = 'SWINDON'

which would show only those rows for which the price is less than £100 and the location is Swindon, or the enquiry:

SELECT DESCRIPTION, PRICE FROM FURNITURE
   WHERE STOCK IS NOT NULL

which would show only those rows which did not have a null stock quantity.

If we only know a part of a value and not the entire value, then we can issue enquiries such as:

> SELECT DESCRIPTION LOCATION
> WHERE LOCATION LIKE 'GLAS%'

which would show all the items held at Glasgow, Glastonbury, and so on, or the enquiry:

> SELECT DESCRIPTION LOCATION
> WHERE LOCATION LIKE '%DON%'

which would show all the items held at Doncaster, London, Swindon, and so on.

In addition to the SUM function SQL offers a number of other functions:

> SELECT AVG(STOCK * PRICE) FROM FURNITURE
> > to obtain the stock and the price for each row, multiply these together, and then display the average of these figures for all the rows.

> SELECT COUNT(*) FROM FURNITURE WHERE LOCATION = 'SWINDON'
> > to display a count of the number of items located at the Swindon stores.

> SELECT DESCRIPTION, MAX(PRICE) FROM FURNITURE
> > to display the maximum price.

> SELECT MIN(STOCK) FROM FURNITURE WHERE
> LOCATION = 'BRISTOL'
> > to display the product which has the lowest stock level at the Bristol stores.

> SELECT PRICE, SUM(STOCK), SUM(STOCK * PRICE)
> FROM FURNITURE
> > to display the price, stock and value (calculated by multiplying the stock by the price) and produce the totals of these figures.

These examples also illustrate the way in which an SQL command can be used to calculate the value of the stock represented by each row of the FURNITURE table by using an element such as:

STOCK * PRICE

SQL uses the IN construction to pick those rows which contain one of a specific set of values:

SELECT * FROM FURNITURE WHERE LOCATION IN ('SWINDON', 'BRISTOL', 'MANCHESTER')

Activity 6

Write down the SQL sentences which would add these rows to the FURNITURE table. Use today's date for the MOVED date.

CODE	DESCRIPTION	STOCK	LOCATION	PRICE	MINIMUM
7001	STEPLADDER	10	LONDON	99.00	10
7002	SIDETABLE	100	MANCHESTER	20.00	30
7003	STEPLADDER	25	SWINDON	99.00	10
7004	SIDETABLE	10	DONCASTER	20.00	60
7005	SETTEE	15	LONDON	50.00	25

Write down an SQL sentence which would increase the prices of all the products by 10%.

When you have produced all thse commands, write out the reports which would be produced by each of the SQL SELECT enquiries shown in the text.

SQL has a great many other features, but we cannot discuss them here.

Assignment 1

Using the SQL language, how would you handle the following situations? Write down the commands which you would use.

(1) To create a new STUDENT table.
(2) To indicate that you want to use the name, address, sex, telephone number, date of enrollment, the student registration number, the fee to be paid, whether the fee has been paid yet

(assume that this is going to be a Y or N), and the degree for which the student is studying.

(3) To add a new student: Miss Mary Byshe of 34 High Street who started to study for a BSc on 9th September 1990. Her registration number is 90/36192. She has no telephone and has not yet paid her fee.

(4) To produce a list of all students who are studying for the MA degree.

(5) To change her record to indicate that Mary Byshe has now paid her fee.

(6) To find the total fees still to be paid.

(7) To delete the record for student 85/13455.

---

dBASE

dBASE – in its various manifestations dBASE II, dBASE III Plus and dBASE IV – is a product of the Ashton-Tate Company. Like much database software, dBASE is screen-oriented, allowing the users to type their enquiries at the keyboard and interacting with the user in a screen-based dialogue. It is also possible to write applications programs in the dBASE language

To illustrate some of the features of dBASE we shall consider the relation FURNITURE which is illustrated in Figure 9.6(a). In this discussion, we shall use the dBASE terminology: **file, record** and **field**.

We must first specify the **structure** for the new file. This is done by means of the:

CREATE

command, as illustrated in Figure 9.6 (b). dBASE then displays a blank structure which we fill in by specifying the name, type, width and format of each field in the file. The structure represents the data dictionary for the file.

We can subsequently change the structure by means of the:

MODIFY STRUCTURE

command.

When the file and the structure have been created, data may be added to the file immediately after the CREATE operation (at which point dBASE will ask you if you want to input any new data records), or you may add them later by means of the:

FURNITURE

CODE	TYPE	COLOUR	MATERIAL	PRICE
4600	DESK	GREY	WOODEN	56.00
3000	SIDEBOARD	BLUE	PLASTIC	175.00
5000	SETTEE	ORANGE	WOODEN	10.00
7000	DESK	WHITE	WOODEN	56.00
8000	CHAIR	RED	SPECIAL	10.00
8763	SIDEBOARD	MAROON	WOODEN	160.00
8077	DESK	RED	PLASTIC	56.00
9134	SETTEE	YELLOW	WOODEN	130.00

(a) FURNITURE relation

CREATE FURNITURE

	FIELD NAME	TYPE	WIDTH	DEC
1	ITEM	NUMERIC	4	
2	CODE	CHAR	10	
3	COLOUR	CHAR	6	
4	MATERIAL	CHAR	8	
5	PRICE	NUMERIC	6	2

(b) CREATE command

Figure 9.6   *Establishing a dBASE file*

APPEND

command. In either case, a blank form will be displayed on the screen – based upon the structure of the file – and the user will be allowed to type in the new data which is to be added to the file.

Records are added – one by one – to the end of a file. They are held in the order in which they are added. dBASE allocates its own record keys and these keys are shown (in the first column of the report) when the file is displayed by means of the:

LIST

command. The output from the LIST command might look like that shown in Figure 9.7. In order to look at the format and structure of the records, we could use the command:

LIST STRUCTURE

as illustrated in Figure 9.7 (b).

There are several statements available if you want to look at specific records:

DISPLAY RECORD 5
to look at a single record.

LIST FOR PRICE > 100

```
LIST

Record £   CODE    TYPE         COLOUR    MATERIAL    PRICE
       1   4600    DESK         GREY      WOODEN       56.00
       2   3000    SIDEBOARD    BLUE      PLASTIC     175.00
       3   5000    SETTEE       ORANGE    WOODEN       10.00
       4   7000    DESK         WHITE     WOODEN       56.00
       5   8000    CHAIR        RED       SPECIAL      10.00
       6   8763    SIDEBOARD    MAROON    WOODEN      160.00
       7   8077    DESK         RED       PLASTIC      56.00
       8   9134    SETTEE       YELLOW    WOODEN      130.00

                     (a) LIST file

LIST STRUCTURE

FIELD    FIELD NAME    TYPE          WIDTH    DEC

   1     ITEM          NUMERIC         4
   2     CODE          CHAR           10
   3     COLOUR        CHAR            6
   4     MATERIAL      CHAR            8
   5     PRICE         NUMERIC         6        2

**Total**                            35

                  (b) LIST STRUCTURE
```

Figure 9.7 *dBASE: LIST command*

LIST FOR COLOUR = 'RED' OR COLOUR = 'MAROON'
LIST FOR COLOUR = 'RED' AND TYPE = 'DESK'
LIST FOR NOT(MATERIAL = 'ASH' OR MATERIAL =
'MAHOGANY')

to look for records which satisfy certain conditions.

LIST FOR SUBSTR(TYPE,1,2) = "SI"

to list all the records of which first two characters of the TYPE are SI; this will show all the SIDEBOARDs in our file. dBASE has a large number of functions.

LIST FOR 'W'/COLOUR

to list all the records which have a W anywhere in the COLOUR field; this will show the WHITE and the YELLOW records.

LIST CODE, COLOUR, MATERIAL, TYPE OFF

to output specific fields. The word OFF suppresses the record number.

LIST CODE, COLOUR+' '+TYPE

to display the code for each record, and the colour and the type concatenated (with a space between them) to form a single string.

These and some other examples are illustrated in Figure 9.8 where we show the dBASE command followed by the output produced.

396

```
DISPLAY RECORD 5

Record £   CODE    TYPE          COLOUR    MATERIAL    PRICE
      5   8000    CHAIR         RED       SPECIAL     10.00

LIST FOR PRICE > 100

Record £   CODE    TYPE          COLOUR    MATERIAL    PRICE
      2   3000    SIDEBOARD     BLUE      PLASTIC    175.00
      6   8763    SIDEBOARD     MAROON    WOODEN     160.00
      8   9134    SETTEE        YELLOW    WOODEN     130.00

LIST FOR COLOUR = 'RED' OR COLOUR = 'MAROON'

Record £   CODE    TYPE          COLOUR    MATERIAL    PRICE
      5   8000    CHAIR         RED       SPECIAL     10.00
      6   8763    SIDEBOARD     MAROON    WOODEN     160.00
      7   8077    DESK          RED       PLASTIC     56.00

LIST FOR COLOUR = 'RED' AND TYPE = 'DESK'

Record £   CODE    TYPE          COLOUR    MATERIAL    PRICE
      7   8077    DESK          RED       PLASTIC     56.00

LIST FOR SUBSTR(TYPE,1,2) = "SI"

Record £   CODE    TYPE          COLOUR    MATERIAL    PRICE
      2   3000    SIDEBOARD     BLUE      PLASTIC    175.00
      6   8763    SIDEBOARD     MAROON    WOODEN     160.00

LIST FOR 'W'\COLOUR

Record £   CODE    TYPE          COLOUR    MATERIAL    PRICE
      4   7000    DESK          WHITE     WOODEN      56.00
      8   9134    SETTEE        YELLOW    WOODEN     130.00

LIST FOR PRICE < 100 AND TYPE = "SETTEE"

Record £   CODE    TYPE          COLOUR    MATERIAL    PRICE
      3   5000    SETTEE        ORANGE    WOODEN      10.00

LIST CODE, COLOUR, MATERIAL, TYPE OFF

CODE    COLOUR    MATERIAL    TYPE
4600    GREY      WOODEN      DESK
3000    BLUE      PLASTIC     SIDEBOARD
5000    ORANGE    WOODEN      SETTEE
7000    WHITE     WOODEN      DESK
8000    RED       SPECIAL     CHAIR
8763    MAROON    WOODEN      SIDEBOARD
8077    RED       PLASTIC     DESK
9134    YELLOW    WOODEN      SETTEE

LIST CODE, COLOUR+' '+TYPE

Record £   CODE    COLOUR+' '+TYPE
      1   4600    GREY DESK
      2   3000    BLUE SIDEBOARD
      3   5000    ORANGE SETTEE
      4   7000    WHITE DESK
      5   8000    RED CHAIR
      6   8763    MAROON SIDEBOARD
      7   8077    RED DESK
      8   9134    YELLOW SETTEE
```

Figure 9.8   *dBASE: LIST and DISPLAY commands*

Like other enquiry languages, dBASE has facilities for counting and totalling. These are illustrated in Figure 9.9.

In addition to simply totalling a field, dBASE will allow you to store the result in a **variable** – we used TOT1 and TOT2 – and then use these stored values for further calculations.

```
LIST TYPE, PRICE, PRICE*0.175

Record £   TYPE          PRICE   PRICE*0.175
       1   DESK          56.00          9.80
       2   SIDEBOARD    175.00         30.63
       3   SETTEE        10.00          1.75
       4   DESK          56.00          9.80
       5   CHAIR         10.00          1.75
       6   SIDEBOARD    160.00         28.00
       7   DESK          56.00          9.80
       8   SETTEE       130.00         22.75

COUNT FOR TYPE = "DESK"
          3 RECORDS

SUM PRICE FOR MATERIAL = "PLASTIC"
          2 RECORDS SUMMED
          PRICE
          231.00

SUM PRICE FOR TYPE = "SETTEE" TO TOT1
          2 RECORDS SUMMED
          PRICE
          140.00

SUM PRICE FOR TYPE = "DESK" TO TOT2
          3 RECORDS SUMMED
          PRICE
          168.00

STORE TOT2 - TOT1 TO DIFTOT
          18.00

AVERAGE PRICE
          3 RECORDS AVERAGED
          PRICE
          81.63
```

Figure 9.9 *dBASE calculations*

Some dBASE commands such as:

GO TOP
GO BOTTOM
GO 2
SKIP 3
SKIP –1
LOCATE FOR COLOUR = 'RED'

will allow you to browse through the file to locate and look at records. These are illustrated in Figure 9.10.

As you browse through the file in the manner illustrated in Figure 9.10, it is convenient to think of dBASE as moving a pointer through the file according to your instructions. The record at which the pointer is positioned at any moment is the *current record*. You may amend the current record, if you wish.

The contents of the current record can be changed by a sequence such as:

```
GO TOP

DISPLAY 2

Record £   CODE    TYPE         COLOUR    MATERIAL    PRICE
       1   4600    DESK         GREY      WOODEN       56.00
       2   3000    SIDEBOARD    BLUE      PLASTIC     175.00

SKIP 2

DISPLAY 1

Record £   CODE    TYPE         COLOUR    MATERIAL    PRICE
       5   8000    CHAIR        RED       SPECIAL      10.00

GO BOTTOM

SKIP -3

DISPLAY 2

Record £   CODE    TYPE         COLOUR    MATERIAL    PRICE
       5   8000    CHAIR        RED       SPECIAL      10.00
       6   8763    SIDEBOARD    MAROON    WOODEN      160.00

GO 2

DISPLAY 1

Record £   CODE    TYPE         COLOUR    MATERIAL    PRICE
       2   3000    SIDEBOARD    BLUE      PLASTIC     175.00

GO TOP

LOCATE FOR COLOUR = 'RED'

DISPLAY 1

Record £   CODE    TYPE         COLOUR    MATERIAL    PRICE
       5   8000    CHAIR        RED       SPECIAL      10.00
```

Figure 9.10 *dBASE: browsing through a file*

LOCATE FOR TYPE = 'DESK' AND COLOUR = 'RED'
REPLACE PRICE WITH PRICE + 10.25

A range of records may be changed by a command such as:

REPLACE ALL TYPE WITH "S/BOARD" FOR TYPE = "SIDEBOARD"

Records can be removed from a file by means of a command of the form:

DELETE RECORD 5

This flags the record(s) for deletion although it does not actually delete them from the file. If you realize that you have made a mistake and you don't really want to delete the records, the RECALL command can be used to cancel the deletion flag. When you are certain that you wish to proceed with the deletion, you will use the PACK command to accomplish this. These commands are illustrated in Figure 9.11.

```
DELETE RECORD 5

LIST

Record £   CODE   TYPE         COLOUR    MATERIAL    PRICE
       1   4600   DESK         GREY      WOODEN       56.00
       2   3000   SIDEBOARD    BLUE      WOODEN      175.00
       3   5000   SETTEE       ORANGE    WOODEN       10.00
       4   7000   DESK         WHITE     WOODEN       56.00
       5*  8000   CHAIR        RED       SPECIAL      10.00
       6   8763   SIDEBOARD    MAROON    WOODEN      160.00
       7   8077   DESK         RED       PLASTIC      56.00
       8   9134   SETTEE       YELLOW    WOODEN      130.00

DELETE FOR TYPE = "SIDEBOARD"

LIST

Record £   CODE   TYPE         COLOUR    MATERIAL    PRICE
       1   4600   DESK         GREY      WOODEN       56.00
       2*  3000   SIDEBOARD    BLUE      WOODEN      175.00
       3   5000   SETTEE       ORANGE    WOODEN       10.00
       4   7000   DESK         WHITE     WOODEN       56.00
       5*  8000   CHAIR        RED       SPECIAL      10.00
       6*  8763   SIDEBOARD    MAROON    WOODEN      160.00
       7   8077   DESK         RED       PLASTIC      56.00
       8   9134   SETTEE       YELLOW    WOODEN      130.00

RECALL RECORD 2

LIST

Record £   CODE   TYPE         COLOUR    MATERIAL    PRICE
       1   4600   DESK         GREY      WOODEN       56.00
       2   3000   SIDEBOARD    BLUE      WOODEN      175.00
       3   5000   SETTEE       ORANGE    WOODEN       10.00
       4   7000   DESK         WHITE     WOODEN       56.00
       5*  8000   CHAIR        RED       SPECIAL      10.00
       6*  8763   SIDEBOARD    MAROON    WOODEN      160.00
       7   8077   DESK         RED       PLASTIC      56.00
       8   9134   SETTEE       YELLOW    WOODEN      130.00

PACK

LIST

Record £   CODE   TYPE         COLOUR    MATERIAL    PRICE
       1   4600   DESK         GREY      WOODEN       56.00
       2   3000   SIDEBOARD    BLUE      WOODEN      175.00
       3   5000   SETTEE       ORANGE    WOODEN       10.00
       4   7000   DESK         WHITE     WOODEN       56.00
       5   8077   DESK         RED       PLASTIC      56.00
       6   9134   SETTEE       YELLOW    WOODEN      130.00
```

Figure 9.11   *dBASE: DELETE, RECALL and PACK commands*

Sorting in dBASE

Since dBASE holds the records in the order that they were added to the file, there must be some means of displaying the records in a specific sequence. This is achieved by means of the:

INDEX

command. Figure 9.12 (a) shows the use of this command to display the records sorted into order of price. We first create the index and call this PINDEX, then we call up this index before issuing the LIST command.

You may also create a new (sorted) version of your file by means of the SORT verb, as illustrated in Figure 9.12 (b). In this particular instance, the new sorted file, called PRODUCTS, contains only the TYPE and the COLOUR from the original FURNITURE file.

```
USE FURNITURE

INDEX ON PRICE TO PINDEX
          8 RECORDS INDEXED

USE FURNITURE INDEX PINDEX

LIST

Record £   CODE   TYPE        COLOUR   MATERIAL   PRICE
       3   5000   SETTEE      ORANGE   WOODEN     10.00
       5   8000   CHAIR       RED      SPECIAL    10.00
       1   4600   DESK        GREY     WOODEN     56.00
       4   7000   DESK        WHITE    WOODEN     56.00
       7   8077   DESK        RED      PLASTIC    56.00
       8   9134   SETTEE      YELLOW   WOODEN    130.00
       6   8763   SIDEBOARD   MAROON   WOODEN    160.00
       2   3000   SIDEBOARD   BLUE     WOODEN    175.00

                    (a) Indexing a file

USE FURNITURE

SORT TO PRODUCTS ON TYPE, COLOUR

LIST PRODUCTS

Record £   TYPE        COLOUR
       1   CHAIR       RED
       2   DESK        GREY
       3   DESK        RED
       4   DESK        WHITE
       5   SETTEE      ORANGE
       6   SETTEE      YELLOW
       7   SIDEBOARD   BLUE
       8   SIDEBOARD   MAROON

              (b) producing a new sorted file
```

Figure 9.12   *dBASE: INDEX and SORT commands*

Assignment 2

This assignment concerns a LIBRARY which is to contain the following information about the books held in the library:

- The book acquisition number. This is a serial number given to each book which the library buys.
- The title.
- The author.
- The price.
- The category. This is the Dewey decimal code which is used in most libraries and consists of a number such as 1.5, 123.45678.

401

- The date on which the book was bought. You can handle the date as a character string in the same manner as the title.

Write down the dBASE command (or commands) which you would use to perform the following:

(1) To create the structure for the file.
(2) To list the contents of the file.
(3) To list the books in category 98.76.
(4) To list the books sorted into order of the authors' names.
(5) To list the computer books bought in 1991.
(6) To find the total cost of books in categories 76 (this is all those which have 76 as the main number: 76.1, 76.2, 76.87654, and so on).
(7) To find how much more we spend on books of category 123.4 than we spend on those of category 234.5.

Processing in dBASE

dBASE allows you to extend fundamental enquiry facilities by creating REPORTs to produce printed output in a formatted manner, and LABELs to produce mailing labels.

The interactive commands of dBASE are augmented by a set of statements which allow conventional programs (or procedures) to be written in the dBASE language. Programs may be created by the dBASE applications generator, or the dBASE commands may be placed in an ordinary file (with the suffix PRG if you are using DOS) and then executed by means of the dBASE DO command. Since there is little functional difference between interactive dBASE and dBASE programs, we shall not look at programming in detail, but a few simple examples will show how they offer the facilities that you would expect of a programming language.

Information may be displayed on the screen by means of statements such as:

```
? 'THERE ARE '
?? REC_COUNT
?? ' RECORDS'
@ 3,1 SAY 'THERE ARE'
@ 3,11 SAY REC_COUNT
@ 3,14 SAY 'RECORDS'
```

The ? and ?? commands are used for producing line by line output (scrolling down the screen): ?? holds the cursor at the end of the output without advancing a line. The first three commands, therefore, have a similar effect to the last three commands except that the @ command offers more powerful screen formatting and – in this example – forces the output to a specific row and column position on the screen.

Data is accepted from the keyboard by statements such as:

INPUT "WHAT IS YOUR USER CODE" TO USER_CODE

Variables are used as on other programming languages, although, unlike languages such as Cobol or Pascal, dBASE does not require variables to be declared before use. Values are assigned to variables by means of statement such as:

STORE 0 TO TOTAL_SALES
STORE SPACE(20) TO CLIENT_NAME

A full range of control statements is provided for structured programming. Some of these are illustrated by the fragments in Figure 9.13.

Statements such as DO ADD_RECORD are the equivalent of CALL or procedure statements in other languages.

```
IF USER_CODE = 'X'
    @ 23,0 SAY 'END OF JOB'
    RETURN
ENDIF

DO WHILE OPTION <> 'X'
    DO PROCESS_ROUTINE
ENDDO

DO CASE
    CASE OPTION = 'A'
        DO ADD_RECORD
    CASE OPTION = 'D'
        DO DELETE_RECORD
    CASE OPTION = 'M'
        DO MODIFY_RECORD
ENDDO
```

Figure 9.13   *dBASE control statements*

Assignment 3

Using the dBASE language, write down the commands which you would use in the following situations:

(1)   To create a new STUDENT file.
(2)   To indicate that you want to use the name, address, sex, telephone number, date of enrollment, the student registration number, the fee to be paid, whether the fee has been paid yet

    (assume that this is going to be a Y or N), and the degree for which the student is studying.

(3) To add a new student: Mr Rashid Khan of 34 Milton Place who started to study for a BA on 9th October 1991. His registration number is 91/7711. His telephone number is 713577 and he has already paid his fee.

(4) To produce a list of all students who are studying for the MA degree.

(5) To change his record to indicate that Rashid Khan's telephone number is now 834354.

(6) To find the total fees still to be paid.

(7) To delete the record for student 85/13455.

QBE – query by example

Most enquiry languages are like SQL and dBASE and allow the user to produce reports and make enquiries by typing English-like sentences.

The QBE – *Query By Example* – language is remarkably different from these, in that it allows the user to make enquiries by *filling in a form*. This has two major advantages: the user does not have remember the names of the various data fields, and there is no quasi-English grammar to learn.

QBE was developed in 1975 by Moshe Zloof, working at the IBM Research Laboratory in New York. Zloof's aim in designing QBE was to produce an enquiry language which would be easy to learn and which would be – as far as possible – error-proof. Like SQL, QBE is concerned with *relational databases* and uses the terms **table**, **row** and **column**.

When the user invokes the QBE processor, a blank form – called a **template** – is displayed on the screen. This is illustrated in Figure 9.14 (a).

Let us suppose that the user wishes to make an enquiry about the STOCK table, then he/she would move the cursor to the appropriate position and enter the name of the table. This is illustrated in Figure 9.14 (b).

Then, by pressing a function key or by some other means, the user would instruct QBE to consult the data dictionary for the STOCK table and display the names of the available columns. This is illustrated in Figure 9.14 (c).

The user would then move the cursor to the required parts of the template and fill in the appropriate columns to indicate the data which is to

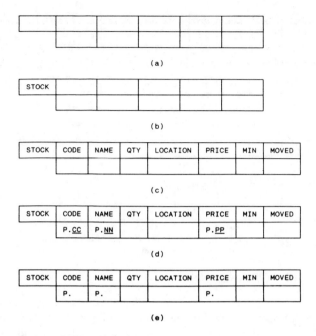

Figure 9.14   *QBE templates*

appear on the output report. Thus, if we wished to look at the stock code, the name and print, we might complete a template like this. This is illustrated in Figure 9.14 (d). The code P. is used to indicate which columns are to be **printed** and the underlined elements representing an **example** of the report which is to be produced – hence *Query By Example*.

On some implementations, you may omit the examples and build a template using just the P. codes. This is illustrated in Figure 9.14 (e).

When the request has been specified, the user will instruct QBE to proceed (again by means of a function key), and the appropriate report will be output. The output will normally be displayed on the screen and there may be facilities to use the function keys to scroll up, down and across the report.

Figure 9.15 shows some further examples of the use of QBE as an enquiry language. We first see two methods of listing the entire contents of the table.

STOCK	CODE	NAME	QTY	LOCATION	PRICE	MIN	MOVED
P.	P.	P.	P.	P.	P.	P.	

(a) Listing all the columns in the table - method 1

STOCK	CODE	NAME	QTY	LOCATION	PRICE	MIN	MOVED
P.							

(b) Listing all the columns in the table - method 2

STOCK	CODE	NAME	QTY	LOCATION	PRICE	MIN	MOVED
P.	P.	P.SUM.ALL			P.		

(c) Totalling the columns

STOCK	CODE	NAME	QTY	LOCATION	PRICE	MIN	MOVED
P.	P.AO(1)			P.AO(3)	DO(2)		

(d) Sorting specifications

Figure 9.15   *QBE examples*

The SUM operation used in the example in Figure 9.15 (c) is one of a number of standard functions offered by QBE. Others include AVG (average), CNT (count), MAX (maximum) and MIN (minimum). These functions operate on all (or selected) values in a column.

As illustrated in Figure 9.15 (d), sorting is achieved by an operator which is similar to these functions, the operator AO specifying ascending order and the operator DO, descending order. The major to minor priority of several sort keys is indicated by a subscript, 1 for the major key, and 2, 3, 4 and so on for the successive minor keys.

Normally, the QBE report will show all the rows in the table. If selection criteria are specified, then only the rows which meet those criteria will appear in the report. Some typical enquiries are shown in Figure 9.16.

Note that if several such conditions are specified, as in Figure 9.16 (b), they have the AND effect. Logical OR and more complex selection criteria may be imposed by using several lines in the template, as we see in Figure 9.16 (e), or the same effect may be achieved by calling up (by means of a function key) a facility which will allow a **condition box** to be declared, as illustrated in Figure 9.16 (f). The underlined LL used here is known as a *variable element*, and behaves rather like a program variable identifier.

If we wished to select on a partial string, such as all the items whose name begins with the letters CHAIR, then we might use the template shown in Figure 9.16 (g). The variable element *X* here represents *any* text string, like the % character in SQL. As before, we could have used any string of characters to denote the variable element where we used the *X* in this example.

STOCK	CODE	NAME	QTY	LOCATION	PRICE	MIN	MOVED
	P.	P.	P.		<100		

(a) items costing less than £100

STOCK	CODE	NAME	QTY	LOCATION	PRICE	MIN	MOVED
	P.	P.	P.	P.YORK	<250		

(b) items costing less than £250 and located at York

STOCK	CODE	NAME	QTY	LOCATION	PRICE	MIN	MOVED
	P.	P.	¬				

(c) items with no quantity

STOCK	CODE	NAME	QTY	LOCATION	PRICE	MIN	MOVED
	P.	P.	¬	SWINDON			

(d) items with no quantity and located at Swindon

STOCK	CODE	NAME	QTY	LOCATION	PRICE	MIN	MOVED
	P.	P.		SWINDON	P.		
	P.	P.		YORK	P.		

(e) items located at Swindon or York - method 1

LL = SWINDON OR LL = YORK

STOCK	CODE	NAME	QTY	LOCATION	PRICE	MIN	MOVED
	P.	P.		LL	P.		

(f) items located at Swindon or York - method 2

STOCK	CODE	NAME	QTY	LOCATION	PRICE	MIN	MOVED
	P.	CHAIRX			P.		

(g) Selecting on part strings

Figure 9.16   *QBE: Selection criteria*

QBE will allow you to derive a list of item(s) from one table and use this to extract data from another table. To do this, the user will indicate that two tables are to be processed and two templates will be completed. For example, an enquiry which SQL might present as:

> SELECT CODE FROM STOCK WHERE NAME = 'YORK'
>   UNION
> SELECT ITEM, PAGE FROM CATALOGUE

might be specified in QBE by means of the two templates shown in Figure 9.17.

STOCK	CODE	NAME	QTY	LOCATION	PRICE	MIN	MOVED
	XXXX			YORK			

CATALOGUE	CODE	ITEM	PAGE	TEXT_ENTRY
	XXXX	P.	P.	

Figure 9.17   *QBE: using two tables – 1*

This QBE enquiry may be read as *find the code(s) of the products on the STOCK table which have the location YORK, and then output the item and the page number for those products from the CATALOGUE table.* As before, any string could have been used for the variable element where we used XXXX, provided that the variable element is the same in both templates, so that QBE will look for matching values. In practice, you would use meaningful names for your variable elements – CODE might have been better than XXXX.

There is sometimes a requirement to extract data from more than one table – in last example, we might have wanted to output the price from the STOCK relation as well as the item and page which are drawn from the CATALOGUE relation. In this situation, QBE allows tables to be processed by means of a *result box.* as shown in Figure 9.18.

Processing in QBE

The data description language, the data manipulation language and the enquiry language of QBE all operate in this same fundamental way. For

STOCK	CODE	NAME	QTY	LOCATION	PRICE	MIN	MOVED
	<u>XXXX</u>			YORK	<u>PP</u>		

CATALOGUE	CODE	ITEM	PAGE	TEXT_ENTRY
	<u>XXXX</u>	<u>II</u>	<u>PN</u>	

RESULT			
P.	<u>PP</u>	<u>II</u>	<u>PN</u>

Figure 9.18   *QBE: using two tables – 2*

data manipulation, the various activities are indicated by means of *codes.* where the enquiry language facilities of QBE use the code:

P.

to print – or output – the values in a column, the data manipulation language uses three further codes:

I. to insert data,
U. to update data, and
D. to delete data.

Thus, to insert a new row into the table, we could use the template illustrated in Figure 9.19, the I. code to indicate that we are inserting an entire new row.

STOCK	CODE	NAME	QTY	LOCATION	PRICE	MIN	MOVED
I.	4567	BOOKCASE	25	SWINDON	250	10	900729

Figure 9.19   *QBE: inserting a row*

To update just one column of an existing row, we could use one of the templates shown in Figure 9.20. Either of template (a) or template (b) would change the current value of the location for product 4567 to YORK. We could extend this to update several columns at one time, as in Figure 9.20 (c).

A more complicated update is represented by Figure 9.20 (d). This would take the current value for the QTY column of the product 4567 (indicated by the variable element Q) and add 10 to this, thus increasing the quantity column of the row by 10.

If we wanted to update the PRICE column of *all* the products or the table, say, increasing the price by 10%, then we could use the template in Figure 9.20 (e).

If we wanted to impose the condition that only those items which cost more than £100 be updated in this way, we could use a composite template with two lines, as in Figure 9.20 (f). This QBE update may be read as *find the code(s) of the products on the STOCK table which have a PRICE greater than 100 and then update the PRICE of those products by 10%*. As before, any string could have been used for the variable element where we used XXXX, provided that the variable element is the same in both lines.

The D. code is used to delete a value or a row from the table. Thus, the template shown in Figure 9.21 would delete the row for product 4567.

STOCK	CODE	NAME	QTY	LOCATION	PRICE	MIN	MOVED
	4567			U.YORK			

(a)

STOCK	CODE	NAME	QTY	LOCATION	PRICE	MIN	MOVED
U.	4567			YORK			

(b)

STOCK	CODE	NAME	QTY	LOCATION	PRICE	MIN	MOVED
U.	4567			YORK	275		

(c)

STOCK	CODE	NAME	QTY	LOCATION	PRICE	MIN	MOVED
U.	4567		Q+10				

(d)

STOCK	CODE	NAME	QTY	LOCATION	PRICE	MIN	MOVED
U.					P*1.1		

(e)

STOCK	CODE	NAME	QTY	LOCATION	PRICE	MIN	MOVED
U.	XXXX XXXX				>100 P*1.1		

(f)

Figure 9.20 *QBE: updating*

STOCK	CODE	NAME	QTY	LOCATION	PRICE	MIN	MOVED
D.	4567						

Figure 9.21 *QBE: deleting a row*

Data description language

The data description task is performed by applying the same QBE activities to a table called TABLES which holds details of all the data on the database. Thus, to find the names of the available tables, we could use the template shown in Figure 9.22 (a), and to insert a new table, that shown in Figure 9.22 (b)

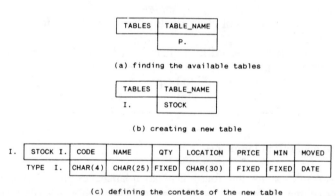

TABLES	TABLE_NAME
	P.

(a) finding the available tables

TABLES	TABLE_NAME
I.	STOCK

(b) creating a new table

I.	STOCK I.	CODE	NAME	QTY	LOCATION	PRICE	MIN	MOVED
	TYPE I.	CHAR(4)	CHAR(25)	FIXED	CHAR(30)	FIXED	FIXED	DATE

(c) defining the contents of the new table

Figure 9.22 *QBE: data description*

Once the table has been created, the column names can be declared by a template such as shown in Figure 9.22 (c).

There are some minor differences between the various implementations of QBE. For example, some require a variable element to be included with every P. code. Others require that all the variable elements be preceded by the underscore character, so that a formula to increase the prices might be:

_PRICE * 1.1

Whichever version of QBE is used, non-technical end-users will find it much easier to learn and to use than many other enquiry languages which use sentences to make enquiries.

411

Assignment 4

Using the QBE language, how would you handle the following situations? Write down the commands which you would use.

(1) To create a new STUDENT table.
(2) To indicate that you want to use the name, address, sex, telephone number, date of enrollment, the student registration number, the fee to be paid, whether the fee has been paid yet (assume that this is going to be a Y or N), and the degree for which the student is studying.
(3) To add a new student: Miss Liu Ying Hui of 1223 Paradise Buildings who started to study for a BSc on 10th September 1991. Her registration number is 91/54322. She has no telephone and has not yet paid her fee.
(4) To produce a list of all students who are studying for the BA degree.
(5) To change her record to indicate that Liu Ying Hui has now paid her fee.
(6) To find the total fees still to be paid.
(7) To delete the record for student 85/13455.

Fourth generation languages

In Chapter 2, we saw that fourth generation languages (4GLs) evolved as a programming medium to offer certain benefits to *commercial* data processing:

- They shorten the development cycle and therefore speed up the production of a new system.
- They remove the programmer from much of the technical detail of the computer solution.
- They offer greater flexibility and thereby allow the solution to be moulded more closely to meet the users' requirements.
- They may even be suitable for end-users to produce their own solutions.
- They can provide a top-down method for developing a system, the programmer gradually enhancing and refining the system.
- The process of enhancement and refinement can be extended after the system has been implemented, thereby removing most of the hazards of maintaining an existing system.

- They interface more closely with the data dictionary and the database itself.

That's what 4GLs do, but how can we recognize a 4GL?

What is a fourth generation language?

At the moment, beyond the characteristics summarized above, there is no real definition of a fourth generation language. But, if we look at some of the software which is described as a 4GL, we can identify a number of common features:

- 4GLs are predominantly used in commercial programming environments. Commercial systems are concerned more with manipulating and organizing large quantities of data, rather than just performing calculations.
- 4GL systems use a data dictionary to specify the format of the data records and values which are being processed and to identify the data names used in the coding and the enquiry sentences.
- 4GL programming tools are easy to learn and to apply. Some people say that you should be able to learn a new 4GL in one day.
- 4GL tools are suitable for all users, from non-technical end-users (such as clerks, managers) through to highly skilled technical staff (such as analysts and programmers). Each user is able to learn and apply the language to the extent that he/she requires.
- 4GL programs are easy to read, write and maintain.
- 4GL programming tools reduce the time and effort needed to develop a system.
- 4GL programming tools improve the productivity of the analyst and programmer.
- 4GL programs are non-procedural. That means that you do not write a sequence of statements which are to be executed one after the other. Instead, the programmer fills in a series of forms and paints a set of screens and report images describing the task which is to be carried out.
- 4GL programming tools focus on the **functionality** (what the program must do) rather than on the mechanics of programming (how the programmer and the program must do it).

The pros and cons of using 4GLs

Because it is a fairly simple matter to learn how to write programs, or even entire systems, in a 4GL, many non-technical users, such as managers and clerks, are now able to write their own systems. This greatly relieves the burden of the programming department and reduces the back-log of outstanding work.

Much of the work of debugging is removed when developing a system in a 4GL. Since the 4GL formalizes the structure of the system (in many cases, offering simple YES/NO choices for the various possiblities and options), the scope for making mistakes is reduced.

By allowing suitably-trained end-users to write their own programs, the resulting computer software is likely to be closer to what those end-users actually want. In many cases, a program which is developed by a team of analysts and programmers may suffer from dilution of the users' original requirements and may not be exactly what the users want.

The technique of prototyping also improves the effectiveness of writing programs.

Many 4GLs (and indeed a great deal of other software) have evolved from specific applications programs which were written and rewritten many years ago. For this reason, 4GLs are not used in one standard form. As a consequence, a programmer moving from one 4GL to another will have to be retrained for the new language. Although there are common principles behind all 4GLs, as we saw above, they each have their idiosyncracies and peculiarities which must be mastered if the programmer is to make full and efficient use of the language.

A programmer who is starting to use any particular 4GL from scratch will not have such retraining problems.

Activity 7

Collect as many computer magazines and journals as you can find. Look through the advertisements and editorial sections to see what information you can find about 4GLs.

Make a list of the names and suppliers of any products which describe themselves as 4GL software.

You may even care to work as a group with your colleagues and request the suppliers to send you more details about the software.

You will find it interesting and useful to compare the features of these 4GLs with those of the enquiry languages which we met earlier and with the SB+ fourth generation language which we shall discuss later.

Prototyping

The name **prototyping** is used to describe a method of developing a computer system in which the outline requirements are obtained and a computer solution is written to meet these requirements; this solution is then reworked and remodelled until it meets the users' precise requirements. There is an exact analogy with the prototyping methods of mechanical engineering where, for example, a wooden or plastic model of a car may be constructed. This will then be refined, changed, extended and modified in the light of wind-tunnel and other experiments, and the reactions from drivers, from the police and traffic authorities, from the motoring organizations and indeed from all interested parties. When an acceptable level of satisfaction has been reached, the design can progress to the next stage where a steel version can be built.

When applying prototyping methods to the development of computer systems, the analyst first talks to the users to obtain a **broad** outline of their functional requirements – this may merely be a rough outline – and a preliminary system is written to meet these requirements. This can be done quite quickly (often in a few minutes, rarely more than half a day) and cheaply. There now starts an iterative process in which this prototype is demonstrated to the users, and modified in the light of their reaction and comments. The modify–demonstrate cycle is then repeated – adding more detail at each pass – until the final system is acceptable to all the users. We can illustrate the process by the diagram in Figure 9.23.

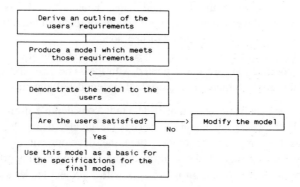

Figure 9.23 *Prototyping*

Such a method has a number of advantages:

(1) The initial prototype can be produced rapidly and cheaply. This quickly gives the user something to look at.

(2) The system can be modified specifically to the users' requirements **as their requirements develop,** by allowing the users to recognize, build up, and specify their own requirements **after they have seen what can be done.** Users rarely know what they do want, but they always know what they **don't** want.

(3) The user is actively involved in design and development.

(4) There is less chance of confusion arising between what the user wants, what the user asks for and what the analyst's solution provides.

(5) There is a gradual, phased user-understanding of the computer system because the user has **grown up with the system** and the user-training requirements are fewer.

(6) There is a shorter development lead time between the initial investigations and a demonstrable solution. A prototype system can be produced within a few hours to give the users a flavour of what the final system will look like.

(7) At this preliminary stage, the user may care to review the feasibility of the proposed system. This encourages the users and leads to an early commitment and involvement on their part.

(8) The system is implemented quickly.

(9) Prototyping implies that any modifications to the system can be made quickly and easily. Because the system is originally developed by the modify–approve sequence, there is no great difference between the fixes and enhancements which take place during development and those which are required later, when the system has to be modified or upgraded.

(10) Because of this, the system has a longer life span and any future modifications are implemented with the same ease and speed as those which made up the original system development.

The major disadvantage is that it demands considerable user-commitment. If the users are unable to accept the greater demands on their time as they review the model, then the development cycle more closely follows that of the traditional methods, with all work being done by the analysts and programmers with a project leader accepting greater responsibility as the representative of the users in observing and approving the system.

Prototyping is an excellent means of identifying and filling in the **detail** of the individual menus, the layouts of the screens, the layout and content of reports and, to a lesser extent, the action of the processes of the system.

When it has been produced and accepted, the model can be taken as the basis for the formal system specification which is then developed in other programming languages using standard programming methods. There are software tools which will take the model derived by the prototyping activity and convert it automatically into a program in a more familiar language, such as Cobol.

The shorter development cycle offered by most fourth generation languages means that they are ideally suited for use as prototyping tools. Some fourth generation languages are such that it is perfectly feasible to use the final model as the final version of the program.

Activity 8

You have been asked to write a computer program to calculate the wages for a small engineering company. The requirements are that the wages clerks will collect the employees' clock cards first thing on Monday morning, and then type in the details of each employee: the name, the clocking-in and clocking-out time. The program will then calculate the wages due to the each employee and print out the pay-slips and the amounts of cash to be collected from the bank to pay the employees.

Write down the stages which you would go through if this system was to be developed by prototyping methods.

Which people would you talk to?

4GL / enquiry language / data manipulation language

There is no clear distinction between a 4GL, an enquiry language and the data manipulation language which is found within a database management system (the DBMS). Indeed, there is considerable overlap between the three, and it may be that, in time, they will all merge into an amorphous collection of all-purpose software. Some points to remember are that:

- All the languages are concerned with processing data on a commercial database. You would, for example, be most unlikely to use any of them to solve a quadratic equation or other mathematical problem. Indeed the pure data manipulation language and the enquiry languages have no facilities for this.

- 4GLs, however, usually have some means of slotting in special processing at various points within the system. These special processes are usually coded in a third generation language such as Basic, or some special 3GL for use within that 4GL. Such a language may be used to perform calculations just like any other 3GL. In this respect, a 4GL can be used very much like any other programming language (albeit with a bias to commercial aspects).

- A 4GL can often be used as an alternative programming medium, alongside Cobol or whatever other languages are used within the organization.

- A data manipulation language, together with the data description language and the data control language are usually bundled together as a part of the database management system. We discuss this in the STUDENTS' GUIDE TO DATABASES. This collection is frequently offered as a complete data processing tool.

- The data manipulation language is used for manipulating the data and has a minimal capability to perform any actions which are not based around the data on the database.

- The data description language is concerned with creating and maintaining the data dictionary, and equipping the DBMS to identify and locate the data which is used in the data manipulation language and the enquiry language.

- The data control language is concerned with setting passwords, security codes and access codes, and equipping the DBMS to prevent users from reaching the parts of the database to which they are not authorized.

- An enquiry language is used primarily as a means of producing reports, but – as we saw with dBASE and the other languages – it can have facilities for data description, data manipulation and data control.

The best thing to do when you are assessing a particular piece of software is – not to attempt to categorize it under any particular heading – but to ask what tasks it is capable of performing:

- Can it be used to produce reports and answer queries just by typing in one set of information, such as a English-like command or a question, or a QBE template? If so, it has some of the qualities of an enquiry language.

- Can it be used to manipulate data by using the same sort of input as is used to produce reports? If so, it has some of the qualities of a data manipulation language.
- Can you write a program which does not depend upon any data on the database? If so, it has some of the qualities of a 4GL.

The most important factors are *what can the software do?* not *what is it called?*

Looking at a 4GL

As an example of a fourth generation language, I want to introduce you to SB+ (pronounced *Ess Bee Plus*). This is a well-established 4GL and was overall winner of the *4GL Grand Prix* held in the UK in 1987, and won two out of the three rounds of the *4GL Grand Prix* held in the UK in 1990. It is derived from an earlier product called *System Builder* which was developed for use on the Pick operating system.

There are two phases of activity with SB+: the first is the *development activity*, during which the analyst and the programmer use the SB+ tools to design and produce the screens, reports and processing routines: the second phase is the *run-time activity*, when the end-users apply the processing routines and use them to do their work.

The driving force behind SB is the *data dictionary* which defines the fields on the database. To illustrate this, let us consider a simple system to maintain the records held on a STOCK file. Some typical records are shown in Figure 9.24. These are held on disk as variable length records, the fields being separated by the ^ character in this illustration. The final field (8432 in the case of record 1000) is a date field and is stored on disk as a numbers of days (since the origin for the Pick operating system clock is on 1st January 1968); so 8432 is 31st January 1991. SB+ converts all dates automatically to the required format.

```
1000^DESK, GREEN-BLUE, ASH^8^MN/17/81^5600^30^2^8432
2000^SETTEE, YELLOW, OAK^18^DN/1/69^10000^30^1^8418
3000^SIDEBOARD, BLUE, ASH^58^MN/5/56^13000^15^2^8395
4000^DESK, BLACK, MAPLE^68^LS/7/87^5600^30^1^8404
1200^DESK, GREY, ASH^16^LS/17/1^5600^30^1^8431
```

Figure 9.24 *Items on the STOCK file*

Like most 4GLs, SB+ is used by filling in a series of definitions and specifications on the screen. We first create the data dictionary definitions for each of the fields on the STOCK file. This is done individually, a definition for each field. Figure 9.25 shows one such definition for the key field on the STOCK file.

```
Field Name          CODE
Field Description   Code
Field Position      0
Type (A/N/D/M)      N
Length Of Field     4
Report Heading      Code
Conversion
Correlative
Allow Amend (Y/N)   Y
Default Value       G10,4
Validation Code     P:4N
Intuitive Help      LIST.CODES
Help Reminder(Y/N)  Y
```

Figure 9.25   *SB+ key field definition*

Note the following points about the information provided in Figure 9.25:

- We chose the name CODE as the field name to identify the key field on the data dictionary.
- The field definition can be specified directly or, as in this case, SB+ will assume that is the same as the field name.
- The key field is declared as field position 0.
- We specify that the key field is to be numeric. The other possibilities are Alphanumeric, Date or Money.
  SB+ will display the data and headings of alpanumeric fields (such as the DESCRIPTION) in a left-justified manner, and all numeric and money fields (such as the PRICE) in a right-justified manner.
- The key field is to be up to four bytes in length.
- The user is to be allowed to amend the key field.
- The default value, when creating a new record, is to be generated from the 10th of a set of standard counters used by SB+ and is to be 4 digits long. These counters are incremented in steps of 1 each time they are used.
- If the user enters a value for the code, SB+ is to validate that it matches a 4 numeric digit pattern.

- The *Intuitive Help* specifies that when the user asks for help (by pressing the F3 function key on his/her terminal), then SB+ is to execute a processing routine called LIST.CODES. This will be written by the programmer and will probably ask the user for some data – such as the colour or the price – which is to be used as a secondary key to identify the record which he/she wants to handle; SB+ will then display the keys of the records which allow him/her to choose the record they want.
- Finally, we say that we wish to specify a help message to remind the user what is to be entered. This help message will be displayed when the user seeks help by pressing the Fl function key. SB+ will ask us to type in the help message when we enter the Y in this field of the definition.

We shall mention other parts of the field definition later.

A similar set of information is used to describe each of the other fields of the record. Definitions for DESCRIPTION (field 1 of the records) and the PRICE (field 4 of the records) are shown in Figure 9.26. The definition for DESCRIPTION is straightforward. That for PRICE needs a few words of explanation:

- We have specified that PRICE is to be of the Monetary field type.
- The *conversion code* of MD2 specifies that, when SB+ displays the PRICE the raw data is to be displayed with 2 places of decimals.

```
Field Name         DESCRIPTION
Field Description  Description
Field Position     1
Type (A/N/D/M)     A
Length Of Field    40
Report Heading     Description
Conversion
Correlative
Allow Amend (Y/N)  Y
Default Value
Validation Code
Intuitive Help
Help Reminder(Y/N) Y
```

```
Field Name         PRICE
Field Description  Price
Field Position     4
Type (A/N/D/M)     M
Length Of Field    10
Report Heading           Price
Conversion         MD2
Correlative
Allow Amend (Y/N)  Y
Default Value      "0"
Validation Code
Intuitive Help
Help Reminder(Y/N) Y
```

Figure 9.26 *SB+ field definitions*

421

- We have specified a default value of "0". This means that if the user does not enter a price for a product, then SB+ will assume a price of zero.

Question

1   Look at the raw data records in Figure 9.24 and use the information there to complete the table in Figure 9.27 showing the data as it would appear when displayed by SB+.

Code	Description	Price

Figure 9.27   *SB+ data output: question*

Activity 9

Write down the field definitions for the other fields of the records.

Derived fields

One feature of SB+ and of the Pick operating system upon which it is founded, is that one data value can be derived from one or more other data fields. We could, for example,

- Pick out the second word of the description in field 1 and identify this by the name COLOUR.
- Use the price (in field 4) and the quantity (in field 2) to display the value of the stock in the store. This is illustrated by the field VALUE in Figure 9.28.
- Read the supplier code (in field 6 of the STOCK records) which is the key to another file (called SUPPLIERS) and use this to bring back data from the SUPPLIERS record for the supplier with that supplier code. This is illustrated by the field SNAME in Figure 9.28.

The *correlative* part of the field definition indicates how this information is to be derived from elsewhere in the database.

```
Field Name           VALUE
Field Description     Value
Field Position        0
Type (A/N/D/M)        M
Length Of Field       10
Report Heading           Value
Conversion           MD2
Correlative          (PRICE * QUANTITY)
Allow Amend (Y/N)    N
Default Value
Validation Code
Intuitive Help
Help Reminder(Y/N)
```

```
Field Name           SNAME
Field Description     Supplier Name
Field Position        0
Type (A/N/D/M)        A
Length Of Field       40
Report Heading        Supplier Name
Conversion
Correlative          (F("SUPPLIERS",<SUPPLIER>)<NAME>)
Allow Amend (Y/N)    N
Default Value
Validation Code
Intuitive Help
Help Reminder(Y/N)
```

Figure 9.28   *SB+ derived fields*

Using the data dictionary

Now that we have defined the fields which we wish to use, we can use them to develop the processing within our system. A typical SB+ system makes very little use of specially written programs. Instead, the input and output screens and the reports are generated from specifications created by the analyst and/or the programmer and submitted to the SB+ run-time software.

There are several ways of producing data input, data enquiry and report systems. One is a *quick-build* facility which allows you to paint your screen layout and create your field definitions at the same time; this is useful for producing cheap and cheerful processing routines and for *prototyping*. The most usual is first to create your field definitions, as we have done, and then paint a screen image using the names on the data dictionary. If we wished to produce a system to maintain records on the STOCK file, we would select the required task for the SB+ menus and then go through a mechanical process of moving the cursor around the screen and when we have reached the required position we should:

423

- type in the text which is to appear on the screen or
- press the F5 function key to instruct SB+ to insert one of your data fields on the screen. SB+ will ask for the name of the field which is to appear on the screen.

As we add a field to our screen, SB+ will display the field description (if required) and a pattern of Xs (for alphanumeric fields), 9s (for numeric fields) or a date mask (for date fields).

The finished screen might look like that shown in Figure 9.29.

```
        Code: XXXX

 Description: XXXXXXXXXXXXXXXXXXXXXXXXXXXXXXXXXXXXXXXXXX

        Price                                       Minimum
     9999999.99                                   9999999999

 Location               Quantity        Date         Value
 XXXXXXXXXXXXXXX       9999999999     31/12/99     9999999.99

 Supplier         Supplier name
 XXXX                   XXXXXXXXXXXXXXXXXXXXXXXXXXXXXXXXXXXXXXXXXX
```

Figure 9.29   *SB+ screen painted by the programmer*

As you *paint* each such screen (and reports are created in exactly the same manner), you will use the function keys to indicate any special requirements. One very important function key is F2, which is generally used to file and finish the current activity. When you are satisfied with your design and finally file the screen or report, SB+ will ask you whereabouts in the menu structure this screen or report is to be inserted. In the case of a screen, SB+ will also ask whether it is to be used for input (that is, for the user to create, change and/or delete records on the file) or for output (that is for enquiries and simple reports). When this has been done, the screen is ready for use as a data input or data enquiry processing routine.

In the same manner, any special processing programs – called *processes* – written in the SB+ processing language or in the dialect of Basic which is offered on the Pick operating system, can also be created and hung on to the menu structure. These processes can be slotted in to almost any point within the SB+ system: before/after a screen is displayed, before/after a data field is input, before/after a record is read from the file, before/after a record is written to the file, and many more; the possibilities are almost endless.

SB+ and the users

When the users switch on their terminals and enter their user identification code, SB+ throws them straight into a menu structure appropriate to their own code. The user then navigates through this menu structure, selecting the work which he/she wants to perform.

SB+ makes extensive use of the functions keys and other keyboard features in order to allow the user to carry out his/her work with a minimum of effort and to reduce the number of keystrokes necessary to perform any task. In addition to F1 (which is used for asking for help) and F3 (which is used for intuitive help), other useful keys include F4 which is generally used to delete the current record and F5 which normally abandons the current activity.

Unlike many pieces of software, SB+ does not entirely disguise the underlying operating; this allows experienced technical users to do all that they want to do. But at the same time it offers a firm structure for the applications system, guiding and helping the user all along the way (there are up to seven levels of help available at some points!).

Assignment 5

Imagine that you are a programmer using a fourth generation language such as SB+. A user has asked to you to write a completely new system which will allow her to process her name and address information.

She needs to hold the following information: name, house number, street, town, postcode, county, telephone number.

(1) In your own words, describe the steps you would take to create the routine to handle your user's name and address records.

(2) Write down the field definitions which you would produce (normally you would not write these on paper; instead, you would type the information straight into an SB+ field definition screen and ask SB+ to print out the definitions when you wanted a hard-copy).

(3) Draw the screen which you would use to maintain the records on the file (normally you would not design your screen on paper; instead, you would paint the screen as described in the text and ask SB+ to print out the screen when you wanted a hard-copy).

(4)   Later, when your system has been working nicely for some time, she wants to add a new field to the records: the date when she last sent a letter to this address. How would you handle this? Describe the steps which you would take.

(5)   Your user has asked what other use she sould make of the information on the name and address file. What would you tell her?

Recap

- There are many ways of giving instructions to a computer. In this chapter, we considered two: procedural and a non-procedural. A procedural language gives a detailed, step by step description of what the computer is to do. A non-procedural language gives an outline of the main action and any detailed processing and then lets the software fill in the rest.

- An early example of a non-procedural language is a report program generator, such as RPG. The user provides a sets of specifications defining the files and the reports, and then lets RPG use this to do the required work.

- A program generator is a software tool which takes an abbreviated description of the processing and from this generates the necessary source code – in Cobol or some other third generation language. This source program can then be edited, compiled and executed as required.

- With the growing use of database technology, most database management systems offer a language for handling the contents of the database. Typically, this includes a data description language (for defining the contents of the database and creating a data dictionary), a data manipulation language (for creating changing and deleting the data held on the database), and a data control language (for controlling the passwords and other security aspects of the database).

- A most powerful tool for use with a database is an enquiry language. These enable the end-users to make their own enquiries about the database and to produce their own reports. In this chapter, we looked briefly at the principal features of the languages SQL, dBASE and QBE.

- Fourth generation languages offer a further means of handling a database. These are generally based around a data dictionary and offer a fairly high-level language for manipulating the data.

- Because of the ease with which 4GLs can be used, they are an ideal medium for the technique of prototyping. This starts with a quick and basic model of the system which, by gradually adding and refining the features required by the user, evolves into a system doing just what the user wants.

Answer to question

1   Your table should look like that in Figure 9.30.

Code	Description	Price
1000	DESK, GREEN-BLUE, ASH	56.00
2000	SETTEE, YELLOW, OAK	100.00
3000	SIDEBOARD, BLUE, ASH	130.00
4000	DESK, BLACK, MAPLE	56.00
1200	DESK, GREY, ASH	56.00

Figure 9.30   *SB+ data output: solution*

10: Applying languages: specialist

Objectives

After reading this chapter, you should be able to:

- Describe the concepts of **concurrent processing, synchronization, and deadlock.**
- Draw a **process diagram** for concurrent processing and transform this into code in the language **Occam.**
- Describe the nature of a **transputer.**
- Describe the features of **simulation languages.**
- Recognize the terms **servers** and **transactions** and represent these on a **queuing diagram.**
- Draw a queuing diagram and use this to develop a short program in a simulation language.
- Describe the nature of **linear programming** applications.

As you have worked through this book, you have seen the gradual flow in the development of computer languages. From the fundamental machine code, through to second and third generation languages. In the previous chapter, we saw how commercial programming has followed its own route via enquiry languages and 4GLs, a route which offers simpler and more powerful facilities for business users. In this present chapter, we shall look at two different ways of using programming languages. One of them even challenges the traditional von Neumann computer architecture. The second shows how the need to visualize a particular problem, that of queuing, in non-procedural terms has resulted in the development of a special, non-procedural language.

Concurrent processing

We saw in Chapter 1 how the von Neumann computer model has influenced our thinking for many years. As a consequence of this, most commercial data processing and therefore most commercial computer programs are designed and written to handle sequential processing. The programmer writes the program as a procedural sequence of imperative instructions and the computer executes these one by one until the processing is completed.

A typical program is organized like this:

- Open the files
- Accept the input data
- Process the input data
- Display the results

Even if we introduce *branching* and *looping* structures,

- Open the files
- Accept the input data
- Loop until end of input data
-    process the input data
-    display the results.
-      accept input data
- end loop

the program still only carries out one step when it has completed the previous step.

There are a great many situations in which we could save time by having more than one part of the program executing at the same time. As a simple example, consider the evaluation of an algebraic expression such as:

$$y = x^2 + 2x - 35$$

for a given value of x. We might solve this problem by a design such as:

- Input value for x
- Calculate y
- Print the value of y

and implement this by means of a Basic program like this:

```
INPUT X
Y = X^2 + 2*X - 35
PRINT Y
```

We could represent this diagrammatically as the sequence of shown in Figure 10.1.

429

Figure 10.1 *Sequential processing*

But if we rewrite the algebraic expression as:

$$y = (x - 5)(x + 7)$$

it would be much **faster** to execute the program if we could arrange the processing as:

- input the value for x
- calculate $x-5$ giving r1   (a)
- calculate $x+7$ giving r2   (b)
- calculate y from $y = r1 *>r2$
- print the value of y

and then arrange to perform the two calculations (a) and (b) in **parallel** instead of sequentially, one after the other.

When two or more processes are to be performed at the same time, they are called parallel or **concurrent** processes. We may depict such concurrent processing by means of a **process diagram** such as that shown in Figure 10.2.

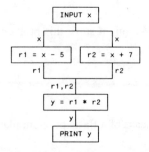

Figure 10.2 *A processing diagram: parallel processing*

Alongside the lines which link the various processing boxes in the process diagram, we have written the names of the values which are travelling along those **links**. You can think of these as being the input parameters and the output parameters for the individual processes.

Question

1   Draw a process diagram to represent the evaluation of the expression:

$$z = (x + 1)(2x - 2)$$

Write the names of the values passing along the links.

2   Draw a process diagram to represent the evaluation of the expression:

$$z = (2x + 3y)(7x - 4y)$$

Write the names of the values passing along the links.

Remember that the four processes (to calculate 2x, 3y, 7x, and 4y) may all be performed concurrently.

A more detailed representation of the process is given by the **annotated** process diagram shown in Figure 10.3. Here, we see quite clearly what each separate processor is doing.

Assignment 1

Draw an annotated process diagram to represent the evaluation of each of the following algebraic expressions:

(a) $y = (x - 5)(x + 7)$
(b) $z = (x + 1)(2x - 2)$
(c) $z = (2x + 3y)(7x - 4y)$
(d) $z = (x + y)(x - y)\ (x^*y) - x$

How does such a system work in practice?

Activity 1

In this activity, I want you to simulate the processes shown in Figure 10.3 using six members of your group, as follows:

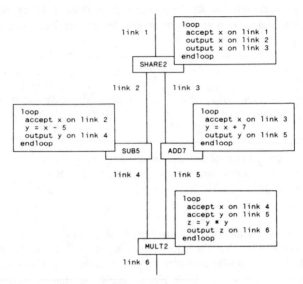

Figure 10.3   *A process diagram: 2*

(a) one member represents the input Link 1 and writes a number (the value of *x*) on a piece of paper and passes it to the member representing SHARE2.

Link 1 then writes another number on another piece of paper and passes this to SHARE2, then another, and another, and . . .

(b) SHARE2 receives the input value of *x*, then writes this on two pieces of paper: one piece is passed to SUB5, the other is passed to ADD7. SHARE2 receives the next number from INPUT and repeats the process.

(c) SUB5 receives the piece of paper from SHARE2, subtracts 5 from it and writes the result on a piece of paper which is passed to MULT7. SUB5 receives the next number from SHARE2 and repeats the process.

(d) ADD7 receives the piece of paper from SHARE2, adds 7 to it and writes the result on a piece of paper which is passed to MULT7. ADD7 receives the next number from SHARE2 and repeats the process.

(e) MULT7 accepts a piece of paper from SUB5, accepts a piece of paper from ADD7, multiplies these two numbers together and writes the result on a piece of paper which is passed to the fifth member representing Link 6. MULT7 receives the next number from SUB5 and then from ADD7 and repeats the process.

(f) Link 6 then writes the result on the board. Link 6 receives the next number from MULT2, writes this on the board and repeats the process.

Make a note of the action of the group. What problems are there? Is anyone too busy? Is anyone to slow? Is anyone spending too much time waiting? Are there are any holdups or bottlenecks? What are the problems? Why?

Summarize the various observations in your own words.

Pay particular attention to the way in which one process communicates with another.

If we arrange our processing in this manner, one important feature is the need for the various boxes on the diagram – the **processes** – to communicate with each other. This not simply so that the data can be passed along the links but it is also necessary so that one process can tell another that it is ready to receive more data. How many times did you hear 'hang on, I'm not ready yet' as you completed the work in Activity 1? You will have realized that, for example,

- a process needs to be able to indicate that it has finished one calculation and is ready to receive the next set of data, and
- a process cannot proceed with its calculation until the necessary set of data has been received from the preceding process (or processes, in the case of MULT2).

In order to be able to implement such a system we need:

(1) a number of separate processors, and
(2) some means of communication between these processors.

Is this feasible?

Synchronization

In order to operate successfully, the various concurrent processes must **synchronize** their activities. Otherwise, one may start without all the necessary information being available for it to complete properly, or, in another situation, one process may attempt to use a resource (such as the printer or a disk file) whilst another is already using it. These two kinds of synchronization are known as **condition synchronization** and **mutual exclusion**.

Condition synchronization

A typical situation in which *condition synchronization* is necessary is where a program is sending output to a printer. The process which generates the output normally sends it to a *buffer* and the printer takes the output from the buffer and prints it character by character. Such a situation is often called a **producer–consumer problem**, because the process which puts data into the buffer (the *producer*) must synchronize with the process which takes data out of the buffer (the *consumer*). If the producer tries to put data into the buffer when it is already full, data may be lost; if the consumer tries to take data out of the buffer before there is any there, the results may be unpredictable.

In this situation, communication between the two processes could be achieved by holding a count of the number of print characters which are held in the buffer. The producer would use this counter to see whether there is room for another character in the buffer; if so, it would add a character to the buffer and add 1 to the count of how many characters are in the buffer. On the other hand, the consumer would use this counter to see whether there are any characters to be taken from the buffer; if so, it would remove a character from the buffer and subtract 1 from the count of how many characters are in the buffer.

Mutual exclusion

Mutual exclusion would be required in a situation where several different users are handling the same data file. Imagine the situation in which there are several different travel clerks using the same computer system and all attempting to book the last remaining seat on the flight SG0001 from Glasgow to Paris: they might all look at the computer record for that flight, see that one seat is available and claim it for themselves, with the result that the flight is overbooked, too many people are sold tickets and attempt to board the plane. We need a system whereby one process (that used by travel clerk A) is able to tell another process (that used by travel clerk B) that the file is busy because someone (travel clerk A) is looking at the record for the Paris flight.

434

Communication between the various processes which require *mutual exclusion* could be made by building up a *busy list* of the flight records which are currently being inspected with a possibility of someone making a reservation. When passenger A comes along with an enquiry about flight SG0001 the process checks whether that flight number appears in the busy list, if not, then the number is added to the list and the enquiry can proceed; when the booking has been made (or declined) the flight number is removed from the list. If passenger B comes along and wants to make an enquiry about flight SG0001 but finds that flight SG0001 is already in the busy list, the process will recognize the fact and it can be arranged to display a message to the travel clerk saying something like 'this flight record is busy, please try again later' and then go on to give the clerk the opportunity to try another flight or wait, or the process may simply wait until the flight number has been removed from the list before proceeding. This latter situation – in which the process does nothing except repeatedly look at the busy list to see whether or not it can proceed – is known as **busy waiting**.

Deadlock

Unfortunately, such mutual exclusion can result in a situation known as **deadlock** or **deadly embrace**. To explain this, let us imagine that passenger A wants to fly from London to Paris on flight LP0001 on January 1st and then on to Zurich on flight PZ0001 on January 2nd; if both flights are possible the passenger will book the two seats and take the tickets. At that same moment, but at another travel agent in another part of town, passenger B is asking to fly from Paris to Zurich on flight PZ0001 on January 2nd and if this is possible, she wants to fly into Paris on flight LP0001 on January 1st; if both flights are possible the passenger will book the two seats and take the tickets. Here we have two passengers wishing to look at the same flight records, but making their enquiries in different ways. Passenger A locks out others from looking at flight LP0001 but cannot complete the bookings (and release flight LP0001) until he has made the booking on flight PZ0001; however passenger B locks out others from looking at flight PZ0001 but cannot complete the bookings (and release flight PZ0001) until she has made the booking on flight LP0001.

If the airline system does not take special precautions – such as only allowing one enquiry to be made at one time – it is possible that a deadlock problem could only be resolved by switching off the entire system!

435

Activity 2

In your own words, describe what you understand by the terms *condition synchronization, mutual exclusion* and *deadlock*.

Consider these situations, and say whether and how condition synchronization and/or mutual exclusion apply:

- A number of people are waiting to collect their pensions at the post office. There is only one counter open.
- A shop assistant is stacking bread on a supermarket shelf for customers to buy.
- There are roadworks where the men are digging a hole in a narrow country road. Only one lane is open and this is controlled by a set of traffic lights.
- Later in the week, a second gang of workmen dig a second hole thirty yards from the first hole. The traffic here is also controlled by signals.

Could deadlock occur?

Describe some other situations in which condition synchronization or mutual exclusion could be involved.

How could deadlock result in any of these situations?

Transputers

Recent developments in computer hardware design have led to the production of the **transputer**. A transputer is a microprocessor on a chip and has a number of independent controllers – known as **link interface controllers** – each of which is able to communicate with other transputers. Several transputers are linked together in a network and the processing is distributed to the various parts of the network. Each transputer uses its interface controllers to let the other transputers know when it is ready to receive data or submit its results. Such an arrangement of hardware which uses several independent processors is known as a **multi-processing** system.

Even without the use of transputers and multi-processing, it is possible for an operating system with a single processor to **simulate** parallel processing. Let us see how this may be done. We can picture the simple *sequential* processing as in Figure 10.4.

By taking advantage of those occasions when one process is unable to proceed – it may be waiting for data to come in from the keyboard or it may be waiting to transfer data to or from the disk – it is possible for

```
┌──── Process 1 ─────┐
│ Process 1 step 1   │
│ Process 1 step 2   │
│ Process 1 step 3   │
│ Process 1 step 4   │
└────────────────────┘
┌──── Process 2 ─────┐
│ Process 2 step 1   │
│ Process 2 step 2   │
│ Process 2 step 3   │
│ Process 2 step 4   │
└────────────────────┘
```

Figure 10.4   *Performing two processes sequentially*

a single processor to perform a step from one process, then a step from the other, then another step from the first, and so on. We can picture such **interleaving** as in Figure 10.5.

```
┌────────────────────┐
│ Process 1, step 1  │
│ Process 2, step 1  │
│ Process 1, step 2  │
│ Process 2, step 2  │
│ Process 1, step 3  │
│ Process 2, step 3  │
│ Process 1, step 4  │
│ Process 2, step 4  │
└────────────────────┘
```

Figure 10.5   *Interleaving the two processes*

The vertical arrow to the left of the diagram represents the flow of time taken to carry out the process. Unfortunately, such interleaving does not always reduce the overall time taken to complete the two processes (in fact, because of the time taken to switch from one process to the other, the total elapsed time may be slightly longer than for sequential processing). Compare this diagram of *interleaved* processing with the representation of true *parallel* processing shown in Figure 10.6.

Occam

Now that computers are able to behave in this concurrent manner – whether by true parallel processing or by simulated parallel processing – there is a requirement for a programming language which will allow the analyst and programmer to specify, design and write concurrent systems. The existing languages are based around the concept of

```
          Process 1              Process 2
     Process 1 step 1       Process 2 step 1
     Process 1 step 2       Process 2 step 2
     Process 1 step 3       Process 2 step 3
     Process 1 step 4       Process 2 step 4
```

Figure 10.6   *True parallel processing*

sequential processing and have no means of indicating that two (or more processes) can be performed at the same time.

One such language is called **Occam**. The Occam language was created by INMOS Limited in the UK and INMOS Corporation in the USA.

Occam has many of the familiar features of any programming language but it also has facilities for:

● Specifying concurrent (parallel) processing.
● Denoting the communication between processes.
● Identifying the various links along which the data is to be passed, received and sent.

To convert the problem:

$$y = (x-5)(x+7)$$

into an Occam definition, we must first draw a process diagram, such as those we used earlier, and then name the various processes and the links or **channels** along which the data is to be passed. We must also take care to draw the channels so that each one is a simple link between two processes with no junctions. We have also added two new channels **keyboard** and **screen**. Our process diagram from Figure 10.2 might then look like that in Figure 10.7.

Assignment 2

Redraw the process diagram shown in Figure 10.7 and, alongside each channel, write the name of the data value (*x*, *y*, and so on) which is travelling along that channel, and add an arrow to show the direction in which the data is travelling.

Redraw your process diagrams from Assignment 10.1 in the same manner.

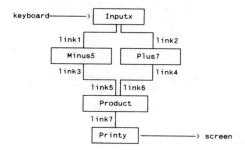

Figure 10.7 *A process diagram for Occam*

If we look at the process *Inputx*, for example, then we see that it takes an input value *x* from channel *keyboard*, and outputs value *x* along channel *link1* and value *x* along channel *link2*. *Inputx* performs no other processing.

Question

3 For each process on the diagram in Figure 10.7, write down

   (a) the names of the channels which it uses, and

   (b) the names of the data values coming along those chan-nels.

An Occam definition

We can now specify each process in turn. An Occam program consists of a set of declarations, constructions and actions. To illustrate this, let us start by looking at the process *Inputx* which we could write as the Occam definition shown in Figure 10.8.

The PROC declaration names the process which we are defining. Note the equal sign after the name.

The CHAN declaration names the channels (the links) which this process has with the outside world and with other processes.

The VAR declaration names the local variables which we shall use in this process.

The SEQ construction specifies that the following statements are to be executed sequentially.

439

```
PROC Inputx =
    CHAN keyboard, link1, link2
    VAR x
    SEQ
        keyboard?x
        link1!x
        link2!x :
```

Figure 10.8   *An Occam process definition*

The statement:

keyboard?x

indicates that this process receives an input value on channel *keyboard* and this value is to be placed in the variable called *x*. If there is no data coming in on the *keyboard* channel, then the process will wait until there is some. As in most programming languages, the names of your channels and variables are arbitrary. The ? indicates that the value is to be input.

The statement:

link1!x

indicates that the value of *x* is to be output on the channel called *link1*. the ! indicates that the value is to be output. The statement:

link2!x

indicates that the value of *x* is then to be output on the channel called *link2*.

There are other statements in Occam. For example, assignment could be performed by statements of the form:

x1 := x2 + 5

The final colon indicates the end of the definition.

The indentation of the Occam statements is important.

Questions

Using the above example as a model, produce an Occam definition for the following processes:

4   The process *Printy*.
5   The process *Minus5*.

6   The process *Plus7*.

7   The process *Product*.

8   You may have felt that there is no real need to separate the *Printy* process and the *Product* process in our process design. We could have combined them into a single process.

Draw the new process diagram corresponding to this new structure and call it *Result*.

Write the Occam definition for the new *Result* process.

Now that we have specified the individual processes, we can specify the whole program. Let us call this *Calculate*. The *Calculate* program will simply call each component sub-process by name, as shown in Figure 10.9. The important feature here is the PAR construction which indicates that the two processes:

Minus5

and

Plus7

may be carried out in *parallel* (concurrently). You should now appreciate why the indentation of an Occam program is important.

More Occam facilities

Our *Calculate* program is only capable of handling one value of *x* at a

```
PROC Calculate(CHAN keyboard, screen)
     SEQ
          Inputx
          PAR
               Minus5
               Plus7
          Product
          Printy :

               (a) using Product and Printy

PROC Calculate(CHAN keyboard, screen)
     SEQ
          Inputx
          PAR
               Minus5
               Plus7
          Result :

               (b) using Result
```

Figure 10.9   *Occam program: 1*

time. Occam has a loop construction will allow us to overcome this. The general form of the *loop* construction is:

WHILE condition

   process

Since we need to keep running indefinitely in order to calculate a large number of values we might use the loop construction in our example as shown in Figure 10.10.

```
PROC Calculate(CHAN keyboard, screen)
    VAR calculating
    SEQ
        calculating := TRUE
        WHILE calculating
            SEQ
                Inputx
                PAR
                    Minus5
                    Plus7
                Result :
```

Figure 10.10   *Occam: looping*

In this program, *calculating* is simply a variable which is set to *true* so that the program will execute over and over again, indefinitely. Having arranged to repeat the processing, we now require some means of terminating the execution. We could do this by adding a test which will stop the execution when a certain value is entered for *x*. Tests are performed by means of the conditional construction. This takes the form of a case-like construction, as shown in Figure 10.11. There may be any number of test conditions with a final TRUE condition to catch the processing in case none of the previous conditions is satisfied.

Applying this to our process, we could write the program so that it will terminate if the user enters a value of 9999 for x, as shown in

```
IF
    condition1
        process1
    condition2
        process2

    TRUE
        processn
```

Figure 10.11   *Occam: conditional / case*

Figure 10.12 (a), or (more elegantly) without the use of the STOP statement, as in diagram (b).

```
PROC Inputx =
    CHAN keyboard, link1, link2
    VAR x
    SEQ
        keyboard?x
        IF
            x = 9999
                STOP
            TRUE
                link1!x
                link2!x :

                        (a)

PROC Calculate(CHAN keyboard, screen)
    VAR calculating
    SEQ
        calculating := TRUE
        WHILE calculating
            SEQ
                Inputx
                IF
                    x = 9999
                        calculating := false
                    TRUE
                        PAR
                            Minus5
                            Plus7
                        Result :

                        (b)
```

Figure 10.12   *Occam program: 2*

Assignment 3

Using the work which you completed earlier, write an Occam program to perform the calculation:

$$z = (2x + 3y)(7x - 4y)$$

The program is to terminate when the value of z is greater than 9999999999.

Priority and selection

Obviously, in our simple examples, there is no great advantage in performing the processes in parallel. There are, however, a great many other problems which can benefit from concurrent processing. For example, an air traffic control program must be capable of performing more than one process at a time. This is illustrated in Figure 10.13.

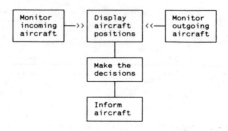

Figure 10.13 *An air traffic control system*

The system must accept input from various radar screens to monitor the positions of the aircraft which are landing and taking off, and display the details to the air traffic controller. The air traffic controller will then make his/her decisions and give the appropriate instructions to the aircraft. Whilst the sequence:

- observe aircraft positions,
- make the decisions,
- give the instructions

is repeated indefinitely, the processes which monitor and display the aircraft positions must be carried out continuously (we indicated this by the use of double-headed arrows in Figure 10.13).

Activity 3

Write down some reasons why it would be unsatisfactory to write a sequential program such as

- loop
-     monitor incoming aircraft positions,
-     display incoming aircraft positions,
-     monitor outgoing aircraft positions,
-     display outgoing aircraft positions,
-     make the decisions,
-     inform incoming aircraft,

- inform outgoing aircraft,
  end loop

to solve the air traffic control problem.

This method of processing is not entirely satisfactory. We do not want to have to wait for, say, the incoming-aircraft-channel before we listen to outgoing-aircraft-channel in case there is no data coming on incoming-aircraft-channel. Otherwise, outgoing aircraft might have to wait all day, until an arriving plane allowed us to proceed with the processing.

When data is coming in on more than one channel, we want to be able to act upon whichever comes in first. Occam has facilities to allow us to address problems such as these. This particular problem is handled by the ALT construction shown in Figure 10.14.

```
ALT
    channel1?a
      b  := a*a
        channel7!b
    channel2?x
        y  := 2*x
        channel7!y
```

Figure 10.14   *Occam: priority – 1*

In this case, the action to be taken is determined by whichever data is received first: the value *a* on *channel1* or the value *x* on channel *2*. There may be any number of such choices.

If we have two actions such as:

    channela?xxx
    channelb?yyy

then the process will wait until data is received on *channela* before it will receive any data sent along *channelb*. This may be inefficient, especially if the program could be doing something useful with the value *xxx* whilst it is waiting for the value *yyy* to come in on *channelb*. This time-wasting can be overcome by use of an ALT construction as shown in Figure 10.15.

If we use the simple ALT construction and data comes in on both channels simultaneously, then the processor will make a random choice as to which is accepted first. If there is to be some priority over the actions, then we could use the PRI ALT construction, as shown in

```
ALT
    channela?xxx
         rxxx := 2+xxx
         channelb?yyy
         ryyy := 3*yyy
    channelb?yyy
         ryyy := 3*yyy
         channela?xxx
         rxxx := 2+xxx
```

Figure 10.15   *Occam: priority – 2*

```
PRI ALT
    channel1?a
         b := a*a
         channel7!b
    channel2?x
         y := 2*x
         channel7!y
```

Figure 10.16   *Occam: priority – 3*

Figure 10.16. In this case, if data comes in on both channels at the same moment, then any data received on channel1 (which is specified first) will be given priority over any which may be received on channel2.

Assignment 4

Write suitable Occam code for the calculations which you considered in the practical work in this chapter.

Simulation problems

Some computer problems have no *exact* solution. How many people will want to buy railway tickets in the rush hour? How long will the queue be at the railway ticket office at 8:25 on a Monday morning? Architects who are designing a railway station and British Rail managers who are making decisions on whether or not to employ extra staff or to buy new ticket machines need to know the answers to such questions.

These problems are inexact because we do not know **exactly** how many people will go to the railway station at any one time. But, by conducting surveys and counting the numbers of passengers which flow through the station, we can produce averages and estimates of typical figures. Using these statistics, we can perform a computer **simulation** of the activity at the station.

Simulation can be applied to many problems:

- The flow of traffic at a busy road junction. We might have some idea of the average numbers of vehicles arriving, which road they use to reach the junction and which road they use to leave it.
- The efficiency of the pumps at a petrol station.

Activity 4

Suggest some other problems which might be studied with the aid of computer simulation.

Simulation languages

It would be possible to write a program in Basic or Cobol to perform the simulation for us, but since simulations are a useful business tool and can be applied to a wide range of topics, a number of **simulation languages** have emerged for specifying and solving such problems: GPSS (the General Purpose System Simulation) language is one of the most widely-used of these languages.

To see how a simulation language is used, let us consider our railway station. Let us propose the following situation:

- Passengers are of two main types: those who buy their tickets for each journey and those who buy season tickets and use these for their journeys. We shall call these **buyers** and **holders**.
- Buyers arrive at the station, queue for a ticket at the ticket office, buy their ticket, then proceed to queue at the barrier.
- Holders who already have their season ticket arrive at the station and proceed directly to the barrier.
- Some holders may decide to buy or renew their season ticket: they arrive at the station, join the queue at the ticket office, purchase (or renew) their ticket, then proceed to the barrier. We shall call these **renewers**.

Based upon this scenario, the railway authorities want to know: how long will a typical passenger have to wait at the ticket barrier?

Activity 5

Suggest some other figures which might be of use to the British Rail manager who is studying the behaviour of the railway station.
   Suggest some figures which might be of interest to:

(1)   A traffic analyst studying a busy road junction.
(2)   A garage owner concerned about the use of the petrol pumps at her service station.
(3)   A bank manager concerned about the service which he gives his clients at the tills.

What is the problem?

Let us consider another, simpler problem: the people arriving to be served at the village post office.

   In order to carry out a simulation of the problem, we need to know two sets of information:

(1)   how frequently do customers join each queue: we shall call this the **inter-arrival time**.
(2)   how long does it take to serve the average customer: we shall call this the **service time**.

Let us suppose that, for the post office these figures are

● (on average) the inter-arrival time is 2 minutes, and
● (on average) the service time is 3 minutes.

What will happen to the queue? Will the queue grow, stay about the same length, or will there never be a queue?

   A pencil-and-paper way of answering these questions is to draw a table with four columns showing the time in minutes since the post office opened, the identity of each customer arriving at the counter, the identities of the customers currently waiting in the queue, and the identity of the customer currently being served.

   We first go down the ARRIVALS column and mark the arrival of one customer every 2 minutes. Each customer is identified by a letter.

   Then we start the complicated part. We go down the table, minute by minute, and look at the AT THE COUNTER column: if the counter is busy, then we add the new arrival to the end of the queue in the IN QUEUE column; if there is no one at the counter, then we move the new arrival to the AT THE COUNTER column and then make 2 further entries for that customer in the AT THE COUNTER COLUMN (because the customer will stay there for 3 minutes). We go down the table, repeating this for each new arrival. The results for the first 30 minutes are shown in Figure 10.17.

Mins after opening	Arrivals	In queue	At the counter
0			
1			
2	A		A
3			A
4	B	B	A
5			B
6	C	C	B
7		C	B
8	D	D	C
9		D	C
10	E	D,E	C
11		E	D
12	F	E,F	D
13		E,F	D
14	G	F,G	E
15		F,G	E
16	H	F,G,H	E
17		G,H	F
18	I	G,H,I	F
19		G,H,I	F
20	J	H,I,J	G
21		H,I,J	G
22	K	H,I,J,K	G
23		I,J,K	H
24	L	I,J,K,L	H
25		I,J,K,L	H
26	M	J,K,L,M	I
27		J,K,L,M	I
28	N	J,K,L,M,N	I
29		K,L,M,N	J
30	O	K,L,M,N,O	J

Figure 10.17 *Times for the village post office*

Since this particular problem is not very complicated, a little thought will show that in, say, 30 minutes, the counter can serve 10 customers, but in that time 15 customers will join the queue. As a result, the queue will grow at the rate of about 5 every half-hour. This is exactly what our pencil-and-paper method showed.

However, if we open a second counter, we can see that in, say, 30 minutes, the counters can serve 20 customers, and in that time, 15 customers will join the queue. As a result, the queue will not form.

In general, we can say that,

● If the inter-arrival time is less than the service time, then the queue will grow indefinitely. This is the first situation above: inter-arrival time is 2 minutes, the service time is 3 minutes.

449

- If the inter-arrival time is equal to the service time, then the queue will be stable, almost one-in, one-out.
- If the inter-arrival time is greater than the service time, then the queue will not form. This is the second situation above: inter-arrival time is 2 minutes, the service time is 1.5 minutes.

Assignment 5

(1) Make a copy of the table in Figure 10.17 and add an extra column to write in the time for which each customer waits in the queue. This is the difference between that customer arriving at the post office and leaving the queue at the counter.

What is the average waiting time?

What is the maximum length of the queue?

What is the average length of the queue?

(2) Let us imagine that there is only one counter open at the post office, but if the queue is longer than 3 people a second counter will be opened. This second counter will close when there are no more people waiting to be served.

Draw a table like that in Figure 10.17 to observe the new situation.

Add an extra column to write in the time that each customer waits in the queue. This is the difference between that customer arriving at the post office and leaving the post office.

What is the average waiting time?

(3) In a queue at the two enquiry desks of a museum, visitors arrive at the rate of one every 1.5 minutes. It takes 3 minutes for one clerk to answer an enquiry, and 1 minute for the other clerk to answer an enquiry (he is more experienced than his colleague). What will happen to the queue? Will the queue grow, stay about the same length, or will there never be a queue?

What will happen if we open a third enquiry desk with a sevice time of 4 minutes?

(4) Construct a table to show the formation of the queues at an airport during the first 15 minutes of business. Each passenger goes to the check-in counter, then to the passport control counter, then the customs channel. There are 2 check-in counters: the inter-arrival time for the passengers is 1 minute, and the service time is 2 minutes. There is one passport control counter: service time is 0.5 minutes. There is one customs channel: service time is 4 minutes.

Queuing diagrams

In order to investigate the railway station problem, we need to know these two sets of statistics, the inter-arrival times and the service times:

(1) How frequently do the buyers, the holders and the renewers arrive at the station?

Our surveys show that, on average, during the period in which we are interested, buyers arrive at the rate of 1 every minute, holders at the rate of one every 2 minutes, and renewers at the rate of one every 30 minutes.

(2) How long does a buyer take to buy a ticket?
Anything between 30 and 70 seconds.

(3) How long does a renewer take to renew a season ticket?
Anything between 1 minute and 3 minutes.

(4) How long does a buyer take to pass the barrier?
Anything between 5 and 20 seconds.

(5) How long does a holder (or a renewer) take to pass the barrier?
10 seconds.

The first step is to draw a queuing diagram. This shows:

(1) the various servers, or facilities which provide the services at the railway station;

(2) the **queues** which form; and

(3) the flow of the **transactions**, the passengers, through the station.

The **servers** are represented by a box with name outside, the *queues* at the servers are represented by a ladder-box, the *transactions* are represented by a box with the name inside. The *flow* of the transactions into the system, from one queue to another and finally out of the system is represented by arrowed-lines. These are illustrated in Figure 10.18.

Question

9 Draw a queuing diagram for the post office using just one counter.

10 Draw a queuing diagram for railway station with one ticket office and one ticket barrier. Show the flow of buyers, holders and renewers.

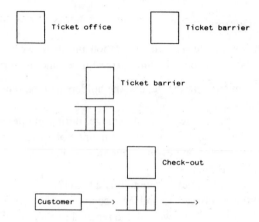

Figure 10.18 *A simulation specification*

A simplified simulation language

In order to specify this situation for the railway station in our simplified simulation language, we first declare the servers and the transactions:

    SERVER TICKETOFFICE
    SERVER TICKETOFFICE
    SERVER TICKETBARRIER

    TRANSACTION BUYER
    TRANSACTION RENEWER
    TRANSACTION HOLDER

The names TICKETOFFICE, HOLDER and so on, are chosen arbitrarily by the person writing the program.

We then go on to specify the figures for the various inter-arrival times and service times:

    BUYERARRIVAL = 60
    BUYEROFFICE = R(30, 70)
    BUYERBARRIER = R(5, 20)
    HOLDERARRIVAL = 120
    HOLDERBARRIER = 10
    RENEWERARRIVAL = 1800
    RENEWEROFFICE = R(60,180)

The times are specified in seconds in this example. There are two types of pattern for the times:

- an exact value, as in

    BUYERARRIVAL = 60

    which indicates that the inter-arrival time for buyers (called BUYER-ARRIVAL) is 60 seconds.

- a random number within a specific range, as in

    BUYEROFFICE = R(30,70)

    which indicates that service time for buyers buying a ticket at the ticket office (BUYEROFFICE) is a *random number* in the range 30 to 70 seconds.

Similarly, the service time for buyers at the ticket barrier BUYERBAR-RIER) is a random number in the range 5 to 20 seconds. The service time for renewers at the ticket office (RENEWEROFFICE) is a random number in the range 60 to 180 seconds. Most simulation languages have facilities for expressing more complicated patterns for the inter-arrival and service times, but we shall not consider them here.

Next, we specify each *transaction* in turn. The simplest case is the holders. We should express this in the simulation language as:

```
GENERATE HOLDER HOLDERARRIVAL
    SEIZE TICKETBARRIER
    HOLD HOLDERBARRIER
    RELEASE TICKETBARRIER
DESTROY HOLDER
```

showing the progress of the *holder* passenger through the system. The first statement:

    GENERATE HOLDER HOLDERARRIVAL

tells the simulation system to imagine that a new holder has arrived at the station and that these passengers arrive at times specified by the expression for HOLDERARRIVAL. The statement:

    SEIZE TICKETBARRIER

requests that the holder be placed in a queue at the ticket barrier. When that holder's turn comes around, the statement:

453

HOLD HOLDERBARRIER

tells the simulation system that the holder will occupy the ticket barrier for a time specified by the expression for HOLDERBARRIER and when this time has passed, the statement:

RELEASE TICKETBARRIER

tells the simulation system that the ticket barrier is now free for the next passenger in the queue. Finally, the statement:

DESTROY HOLDER

will allow that holder to pass out of the system completely.

For the *buyers*, the specification would be slightly more complicated since each new buyer will first occupy a place in the queue for the ticket office and then go on to occupy a place in the queue at the ticket barrier. This, and the specification for *renewers* can be seen in the complete specification in Figure 10.19.

```
SERVER TICKETOFFICE
SERVER TICKETOFFICE
SERVER TICKETBARRIER

TRANSACTION BUYER
TRANSACTION RENEWER
TRANSACTION HOLDER

BUYERARRIVAL = 60
BUYEROFFICE = R(30,70)
BUYERBARRIER = R(5,20)
HOLDERARRIVAL = 120
HOLDERBARRIER = 10
RENEWERARRIVAL = 1800
RENEWEROFFICE = R(60,180)

GENERATE HOLDER HOLDERARRIVAL
       SEIZE TICKETBARRIER
            HOLD HOLDERBARRIER
       RELEASE TICKETBARRIER
DESTROY HOLDER

GENERATE BUYER BUYERARRIVAL
       SEIZE TICKETOFFICE
            HOLD BUYEROFFICE
       RELEASE TICKETOFFICE
       SEIZE TICKETBARRIER
            HOLD BUYERBARRIER
       RELEASE TICKETBARRIER
DESTROY BUYER

GENERATE RENEWER RENEWERARRIVAL
       SEIZE TICKETOFFICE
            HOLD RENEWEROFFICE
       RELEASE TICKETOFFICE
       SEIZE TICKETBARRIER
            HOLD RENEWERBARRIER
       RELEASE TICKETBARRIER
DESTROY RENEWER
```

Figure 10.19 *A simulation specification*

The simulation language specification represents a model of our station system. Having produced the model, we would submit it to the simulation system. The system would then generate a stream of random numbers representing the arrival, service and departure of the passengers according to the rules we specified. There would be facilities for us to indicate how long the simulation is to run: we might ask for the simulation to represent the passage of 100 passengers through the system, or we might ask it to run for a simulated period of 1 hour from the start of business, or we might say that we want the system to become stable (with the queues neither growing nor shrinking) and then observe its progress over the next hour. When the simulation has finished, a set of statistics would be produced by the system, including:

- the average queue length at each of the servers;
- the average times for which the transactions wait at each of the servers.

The system may also display details of the queues so that we can imagine that we are watching the station in action, with the queues forming, growing, shrinking, disappearing as time goes by.

Question

11 Write a simulation language specification for the post office with one counter.

From the figures output by the simulation system, it would be possible to make a decision as to whether the queues were satisfactory or whether they were too long. The railway authorities might decide to open another ticket office.

You could represent several ticket offices on a queuing diagram as shown in Figure 10.20. where we assume that only one queue is formed and the head of the queue goes to the first empty ticket office.

We would change our server specification to:

SERVER TICKETOFFICE (2) QUEUES (1)

and then run the simulation again to compare the results.

You will notice that we have imagined that the passengers will form a single queue and then move to a ticket office window as it becomes

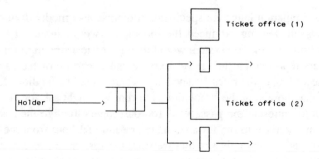

Figure 10.20 *Railway station: two ticket offices*

vacant. This form of queuing is found in many places, such as post offices, banks and government offices. If we were to allow two separate queues to form, one at each ticket office, then we should have to introduce a further complication by specifying the manner in which a passenger selects either of the two queues. We shall not discuss this here.

Assignment 6

(1)   The model of the railway system now includes 3 ticket offices. Passengers form a single queue and go to whichever of the three ticket offices is free.

   Draw a queuing diagram for the new model.

   Change the simulation language specification to show the extra office.

(2)   We need to change the model of the railway system as follows:

   ● There is one ticket office for season ticket sales.
   ● There are three ticket machines.
   ● There is one ticket just for today's ticket sales. This is for people who don't have the correct change for a ticket machine.

   Draw a queuing diagram for the new model.

(3)   Using the following information, produce a simulation language specification equivalent to your queuing diagram for the new model:

   ● Buyers using the ticket machines arrive at the rate of 1 every 70 seconds.

- Buyers using the ticket office arrive at the rate of 1 every 5 minutes.

What else is there?

The use of the word *model* in the discussion reminds us that the simulation language is not a programming language in the sense we have been using it in this book. The language merely allows us to construct our model and then submit this description of our model to a piece of very specialized software. It would not be possible, for example, to use the simulation language to print a railway timetable or to perform any general-purpose programming such as printing out invoices or sales orders.

Linear programming

Another type of software which falls into this modelling category is that of **linear programming**. We should perhaps mention it because it uses the word *programming* in its name which rather implies that it is a programming language or method.

Linear programming is not a way of programming a computer. It is a method of solving certain types of mathematical problems. Let us look at a typical problem which might be solved using linear programming techniques:

A company manufactures three different products: chairs, tables and dressers. A chair costs £36 and it takes one employee 4 hours to make one chair; a table costs £56 and it takes one employee 5 hours to make one table; a dresser costs £72 and it takes one employee 6 hours to make one dresser.

The company employs five workers and each employee works 42 hours per week.

The problem is to find the best means of organizing the employees in producing the various items of furniture so that the income from the sales is as great as possible.

To solve this mathematically, we must first write the problem down as a series of equations (and inequalities). If we let C represent the number of chairs to be manufactured, T the number of tables, and D the number of dressers, then the following equations can be written down to represent the ideal solution:

Income = 36*C + 56*T + 72*D pounds
Hours taken = 4*C 5*T 6*D <= 210 hours

The restrictions on the values of C, T, and D are that they must be integers and they must be 0 or more (since we cannot produce a negative quantity of chairs, nor – in this particular problem – can we make half a chair or 0.345 dressers):

$C, T, D > = 0$

Our aim is to *maximize* the income, that is, to discover what the greatest possible income is whilst still obeying the equations and satisfying all the constraints.

Looking at the second equation, we see that the number of chairs will be in the range 0 to 52 (we cannot make fewer than 0 nor more than 52 chairs because 53 chairs would take 214 hours), the number of tables will be in the range 0 to 42, and the number of dressers will be in the range 0 to 35.

The naive solution would be to write a program made up of a set of loops within loops and try every conceivable combination of numbers of products to see which produces the maximum income. But this would require us to perform 76440 iterations (that is, 52 times 42 times 35 loops) and is clearly not very efficient. This particular problem is fairly straightforward since the quantities are integers. But certain types of problem are not so simple and would require us to have a small step value for each of the loops, thereby increasing the number of iterations by several orders of magnitude.

Linear programming software accepts a specification of the problem in the form of equations and constraints and then, by using standard mathematical techniques, produces the feasible solutions. Just as our simulation program accepted our specifications and then hummed away for a time before printing out the required figures, so a linear programming system would accept our parameters and, after some time, would output a mass of figures about the model including:

- what the maximum possible income would be, and
- how many tables, chairs and dressers we should produce.

Once again, as we have done many times before in this book, we have come to a grey area where the distinction between a programming language and applications software becomes ill-defined.

Recap

- The majority of programming languages are based upon the von Neumann computer model and present their instructions as a sequence of imperative instructions.
- Certain types of problem are more efficiently solved with the aid of concurrent or parallel processing. Recent hardware developments in connection with parallel processing have produced transputers. These are independent processors which simultaneously perform a small part of a large task. The overall task is thereby completed much more quickly than if each step were performed in sequence.
- An important feature of such processing is the way in which the various processing elements communicate with each: they must pass data from one to another and they must be capable of indicating when they are ready to send and to receive data from the other processors. This synchronization is achieved by several means. We looked at condition synchronization and mutual exclusion, and we saw how casual use of mutual exclusion can result in deadlock.
- A parallel process can be represented by a process diagram. This shows the action of each process, the data which they receive and send and the channels along which the data flows. Each process may then be represented in a suitable simulation language.
- We also looked at the technique of simulation and applied it to several situations. By drawing a queuing diagram to depict the flow of, in our case, customers through a railway station, it was possible to derive a model of the station. By adding statistics for the inter-arrival time between customers and the time taken to serve each customer, it was possible to create a description of the model which could be submitted to a simulation language. The software would then tell us how long the queues would be, how long the average customer must wait. The final figures might be of use in making management decisions about the station and the future organization of resources.
- Finally, we took a brief look at the sort of multi-variable problems which can be solved with the aid of linear programming software.

459

Answers to questions

1 See Figure 10.21. Your solution may have calculated $2x$ first and then used this to calculate $2x - 2$.

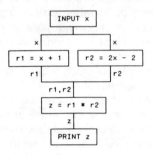

Figure 10.21 *A process diagram: solution 1*

2 See Figure 10.22. Your answer may have shown two separate boxes for the input of the values x and y.

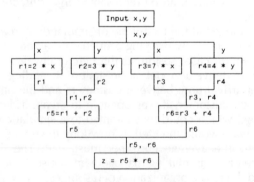

Figure 10.22 *A process diagram: solution 2*

3 Process *Minus5* uses channels *link1* and *link3*. Value x is input on channel *link1*, and value $r1$ is output on channel *link3*.
   Process *Plus7* uses channels *link2* and *link4*. Value x is

input on channel *link2* and value *r2* (obtained by adding 7 to the value of *x*) is output on channel *link4*.

Process *Product* uses channels *link5, link6* and *link7*. Value *r1* is input on channel *link5*, value *r2* is input on channel *link6*, and value *y* (obtained by multiplying value *r1* by value *r2*) is output on channel *link7*.

Process *Printy* uses channels *link7* and *screen*. Value *y* in input on channel *link7* and output on channel *screen*.

4 See Figure 10.23.

```
PROC Printy =
      CHAN link7, screen
      VAR y

          link7?y
          screen!y :
```

Figure 10.23 *Occam definition: Printy*

5 See Figure 10.24.

```
PROC Minus5 =
      CHAN link1, link3
      VAR x, r1
      SEQ
          link1?x
          r1 := x-5
          link3!r1 :
```

Figure 10.24 *Occam definition: MINUS5*

6 See Figure 10.25.

```
PROC Plus7 =
      CHAN link2, link4
      VAR x, r2
      SEQ
          link2?x
          r2 := x+7
          link4!r2 :
```

Figure 10.25 *Occam definition: Plus 7*

7 See Figure 10.26.

461

```
PROC Product =
     CHAN link5, link6, link7
     VAR r1, r2, y
     SEQ
         link5?r1
         link6?r2
         y := r1*r2
         link7!y :
```

Figure 10.26   *Occam definition: Product*

8   See Figure 10.27.

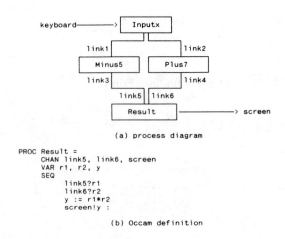

(a) process diagram

```
PROC Result =
     CHAN link5, link6, screen
     VAR r1, r2, y
     SEQ
         link5?r1
         link6?r2
         y := r1*r2
         screen!y :
```

(b) Occam definition

Figure 10.27   *Occam definition: Result*

9   See Figure 10.28.

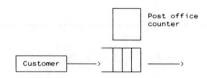

Figure 10.28   *Post office: queuing diagram*

10 See Figure 10.29.

11 The solution shown in Figure 10.30 specifies the times in minutes. You may have specified the times in seconds. You have probably used different names for the servers and for the transactions.

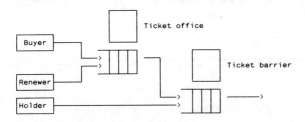

Figure 10.29 *Railway station: queuing diagram*

```
SERVER COUNTER

TRANSACTION CUSTOMER

CUSTOMERARRIVAL = 2
CUSTOMERSERVICE = 3

GENERATE CUSTOMER CUSTOMERARRIVAL
        SEIZE COUNTER
            HOLD CUSTOMERENQUIRY
        RELEASE COUNTER
DESTROY CUSTOMER
```

Figure 10.30 *Post office simulation program*

11: Other language models

Objectives

After reading this chapter, you should be able to:

- Name some of the models upon which a programming language may be founded.
- Explain what is meant by the term **orthogonality**.
- Describe the main features of a **functional-oriented programming language**.
- Use the **lambda notation** for declaring functions.
- Describe and use the principal features of the **LISP** language.
- Describe the main features of a **logic-oriented programming language**.
- Describe and use the principal features of the **Prolog** language.
- Describe the concept of **backtracking**.
- Describe the main features of an **object-oriented programming language**.
- Describe and use the principal features of the **Smalltalk** language.

After working through this book, you will have built up an image of the skill of programming as being:

- a way of visualizing data; together with
- a design for some method of processing that data.

This leads us on to a programming language as being:

- a formal system for describing the form and nature of the data; together with
- a prescription for the processes which are to manipulate that data.

This fits in very well with all the languages which we have covered, from machine code to 4GLs. It also lets us include less-obvious tools such as *spreadsheets* and *simulation.*

In this chapter, we shall look at some other models upon which we could base our implementation of a programming language. These fall into three broad categories:

- **Functional-oriented languages.** These are designed around *mathematical functions.* A typical functional-oriented language is LISP, the list processing language.
- **Logic-oriented languages.** These are based upon the concepts of *symbolic logic* which tests whether a given statement is *true* or *false.* A typical logic-oriented language is Prolog.
- **Object-oriented languages.** These concentrate their attentions upon the *data and data structures* which are used in solving a problem and then add to these a set of processing operations which manipulate that data. This approach has many similarities to the concept of abstract data types which we discussed earlier. A typical object-oriented language is Smalltalk.

We shall see how some of the languages are intended for general application, whilst others are aimed at fairly specialized users.

One important point which I have tried to convey is how it is possible to conceive a programming language which does not specify its requirements as a purely sequential series of instructions.

Functional programming languages

The functional programming model attempts to apply the concepts of mathematical functions to problem solving.

Although a functional programming language uses a data structure for storing data, the traditional use of variables and assignment statements is removed. The tools of the language are **function definitions** and **function specifications** and the execution process is concerned with the **evaluation** of the specifications.

The functions may be specified in the manner very much like that which we considered earlier. Thus, a definition such as:

$$\text{funca}(x) \equiv (x + 2)/(x - 2)$$

maps each number x in the *domain* to a real number in the *range.* Some examples are shown in the table in Figure 11.1.

Domain	Mapping
1.5	-7
-4	0.333
1	-3
2	0
4	3
7	1.8
-7	0.556
-6	0.5
6	2
-3	0.2
3	5
-2	0
-1	-0.333
5	2.333
-5	0.429

Figure 11.1   *Mapping of funca*

This tells us that funca(1) returns the value −3, funca(−3) returns the value 0.2, funca(3) returns the value 5, and so on. For any value, *x*, the function returns a unique value for funca(*x*). This is exactly the same as the more familiar functions such as

PRINT SQRT(B*B−4*A*C)
LOGN = LOG(NUMBER)
ROOT = EXP(LOGN/10)

which are used in Basic and other programming languages.

Lambda notation

An alternative way of writing down a function, known as a **lambda expression** was developed by Church in 1941 and allows us to define our function as:

funca ≡ λx.(x+2)/(x−2)

or, omitting the name, we could provide the definition:

λx.(x+2)/(x−2)

Using this **lambda notation**, a lambda expression consists of the Greek letter *lambda* λ followed by the element (or elements) in the domain, then a dot followed by the definition.

If this notation is used, applications of the function are written as:

funca : 1.5

or

λx.(x+2)/(x−2) : 1.5

either of which would, as we saw above, return a value –7. Note that we do **not** use the bracketed notation funca(1.5).

There may be more than one argument. For example, a function to add two numbers together could be defined by any of the forms:

sum2(x,y) ≡ x+y
sum2 ≡ λx,y . x+y
λx,y . x+y

The fundamental operations

+
–
/
*

are available for use in lambda expressions.

Questions

1 Write each of the following functions using all *three* notations illustrated in the text:

(a) A function to return the product of two input numbers.
(b) A function to return the lower of two input numbers.

2 Write the following mathematical expressions using the two forms of the lambda notation introduced in the text:

(a) $x - 7$
(b) $x^3 + 2x^2 - 7x + 3$

3 Write down the values of the following expressions:
(a) λx. 3*x : 7.5
(b) λx. x–3 : 0
(c) λx,y. 2*x – 3*y : 1,2
(d) λa,b,c. b*b – 4*a*c : –2,–3,4

The operation can be more than just an arithmetic calculation. We could define a function:

maximum ≡ λx,y. if x>y then x else y

It is this feature which makes it possible for an entire language to be constructed from such functions.

Question

4 Use the lambda notation to write down the following functions:

(a) A function which will look at the two input numbers and return a value of *true* if the first is lower than the second, otherwise it will return a value of *false*.

(b) A function which will look at the two input numbers and return the positive difference between them. For example, the expression:

func2(2,3)

will return the value 1, and the expression:

func2(3,2)

will also return the value 1.

A functional-oriented language uses a small number of *primitive* functions to construct the required repertoire of complex functions. We could, therefore, use the *maximum* function in the definition of another function – called *absolute* – which is to return a number without its arithmetic sign:

absolute ≡ λx. maximum : x, –x

Going further, we could use this in another definition:

sqrt ≡ λx. square root of (absolute : x)

In this definition, the brackets have been included to show the range of the square root activity.

Orthogonality

The extent to which a programming language uses a relatively small number of primitive constructs to build a large number of more complex constructs is known as **orthogonality**. The more *orthogonal* the language, the fewer forms there are and the easier it is to learn and to use the language. The less *orthogonal* the language, the more special forms, exceptions and special rules there are for the programmer to learn, and the more difficult it will be to remember and to use and exploit all these forms.

To illustrate the concept of orthogonality, we could consider the Basic operator:

^

which is used to raise a number to a power. We can use this to take the square root of a number by writing a statement such as:

A = B ^ 0.5

But Basic also offers the square root function:

A = SQRT(B)

The SQRT function is restricted in its action (it can only find square roots), but the ^ operator is much more powerful (it can be used to calculate roots and powers). So Basic is *less orthogonal* than a language which only offers the ^ operator.

When duplicate facilities are offered, thereby making the language less orthogonal, this is usually done to save time and effort: the SQRT function will probably be faster than using the ^ operator, and it is also easier to remember.

If the language is less orthogonal and has a great many facilities, most programmers will work only with a subset of those facilities, using only those which they can remember, understand and use. As a result, there may be many powerful and efficient operations which they forget and do not use.

Activity 1

Consider any of the programming languages which you have used.

(1) Give some examples of operations which can be performed in more than one manner.
(2) Look through the reference manual and make a list of those statements and functions which you have never (or rarely) used.

Composition of functions

It is possible to use the result of the evaluation of one function as the argument to a second function. We have seen with our original function,

funca(4) returns a value of 3, and
funca(3) returns a value of 5

so the expression:

funca(funca(4)) returns a value of 5

The lambda notation allows us to define a new function which represents the **function composition** of one or more functions. In this particular case, we could use the definition:

funcb ≡ funca **o**

so that

funcb(4) returns a value of

The special symbol

o

indicates that the two functions are to be performed one (the left-most) *after* the other (the right-most).

Other examples might be:

funcc ≡ funca **o** absolute

In this example, the right-most function (*absolute*) is applied first, and the result of this is the input to the next function (*funca*), so that:

funcc(4) represents funca(absolute(4))

which is equivalent to:

funca(4)

and therefore returns the value 3.

Notice that the order in which the functions are composed is important. In general:

funcq1 ≡ funcx **o** funcy

does not return the same value, and is not the same function as

funcq2 ≡ funcy **o** funcx

Any number of functions may be composed in this manner. For example:

funcq3 ≡ funcz1 **o** funcz2 **o** funcz3 **o** funcz4

is perfectly acceptable, provided that the functions *funcz1* to *funcz4* have been defined, and that the range of each function is within the domain of its neighbour to the left.

Question

5   Using the function definitions for *funca, absolute* and *sqrt* given in the text, evaluate the following:

funcx1 ≡ absolute **o** funca
funcx2 ≡ funca **o** absolute
funcx3 ≡ sqrt **o** absolute
funcx4 ≡ absolute **o** sqrt

for integer input values over the range –7 to 7.
   Indicate any parts of their domain for which any of these functions are undefined.

As an example of a functional-oriented language, let us look at LISP.

LISP: list processing

The name LISP is an acronym derived from **LIST** processing, and the language is one of a number which have been associated with *artificial intelligence* applications. LISP is available on large and small computer systems, and there are a number of machines dedicated to the use of that language alone. As with many of the current programming languages, LISP statements can be typed in and executed immediately, in an interactive manner, or a group of statements may be stored for execution as a program later.

   The language was developed in the later 1950s by an American called John McCarthy in an attempt to produce a programming medium that was more intelligible than the assembly languages which were used at that time.

   As the name implies, LISP is essentially concerned with the manipulation of data which is held in *lists*. A simple list consists of a sequence of **members** separated by spaces and enclosed in parentheses. Superfluous spaces are ignored by the LISP processor. Here are some LISP lists:

> (mother father sister brother)
> (x   father sister brother)
> (1 4 9 16 25 36)
> (elephant hippopotamus rhinoceros)
> (1234 wild-cat coelocanth laughing-hyena –9876)
> (computer)
> (computer   )

A member of a list may be an **atom** or another list. An atom is any string of characters, except spaces. An atom which contains only digits (with or without a preceding – or + sign) is considered to represent a numeric value and is called a **number**, and an atom which does not represent a numeric value is known as an **identifier.** Thus, atoms such as *x* and *mother* in our examples are both identifiers. You may like to think of an identifier as being used like a program variable, so the list:

> (mother father sister brother)

can be considered to be a list of variable names.

Question

6 Write down the *members*, the *atoms*, the *numbers* and the *identifiers* in this LISP list:

> (1234 wild-cat VALUE coelocanth laughing-hyena –9876)

A member of a list may be an atom or another list:

> (cat (dog fox) sheep)

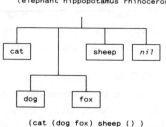

Figure 11.2   *LISP lists as trees*

An **empty list** may also be included as a member of a list. The empty list is represented by ( ) and is referred to by the name *nil*:

(cat (dog fox) sheep ( ))

It is often convenient to visualize lists as tree structures, as shown in Figure 11.2.

Questions

7 Write down a LISP list which is to be used by an export company and which represents the continents: Europe, America, Asia, Australasia and Oceania.
8 Modify your list so that Europe is replaced by the list consisting of Britain, Ireland, France, Germany and Holland, and America is replaced by North-America and South-America, and Asia is replaced by India, China and Malaya.
9 Modify your list further so that Britain is replaced by the list comprising England, Scotland, Wales and Northern-Ireland.

Draw your own tree structures to represent these lists.

Processing with LISP

In the LISP language, not only data, but processing instructions are also held as lists. These lists are called *functions* or *S-expressions* (that is, *symbolic expressions*). These have the general form:

(name parameters)

which specifies the name of the function and a sequence of parameters which are to be processed by the function. For example, an expression such as:

(SETQ England 100)

can be used to put the value 100 into the identifier called *England*.

Whereas most languages offer some form of assignment statement, such as:

LET England = 100   in Basic
MOVE 100 TO England.   in Cobol
England := 100   in Pascal

and use the concept of *assigning* a value to a variable, LISP **binds** a value to an identifier. Thus, the statement:

(SETQ England 100)

is said to *bind* the value 100 to the identifier *England*.

Arithmetic in LISP

Functions are used to carry out arithmetic calculations and other processing. The function to add two numbers might be:

(PLUS 123 456)

which has a value of 579.
  Other arithmetic functions are represented by functions:

(TIMES 123 456)
  which multiplies the two numbers together and has a value of 56088 in this instance.

(DIFFERENCE 123 456)
  which calculates the difference between the two numbers and has a value of –333 in this instance.

(DIVIDE 369 123)
  which divides 369 by 123 and has a value of 3 in this instance.

(QUOTIENT 456 123)
  which takes the integer result of dividing 456 by 123 and has a value of 3 in this instance.

(REMAINDER 456 123)
  which takes the remainder of performing integer division and has a value of 87 in this instance.

Some implementations use the familiar arithmetic symbols:

+ * – /

for arithmetic functions.
  More complex operations can be carried out by using the fact that any member may be another list. Thus, the list:

(SETQ result (PLUS (TIMES 12 34) (DIFFERENCE 34 12)))

would be evaluated step by step as a composite expression, like this:

(SETQ result (PLUS 408 (DIFFERENCE 34 12)))
(SETQ result (PLUS 408 22))
(SETQ result 430)

finally binding the value 430 to the identifier *result*.

Some versions of LISP only handle integer numbers in the range −32768 to +32767, whilst others are capable of handling characters, floating point-numbers and integers with up to 77,000 decimal digits.

Questions

Using the arithmetic functions described in the text, write LISP lists which are equivalent to these Pascal statements:

10   A := 42
11   Answer := 1099 + 133 − 988
12   Tax := (53*43) − (63/9)

Input and output

Unfortunately, there seems to be no standard version of LISP at the time of writing. Each implementation offers different facilities. In fact, the only real differences are that some versions offer more **standard functions** than others. The underlying model of list processing applies across all implementations of the language. In our discussion, we shall use the simplest forms of those which are available.

There are facilities for reading and writing data to disk or other device (typically by means of OPEN, READ, PUT and CLOSE functions) and for outputting to the terminal screen and inputting from the keyboard.

To print out the contents of any identifier, we could use the PRINT function:

(PRINT England)

or we could simply type in the name of the identifier:

England

To input data into an identifier, we could use the INPUT function:

(INPUT England)

When this is encountered, the user will be invited to enter a LISP list (or an atom) and this will be bound to the identifier *England*. This will normally be used only in stored LISP programs.

The QUOTE function

When you are using LISP interactively, the LISP processor will attempt to evaluate anything that you type in. So if you wished to assign the list:

(Scotland Wales Ireland England)

to the identifier:

Britain

and you were to type in the list:

(SETQ Britain (Scotland Wales Ireland England))

then, the LISP processor will attempt to evaluate the list:

(Scotland Wales Ireland England)

It will interpret the head of the list – Scotland – as the function name. Since it is unlikely that you have a function called *Scotland*, the LISP processor will detect an error. To overcome this, we could use the QUOTE function, like this:

(SETQ Britain (QUOTE (Scotland Wales Ireland England)))

or

(SETQ Britain '(Scotland Wales Ireland England))

which instructs the processor to leave the list exactly as it stands without attempting to evaluate it and place the list into the identifier *Britain*. The alternative form uses the apostrophe ' and does not require the further set of parentheses. The importance of QUOTE can be demonstrated by some further examples. The statement:

(SETQ China 32)

would bind the value 32 to the identifier *China*, and the statement:

(SETQ China (TIMES 4 8))

would also bind the value 32 to *China*. But, if we use the quote function, the statement:

(SETQ China '(TIMES 4 8))

would bind the value:

(TIMES 4 8)

to *China*. Then, if we subsequently typed in the function:

(China)

the LISP processor would output the value:

32

Similarly,

(SETQ Britain (QUOTE UK))

or

(SETQ Britain 'UK)

can be used to bind the value UK to *Britain*. Note that the forms:

(SETQ Britain (QUOTE (UK)))

or

(SETQ Britain '(UK))

will put a *list* with a single member (UK) into the identifier.

The COND function

The LISP equivalent of the IF and CASE structures is achieved by the *COND* function together with *comparison operations* of the form:

(= X 12)
   which is true if X has a value 12;

(< X 123)
   which is true if X has a value less than 123;

(> X 35)
   which is true if X has a value greater than 35;

(= 0 X)
   which is true if X has a value 0.

Compare this **pre-fix** notation (or *Polish* notation) with the **post-fix** notation (or *Reverse Polish* notation) which we discussed in Chapter 8.

477

Some implementations of LISP offer the following operations for comparison:

> EQ instead of =
> GREATERP instead of >
> LESSP instead of <

together with others such as:

ATOM
> to test whether a member is an atom (and not a list);

LIST P
> to test whether a member is a list (and not an atom);

NUMBERP
> to test whether a value is a number;

NULL
> to test whether a value is null (or *nil*);

ZEROP or =0
> to test whether a value is equal to zero;

ONEP
> to test whether a value is equal to 1.

The COND function has the general form:

> (COND (comparison action)
>   (comparison action)
>
>   (comparison action))

and each comparison is performed and a value of T (*true*) or nil (*false*) is returned. When a *true* result is detected, the associated action is performed. The special LISP identifier T can be used as a catch-all (otherwise) condition in case all the preceding conditions are false.

To take some specific examples, we see that the statement:

> (COND ((< X 1) (TIMES –1 X)))

or the equivalent indented statement:

```
(COND (
                    (< X 1) (TIMES –1 X)
          )
)
```

has the same meaning as the Basic statement:

    IF X<1 THEN X=–1*X

The statement:

    (COND ((< B 1) (SETQ B 0) (T (SETQ B 200))))

or

```
(COND (
                    (< B 1) (SETQ B 0)
                    (T       (SETQ B 200)
          )
)
```

has the same meaning as the Basic statement:

    IF B<1 THEN B=0 ELSE B=200

Some LISP users find it useful to lay out the statement in the indented manner, as we have done here. This makes the statement easier to read. A great source of error is that of suplying the correct number of brackets. This is particularly troublesome when the LISP statements are being entered interactively. As a partial solution to this, some implementations offer the **superbracket** – this is written as] – which closes all bracketed sets up to that point. Thus, we could use the statements:

    (COND ((< X 1) (TIMES –1 X]

    (COND ((< B 1) (SETQ B 0) (T (SETQ 200]

instead of those shown above. The open superbracket, written as [, is also available.

A more complex CASE structure is represented by the statement:

    (COND ((> Value 100) (SETQ Discount 4)) (> Value 50)
    (SETQ Discount 3)) (> Value 20) (SETQ Discount 2)) (T
    (SETQ Discount 1))))

or

(COND ((> Value 100) (SETQ Discount 4)) (> Value 50)
(SETQ Discount 3)) (> Value 20) (SETQ Discount 2)) (T
(SETQ Discount 1]

or

(COND (

       (> Value 100) (SETQ Discount 4))
       (> Value 50) (SETQ Discount 3))
       (> Value 20) (SETQ Discount 2))
       (T   (SETQ Discount 1))

)

)

Even more complicated conditions can be constructed by means of the AND, OR and NOT operators:

(AND (= Malaya China) (= China Peru))
   which will be true if *Malaya* is equal to *China and China* is equal to *Peru*;

(OR (= Malaya China) (= Malaya France))
   which will be true if *Malaya* is equal to *China or Malaya* is equal to *France*.

(NOT (= Malaya China))
   which will be true if *Malaya* is not equal to *China*.

Activity 2

(1) Rewrite the three COND statements illustrated above in any of the languages which you have used in your programming work.
(2) Rewrite these Basic fragments using the LISP forms which we introduced in the text:

    (a) A = 1
         B = 2
         C = A + B
    (b) TOTAL = 0
         FOR X=1 TO 10
             TOTAL = TOTAL + X
         NEXT X
         PRINT TOTAL

(c) PRINT 'PLEASE ENTER THE START OF THE RANGE'
     INPUT S
     PRINT 'PLEASE ENTER THE END OF THE RANGE'
     INPUT E
     TOTAL=0
     FOR X=S TO E
         TOTAL = TOTAL + X*X
     NEXT X
     PRINT ' THE SUM OF THE SQUARE IS '
     PRINT TOTAL

Defining your own LISP functions

LISP allows you to define your own functions by means of the DEFUN function. If we wished to define a function, with the name SQUARED, which is to return the square of a number, we might do this by means of the expression:

(DEFUN SQUARED (X) (TIMES X X))

and we could then use the name SQUARED exactly as we use TIMES, PLUS and the other built-in LISP functions.

Function names may be used recursively. A function to calculate factorials could be defined as:

(DEFUN Factorial (X) (COND ((< X 1) 1) (T (TIMES X
(Factorial (MINUS X 1))))))

or

(DEFUN Factorial (X) (COND ((< X 1) 1) (T (TIMES X
(Factorial (MINUS X 1]

or

(DEFUN Factorial (X)
     (COND
             ((< X 1) 1)
             (T (TIMES X (Factorial (MINUS X 1))))
)
)

Activity 3

(1)   Write LISP definitions for the functions in Questions (1) to (5).
(2)   Write small LISP programs which could be used to demonstrate and test these functions.

Heads and tails

A LISP list is made up of two parts: a **head** and a **tail**. The *head* is the
first member of the list, and the *tail* is a list consisting of the remaining
members of the list. Thus, if we consider the list:

(1234 wild-cat coelocanth laughing-hyena –9876)

The head is the member:

1234

(an atom), and the tail is the list:

(wild-cat coelocanth laughing-hyena –9876)

In the case of the list:

(( ) cat)

the head is the member:

( )

(the empty list), and the tail is the list:

(cat)

Questions

Write down the head and the tail of each of these lists:

13   (1 4 9 16 25 36)
14   (elephant hippopotamus rhinoceros)
15   ((Britain Ireland France Germany Holland) (North-America
South-America) (India China Malaya) Australasia Oceania)
16   (cat (dog fox) sheep ( ))
17   (North-America South-America)
18   (computer)

CAR and CDR

There are two LISP functions which will return the head and the tail of a list. The function:

(CAR listname)

will return the head of the list, and the function:

(CDR listname)

will return the tail of the list. For example, the function:

(CAR '(friday saturday sunday monday))

will return the head of the list:

friday

and the function:

(CDR '(friday saturday sunday monday))

will return the tail of the list:

(saturday sunday monday)

In case you are wondering: CAR stands for *contents of the accumulator register*, and CDR stands for *contents of the decrement register*. These names are relics of the terminology used in the first implementations of LISP.

Just as CAR returns the head of the list and CDR returns the tail, the extended forms:

CAAR
will return the head of the head of the list,

CDDR
will return the tail of the tail of the list,

CADR
will return the head of the tail of the list. In this case the D (that is, CDR) is evaluated first, and then A (that is, CAR) is applied to the result.

CDAR
will return the tail of the head of the list,

and so on with more and more complicated forms such as **CDDAR** and **CAAAR**.

Questions

Evaluate the following functions:

19   CAR (the cat sat on the mat)
20   CDR (the cat sat on the mat)
21   CADR (the cat sat on the mat)
22   CDAR (the cat sat on the mat)
23   CADDR (the cat sat on the mat)
24   CDDDR (the cat sat on the mat)

The reverse of CAR and CDR is the CONS function which constructs a new list from the head and tail which are supplied as parameters. Thus:

(CONS 'january '(february march))

will produce a new list:

(january february march)

Activity 4

(1)   Write LISP expressions which, for each of the lists in Questions (13) to (18), will put the head into an identifier called FRONT-OF-LIST and the tail into an identifier called BOTTOM.

(2)   Write LISP expressions using variants of the CAR, CDR and CONS functions on the list:

(the cat sat on the mat)

to display the following output:

(a)   the
(b)   cat
(c)   mat
(d)   the mat
(e)   cat on the mat
(f)   the mat sat on the cat

Implementing LISP

LISP is frequently implemented by means of **cells**. Each cell contains two *pointers*: the first of these is the CAR pointer which tells the processor the actual address at which the head of the list can be found; the second pointer is the CDR pointer which tells the processor where to find the rest of the list. This is shown by the diagram in Figure 11.3. This shows a **CONS-cell diagram**. The end of a list is denoted by a cell with a diagonal through the CDR representing a pointer to an empty list or *nil*.

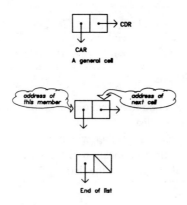

Figure 11.3 *CONS-cells*

Some particular instances of CONS-cell diagrams are illustrated in Figure 11.4 which represents the three lists:

( )
(mouse horse sheep)
(mouse (dog fox) sheep)

The first cell in the sequence contains a CAR pointer indicating the location of the first data member of the list – *mouse* – and a second pointer indicating the location of the next cell. The LISP processor can follow up this CDR pointer to find the next cell. This second cell contains a CAR pointer to the location of the member – *horse* – and a CDR pointer indicating the location of the next cell. Following this second CDR pointer, the LISP processor can locate the next cell which contains a CAR pointer to the location of the member – *sheep* – and the

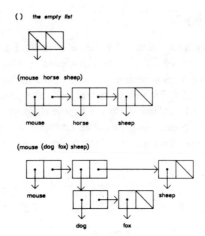

Figure 11.4 *LISP lists*

final CDR pointer is found to have a diagonal line through it, indicating that this is the end of the list.

When the list contains a member which is itself a list, there is a cell at the top level indicating the location of the start of the sublist. This is illustrated by the cell diagram for the list:

(mouse (dog fox) sheep)

Question

25 Write down the LISP list which is represented by the CONS-cell diagram in Figure 11.5.

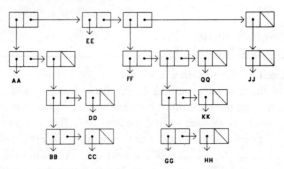

Figure 11.5 *CONS-cells for a list*

Activity 5

Draw cell diagrams for the following lists:

(a) (1 4 9 16 25 36)
(b) (11 22 (33 44) 55 66)
(c) (AA (BB CC) () (() DD) EE)
(d) (sloth (kangaroo wallaby) lion (giant-panda yeti))
(e) (cat (dog fox) (merino black-face) ( ))
(f) (North-America South-America)
(g) (computer)
(h) ((AA ((BB CC) DD)) EE (FF ((GG HH) KK) QQ) (JJ)))

Cells and binding

Much internal handling of the lists is achieved by means of pointers. Of particular interest is the effect of the binding which is achieved by the SETQ statement. After executing statements such as:

(SETQ Malaya '(12 34))
(SETQ Peru '(12 34))
(SETQ China '(AA BB))

the symbol table (telling us where to find the lists *Malaya*, *Peru* and *China*) and the CONS-cells will look like that shown in Figure 11.6 (a). After issuing a further statement:

(SETQ China Peru)

the situation will look like that shown in Figure 11.6 (b).

It has probably occurred to you that space (and processing time) could be saved by using the second pointer in a CONS-cell to point to the actual data, rather than to another CONS-cell which itself points to the data. This can be achieved by writing a list in the form of a *dotted* pair. Figure 11.7 shows LISP would use CONS-cells to represent the dotted pair produced by a statement such as:

(SETQ Malaya '(AA . BB))

Only *pairs* of members may be linked in this manner, so we have to construct longer lists as an arrangement of dotted pairs by specifying them in forms such as:

(mother . (father . (sister . brother)))

487

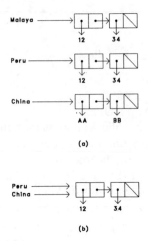

Figure 11.6   *CONS-cells and binding*

Activity 6

(1)   Draw a CONS-cell diagram for the list

(mother . (father . (sister . brother)))

(2)   Rewrite the list in Questions (13) to (18) as dotted pairs and draw the equivalent CONS-cell diagrams.

Logic programming

During our study of the way in which programming languages are constructed, we saw that there are sequences, iterations and selections used in many languages. This is particularly true of the first, second and third generation languages.

Programs are organized in this manner for largely historical reasons. But that does not mean that there are no other ways of thinking about computer solutions. We have already met parallel processing and concurrent processing. In this chapter, we shall look at another means of writing programs: **logic programming**.

The languages which use logic programming do not present a series of assignment statements, loops and selections. Instead, they are written as a series of **declarations** and the languages themselves are said to be

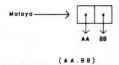

(A A . B B)

Figure 11.7 *A dotted pair*

declarative languages or **non-procedural languages.** This distinguishes them from the more familiar imperative languages or procedural languages, such as Cobol, Basic and Pascal, which give a set of instructions telling the computer exactly how to perform a particular task. Indeed, this is one great disadvantage in using procedural languages, because the analyst and the programmer have to know *exactly* what is required before they can start to write the program.

In contrast, a non-procedural language describes not the *route* to producing the results, but rather the *form* and the *nature* of the results, together with a set of information and a method by which the result can be deduced from this information.

We can illustrate this by a simple example drawn from the *Prolog* language which we shall look at in depth later. I can provide the Prolog processor with a set of **facts** such as:

```
ruler(elizabeth_i, england).
ruler(elizabeth_ii, england).
ruler(alfred, england).
ruler(charles_i, england).
ruler(louis_xiv, france).
```

declaring that Elizabeth I is/was a ruler of England, Louis_XIV is/was a ruler of France, and so on. Then I can give it a set of **rules** which use those facts:

```
english(x) :– ruler(x,england).
french(x) :– ruler(x,france).
```

indicating that a person (known as *x*) is/was English if he or she is/was a ruler of England, or the person *x* is/was French if he or she is/was a ruler of France.

I can then ask questions such as:

```
? english(elizabeth_ii).
```

to which Prolog will respond with the answer:

yes

since Elizabeth II is/was a ruler of England (this is a fact) and she is/was, therefore, English (according to our rule). If we ask the question:

? english(louis_xiv).

then Prolog will answer:

no

since, according to our facts and rules, this cannot be found to be true. If we ask a further question:

? english(william_i).

then Prolog will again answer:

no

since, according to our facts and rules, this cannot be found to be true.

Prolog – Programming in logic

Prolog expresses the users' requirements in a declarative manner, rather than as a procedural specification, and offers a facility for **PRO**gramming in **LOG**ic.

Since its first implementation at the University of Marseilles in the early 70s, Prolog is becoming increasingly used in work on expert systems and **artificial intelligence** and other application areas and it has been adopted as the principal language for the Japanese **fifth generation project** at the Institute of New Generation Technology. Because of its use in AI, the data which is handled by Prolog and similar languages is frequently referred to as a knowledge-base (KB) and is manipulated by a knowledge-base management system (KBMS), rather than the more familiar DB (database) and DBMS (database management system). We shall ignore these terms for our present purposes.

Prolog is available in several versions: DEC 10 Prolog developed in Edinburgh and another – called IC-Prolog or micro-Prolog – developed at Imperial College in London, with further dialects coming from the USA. Micro-Prolog is available on a number of machines, including MS-DOS and the Sinclair ZX Spectrum. The examples shown below will (taking a few liberties for the sake of clarity) be based upon these versions.

Prolog allows the user to express certain **facts, relations** and **rules** and then uses these to answer queries and to draw logical conclusions based upon this information. The principle behind logical programming is based upon a logical form known as a Horn clause, originally developed by Alfred Horn in the 1950s. A **Horn clause** is a statement which implies just a single conclusion: thus, in a sentence such as:

If Michael is the parent of John, then John is the child of Michael

there is just one conclusion: *John is the child of Michael.*

This contrasts with the non-Horn clause such as:

If Michael is the parent of John, then John is the son of Michael and Michael is a boy

which has two conclusions: *John is the son of Michael,* and *Michael is a boy.*

It was from such a basis that the impetus came to attempt to use computers to prove theorems, and from this came languages such as Prolog.

Let us start by looking at a Prolog *relation* called *parent* which might be represented by a set of *facts* such as:

```
parent(michael,john).
parent(peter,mary).
parent(michael,joanne).
parent(susan,william).
parent(frederick,peter).
parent(stanley,florence).
parent(stanley,william).
```

meaning that Michael is the parent of John, Peter is the parent of Mary, and so on. Syntactically, a fact consists of a **predicate** – parent, in these facts – followed by one or more **arguments**. The words *stanley, peter, mary* and so on, are called **atoms** and are similar to non-numeric constants in other programming environments.

Activity 7

Copy the above facts about the parent relation on to a sheet of paper.

491

To this list, add the following facts:

Anne is Stanley's parent.
Victor is Mary's parent.
The parent of Diana is Ruby.
The parents of Ruby are Cynthia and George.

Add the members of your own family to the facts in our database. Include your own parents, your brothers and sisters, and your grandparents.

We could equally well have chosen other forms for the predicates and the arguments. For example, we could have written these as:

is_the_parent_of(michael,john).

or

parent(michael, the_little_girl_with_plaits).

I might even have conceived the significance of the arguments differently, putting the arguments in the reverse order, and expressing the same facts in a form such as:

parent(john,michael).

which I take to mean that the parent of John is Michael. Obviously, once I have made the decision to write the arguments in a certain order, then I must continue with that convention.

In another situation, I may have decided to use a predicate such as

son_of_john(michael).

with a single argument.

The number of arguments entirely depends upon the nature of the relation which I am using. Our parent relation is a **two-place predicate** because it requires two ordered arguments; a relation such as:

british(william).

is a **one-place predicate**; a relation such as:

gives(mary,dog,richard).

is a **three-place predicate.** It is even possible to have a predicate such as:

soluble

which has no arguments.

Prolog behaves interactively, displaying a prompt in readiness for the user's input, and storing the facts and responding to the queries posed by the user.

On some implementations, each statement – except for the variables mentioned later – must be entered in lower-case letters, and the full stop is used to terminate each piece of data entered to Prolog. This also applies to the facts shown here (and also the rules and queries which we discuss below).

For example, to interrogate the facts shown above, a typical **query** might look like this:

? parent(michael,john).

This asks:

'*Is it true that* michael is the parent of John?'

Prolog would then scan the database, interpreting the available facts, and – in this instance – display the answer:

yes

since Michael *is* the parent of John, whereas, the query:

? parent(susan,mary).

would display the answer:

no

since according to the facts here, Susan is not the parent of Mary. Prolog regards such a query as a **goal** which must be *satisfied*.

Questions

For these questions, use only the database which you produced in the last activity and no other knowledge.

Write down, in your own words, the meaning of the following Prolog queries and write down the response which Prolog would give:

26 parent(anne,stanley).
27 parent(florence,stanley).

28   parent(frederick,peter).
29   parent(george,ruby).
30   parent(joanne,michael).

Write down the queries which you would pose to Prolog to answer the following questions and give the answer in each case using just the database which you produced in the last activity and no other knowledge.

31   Is Michael the parent of Joanne?
32   Is Ruby Diana's parent?
33   Is Stanley the parent of Daphne?
34   Is William Susan's parent?
35   Is Mary the child of Victor?

Activity 8

Write down the queries which you would pose to answer the following questions about the facts in the database which concern your own family. Use the actual names of the people.

Write down the response which Prolog would give in each case.

Is your_father the parent of your_brother?
Is your_father your parent?
Is your_father your_sister's parent?
Is your_grandfather the parent of your_sister?
Is your_grandfather your parent?
Is your_grandfather your_father's parent?
Is your_grandmother the parent of your_mother?
Is your_grandmother your parent?
Is your_grandmother your_father's parent?
Is your_mother the parent of your—sister?
Is your_mother your_brother's parent?

AND / OR

A query may have more than one goal. For example, there are two goals in the query:

?parent(michael,john), parent(peter,mary).

Separating the separate goals by a comma in this manner means that *both* goals must be satisfied. The comma has the meaning of AND, and you can think of the query as asking:

'Is it true that Michael is the parent of John and also that Peter is the parent of Mary?'

Prolog will attempt to satisfy each goal in turn, and only when *both* goals have been satisfied – as would be the case with our data – will the answer be:

yes

Similarly, using the facts in our database, the query:

? parent(michael,john), parent(john,michael).

would produce the answer:

no

since only one of the goals is satisfied, not both.
If we separate the goals by a semi-colon:

? parent(michael,john); parent(peter,mary).

this means that *at least one* goal must be satisfied. The semi-colon has the meaning of OR, and you can think of this query as asking:

'Is it true that Michael is the parent of John or that Peter is the parent of Mary?'

Prolog will attempt to satisfy each goal in turn, and if *either* goal – or both goals – can be been to be satisfied the answer will be:

yes

Similarly, the query:

? parent(michael,john); parent(john,michael).

would also produce the answer:

yes

since one of the goals (the first in this instance) is true. But if we were to ask:

? parent(john,peter); parent(john,mary).

then the answer would be:

no

since the facts in our database do not allow either of the goals to be satisfied.

Questions

What responses would Prolog give to these queries about our database?

36 parent(william,susan), parent(joanne,michael).
37 parent(michael,joanne); parent(victor,mary).
38 parent(ruby,diana), parent(george,ruby).
39 parent(stanley,anne); parent(michael,john).
40 parent(susan,william), parent(florence,stanley).
41 parent(anne,miriam); parent(peter,frederick).

Instead of using specific **constants** – such as *susan* and *mary* in our examples – we can use **variables** in our queries. For example:

> ? parent(X,mary).

means:

> 'Who is the parent of Mary?'

and would cause Prolog to seek through the available facts for an instance of X which would satisfy the query and produce the answer:

> X = peter

You may use any letter or word as the variable, provided that it begins with a capital letter (some versions of the language require variables to be prefixed with an asterisk). Another query:

> ? parent(michael,Whom).

meaning 'Michael is the parent of whom?' or 'of whom is Michael the parent?' would produce the answer:

> Whom = john

and then Prolog would return to wait for another query from the user.

Note that Prolog only tells you the first solution to your query. If you enter a semi-colon in response to this display, Prolog will continue the search and report another solution:

Whom = joanne

If you enter a semi-colon again, Prolog will respond:

no

meaning that there are no further solutions to your query.

Activity 9

Write down the queries which you would pose to answer the following questions, and write down the answers which Prolog would give using the facts in your database:

Who is the parent of John?
Whose parent is Mary?
Who is your parent?
Whose parent is Ruby?
Who is Ruby's parent?

Backtracking

During its attempt to find a satisfactory solution, Prolog carries out a process called **backtracking**. We can illustrate backtracking by considering what happens when we use the facts:

friend(michael,philip).
friend(mary,joanne).
friend(paul,peter).
friend(michael,john).
friend(william,mary).
friend(michael,joanne).
friend(stanley,john).
friend(mary,john).
friend(mary,philip).

and ask:

? friend(X,john), friend(X,joanne).

in order to answer the question 'who is a friend of both John and Joanne?' We can represent the enquiry by the tree structure shown in Figure 11.8.

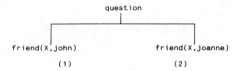

Figure 11.8 *A query as a tree structure*

Prolog first attempts to satisfy the *left-most* branch of the tree, goal (1):

friend(X,john).

and searches through the facts one by one from the beginning:

friend(michael,philip) is not a solution
friend(mary,joanne) is not a solution
friend(paul,peter) is not a solution

until we find that a solution is given by the fact:

friend(michael,john).

So *X* is now **bound to** *michael*, and this value of *X* (*michael*) is carried over and used in the next branch of the tree to see whether goal (2) is satisfied. This goal is now:

friend(michael,joanne).

Prolog searches through all the facts *from the beginning* and finds that goal (2) is satisfied, so the first answer to the entire query is displayed:

X = michael

If the user now types a semi-colon to look for more solutions, *X* is unbound from *michael* and the search through the facts continues from the previous solution:

friend(michael,john).

in an attempt to find a further solution to goal (1):

friend(X,john).

We find that:

498

> friend(william,mary) is not a solution
> friend(michael,joanne) is not a solution

then, we find the solution:

> friend(stanley,john).

and *x* is bound to *stanley*. but, Prolog cannot find a fact to satisfy goal (2):

> friend(stanley,joanne).

so this fails.

X is now unbound from *stanley* and the search resumes to find another solution to goal (1):

> friend(X,john).

This time, we find a solution:

> friend(mary,john).

and *X* is bound to *mary*. Prolog now attempts to satisfy goal (2).

> friend(mary,joanne).

a search of the facts proves that this is satisfied, so a further solution is:

> X = mary

Prolog attempts to find another solution to goal (1):

> friend(X, john).

and the only remaining fact:

> friend(mary,philip)

is not a solution so we can can conclude that there are no more solutions, since we have searched the entire fact base for solutions to goal (1), so the query is terminated.

To do all this, Prolog keeps a pointer to which facts it is considering at any one time for each goal of the query. When it resumes its backtracking, it continues from where the pointer got to for that goal. So in our example, it passes once through the facts looking for solutions to goal (1), and for each satisfactory solution to goal (1) it passes once through the facts looking for satisfactory solutions to goal (2).

Activity 10

Write down, in the manner of the above description, exactly what happens when the following queries are asked of the Prolog *friend* facts.

? friend(Y, joanne), friend(Y, john).
? friend(peter, Z), friend(Z, paul).
? friend(michael, F), friend(mary, F).

At each stage of the search, indicate:

    (a) The goal which is being satisfied.
    (b) The current solution.
    (c) The current fact which is being checked.

Write predicate

To instruct Prolog to print all the possible solutions, instead of proceeding one by one, some implementations provide the *write* predicate:

    ? parent(michael,Y), write(Y).

which would display all the solutions to this query, one by one:

    john
    joanne

If we wanted to find all pairs of brother/sister occurrences amongst our facts, we could pose a query such as:

    ? parent(X,Y), parent(X,Z), write(Y), write(Z).

which may be read as:

    'Display the pairs of Y and Z for which X is the parent of Y and X is also the parent of Z.'

In our case, Prolog would display:

    john   joanne
    florence william

In addition to facts, we can also define *rules* for our database. A rule is a conclusion which can be drawn from one or more known facts. So if we are likely to need our brother/sister relationship frequently, we could simplify the query by defining a rule:

sibling(Y,Z) :– parent(X,Y), parent(X,Z).

Note that we are not concerned with the identity of *X*, the parent, only that *X* is parent of both *Y* and *Z*. We could then use this rule in queries such as:

? sibling(florence,william).

which would produce the answer:

yes

or

? sibling(joanne,Who).

to which Prolog would respond:

Who = john

since Florence and William have a common parent (Stanley, according to the facts). The query:

? sibling(florence,mary).

would produce the answer:

no

Questions

42 Write a rule for a relationship called *child* which declares that someone is a child if someone else is his/her parent.
   Write down the answers which Prolog would give to these queries, using the facts shown in the text:

(a) child(stanley).
(b) child(michael).
(c) child(W).

New facts, relations and rules may be added to the database at any time.
   To introduce new relations *male* and *female*, we could provide further facts such as:

```
female(florence).
female(joanne).
female(mary).
female(susan).

male(frederick).
male(john).
male(michael).
male(peter).
male(stanley).
male(william).
```

then we could define *father* and *mother* rules:

father(X,Y) :– parent(X,Y), male(X).

which means that *X* is the father of *Y* *if X* is the parent of *Y and X* is male.

Remember that the comma has the meaning *and*, as we saw above, and the semi-colon has the meaning *or*.

Questions

43 Using the rule *father* as a model, declare a rule *mother*.
44 Declare a rule *grandfather*.
45 Declare a rule, such that:

  related(X,Y)

  is true if *X* is the parent of *Y* or *Y* is the parent of *X*.

Prolog in business

In relational database terms, we could represent the facts as the rows of the *parent* relation, each having two columns (or fields) indicating that the person named in the first column is the parent of the person named in the second column. We could then use Prolog as a query language. The answer *yes* would mean that there is one (one or more) rows which satisfy the query, and the answer *no* would mean that there are no rows which satisfy the query.

To put the language in a commercial context, let us imagine that we wish to represent the stock in a warehouse by a series of facts. We could define the stock by the Prolog facts:

    stock(1000,desk,green,ash,8,mn/17/81,56,30,2000,06/11/93).
    stock(2000,settee,yellow,oak,18,dn/l/69,100,30,1000,23/10/93).
    stock(3000,sideboard,blue,ash,58,mn/5/56,130,15,2000,30/9/93).
    stock(4000,desk,black,maple,68,ls/7/87,56,30,1000,09/10/93).
    stock(5000,settee,orange,ash,24,dn/19/3,10,30,1000,28/9/93).

This tells us, in the case of the first fact, that this is product number *1000*, is of product type *desk*, has the colour *green*, is made of *ash*, has a stock of *8*, is stored in location *mn/17/81* in the warehouse, costs *56*, has a minimum stock level of *30*, is bought from supplier number *2000*, and the last stock was bought on *06/11/93*.

We could then define each part of the stock items by Prolog rules:

    partno(X) :- stock(Z,_,_,_,_,_,_,_,_,_), item(1,Z,X).

using the built-in rule *item*, and specifying that the part-number is the first item (column) of the stock relation, no matter which stock relation we consider. The underscore represents any value. We could use this rule to check for the existence of a specific part-number on the file:

    ? partno(1000).

would produce the reply:

    yes

whereas, the query:

    ? partno(9999).

would produce the reply:

    no

The rest of the columns might be defined as:

    type(P,X):-
        stock(Z,_,_,_,_,_,_,_,_,_),
        item(1,Z,P), item(2,Z,X).

with an actual query using this rule:

> ? type(1000,TYPE).

giving the reply:

> TYPE = DESK

The remaining columns would be declared in the same manner:

```
colour(P,C):-
     stock(Z,_,_,_,_,_,_,_,_,_,_,),
     item(1,Z,P), item(3,Z,C).
quantity(P,C):-
     stock(Z,_,_,_,_,_,_,_,_,_,_),
     item(1,Z,P), item(5,Z,C).
minimum(P,C):-
     stock(Z,_,_,_,_,_,_,_,_,_,_),
     item(1,Z,P), item(8,Z,C).
date(P,D):-
     stock(Z,_,_,_,_,_,_,_,_,_,_),
     item(1,Z,P), item(10,Z,D).
```

and so on.

Activity 11

In your own words, write down the meaning of these rules, as they are presented in the text:

```
partno(X)
type(P,X)
colour(P,C)
quantity(P,C)
minimum(P,C)
date (P,D)
```

Give some examples of queries using these rules, explain in your own words what the query is asking and write down the response which Prolog would give and what this means.

To produce a listing of the part-number, type and price of all the items on the stock file, we might issue a query such as:

```
? partno(X),
      type(X,Y),
      price(X,Z),
      write(X),
      write(Y),
      write(Z).
```

Notice how we can enter the query in fairly free-format because the full stop terminates the statement.

To select specific items, we might use one of the built-in predicates, *less*, in a query such as:

```
? partno(X), price(X,Y), less(Y,25), write(X), write(Y).
```

which would display the part-number and the prices of all products which have a price of less than £25. We could list details of all products within a specific price range by means of a query such as:

```
? partno(X), price(X,Y),
      less(25,Y), less(Y,100),
      write(X), write(Y).
```

to show all those which cost between £25 and £100.

Since we have rules defining quantity and minimum, we could define a further rule to represent the below-minimum situation:

```
low(P) :- quantity(P,Q), minimum(P,M), less(Q,M).
```

such that the query:

```
? low(1000).
```

would return the answer:

yes

since we have only 8 of item 1000 and the minimum level is 30.

Some versions of Prolog have logical operators:

```
<
>
=
>=
<=
```

he *low* rule could be rewritten as:

low(P) :– quantity(P,Q), minimum(P,M), Q < M.

Let us look at some other ways in which we may pose queries about our STOCK database:

(1) Produce a list of the part-numbers of all the *desk* products:

　　　? stock(X,desk,_,_,_,_,_,_,_,_), write(X).

Prolog would then reply:

　　1000
　　4000

We might also have specified this query as:

　　　? TYPE=desk, stock(X,TYPE,_,_,_,_,_,_,_,_), write(X).

(2) Produce a list of the part-number, colour and quantity of all *ash settees*:

　　　? stock(X,settee,Y,ash,Q,_,_,_,_,_),
　　　　write(X), write(Y), write(Q).

(3) Produce a list of the part-numbers and description of all the products which are below the minimum stock level:

　　　? stock(P,T,C,M,Q,_,_,M,_,_), Q < M,
　　　　write (P), write(T), write(C), write(M).

The goal *Q* < *M* is satisfied if the value of *Q* is less than the value *M*.

(4) Produce a list of the part-numbers of all products which cost less than £50 and are made of ash:

　　　? stock(P,_,_,ash,_,_,PR,_,_,_), PR < 50, write(P).

To produce a program in, say, Pascal with the same facilities would require much time and effort.

Processing data in Prolog

In addition to the facilities for handling enquiries, Prolog has a number of features which allow you to produce processing routines in the language. For arithmetic calculations, there are predicates such as:

　　sum(3,4,X).

which would return the answer:

X = 7

We could use this same predicate for *subtraction*:

sum(3,ANSWER,7).

which would give the reply:

ANSWER = 4

There are further facilities, as illustrated by these queries and their responses:

```
times(2,3,X).      X = 6
sign(4,S).         S = 1
int(4.5,XX).       XX = 4
```

Most arithmetic processing can be performed with the help of these rules. The application of **recursive rules** which use themselves, makes the language particularly powerful. Thus, we might define a *factorial* rule like this:

```
factorial(NUMBER, FACTORIAL):–
    sum(NUMBER,–1,LOWER),
    factorial(LOWER,LOWERFACT),
    times(NUMBER,LOWERFACT,FACTORIAL).
```

This specifies that in order to calculate the FACTORIAL value of a NUMBER, we find the number LOWER which is one less than NUMBER and then find the factorial value of LOWER (calling this LOWERFACT), then FACTORIAL is simply LOWERFACT multiplied by NUMBER. In a real instance, this tells us that factorial 4 is 4 times factorial 3; factorial 3 is 3 times factorial 2; factorial 2 is 2 times factorial 1. We must also have previously defined factorial 1 as:

```
factorial(ONE,1) :– less(0,ONE), less(ONE,2).
```

or

```
factorial(LOW,1) :– less(LOW,2).
```

or

```
factorial(LOW,1) :– LOW < 2.
```

in order to terminate the recursion.

On some versions of Prolog, an alternative means of assigning values, and of performing long calculations, is provided by the:

is

operator. Unlike the predicates which we have seen so far, this is used in queries of the form:

? X is (1+2) * (3–4) + 5.

to which Prolog would reply:

X = 2

An important point is demonstrated by a rule such as:

increment(X,Y):– Y is X+1.

which adds 1 to the value of *X* and puts the result in *Y*. Prolog does not allow us to use a rule such as:

add_one(X) :– X is X+1

since a new variable must be used to receive the result and not one of the input arguments; in other words, the same variable may not appear on both sides of the *is* operator.

Instantiation

The Prolog processor performs a task known as **instantiation** which is similar to the concept of assignment in other languages. We can illustrate this by looking at the query:

? X is A + B

If *A* and *B* have been instantiated (assigned a value) and *X* has not been instantiated, then the contents of *A* and *B* will be added together and the clause will be satisfied and the result used to instantiate *X*. However, if either (or both) of *A* and *B* has not been instantiated then the clause will not be satisfied and *X* will not be instantiated; furthermore, if *X* has already been instantiated then the clause will not be satisfied and *X* will not be instantiated. It is for this reason that, unlike the equivalent assignment statement in, say, Basic,

?X is X+1

can never work successfully in Prolog.

There are also terminal input-output facilities. We have already met:

write(X).

There is also:

nl

to skip to a new line between output from write statements, and:

read(X).

to accept input from the user's keyboard. The various implementations of the language also offer facilities for handling files.

We could use our relations and rules in a simple program to ask for the part-number of a product and an order quantity, and then display the details of the product and whether or not the order can be fulfilled. This might be implemented by a program, as shown in Figure 11.9. The program in Figure 11.9 (a) could then be used in a sequence such as those in Figure 11.9 (b).

```
check_stock:-
        write('Enter the part-number of the product: '),
        read(X),
        type(X,T),
        colour(X,C),
        material(X,M),
        quantity(X,Q),
        write(T), write(C), write(M), write(Q),
        nl,
        write('Enter the order quantity: '),
        read(Y),
        sum(Q,1,UPPER),
        less(Y,UPPER).

                        (a)

? check_stock.
Enter the part-number of the product: 1000
DESK GREEN ASH 8
Enter the order quantity: 5
yes

? check_stock.
Enter the part-number of the product: 1000
DESK GREEN ASH 8
Enter the order quantity: 33
no

                        (b)
```

Figure 11.9 *Prolog: a processing routine*

Relations and rules can be added to the database as required, and the support processor for the language has full facilities for creating, editing, saving, maintaining and combining databases.

It could be said that Prolog is not user-friendly, and it is certainly true that the user must pay attention to the brackets and other punctuation of the queries and rules. The most common mistake is to forget the full stop, and then have to wait for ages until you realize what's gone wrong. For this reason, front-end processors have been provided which allow the user to type in queries and declarations in natural language and in virtually free format; these are then parsed and converted into a suitable form for Prolog processing.

Expert systems

Data is a set of letters, numbers and other characters which represents the resources used by an organization. By applying structure to those data, we derive **information**. If we now impose context and rules upon that information, then we obtain **knowledge**. We can illustrate this with a simple example. If I look at a document – a piece of paper or a piece of magnetic tape – I might encounter the characters:

–12345

This is the raw **data**. I can give this structure which will enable me to interpret it as a sum of money:

£123.45 DR

This gives me **information**. If I put this in the context of my bank account, and apply a simple rule of banking, I gain the **knowledge** that:

My bank account is overdrawn and I shall soon be getting a letter from my bank manager.

The ability to capture and apply rules such as:

If the balance of the account is less than the agreed credit limit, then the account is overdrawn and a letter should be sent to the customer.

is the basis of computer software known as an **expert system**.

The rules which are appropriate for the specific task in hand are submitted to the expert system in much the same way that source program statements – in a language such as Cobol or Basic – are submitted to a compiler. The similarity between expert systems and other programming devices has led some writers to use the term **fifth generation languages** to describe such high-level media.

Unlike many programming languages, however, the features of an expert system can be applied both to conventional business situations and also to less **numerate** areas such as medical diagnosis and legal interpretation. This is possible because the rules such as:

> If the patient has a temperature of ... and there is pain in the . . . accompanied by loss of . . . then . . .

or

> if the defendant has admitted that . . . and the past record shows that . . . then . . .

can be provided by experts in the relevant subject and disciplines. The expert system will first accept the experts' rules. It will then solicit the necessary information from the end-user – the facts of the case. A complex process of cross-referral and correlation of the input data with the various rules will then be performed, and the results will be displayed, together with an explanation of how and by which rules the final decision was reached.

Care must be taken with the compatibility of the rules. They must not conflict – or if they do, there must be some indication of the priority of one rule over another. If there are too many rules – one package suggests a maximum of fifty rules – then it may be impossible or time-consuming to make an interpretation.

Object-oriented programming

Most of the languages that we have considered look at the programming task in terms of what *processing* is required, what is to be done with the data. In contrast, **object-oriented programming** languages concentrate upon data structures and then add a processing capability to handle those data structures. Some examples of object-oriented languages are *Smalltalk*, which we shall look at briefly in this section, and the extension of the C language known as C++.

The original concept of object-oriented programming was developed in the late 1960s when Alan Kay, working at the University of Utah, devised a system which was based around a typical office desk. The intention of the system was to make computers more accessible to non-technical users. The system, called *Dynabook*, simulated a desktop on which there were laid a number of documents, some lying on the top of others in the manner of the current fashion for windows and pop-up menus, as illustrated in Figure 11.10.

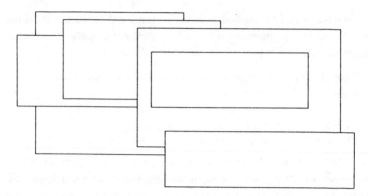

Figure 11.10   *Windows and pull-down menus*

The user controls the environment by means of a mouse, a touch-screen or some other pointing device. The programming language which supported the Dynabook system came to be known as Smalltalk. The illustrations shown below are based upon the Smalltalk language.

A program written in an object-oriented language consists of a number of **objects**. This term covers everything from a simple constant to an entire program. An object is a chunk of information plus a description which indicates how that information is to be manipulated.

Each object has its own local storage areas and some means of communicating with other objects, and communicates with other objects by sending **messages** or by receiving messages which ask for an operation which the objects provide.

Classes

Objects are organized into **classes** and each class represents a model for the objects in that class and lays down the **public properties** and the **private properties** which apply to all objects of that class.

The *public properties* describe the data structure, the processing and the means of communication for all objects in that class. Each real example of an object in a class is known as an **instance** of the class.

Thus, if we wanted to define a new class of object called *Report*, we might do this by declaring that it is a **subclass** of the general class of Objects, as shown in Figure 11.11.

The data used by a class is made up of instance variables (account-number, name, detail and account in this example) which are the vari-

```
Object subclass: £Report
    instancevariablenames
        'accountnumber name detail amount'
    classvariablenames
        'Totals Linesprinted'

!Report class method!

cleardown
    Totals <—— 0.
    Linesprinted <—— 0.
```

Figure 11.11 *A class and one of its methods*

ables which are used by all instances of this class and class variables
(*Totals* and *Linesprinted* in this example) which are the variable shared
by all instances of this class.

The processing is described by the **methods** for that class. The *clear-
down* class method applies to all instances of the *Report* class. The
description of the communication for a class – known as the **interface**
– lists the sort of messages which objects of this class can accept.

The *private properties* of a class distinguish one instance of that
class from another instance and detail the actual values of the instance
variables and the actual set of operations which make up the processing
methods for this instance. These are illustrated by method for the
Report class shown in Figure 11.11.

Some of these features – the set of values and the set of operations –
remind us of the definition of an *abstract data type* which we met earlier. There are, indeed a number of standard abstract classes available in
most implementations of Smalltalk; these include *Magnitude, Stream*
(used for input and output, as we shall see later) and *Collection* (which
includes *Array, String, Set* and *Dictionary*).

One class may be the **descendant** or **subclass** of another class (or
classes) and will **inherit** the characteristics of the **ancestor** class.

It is these notions of objects and classes, abstract data types, and
inheritance which distinguish object-oriented languages from the other
languages which we have considered.

Messages

A message is an instruction or a request to perform an action, it is not
an indication of how the action is to be performed, nor is it information.
Each Smalltalk **statement** is made up of a **receiver** object, a **selector**
indicating the nature of the action and, possibly, **arguments** indicating
the objects which are specific to that particular instance of the message.

Thus, one object might send a message:

> top / bottom

in which *top* is the *receiver,* and / is the *selector* / and *bottom* is the *argument.* The assignment statements:

> answer ⟵ 22
> total ⟵ result

are easily recognizable, but the argument may itself be a message, giving the forms:

> value ⟵ part 1 + part2
> answer ⟵ answer + 1

Some messages do not require arguments. For example:

> 8 factorial
> anglex sin
> 99 negative

Methods

The **method** of a class describe the sequence of actions which are to be performed by all instances of that class. A method is defined as a sequence of messages separated by full stops, for example:

> a1 ⟵ 0.
> b1 ⟵ 32.
> tax ⟵ tax + 1.
> balance ⟵ balance – debit + credit.

The messages themselves are made up of of **expressions**. In Smalltalk, there are four kinds of expression: **variable names, literals, message expressions** and **block expressions.**

There are two kinds of variable: **private** or local variables, and **public** or global variables. As in other languages, variables are identified by names consisting of a letter followed by one or more letters and/or digits. A private variable begins with a lower-case letter, and a public variable with an upper-case letter.

Local variables are declared on a statement such as:

> | val1 tax balance credit debit |

with the names enclosed between vertical bars. In use, literals are similar to those of other languages and are of several types, including:

(1)   Numeric literals of class *Integer*;

> 123
> −100
> 0

of class *Float*:

> 3.14159
> 1.5
> 1.23e20
> 5.5e−10

or of class *Fraction*;

> 1/2
> 100/3

(2)   Character literals, declared as a dollar sign followed by a single character:

> $A
> $!
> $$
> $+

(3)   String literals, enclosed in apostrophes:

> 'End of job'

Blocks

A **block** is a sequence of messages, separated by full stops and enclosed in square brackets. For example:

> [tax x ⟵ 0. gross ⟵ 0]

will establish a block to zeroise variables *tax* and *gross*. To execute a block, we use the special message *value*, like this:

> [age ⟵ 0. service ⟵ 0] value

An even more powerful feature of Smalltalk is that of **binding** a block to a variable. Thus, a statement such as:

```
clearall ←—— [ tax ←—— 0. gross ←——0]
```

binds the set of messages, zeroising variables *tax* and *gross*, to the variable *clearall*. As before, we could *execute* this block by means of the *value* message:

```
clearall value
```

We might have a more general block which accepts parameters, like this:

```
[ :x :y I total ←—— total + x + y ]
```

Let us look at a method which we have called *older*. This returns the greater of the two input values. The variable called *work* is a local variable, and the character ˆ indicates that the contents of work are returned by the method.

```
older
    first: val1 second: val2
        I work I
    work ←—— val2.
    (val1 >= val2) iftrue [work ←—— val1]
ˆ work
```

To use this method, we might subsequently include statements such as:

```
which1 ←—— older first: john second: joan
```

in order to find the greater of the two values in the variables *john* and *joan*. Observe how the input values are identified by the keywords *first* and *second*, thereby associating *john* and *joan* with the variables *val1* and *val2* inside the method.

Selection and iteration

The Smalltalk language offers other facilities resembling those of the imperative languages. The messages:

```
iftrue:
iffalse:
whiletrue:
whilefalse:
timesrepeat:
```

and the more complex:

516

to: by: do:

structure are used in the control of selection and iteration. These would be used in contexts like those in Figure 11.12.

Activity 12

In your own words, describe the action of the selection and iteration processes which are shown in Figure 11.12.

```
(val1 > val2) iftrue: [val1 <— 0]

(val1 > val2) iftrue: [val1 <— 0];
              iffalse: [val2 <— 0]

ctr <— 1.
total <— 0.
(ctr < 10) whiletrue: [total <— total + ctr.
                       ctr <— ctr + 1]

ctr <— 1.
total <— 0.
(ctr >= 11) whilefalse: [total <— total + ctr.
                         ctr <— ctr + 1]

factor <— 1.
10 timesrepeat: [factor <— factor * number]

1 to: 10 do: [ :val | total <— total + val]

1 to: 10 by: 2 do: [ :val | eventots <— eventots + val]
```

Figure 11.12   *Smalltalk: selection and iteration*

Input / output

Input and output are achieved by means of a number of standard classes of type *Stream*. This has subclasses *Terminalstream, Printstream, Filestream, Readstream, Writestream* and *Readwritestream*. A typical use of these might be:

finalreport ←— Printstream with: totals

These, and some of the other classes mentioned here, are not a standard part of the Smalltalk language but they, or similar objects, are increasingly provided on the various implementations of the language.

The language is currently available in a number of versions for use on IBM PC and compatible computers and on Apple Macintosh machines.

Questions

Transform the following into Smalltalk code:

46 The Basic loop:

```
FOR FAHR = 212 TO –32 STEP –1
    CENT = (FAHR –32)*5/9
NEXT FAHR
```

47 The design:

```
case depending upon code
    case code = "+" add current to total
    case code = "–" subtract current from total
    case code = "C" clear total to zero
end case
```

Activity 13

In your own words, consider the facilities of any third generation language which you have used (such as Cobol or Basic) and compare these with those of LISP, Prolog and Smalltalk.

Why do you think that a user might prefer to use a functional-oriented language to a more familar 3GL?

Why do you think that a user might prefer to use a logic-oriented language to a more familar 3GL?

Why do you think that a user might prefer to use an object-oriented language to a more familar 3GL?

Recap

- Besides the familiar imperative model for a programming language, there are other ways of expressing processing requirements.
- In this chapter, we looked at three possible models: functional-oriented languages, such as LISP, which are designed around the concept of mathematical functions; logic-oriented languages, such as Prolog, which are based upon the concepts of symbolic logic; object-oriented languages, such as Smalltalk, which concentrate their attentions upon the data and data

structures which are to be used in solving a problem and then add to these a set of processing operations which manipulate that data.

Answers to questions

1 (a) product2(x,y) ≡ x∗y
product2 ≡ λx,y. x∗y
λx,y. x∗y
(b) minimum(x,y) ≡ if x<y then x else y
minimum ≡ λx,y. if x<y then x else y
λx,y. if x<y then x else y

2 (a) func1(x) ≡ x–7
func1 ≡ λx. x-7
λx. x–7
(b) quadratic1(x) ≡ x∗x∗x + 2∗x∗x – 7∗x + 3
quadratic1 ≡ λx. x∗x∗x + 2∗x∗x – 7∗x + 3
λx. x∗x∗x + 2∗x∗x – 7∗x + 3

3 (a) 22.5
(b) –3
(c) –4
(d) 41

4 (a) inorder ≡ λx,y. if x>y then *true* else *false*
λx,y. if x>y then *true* else *false*
(b) pdifference ≡ λx,y. if x>y then x–y else y–x
λx,y. if x>y then x–y else y–x

5 The results are shown in Figure 11.13. I have put ?? where the function is undefined.

Input	funcx1	funcx2	funcx3	funcx4
-7	0.5555	1.8	2.6457	??
-6	0.5	2	2.4494	??
-5	0.4285	2.3333	2.236	??
-4	0.3333	3	2	??
-3	0.2	5	1.732	??
-2	0	??	1.4142	??
-1	0.3333	-3	1	??
0	1	-1	0	0
1	3	-3	1	1
2	??	??	1.4142	1.4142
3	5	5	1.732	1.732
4	3	3	2	2
5	2.3333	2.3333	2.236	2.236
6	2	2	2.4494	2.4494
7	1.8	1.8	2.6457	2.6457

Figure 11.13 *Composition of functions*

6 Members: 1234 wild-cat VALUE coelocanth laughing-hyena –9876

Atoms: 1234 wild-cat VALUE coelocanth laughing-hyena –9876

Numbers: = 1234 – 9876

Identifiers: wild-cat VALUE coelocanth laughing-hyena

7 (Europe America Asia Australasia Oceania)

8 ((Britain Ireland France Germany Holland) (North-America South-America) (India China Malaya) Australasia Oceania)

9 ((((England Scotland Wales Northern-Ireland) Ireland France Germany Holland) (North-America South-America) (India China Malaya) Australasia Oceania)

10 (SETQ A 42)

11 (SETQ Answer (DIFFERENCE (PLUS 1099 133) 988))

(SETQ Answer (PLUS 1099 (MINUS 133 988)))

12 (SETQ Tax (DIFFERENCE (TIMES 53 43) (QUOTIENT 63 9)))

13 head: 1; tail: (4 9 16 25 36)

14 head: elephant; tail: (hippopotamus rhinoceros)

15 head: (Britain Ireland France Germany Holland); tail: ((North-America South-America) (India China Malaya) Australasia Oceania)

16 head: cat; tail: ((dog fox) sheep ())

17 head: North-America; tail: (South-America)

18 head: computer; tail: () or *nil*

19 the

20 (cat sat on the mat)

21 cat

22 () or *nil*

23 sat

24 (on the mat)

25 ((AA ((BB CC) DD)) EE (FF ((GG HH) KK) QQ) (JJ))

26 Is Anne the parent of Stanley? yes

27 Is Florence Stanley's parent? no

28 Is Frederick the parent of Peter? yes

29 Is George the parent of Ruby? yes

30 Is Joanne the parent of Michael? no

31 parent(michael,joanne). yes

32 parent(ruby,diana). yes

33 parent(stanley,daphne). no

34 parent(william,susan). no

35 Strictly speaking, we cannot answer this question because there are no facts concerning the relationship *child*. If we were to write:

> parent(victor,mary).

we should be assuming knowledge about the connection between *parent* and *child*. We know this relationship, but Prolog only knows the facts which we give it. We shall see how to overcome this particular problem later.

36 no
37 yes
38 yes
39 yes
40 no
41 no
42 child(X) :- parent(Y,X).

    (a)   yes.
    (b)   no.
    (c)   W = john   This would be the first response. I'll leave you to write down the rest.

You may use any names for the variables used in the rule, provided that they begin with a capital letter.

43 mother(X,Y) :- parent(X,Y), female(X).
44 grandfather(X,Y) :- male(X), parent(X,Z), parent(Z,Y).
45 related(X,Y) :- parent(X,Y) ; parent(Y,X).
46 fahr ⟵ 212.
    (fahr >= –32) whiletrue:
                [work1 ⟵ fahr –32.
                work1 ⟵ work1*5.
                work1 ⟵ work 1/d.
                fahr ⟵ fahr–1]
47 (code = $+) iftrue: [total ⟵ total + current].
    (code = $–) iftrue: {total ⟵ total – current].
    (code = $C) iftrue: {total] ⟵ 0]

Index

4GL Grand Prix, 419
4GL, *see* Fourth generation language
Abstract data type, 185, 191
Accumulator, 13
Ada, 134
Address, 15, 43
ADT, *see* Abstract data type
AI, *see* Artificial intelligence
Algol, 46
APL, 135
Architecture, 9, 11
Argument, 248, 491
Arithmetic, 220, 350
Array table, 338, 343
Array, 145, 342
Artificial intelligence, 471, 490
ASCII, 98
Assembler, 27
Assembly code, 24, 25
Assignment statement, 219
Atom, 472, 491

Backtracking, 497
Backus-Naur form, 269
Bag data type, 207
Base address, 56
Base, radix, 117
Basic, 132
Binary data, 92, 93, 95, 96
Binary operation, 55
Binary/decimal conversion, 95
Binding, 474, 487, 498, 515
Bit, 91
Block, 249, 515
Block-structured language, 249

BNF, *see* Backus-Naur form
Boolean data type, 128
Branching, 18, 29
Buffer, 15
Busy waiting, 435

C, 141, 228, 511
C++, 511
Call by reference, 255
Call by value, 253
Calling a module, 253
Carry flag, 57
CASE structure, 221
Cell, 485
Channel, 438
Character data type, 105
Character set, 105
Chip, 11
Class, 512
Cobol, 136, 228
Code generator, 381
Common data, 256
Comparison, 13, 18
Compiler, 47, 61, 334
Complex numbers, 138, 141
Composition of functions, 468
Concurrent processing, 428
COND function, 476
Condition synchronization, 434
Constant, 340
Constant table, 338
Constraint error, 134, 209
Consumer-producer, 434
Context-free grammar, 285
Context-sensitive grammar, 286

Converting binary numbers to decimal, 92
Converting decimal numbers to binary, 95
Converting in-fix expressions to post-fix, 355

Data control language, 385, 418
Data description language, 385, 411, 418
Data dictionary, 389, 395, 411, 413, 419, 423
Data manipulation language, 385, 409, 418
Data name, 28, 132
Data store, 14
Data type, 91, 104, 130, 185
Database 381, 384, 417
Database language, 381
dBASE, 394
DCL, *see* Data control language
DDL, *see* Data description language
Deadlock, 435
Deadly embrace, 435
Debugging, 64
Decimal number, 95
Declarative, 29
Declarative language, 489
Deriving a sentence from a grammar, 272
Describing a function, 308
Difference, 170, 299
Dimensions of an array, 152
Directive, 29
DML, *see* Data manipulation language
Domain, 303, 308
Dope vector, 146
Double-precision, 125
Double-word, 110
Dummy arguments, parameters, 248
Dyadic operation, 351
Dynabook, 511
Dynamic array, 207

E-notation, 125
EBCDIC, 98
EBNF, *see* Extended Backus-Naur Form
Empty set, 299
End-user, 2, 414, 425
Enquiry language, 381, 385, 417
Enumerated data type, 135, 157
Escape sequence, 106
Evaluating a post-fix expression, 359
Exception condition, 231
Expert systems, 510
Exponent, 117, 122
Extended Backus-Naur form, 269, 277, 280
External processing module, 243

Fact, 489
Field, 156
Fifth generation language, 510
Fifth generation project, 490
First generation computer, 9
First generation language, 24
Fixed data type, 109
Fixed point number, 115
Flag, 57
Floating point number, 117
Formal description, 317
Formal parameter, argument, 248
Formal specification, 203
Fortran, 45, 137, 228
Fourth generation computer, 9
Fourth generation language, 49, 50, 412
Fraction, 115
Function, 240, 244
Functional programming language, 465
Functionality, 51

Generations of computers, 9
Global variable, 249
Goal symbol, 270

Grammar, 266
Graph data type, 208

Half-word, 110
Head, 482
Heap data type, 207
Heterogeneous array, 151
Hexadecimal notation, 100, 103
High-level language, 46
Homogeneous array, 151
Horn clause, 491
Host language, 388

Immediate instruction, 56
Imperative language, 9, 216, 376
Implementing an ADT, 193, 207
Implicit naming, 137
In-fix notation, 351, 355, 359
Index register, 56
Information hiding, 211, 243
Input set, 303
Input/output, 3, 58, 517
Instance, 512
Instantiation, 508
Instruction format, 21, 42
Instruction set, 12, 17, 20, 29, 51, 54
Instruction store, 13
Integer data type, 109
Internal processing module, 240
Interpreting, 59
Intersection, 171, 299
Intrinsic function, 244
Iteration 224, 516

KBMS, Knowledge-base management system, 490

Label, 29
Labelled COMMON, 259
Lambda notation, 466
Large number, 116
Lexical analysis, 336
Linear programming, 457

Link editor, linking, 62
Linked list, 165
LISP, 465, 471
List processing, 207, 471
Loader, loading, 62
Local variable, 249, 251
Logic-oriented language, 465, 486, 488
Logical error, 61
Logical expression, 222
Loop structure, 224, 442

Machine code, 22
Macro, 32
Maintainability, 64
Mantissa, 117, 120
Map, 337, 339
Mapping, 304
Member, 167, 298
Memory, 43
Message, 512, 513
Meta-statement, 382
Metalanguage, 269
Metasymbol, 270
Method, 513, 514
Mnemonic, 25
Modular programming, 237
Mutual exclusion, 434

Negative number, 110
Network data type, 208
Non-procedural language, 51, 376, 489
Non-terminal symbol, 269
Normalized number, 118

Object, 512
Object program, 38, 61, 360, 366
Object-oriented language, 465
Object-oriented programming, 465, 511
Occam, 437
Off-line equipment, 377

Op-code, 20
Operand, 20
Optimization, 366
Ordinal data type, 158
Orthogonality, 65, 468
Output from a function, 294
Output set, 305
Overflow, 15, 58

Packed decimal data type, 126
Parallel processing, 430, 436, 441
Parameter, 248
Parity flag, 58
Parsing, 273
Partial function, 310
Pascal, 140, 228
Pass by reference, 255
Pass by value, 253
Pick operating system, 419 PL/1, 141
Pointer, 161
Polish notation, *see* Pre-fix notation
Port, 58
Portability, 44, 49
Post-condition, 202
Post-fix notation, 351, 355, 359, 477
Pre-condition, 202
Pre-fix notation, 355, 359
Precision, 115, 125
Predecessor, 159
Predicate, 491, 492
Primitive, type 131, 301
Priority, 443
Private property, 512
Procedural language, 376
Process diagram, 430
Producer–consumer, 434
Production, 269
Program generator, 381
Program status word, 15
Programmer, 5
Programming language, 1, 63, 130, 263
Prolog, 465, 490

Property of a class, 512
Prototyping, 387, 415
Pseudo-code, 226
PSW, *see* Program status word Public property, 512
Punched card, 377

QBE, Query By Example, 404
Quartet, 101
Query, 493
Query language, *see* Enquiry language
Queue data type, 192
Queuing diagram, 451
QUOTE function, 476

Radix, 117
Railroad diagram, 283
Range, 305
Readability, 63
Real number, 117, 119
Record, 156, 165
Recursion 267, 285, 322, 481, 507
Recursive rule, 267
Register, 11, 13, 14
Relational database, 388
Report program generator, 377
Reverse Polish notation, *see* Post-fix notation
RPG, 378
Rule, 489
Run-time processor, 62, 64

SB+, 419
Scope, 249, 363
Scope-checking, 363
Second generation computer, 9
Second generation language, 25
Security, 418
Selection, 221, 443, 516
Semantic, 263, 287, 309
Sentence, 270
Sequence, 207, 219

Set 167, 297
Set notation, 298
Set data type, 167
Sign flag, 58
Simulation, 5, 446
Simulation languages, 447, 452
Single-precision, 125
Small number, 116
Smalltalk, 465, 511
Software, 38
Sorting, 376
Source program, 61, 366
Specification by example, 288
Specification by narrative description, 287
Specification by substitution, 289
Specification of a function, 294
Specification of a programming language, 263
Specification of an ADT, 197, 205
Specification of an operation, 201
Spreadsheet, 385
SQL, 388
Start symbol, 270
Statement, 29
Storage Map, 339
Stored program, 37
String, 106, 107
Structured English, 226
Structured programming, 216
Subclass, 512
Subroutine, 39, 240
Subscript, 145, 147
Successor, 159
Surface structure, 218, 226
Symbol table, 61, 161, 337, 342
Symbolic expression, 473

Symbols, 336
Synchronization, 433
Syntax analysis, 345
Syntax checking, 347
Syntax diagram, 283
Syntax error, 61, 349
Syntax of a language, 263
Syntax of an operation, 202
System Builder, 419
Systems analyst, 4

Tabulator, 377
Tail, 482
Terminal symbol, 269
Third generation computer, 9
Third generation language, 44
Total function, 310
Transputer, 436
Tree data type, 207
Tree diagram, 233
Twos complement form, 113
Type checking, 143, 187, 338

Union, 168, 170, 299
Unnormalized number, 119
User-defined function, 247
Utility program, 37

Variable, 340
VDM, Vienna Development Method, 189
Von Neumann architecture, 9

Word, 42, 110

Zero flag, 58